Australian
Fish & Seafood Cookbook

The ultimate kitchen companion

Susman, Huckstep, Swan & Hodges

MURDOCH BOOKS
SYDNEY · LONDON

'I've been waiting for a book like this for some time. For anyone who enjoys seafood, this is an essential tool. Packed full of clear, beautiful shots with relevant, concise and really useful information. It excites and inspires ... an absolute game-changer.'
Darren Robertson

'A book Australia not only wants, but needs, written by the only people in the country truly equipped to tackle the task. Essential.'
John Lethlean

'John Susman is a hero of mine. He has so much knowledge to share, which he does with such enthusiasm and generosity with cooks and fishermen alike. I just love his never-ending quest for the best seafood in the most perfect condition possible from the sea to the table. This tome is the next best thing to having him expand on his fascinating subject in person.'
Maggie Beer AM

'I first met John Susman in the early eighties and our professional and personal lives have been entwined ever since. First as an employee, then as a supplier, always as a friend. Apart from sport, fish is the usual topic of conversation with us – you learn a lot as that much time passes. I couldn't imagine a more qualified person to speak on the subject. John has gathered a stellar troupe of seafood aficionados, making this a must-have for everyone from restaurant chef to home cook. It's the bible for seafood. The only book you'll ever need on the topic.'
Neil Perry AM

'When it comes to Aussie fish, Susman and Hodges are the absolute OG seafood slayers! This is the only book I need when it comes to knowing how to handle, look for, research, prepare and cook Australian seafood.'
Dan Hong

'I thought I had some grounded seafood knowledge after being in the game for 20 years until I met John Susman, undoubtedly one of the world authorities on seafood from every aspect, including taste, cooking, catching and, of course, sustainability. His enthusiasm and knowledge are highly infectious. Combined with Chef Hodgie, this book is a once in a lifetime opportunity of knowledge.'
Mitch Tonks

'For more than 30 years, John Susman has been introducing me to some of the best and most interesting fish and seafood in the country to enliven my menus, and they always come out tops. Now it's all in the book. Good on you, Susman.'
Cheong Liew OAM

CONTENTS

Preface	6
An introduction to Australian seafood	9
Catching & handling methods	12
Sustainability	16
Selection & storage	18
Fish A–Z guide & recipes	**20**
Shellfish A–Z guide & recipes	**296**
Preparation & cooking techniques	426
Sauces, stocks & accompaniments	454
Seasonality guide	464
Index	466
Acknowledgements	476
About the authors	478

PREFACE

Seafood has become my life. After 30 years of plumbing the depths in the fish caper, spanning everything in the supply chain from catcher to cook, I'm surprised I haven't grown scales and a dorsal fin.

Whether you're on the end of a line, working in a processing factory, delivering fish to a chef, or cooking and serving seafood in a restaurant, there's something about seafood that sets it apart from terrestrial foods.

I've seen massive change over the years in a business that is arguably one of the toughest in the food game. Constantly wet, cold, smelly and slimy, and surrounded at times by various lying, cheating, thieving pirates – the seafood business is not for the faint-hearted. But the bounty beneath the ripples of deep blue is worth every effort.

My life changed forever when, as a young hotel-school graduate with a background working in some terrific restaurants in Adelaide, I found myself in awe of a piece of chargrilled kingfish. It was the early 1980s, and a young Neil Perry was on the pans at Barrenjoey House in Palm Beach, north of Sydney. Suddenly it all made sense – a simple piece of perfect fish, handled with care and cooked with respect, delivered an amazing meal.

Inspired by this experience, my professional career in seafood commenced. Through a serendipitous confluence of good luck and good fortune, I found myself working with some of the best catchers and cooks of seafood in the world. I've gone from working at the Rungis fish markets in Paris and the tuna halls of the Tsukiji fish market in Tokyo to running fish catching, processing and distribution businesses in Australia and Asia. I've been hooked on seafood – and especially how it's handled and cooked – my entire life.

Seafood is without doubt the most distinctive, special and downright deliciously addictive of all foods. It also engenders great memories. I can still taste a spectacular dish I first enjoyed at a long-closed restaurant on Sydney's lower north shore, Puligny's: a mousse of Jervis Bay scallop, wrapped in a light puff pastry and served on a creamy lobster bisque. The chef who cooked that dish, Steve Hodges, remains not only a great mate but one of the world's greatest seafood cooks. Throughout his time at the iconic Pier Restaurant in Sydney's Rose Bay and his quirky Darlinghurst diner, Fish Face, 'Hodgie' has retained almost a savant's approach to seafood cookery.

I first met restaurant critic and writer Anthony 'Huck' Huckstep more than fifteen years ago when we were both in disguise as restaurant critics (he as a professional, I as a stand-in). We were peering over menus at each other, smirking at the concept of a dish where the principal ingredient was the chef's ego. Huck has always had a 'no bullshit' approach to food reviewing, and he's been a constant source of inspiration to me.

In an industry renowned for ego and attitude over objectivity, Huck is a rare voice of reason in the food media. With a palate that has as much in common with those of ordinary folk as of gourmets, Huck understands the intimate and symbiotic relationship between great produce, great cooking and great food. He's also a dab hand at penning interesting food pieces that are lessons in brevity, precision and clarity.

Huck and I have been talking about writing a book like this for years, but it wasn't until we filed the very first species – flathead – that we realised why no one had undertaken such a task before. It's been the albatross around our necks for two years, but the end result is worth it.

While Huck agreed to ride shotgun on this project with me, as well as capture Hodgie's piscatorial genius, the job of interpreting Hodgie's restaurant-kitchen approach and rendering the recipes home-kitchen ready has been that of chef Sarah Swan. I've known 'Swannie' for a quarter of a century, since her emergence as a young chef at Sydney's Bayswater Brasserie, through her time on the line at seafood temple Rockpool, which culminated in her assisting Neil Perry in the development of concepts, dishes and recipes. She's now chef patron of 100 Mile Table, one of the New South Wales Northern Rivers' finest food operations. Swannie's style, understanding and technical cooking ability are unmatched.

I feel privileged to have worked with this team on this book. It is a collaboration of passion, skill and knowledge. Huck, Hodgie, Swannie and I all truly love seafood and are keen to share our experiences, thoughts and ideas.

There are several thousand types of seafood swimming in the Australian and New Zealand waters, but we have selected a little over 60 main species and a total of about 120 common species to consider for your dinner. We've hauled in nets brimming with information that we hope will help inspire you to try new and different seafoods and to enjoy the amazing world that is seafood cooking. This, coupled with the most stunning species photography, means there truly is no book quite like this on the planet.

We've tried to cover everything, from catching methods to the environment each species calls home, through their culinary applications and master classes in kitchen techniques, to over 130 accessible recipes presenting each species at its optimum. We hope we've given you the tools you need to break the surface of the water and get more than just your toes wet.

And remember, many fish can be substituted for other species in a myriad of recipes, so get to know your fish and be adventurous.

Mostly, though, we hope you enjoy this book and, even better, that you eat more seafood.

John Susman

AN INTRODUCTION TO AUSTRALIAN SEAFOOD

How do you feel about fish? While many of us love the flavour and texture of beautifully cooked fish and seafood, and realise the many nutritional benefits of eating this lean form of protein, most of us don't cook much fish ourselves at home. We might buy salmon or ling once a fortnight and cook the same old recipe, or throw some prawns into a stir-fry every now and then, but we don't always consider fish or seafood a staple item on our shopping lists, and we don't necessarily know enough about it to really feel confident buying it or cooking with it regularly.

We want to change this. This book aims to give you the confidence to make the right choices when it comes to buying and cooking fish. It's no harder to prepare than chicken or red meat once you know the basics, and these skills can be easily learnt. Whether you buy from your trusted fishmonger or from the local supermarket, we want to arm you with the knowledge you need to know which questions to ask and what to look for. We don't see why fish and seafood shouldn't be on the menu in everyone's homes more often – after all, it's versatile, widely available and affordable when in season, quick to cook and delicious.

Ask any Australian and they'll tell you this country has a bounty of seafood. Some 6000 marine species can be found in our waters, but only a fraction of these is harvested commercially. Our fishing grounds are the third largest in area, ranging across all five oceanic zones, and from the tropics to the Antarctic. For production by volume, however, we come in at around number 80.

The fact is, our waters are, relatively speaking, sparsely populated. The New Zealand fishing industry catches more of one species (some 250,000 tonnes of the fish and chips staple blue grenadier or hoki) than we produce in all of our wild and aquaculture fisheries combined. This is due to a combination of factors. Ours is the driest continent on the planet, and the waterways that feed our coastal zones are especially low in nutrients, reflecting the natural state of our soils. This, in addition to frequent drought, means our oceans are not exactly teeming with marine life. So while we have an enormous fishing area and a prodigious range of species available, production on a large scale just isn't possible.

But our consumption of seafood provides a stark contrast to our production figures. Australians now eat almost 18 kg (40 lb) of seafood per person per annum. This is way below the massive consumption of seafood in Japan – 213 kg (470 lb) per person per annum – and even well below the more than 150 kg (330 lb) of other meats (beef, lamb, pork and poultry) we each consume annually. Yet it's a dramatic increase from the 8.5 kg (19 lb) of seafood we consumed annually only fifteen years ago. And for a country that prides itself on having lived off the sheep's back, it's interesting to note that we now consume almost 20 per cent more seafood each year than we do lamb.

Seafood has become the protein of choice in the food-service industry, where it punches well above its weight in menu listings. But how are we supplying this rampant growth in demand for seafood if our fisheries are small and production relatively low? The bottom line is, we're not. Australia imports nearly 75 per cent of the seafood we consume! This includes supply from our close cousins the Kiwis – New Zealand is now the largest supplier of fresh fish to the Sydney Fish Market. Our exports are predominantly high-value species – rock lobster, abalone, prawns and tuna – while our imports are generally lower value skinless boneless fish, calamari, octopus and farmed prawns.

We live in a global village these days, so the idea that the seafood caught or processed within seagull flight of your place is the freshest, cheapest or best no longer applies. Conversely, just because a seafood is imported doesn't mean it's lacking in culinary or commercial qualities.

This book aims to celebrate what's caught and grown here in Australia and across the Tasman in New Zealand. It can seem like understanding seafood involves a complex matrix of seasons, regions, catching methods, handling, processing and preparation, but just a little knowledge can go a long way. Let's take time to understand what we have here and to celebrate how wonderful it is.

Our fisheries

Australia has some of the most technologically advanced and sustainable commercial fisheries in the world. The vast fishing grounds and the limited resources available demand that we care for our fisheries. Including the Australian Fisheries Management Authority (AFMA), there are eight separate agencies responsible for the management and control of commercial activities in fishing, most of which are regarded worldwide as standout examples of fisheries management. Indeed, the Spencer Gulf king prawn, Gulf of Carpentaria prawn, and western and southern rock lobster fisheries, to name a few, are not only standout but world's best. The subantarctic toothfish fishery is regarded as the high watermark in sustainable fishing – and the premium it returns reflects this.

The major issue for Australian seafood is that it's relatively costly to produce – licences and quotas have among the highest prices in the world, labour costs are relatively high, we don't have a huge stock to draw upon, and the size of the country means transport is expensive. There are also other stakeholders whose considerations impact the availability of seafood in Australia.

Recreational fishing is the number-one sport in the country, according to the Australian Recreational Fishing Foundation. With more than four million recreational anglers wetting a line every weekend and holiday, the volume of seafood caught by amateurs is significant. There's also an imperative to recognise the rights and needs of the Indigenous population of Australia and their seafood requirements.

Thus the dilemma for fisheries management is how to care for a limited resource while meeting not only the commercial needs of the food-service and retail sectors, but also the social needs of recreational fishers and Indigenous peoples, all while maintaining availability, consistency and affordability.

Aquaculture

Aquaculture is defined by the United Nations Food and Agriculture Organization as 'the farming of aquatic organisms including fish, molluscs, crustaceans and aquatic plants' with some sort of 'intervention in the rearing process to enhance production, such as regular stocking, feeding, protection from predators'. Although aquaculture seems like a contemporary form of farming, history shows that it was one of the first forms of agriculture – there are clear signs of oyster farming occurring some 6000 years ago.

In recent times aquaculture has become an essential part of our seafood industry, growing in importance as the global supply of wild-caught seafood has dwindled. So much so, that it has become an equal partner in the supply of seafood globally, now accounting for more than 50 per cent of all seafood consumed. As the popularity of seafood increases, so too does the need for improved, sustainable means to produce it. Aquaculture is the answer.

Aquaculture has been one of the fastest growing parts of global food production in recent decades, increasing by more than 10 per cent a year. In part this is because fish and other farmed seafood species need far less food than do terrestrial species (cattle, sheep and so on) to produce the same amount of protein.

In Australia, aquaculture occurs in ponds, tanks, pens and floating cages, in fresh water, brackish water or sea water. The Australian Department of Agriculture defines aquaculture as extensive, semi-intensive or intensive according to the inputs and outputs involved. With intensive aquaculture, farmers intervene in the growing stages by such means as supplementary feeding and, in prawn farming, water aeration. In extensive aquaculture, by contrast, the seafood is allowed to grow on its own, using natural food sources and conditions. This is the case with oyster and mussel farming, for example. Semi-intensive is, as the name implies, somewhere in between. In some instances, aquaculture is integrated with other agricultural activities, for example farming fish in a rice field, or aquaponic systems where water from fish tanks is used to grow green leafy vegetables then cycled back to the tanks.

As for most other industries, the cost of production is much higher in our part of the world than, say, in Asia, but our unique geographic location, the quality of our water and the laws governing environmental management mean that the seafood grown here is among the best, safest, most environmentally friendly – and expensive – in the world. The growth in artisan aquaculture is particularly exciting, producing everything from oysters and mussels grown by season and region, to indigenous fish species such as barramundi, Murray cod and silver perch. The focus is not only on producing delicious seafood but also on minimising environmental impact.

CATCHING & HANDLING METHODS

Australian seafood is subject to some of the most stringent management laws in the world, and fishing techniques are a vital component in the sustainability of wild-caught seafood. A range of equipment and methods is used, some specifically designed to target a single species, others for higher volume production, which are less discriminating. The trend in modern fisheries management is in favour of targeted fishing, which yields a higher quality catch and reduces bycatch.

Whatever the method, fishing is wet, often hot or cold and always dangerous work. The fisher is a hunter, one of the last targeting wild protein. What they do on a daily basis goes well beyond the activities of a terrestrial farmer, and along with skill it requires guile and sometimes outright good luck. Most commercial fishers are away from home for weeks, sometimes months, and yet they're some of the more underrated contributors to the food industry. Wild-caught seafood is unique, and the commercial methods employed to harvest it are largely misunderstood.

Fish live in almost every available body of fresh and salt water, including rivers, lakes, oceans and streams. They also live at various water depths, some preferring deep water and others staying close to the surface. Most of the fish we eat are caught in waters from the surface to 200 m (650 ft) depth, although some are caught much deeper.

Some fish – such as flathead, flounder and gurnard – will only live in the benthic (or sea-floor) zone, where they feed on molluscs, crustacea and other sea-floor dwellers. Others – such as sardines, anchovy, whiting and garfish – will live predominantly near the surface, where they feed on algae and seaweed. Still others will traverse various depths, chasing other fish as well as the molluscs and shellfish on the sea floor. These pelagic fish include broad-roaming species such as tuna, swordfish, mahi mahi and marlin.

Here's a brief summary of the main commercial fishing methods used in Australian waters.

Nets

One of the most important types of net is a seine net, which hangs vertically in the water thanks to floats buoying its top edge and weights holding down its bottom edge. Seine nets are used in several different techniques.

Beach seines are set by a small vessel parallel to a shoreline some distance off a beach, with one haul line still attached to the beach. The dinghy moves to the far end of the beach, then both ends of the net are hauled towards the beach until the seine net and fish are dragged to shore. Beach seining, generally species-specific, is used to catch salmon, mullet, sand whiting, garfish and bream.

Danish seines involve a line and net laid out in a pear shape then hauled back to a stationary or slow-moving vessel – which is similar to bottom trawling (see page 14). They're used on the continental shelf for deepwater flathead, redfish and morwong.

Purse seines are made with mesh smaller than the fish being targeted. A small dinghy or barge anchors the net as it sets around a school of fish. A 'purse line' is then pulled to close the bottom of the net. Purse seine nets are used in coastal and oceanic waters to target high-volume schooling species, including mackerel, trevally and some tunas. Purse seines have no impact on the sea-floor habitat, and bycatch is rarely an issue.

Other common types of net include lampara nets and gillnets. **Lampara nets** are similar to purse seines but have tapered panels that give them a scoop shape. The net is set around a school of fish, and once both ends of the net are retrieved the vessel tows it forward, closing the bottom and top of the net. This method is used to catch garfish, pilchards and anchovy in inshore waters. It has a limited impact on the environment, with no effect on the seabed and very little bycatch.

The panels of a **gillnet** are set vertically in the water column – either in contact with the seabed or with the surface – to entangle fish. The size of the mesh determines the size of the species caught – smaller fish can swim through the mesh while larger fish bounce off. Intertidal and subtidal gillnetting are effective means of targeting specific species, including Marine Stewardship Council–certified Coorong mullet, mulloway, wild barramundi and mangrove jack.

Lines

Fishing lines are used in an ingenious set of ways, from the simple line and hook we all know to complex arrangements of lines, hooks and floats.

Handlines consist of a single line, often with multiple hooks, operated by a single fisher who will return the line either manually or with a semi-mechanical retrieval device. This method is species-specific and delivers only small volumes of catch. It's rarely used in open-ocean or deepwater commercial fisheries, so be careful of ambit claims that this method was used in the harvesting of deep-sea species such as john dory. The handline method is generally used for snapper, garfish, King George whiting and southern calamari squid.

Pole and line is used for some tuna fishing. Here surface-swimming schools of tuna are attracted to a fishing vessel using live or dead bait. The tuna engage in a pure feeding frenzy, and are hauled aboard via a pole and short fixed line once they take a barbless hook and lure.

Hook and line trolling involves one or more fishing lines, baited with lures or baitfish, being drawn through the water. This may be behind a moving boat, or by slowly winding the line in from a static position, or even sweeping the line from side to side (used particularly in the Spanish and grey mackerel fisheries).

It might sound like a dance, but a **squid jig** is not, although it does occur at night, and bright lights are used to attract the squid to a vessel. Lines with barbless lures are 'jigged' up and down, and squid caught on the lures are hauled onto the vessel using automated jigging machines. Squid are fast-growing, prolific breeders, and this method ensures a sustainable, targeted catch.

Setlines, sometimes called trotlines, consist of a series of baited hooks attached at intervals to a single line by means of branch lines or snoods. This method is used in pelagic longlining, droplining and bottom longlining.

With a **pelagic longline**, a mainline is suspended horizontally by floats, while branch lines, each with a single baited hook, are attached to it at regular intervals. The line is left for several hours before retrieval. This method is used to catch tuna, swordfish, mahi mahi and other billfish in oceanic waters, where the hooks are usually set shallower than 300 m (980 ft). There's minimal bycatch and strict quotas are maintained.

Droplines consist of a single mainline with numerous baited hooks attached. The mainline sits vertically in the water column between a surface float and a bottom weight. Droplines are often set to depths in excess of 500 m (1640 ft) to catch popular species such as snapper, blue-eye trevalla and hapuka. This species-specific method generally results in fish of premium quality, and is often coupled with ike jime brain-spiking (see opposite) and bleeding of live fish.

Bottom longlines consist of a mainline with attached branch lines and hooks set across the seabed. They are used to target specific species, such as blue-eye trevalla, ling and school shark. They have minimal impact on the environment.

Trawls

Trawling involves dragging a net or another device through the water behind a boat or several boats. The net used is called a trawl. When no net is involved, the technique is called dredging.

With a **bottom otter trawl**, sometimes referred to as a demersal trawl, an open, cone-shaped net is held across the seabed by hydrodynamic plates called otter boards. The otter boards are attached to a net by lines called sweeps that aid in herding fish towards the net mouth. As the net is pulled along, fish accumulate in the rear section of the net. Bottom otter trawling can occur to depths of 1500 m (5000 ft), but generally less than 1000 m (3250 ft). Some believe it's neither selective nor good for the catch, but it remains the principal method for harvesting species such as flathead, redfish, ling, and john and mirror dory. Much work has been done in recent times to minimise the impact of bottom otter trawling, in particular the simultaneous use of devices that exclude bycatch.

Mid-water trawls, sometimes referred to as balloon trawls, are much larger than bottom otter trawls, and are designed for fishing off the seabed in open-ocean waters. They're used to target species such as blue grenadier (hoki) off western Tasmania and Victoria, and in New Zealand for harvesting a number of popular fish, including blue-eye trevalla, snapper and dory. Contemporary developments in technology, including the use of net-based cameras and exclusion devices, have aided in limiting non-target and bycatch species.

Prawn trawl nets are similar to bottom otter trawls but do not use sweeps. Rather, chains hang below a footrope to disturb the prawns (which like to bury themselves in mud), causing them to 'jump' into the path of the oncoming net. A single vessel commonly tows two, three or even four such nets. Prawn trawling of this type is limited to waters shallower than about 80 m (260 ft).

Scallop dredges are mainly box-shaped and are dragged along the seabed, digging into the substrate and collecting the sea creatures within it. They're used in shallow continental shelf waters to a depth of 100 m (330 ft). The outcome of this fishing may be delicious, but scallop dredging is not highly regarded due to its environmental impact.

Hand collection

Several important species are still collected by hand, sometimes directly by diving, and in other cases after they're first trapped in some way.

Diving is used to harvest abalone, sea urchins, scallops and clams, and requires a high level of direct human involvement by skilled divers doing dangerous work. It's used mostly for specialised, high-priced, premium seafood.

Hand-raking is used for harvesting cockles, pipis and clams. Using a broad-mouthed net and a shallow rake, fishers collect the shellfish by standing in shallow water and raking on the outgoing waves.

Pots, **traps** and **hoop nets** are used to catch crustaceans such as lobsters and crabs, and some fish, particularly some premium tropical species. The devices are baited then placed on the seabed with a line linking them to a surface float and left for a period of time. The Queensland spanner crab fishery uses a variation of a hoop net colloquially called a dilly, which consists of a piece of flat wire mesh and a centrally located bait holder. All these devices can be set at a range of depths from just a few metres to more than 200 m (650 ft). It creates very little bycatch, and what little there is can be kept alive and discarded without harm.

The art of ike jime

Ike jime (also known as iki jime) is a handling technique used during harvesting to increase the quality of the seafood being processed. Essentially, it's a method of paralysing and bleeding fish. It originated in Japan, but is now the method of choice throughout the better fisheries worldwide.

Traditionally, after a fish has been landed, it's left to die by asphyxiation before being gutted and chilled. Although the flesh may still be of high quality, the fish rapidly stiffens and this may cause tearing of the flesh and also affect the texture and taste. High levels of residual adrenaline in a fish that was stressed during death will result in a slightly bitter or sour flavour and vastly shorten the shelf life. The flesh of a fish can also be liable to gaping and blood spotting.

The ike jime process, by contrast, causes immediate brain death through the quick insertion of a spike directly into the hind brain of the fish, which is usually located slightly behind and above the eye. When spiked correctly, the fish will flare its fins then relax and cease all motion. The process not only delivers a quick death, but causes the blood in the flesh to retract to the gut cavity, yielding a fillet with a better colour and flavour. Ike jime also helps reduce adrenaline production at harvest because the fish is less stressed.

Killing the fish quickly and immediately after capture delays the stiffening process. Complete destruction of the hind brain means there is no movement from the fish and therefore all the fuel remaining in the muscle tissue goes towards maintaining cellular structure post-harvest. This results in flesh of a far superior quality. The texture is also improved – almost 'crisp' yet still supple. The taste of an ike jime fish is more refined, with complex notes rather than an overwhelming taste of fish fat.

The art of ike jime, which is practised on both wild and farmed fish, requires a specialist tool designed for efficiency and effectiveness, and great skill in its use. Imagine carrying it out on the slippery deck of a boat rolling around on an 8 metre (26 foot) swell! Ike jime is not just marketing hype – it's the real deal in delivering the best eating fish.

SUSTAINABILITY

Nothing causes more heated debate than the issue of sustainability in seafood production. For most of us the argument is an emotional one, because we're so far removed from fisheries practice and data collection. In addition, the increasing number of agencies involved, and differences of opinion as to what actually constitutes sustainability, have made the issue ever more confusing.

In its strictest sense, sustainable seafood means farmed or wild seafood harvested without harm to its population or habitat or to any other species in its ecosystem. But translating this simple-sounding concept into workable policies and wise purchasing decisions can be fraught.

In Australia and New Zealand, seafood is subject to some of the most stringent management laws in the world. These laws effectively prohibit unsustainable fishing and growing practices in commercial fisheries. The level of investment in marine science in this part of the world is the highest of any commercial fisheries on the planet.

Third-party certification agencies, such as the Marine Stewardship Council, Friend of the Sea and Best Aquaculture Practices, offer independent assessment to fisheries and enterprises. These evaluations, undertaken at great cost to the fishing companies themselves, give us a clear indication of the sustainability of both local seafood and imported products.

We have used science gathered by the Fisheries Research & Development Corporation (FRDC) to validate our claims of the sustainability of each species in this book. Their biennial report, the 'Status of Key Australian Fish Stocks', is developed in consultation with fisheries agencies across the country to determine the status of Australia's wild-catch fish stocks against a nationally agreed reporting framework, and is a valuable resource designed to inform the public, policymakers and industry on the sustainability of stocks.

In our view, discussions on sustainability also need to consider the cultural viability of the communities involved in catching and growing seafood, and the commercial sustainability of the fisheries upon which they rely. In Australia, for every fisher out fishing, there will be at least four others onshore depending on the catch for their income. Then there are the countless fishmongers and cooks working with seafood upstream.

Sustainability should be part of your seafood-purchase decision. Understand what you're getting, where it's from and how it was raised or harvested. Ask your fishmonger about the farms and fisheries from which they purchase the seafood they sell. Was it produced to first-world food-safety standards? Does it come from a fishery, region or country that observes United Nations labour standards? The principle of nose-to-tail eating also applies to fish and seafood (we call it fins-to-scales). Buying whole fish rather than fillets, and learning how to use every part, right down to making stock from the bones and heads, reduces waste and makes the very best of each and every catch.

Sustainability is as complex as it is fast-changing. The best you can do is undertake to buy seafood of the highest culinary quality you can, whatever the species. You can do this safe in the knowledge that in Australia there's always a strong correlation between the best tasting seafood and a commitment to best sustainable practices. Simply put, people who care about how seafood tastes inevitably care about how it's produced.

For us, sustainable seafood is about honouring what we catch and grow in Australia and New Zealand. Produced to first-world environmental, labour and culinary standards; owned, operated and managed by locals who live in and support regional towns – our seafood is special, sustainable, bloody delicious and worth celebrating!

SELECTION & STORAGE

The secret to a perfect seafood meal lies in the raw material – the seafood itself must be of impeccable quality, whether fresh or frozen. Often, the reason we seem to have a better seafood meal in a restaurant than at home lies in the careful sourcing, storage and handling of the seafood, even before it hits the pan or the plate.

The key to buying good seafood is having access to it. As in so many other parts of the food chain, supermarkets are now a significant channel to market for many seafood producers. Although the nature of seafood – sporadic availability, variable storage and handling and high perishability – makes running seafood departments in large supermarkets a complex task, the quality and range of seafood available in supermarkets has improved dramatically over recent years, especially in the freezer section. While this growth has contributed to the gradual demise of many independent fishmongers, a specialist fishmonger is still more likely to offer a more dynamic range, as they are more likely to be directly involved in sourcing seafood on a daily basis.

Seeking out a good fishmonger is important. Whether they're behind the counter of a major supermarket or running their own store, find someone who cares about seafood, is excited by seafood and, most importantly, is an avid fan of eating seafood. Wherever you are, don't treat buying seafood the same as buying sausages or frozen peas. Make it an occasion and try to eat it on the same day – you don't see people buying seafood at the markets of Europe or Asia to eat next week!

The process starts with selection. As frustrating as it might seem, you need to have an open mind when buying seafood. Don't think that just because you want to cook the hapuka recipe on page 113 on Friday night, you'll be able to go out and buy hapuka. Availability depends on the vagaries of the season, fishing conditions and general supply – there simply may not be any fresh hapuka the day you're looking for it. Where possible, we've tried to offer alternatives in the descriptions, but as a general rule, head to the fishmonger first, then plan the menu or dish based on what you find.

It's also important to consider frozen seafood. It can be not only a safe, reliable option, but in some instances it's the only option – the beautiful subantarctic toothfish or deepwater scampi simply never find their way to market fresh. But note that freezing is not like embalming – seafood remains highly fragile and subject to rapid deterioration. Even if a prawn has been deep frozen at –50°C (–58°F) on board the vessel it was caught from within minutes of coming out of the water and using the latest technology, its shelf life is limited. Your domestic freezer, which runs variously at –6 to –8°C (18–21°F), is not the place to store frozen seafood for much longer than two months.

Use your senses when buying seafood. Look, smell and, where possible, taste. It might seem pushy to demand of your fishmonger a feel, sniff or bite, but it will save you much anxiety (and money) when you get home and find that your selection doesn't need to be thrown out. Learn to recognise fresh seafood – stop by your fishmonger often and get to know their sources. Take their advice as to what's in season, what's coming through and, importantly, what they're taking home for dinner – a surefire tip to the best in the shop.

As we've seen, sustainability is also important. The easiest way is to try to buy the best looking seafood – inevitably, this will have come from a source that cares about the welfare of the fisheries.

Tips on buying and storing fish

These are general guidelines – specific instructions are given if necessary in the individual fish and shellfish descriptions that follow.

Always try to buy whole fish where possible – except if the fish is large, such as tuna or swordfish. Whole fish will keep for longer and the flesh will stay in better condition. It also allows you to scrutinise the quality closely: the eyes should be clear and plump, not sunken or discoloured. The aroma should be a clean, fresh smell of the sea with a soft, buttery sweet note. Good-quality whole fish should look visually stunning – there should be a consistent covering of scales with no obvious indents or bruising. The fish should be covered in a clear, clean protective coat of natural fresh sea 'slime' (believe us, this is a good thing!) that has a distinct marine aroma. If a whole fish doesn't have this, it's probably been washed and rewashed in fresh water, which shortens the shelf life and removes a great deal of flavour.

If you don't have the confidence to fillet whole fish, ask your fishmonger to do it for you. Be sure to ask for dry-filleting, which means the fish isn't soaked in water before or after cutting. Remember, *fresh water is the enemy of fresh fish*. It rips the essential oils out of the flesh, increases the core temperature and dramatically reduces shelf life.

Having said that, don't be afraid to give filleting a go (see pages 428–29 and 431–33 for techniques), as fish that's been filleted just before use will undoubtedly provide the best eating experience. Make sure you have an appropriate sharp knife, then practise on some simple, inexpensive 'round' fish, such as blue mackerel or mullet. You'll be surprised how quickly you can learn the basics. You could ask your fishmonger to gill, gut and scale the fish for you, leaving the mess with them. Have them wrap your 'dressed' fish, then, at home, rewrap the fish in muslin (cheesecloth) or freezer film (plastic wrap designed for freezer use). Prepare an airtight container with a layer of ice on the bottom and a drip tray sitting above. Rest the wrapped fish on the drip tray, seal and store in the driest part of the fridge – the vegetable crisper – until required. Always fillet as close to the time of use as possible, as cut flesh has a tendency to oxidise quickly. If your fishmonger fillets the fish for you, remind them to dry-fillet and to wrap the fillets tightly in freezer film or butcher paper. Once home, store them the same way as whole fish.

When buying fillets, look for those with a translucent sheen, a bright sparkling colour and a fresh, clean aroma. Wrap them tightly in freezer film, then in plastic wrap, as the fillets will oxidise even more quickly than whole fish, then store them in the same way. Always use fresh fillets as soon as possible. If you choose to freeze fresh fillets at home, be aware that both their culinary quality and shelf life will be very limited. If you want to use frozen fillets, try to purchase them pre-frozen, as these are usually produced using professional deep-freeze technology and packaging. If frozen fillets aren't vacuum-sealed, wrap them tightly in plastic wrap then again in newspaper or butcher paper. To thaw, place unwrapped frozen fillets on a drip tray in an airtight container and leave overnight in the fridge, then use immediately.

FISH
A–Z GUIDE
& RECIPES

BARRAMUNDI

Barramundi (*Lates calcarifer*) is an iconic table fish revered as a quintessential Australian brand – the name barramundi, after all, is derived from an Australian Aboriginal word meaning 'large-scaled river fish'. Its status is justly deserved – the flavour and texture of a wild, ocean-swimming barramundi make for a truly unique experience. It's a special fish, as beautiful in reality as in the dreams of many anglers and chefs, but such is the demand for barramundi that a substantial amount consumed in Australia is actually imported.

This member of the sea perch family has a distinct pointed head, concave forehead, large jaw and rounded tail fin. It has two dorsal fins, one with seven or eight strong spines and a second of ten or eleven rays. Along with thick shoulders and a powerful tail, it has characteristically large scales. It can vary in colour from silver for a sea-run fish to very dark chocolate brown for a fish caught or farmed in a freshwater pond or waterway. It's hermaphroditic, starting life as a male and changing after a few years into a female.

These quirky fish can live happily in a broad range of salinities, from turgid fresh water to oceanic salt water. They prefer to inhabit the bottom of the sea, river or billabong, from where they ambush their prey.

They're prolifically farmed throughout the tropical waters of Australia and Asia. When sea-run or grown in saltwater ponds and kept swimming against tides or currents rather than raised in still freshwater ponds, they're typically firmer, with a cleaner flavour.

SEASONALITY Wild: season closed November–February; farmed: year round

CATCHING METHOD Monofilament gillnet on inshore tidal mudflats and rivers

COMMON LENGTH 60–90 cm (24–35½ in)

COMMON WEIGHT 2–8 kg (4 lb 8 oz – 17 lb 10 oz)

IDENTIFIABLE FEATURES Small head, large mouth and eyes, thick shoulders, rounded tail fin, silver to chocolate brown, belly always silver

SUSTAINABILITY Stock status good

BARRAMUNDI IN THE KITCHEN

It's worth hunting down wild barramundi when it's in season; specimens of 4–5 kg (8 lb 13 oz–11 lb) or more offer the most distinctive taste of any fish in Australia. An intense, earthy, almost mushroom-like flavour combines with soft flesh that stays moist. If the flesh is lacking a little in firmness, especially with farmed fish, salting the fillets for 12–24 hours before cooking can firm up the flesh.

It's beautiful in fillet form – cook it on a hotplate with a bowl over it so it will poach while the skin crisps up. As it can spend time in both fresh and salt water, its fat content can vary, but it's always quite fatty, so the flesh retains its moisture and the skin crisps up like pork crackling. Plate-sized (1 kg/2 lb 4 oz) fish are best steamed or fried.

With such a great flavour, the accompaniments should be simple – something as basic as crushed peas would suffice, so you can enjoy the natural mild sweetness and nuttiness of the fish. Autumnal vegetables, simple salads and plain butter sauces also allow the fish to shine.

A number of farms in Australia have worked hard to replicate the flavour and texture of wild fish. Of particular note are the sea-cage operation at Cone Bay in Western Australia, and the farms off Humpty Doo in the Northern Territory and the Daintree and Coral Coast in Queensland. These all produce fish of exceptional quality and great consistency.

BEST COOKING METHODS Pan-fried with crisp skin (fillets, see page 437), steamed or fried (plate-sized)

TEXTURE Soft to medium–firm and generally moist once cooked

AROMA Intense, with a fresh shiitake mushroom character

FLAVOUR Clean, with autumnal notes – cooked egg yolk, mushroom and sweet cooked carrot

APPEARANCE Flesh light grey to white with pink hues when raw; dull white to arctic white once cooked

YIELD Boneless flesh about 40% of whole weight

SUBSTITUTES Blue-eye trevalla, mulloway (including jewfish)

Steamed barramundi with tomato consommé

To make the tomato consommé, place the ripe tomatoes, chilli, salt, brown sugar, coriander root and garlic in a narrow, deep bowl. Blitz until smooth using a hand-held blender. Strain the tomato mixture through a conical sieve lined with muslin (cheesecloth), collecting the liquid in a small saucepan.

Warm the tomato consommé over medium heat and bring to a simmer.

Place the fish fillets in a prepared electric steamer or other steamer (see note) and cook for 5 minutes. Remove and leave to rest for a minute. Gently peel off the fish skin and discard.

Meanwhile, blanch the roma tomatoes by making a small cross in the base of each one, leaving the green stem attached. Plunge the tomatoes into boiling water for 7–8 seconds then transfer to a bowl of iced water to refresh. Gently remove the tomatoes from the iced water and peel – the skin should come off easily.

Pour the consommé into four bowls. Add one barramundi fillet, two whole blanched tomatoes with stems, a coriander sprig and a drizzle of lemon oil to each bowl. Sprinkle a pinch of sea salt over the fish and serve.

NOTES: Lemon oil is available in gourmet grocery stores and good supermarkets, but you could use quality extra virgin olive oil with perhaps a squeeze of fresh lemon.

Cooking times may vary a little depending on whether you use an electric steamer, a Chinese steamer, a double boiler or choose to steam in the oven, so take care not to overcook the fish.

SERVES 4

2 kg (4 lb 8 oz) ripe tomatoes
1 long red chilli, split lengthways, seeds removed, finely chopped
2 teaspoons sea salt, plus extra to serve
2 tablespoons light brown sugar
4 coriander (cilantro) roots, washed, finely chopped
4 garlic cloves, peeled
4 × 200 g (7 oz) barramundi fillets, skin on, pin-boned
8 small ripe roma (plum) tomatoes, with stems
iced water, as required, to refresh
4 coriander sprigs (cilantro)
lemon oil, to serve (see note)

Barramundi with crushed peas and sour cream

SERVES 4

4 × 200 g (7 oz) barramundi fillets, skin on, pin-boned
2 tablespoons rice flour
80 ml (2½ fl oz/⅓ cup) ghee (see note)
Crushed Peas (page 459)
85 g (3 oz/⅓ cup) sour cream
sea salt, to taste
lemon oil, to serve (see note page 25)

To prepare the barramundi fillets for pan-frying with crisp skin, lay them on a work surface and dust the skin sides with the rice flour. Place each fillet, flesh side down, on a sheet of baking paper large enough to cover the fillet.

Heat a large cast-iron or heavy-based frying pan over medium–high heat (or two smaller pans – it's essential that the fish is not overcrowded in the pan; see note) and add the ghee. When the pan is hot and the ghee translucent, place the fillets in the pan, skin side down, leaving the paper on the flesh side. Place a 1 kg (2 lb 4 oz) weight – such as a heavy pot or another pan – on top of the fillets and cook for 4 minutes, lifting the weight once or twice then moving the fillets gently around the pan so they don't burn. Reduce the heat to low. Remove the weight and the paper, then, using a spatula, gently flip each fillet to quickly seal the other side. (Cooking times may vary depending on the size of the fish from which the fillets were cut; for more information, see page 437.)

Serve the barramundi immediately, skin side up, with the crushed peas, sour cream and a liberal pinch of sea salt on the fish skin. Add a splash of lemon oil over the sour cream.

NOTES: Ghee is a type of clarified butter, made by heating the butter to separate the water, fat and milk solids. The water is discarded and the milk solids are left to caramelise with the fat to form a clear, nutty liquid. Good-quality versions are available in gourmet grocery stores and some supermarkets. Although it is used in the recipes throughout this book, feel free to use your favourite oil instead.

If you don't have a pan large enough for all the fillets, or two smaller pans, cook the fish in two batches. Keep the first batch warm while you cook the second.

Bass groper

BASS GROPER & BAR COD

The bass groper (*Polyprion moeone*) is a member of the wreckfish family, which includes the bar cod, hapuka and blue-eye trevalla. They are all well regarded for their broad scalloping flesh and moderate fat content, which keeps the flesh moist and delicious when cooked. The bar cod (*Epinephelus ergastularius*) and bass groper are almost interchangeable, although some aficionados prefer the slightly fattier bar cod and others the slightly firmer but more densely flavoured bass groper.

Bass gropers inhabit the deep offshore waters all around New Zealand, off Australia's southern coast, off the western coast from Coral Bay in the north to Geographe Bay in the south, and in deepwater locations off the eastern coast, from Tasmania to northern New South Wales. These bottom-dwelling predators feed on fish and crustaceans, with a particular passion for the ever-tasty rock cod, which is perhaps what gives them such a delicious flavour.

Although they're not abundant in Australian waters, the New Zealand fishery is consistent, providing a ready supply to the Australian market, where they're hugely popular with chefs, especially for Vietnamese cuisine. Due to their high value, the fish are rarely found in fillet form, but the head and wings are particularly meaty and can form a meal in themselves. The liver of winter fish is delicious and worth seeking out.

SEASONALITY NZ: year round, with a peak in winter–spring; southern Australia: autumn–spring

CATCHING METHODS Dropline, setline, some bottom otter trawl

COMMON LENGTH 30–100 cm (12–39½ in)

COMMON WEIGHT 1–30 kg (2 lb 4 oz – 66 lb)

IDENTIFIABLE FEATURES Mottled fawn colouring, bar cod with faint pale vertical bands

SUSTAINABILITY Managed by quota in Australia and NZ

BASS GROPER & BAR COD IN THE KITCHEN

Some chefs believe these are the best fish in Australian waters, and they're certainly among the most versatile. Although quite expensive, with a relatively low yield, they're worth every cent. The immense and sweet fish flavour will remind you just how special our waters are.

Baked, roasted, grilled (broiled), pan-fried with crisp skin or cooked in curries – bass groper and bar cod will shine in any culinary application. Bass groper cooked in a curry is the most gelatinous, more-ish of eating experiences. It's also delicious poached, steamed or cooked under a classic French fish weight (or another flat weight of about 1 kg/2 lb 4 oz, such as another pan). It's not done widely because of its cost, but it's delicious when battered and fried.

The one thing you shouldn't do is cook them in a really hot oven – this will split the protein in no time, creating a broken, grainy texture that isn't much fun to eat. Choose your cooking method based on the size of the fish; if you want to eat it raw, as sashimi or carpaccio, you need a small fish, but a 3–4 kg (6 lb 12 oz – 8 lb 13 oz) groper is ideal for cooking with crisp skin or in a curry. Large fish over 4 kg produce a deep, thick fillet which is ideal for pan-frying, roasting or steaming. Always undercook it a little, to experience its unique sweetness. If you cook it longer, it will take on a bigger flavour but will be more savoury. The less you cook this fish, the lighter the accompaniment it needs.

They can both be salted (see page 462), but also work well cooked simply and served with roasted vegetables – carrots, pumpkin (winter squash), cabbage, eggplant (aubergine) and witlof (chicory) – and can take small sweet flavours, Asian tastes and even Mediterranean.

BEST COOKING METHODS Grilled (broiled), poached, steamed, fried, pan-fried with crisp skin (fillets, see page 437), roasted, salted
TEXTURE Broad flake with a soft, rich mouthfeel
AROMA Deep, rich, intense
FLAVOUR Sweet, rich, mild yet lasting
APPEARANCE Flesh translucent grey–pink when raw; pearl white once cooked
YIELD Flesh about 35% of whole weight
SUBSTITUTES Blue-eye trevalla, hapuka, pink snapper

Bass groper with salt-roasted celeriac and yoghurt

Make breadcrumbs by frying the rye bread in the butter in a frying pan over high heat until golden. Chop into rough crumbs, or blitz in a food processor.

To prepare the bass groper fillets for pan-frying with crisp skin, lay them on a work surface and dust the skin sides with the rice flour. Place each fillet, flesh side down, on a sheet of baking paper large enough to cover the fillet.

Heat a large cast-iron or heavy-based frying pan over medium–high heat (or two smaller pans – it's essential that the fish is not overcrowded in the pan; see note) and add the ghee. When the pan is hot and the ghee translucent, place the fillets in the pan, skin side down, leaving the paper on the flesh side. Place a 1 kg (2 lb 4 oz) weight – such as a heavy pot or another pan – on top of the fillets and cook for 4 minutes, lifting the weight once or twice then moving the fillets gently around the pan so they don't burn. Reduce the heat to low. Remove the weights and the paper, then, using a spatula, gently flip each fillet to quickly seal the other side. (Cooking times may vary depending on the size of the fish from which the fillets were cut; for more information, see page 437.)

Place a scoop of the salt-roasted celeriac on each plate and top each with 1 tablespoon yoghurt and ½ teaspoon chives. Lay a bass groper fillet, skin side up, on each plate and sprinkle the skin with a little sea salt.

To finish, scatter breadcrumbs over each plate and add a drizzle of lemon oil.

NOTE: If you don't have a pan large enough for all the fillets, or two smaller pans, cook the fish in two batches. Keep the first batch warm while you cook the second.

SERVES 4

3–4 slices rye bread
20 g (¾ oz) butter
4 × 200 g (7 oz) bass groper fillets, skin on, pin-boned
2 tablespoons rice flour
80 ml (2½ fl oz/⅓ cup) ghee (see note page 26)
4 serves Salt-roasted Celeriac (page 463)
95 g (3¼ oz/⅓ cup) plain yoghurt
2 teaspoons chopped chives
sea salt, to taste
lemon oil, to serve (see note page 25)

Salted bar cod salad with poached egg, wild rocket and salmon roe

SERVES 4 AS AN ENTRÉE

400 g (14 oz) Salted Fish (page 462) made with bar cod
4 eggs, ideally very fresh
white wine vinegar, for poaching
2 handfuls wild rocket (arugula), leaves and stems
extra virgin olive oil, to serve
freshly ground black pepper, to serve
1 tablespoon salmon roe

To prepare the salted fish for cooking, rinse the salt off gently under cold running water, without washing it thoroughly. Fill a deep frying pan with fresh water and bring to the boil over high heat. When the water is boiling, remove the pan from the heat and add the fish. Leave the fish to poach for 2 minutes, then remove with a slotted spoon. Flake the fish roughly and set aside.

To poach the eggs, fill a very clean, small saucepan with water. Bring to the boil over high heat, then add a good dash of the vinegar. Return the water to the boil, then reduce the heat to low and gently add the eggs (see note). Using a spoon, slowly move the eggs around to create clean-edged poached eggs. Using a slotted spoon, remove the eggs carefully from the water, one at a time, as soon as the whites are set.

Place the rocket on serving plates and scatter the flaked fish over. Gently place a poached egg on each plate, then dress with a splash of olive oil and a little pepper. Top each with a teaspoon of salmon roe.

NOTE: When poaching eggs, break each egg separately into a small bowl first – this makes it easier to slip them into the boiling water.

BLUE COD

The blue cod (*Parapercis colias*) is endemic to New Zealand, where it has cult status with consumers something akin to the All Blacks rugby team. They live in shallow waters around the rocky coasts and to a depth of 150 m (500 ft) around the Chatham Islands to the east and Stewart Island to the south. They feed mainly on small fish, abalone and crabs.

With a large head and a tapering body, they're bluish green to blue–black on top and grey towards the belly. Blue cod are strongly territorial and will defend their area aggressively if disturbed. They spawn in spring, and can change gender from female to male during their lifetime.

The pot fishery is especially environmentally friendly and sustainable, as it eliminates large amounts of bycatch, but all blue cod is caught under a strict New Zealand Government quota system.

SEASONALITY Year round, with a peak in winter
CATCHING METHODS Baited pot, trawl
COMMON LENGTH 30–50 cm (12–20 in)
COMMON WEIGHT 1–3 kg (2 lb 4 oz – 6 lb 12 oz)
IDENTIFIABLE FEATURES Large, bluish green to blue–black on top, brownish grey on sides, smoothly sloped head and snout, short low first dorsal fin, long second dorsal fin
SUSTAINABILITY Highly sustainable

BLUE COD IN THE KITCHEN

Blue cod has a mild, slightly grassy flavour and soft yielding flesh. To any New Zealander it's the fish that fits any occasion. It can be cooked in many ways, including smoked, baked, fried, or in a soup or chowder.

Try it steamed with leafy greens such as cos (romaine) lettuce or celery hearts. But the best way to enjoy blue cod is to take full advantage of its delicate flaky texture – sear it in a pan until the flesh just turns white (leaving the middle slightly translucent), and it will fall apart into medium flakes and remain tender and succulent.

BEST COOKING METHODS Pan-fried with crisp skin (fillets, see page 437), baked, poached, steamed
TEXTURE Soft, yielding flesh with a broad scalloping flake
AROMA Clean, light, with a grassy iodine note
FLAVOUR Mild, sweet, with light notes of seaweed and moss
APPEARANCE Flesh translucent and pale when raw; arctic white once cooked
YIELD Flesh 35–40% of whole weight
SUBSTITUTES Gurnard, latchet, ling

Blue cod fillets with steamed celery and lettuce

SERVES 4

2 baby cos (romaine) lettuces, cut in half lengthways
4 pieces celery heart, with leaves
4 × 200 g (7 oz) blue cod fillets, skin removed, pin-boned
95 g (3¼ oz/⅓ cup) plain yoghurt
1 spring onion (scallion), outer layer removed, thinly sliced on the diagonal
lemon oil, to serve (see note page 25)
sea salt and freshly ground black pepper, to taste

Fill a Chinese steamer, wok or saucepan with water and bring to the boil over high heat.

Line two metal or bamboo steamer baskets with baking paper to prevent sticking. Place the cos and celery in one steamer basket and the cod fillets in the other.

Set the baskets over the steamer, with the fish on the bottom layer, and cover with a tight-fitting lid. Steam the vegetables for 1 minute, or until wilted and soft. Remove from the steamer and keep warm. Replace the lid to allow the cod to cook for a further 4 minutes (see note).

Place the steamed cod fillets on serving plates and top with the cos and celery. Spoon a tablespoon of yoghurt beside the fish and scatter with the spring onion. Drizzle a little lemon oil over the yoghurt. Season with salt and pepper to serve.

NOTE: Cooking times may vary according to the size of the fish and the thickness of the fillets, and whether you use a Chinese steamer or a double boiler, so take care not to overcook the fish.

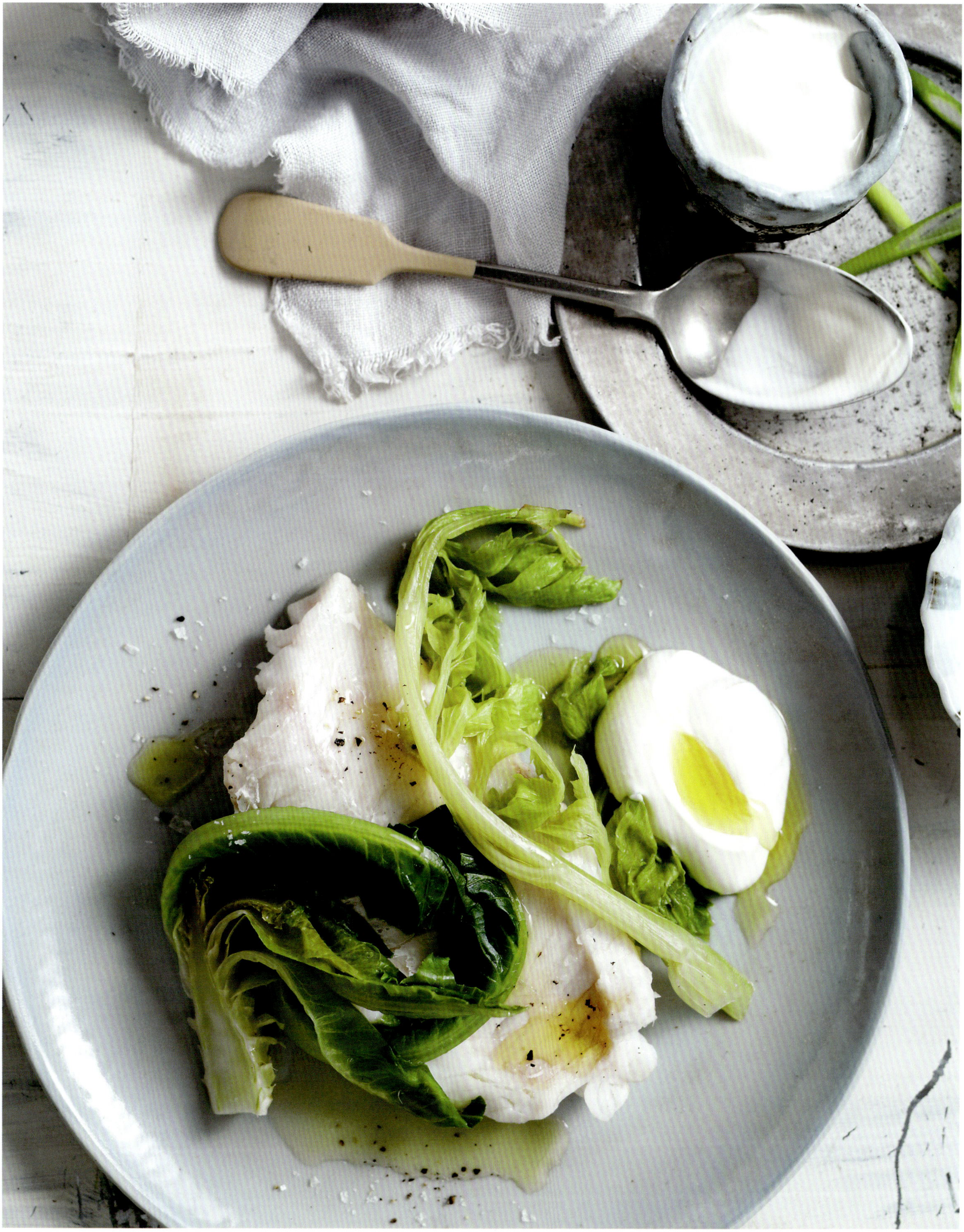

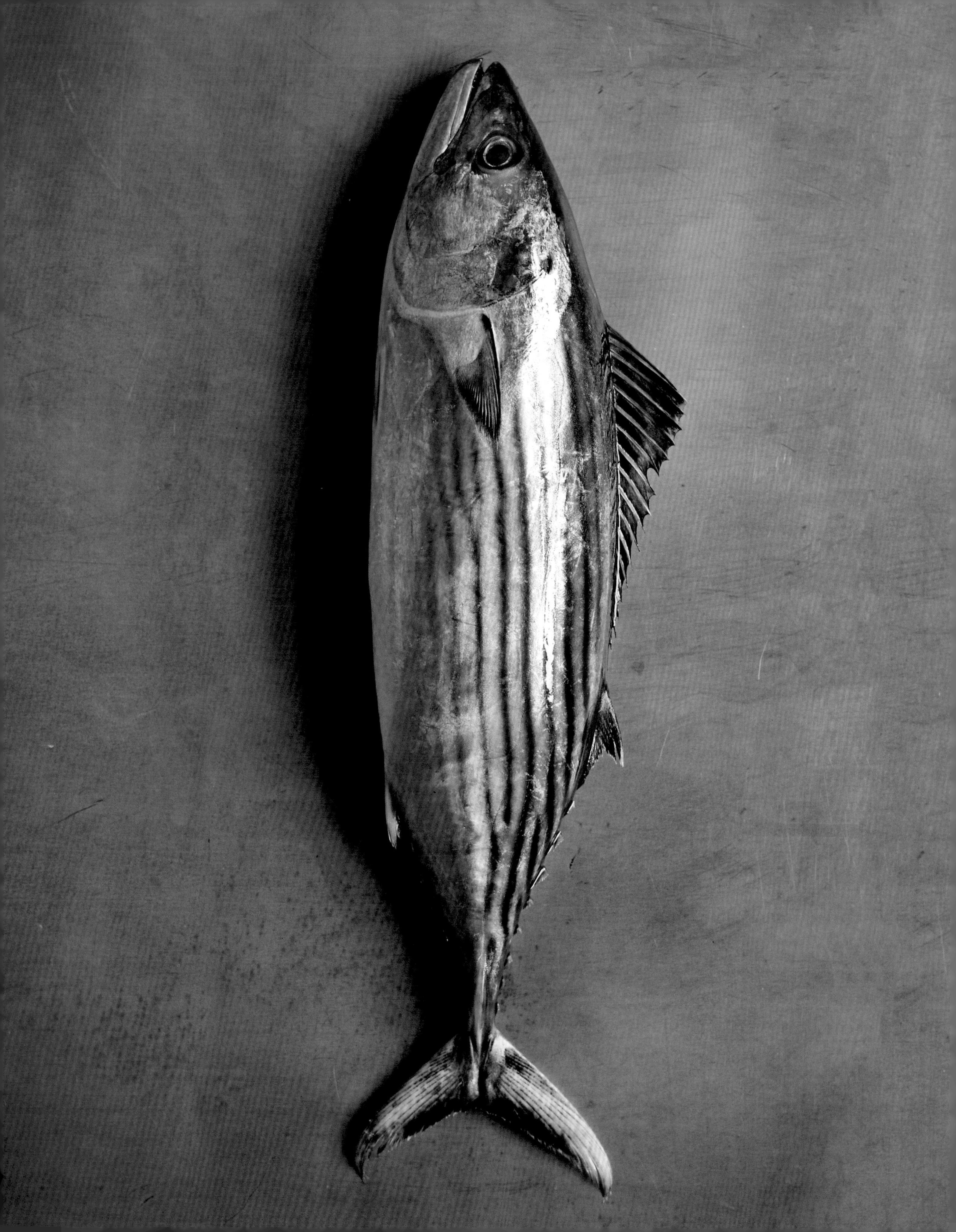

BONITO

Australian bonito (*Sarda australis*), a member of the tuna family, sometimes goes by the ungainly name horse mackerel, in reference to its habit of riding along with shoals of other ocean-going fish. The popularisation of bonito has been assisted by our growing interest in Japanese food; in Japan, dried bonito (or katsuobushi) is a vital ingredient of the stock called dashi, while fresh fish are grilled (broiled) tataki style or marinated in soy sauce and served with sliced garlic (zuke).

Of the three main species found in Australia, *Sarda australis* is the most commonly harvested for food. They feed on shoals of pilchards, anchovies and other smaller fish. The other two common species are oriental or striped bonito (*Sarda orientalis*) and leaping bonito (*Cybiosarda elegans*).

Caught mostly around the south-eastern corner of Australia, from southern Queensland to the South Australian border, the bonito is generally a bycatch of the longline and purse-seine fisheries hunting tuna, flathead or ling. As a fast-swimming, tough, hard-fighting little fish, it's also highly regarded by sports anglers, and is popular among game fishers as live bait.

Although bonito has a lower fat content than other members of the tuna family, it's quite soft-fleshed, bruising easily if poorly handled and becoming quite dark when left unbled. It's at its best when dispatched rapidly on harvest – knocked on the head immediately, then ice-slurried to protect the flesh.

SEASONALITY Year round, with a peak in summer to late autumn
CATCHING METHODS Pelagic longline, purse seine
COMMON LENGTH 40–50 cm (16–20 in)
COMMON WEIGHT 400 g – 2 kg (14 oz – 4 lb 8 oz)
IDENTIFIABLE FEATURES Bright blue–green or blue–black back, dark horizontal stripes, silver belly
SUSTAINABILITY Stock status strong

BONITO IN THE KITCHEN

Until recently underused by many chefs, this glorious little fish is now in hot demand, particularly thanks to enthusiastic use by Japanese chefs, and has become hard to get. The bigger the bonito, and the duller colour of its skin, the more buttery and enjoyable it will be to eat. Perfect at about 800 g (1 lb 12 oz), it makes a good sashimi fish, but it's best to set the protein with a little heat. Unless it's marinated first, it's not a great fish for cooking, as it quickly drops its fat.

The flesh has a very soft texture, so to firm it up try this: score the skin, rub a little salt on it, then pour boiling water over it to set the outside of the protein. Or set skinless fillets by pouring boiling water over them. Don't cook it, but let it set to a firmness that makes it easier to slice. Some like to blowtorch the skin before slicing it for sashimi or for a tartare with French shallots.

SPECIAL STORAGE AND HANDLING Handle carefully; gut, wrap in freezer film, then store as usual. Do not store for longer than 48 hours; fillet just before preparation.

BEST COOKING METHOD Raw as sashimi, with blowtorched skin

TEXTURE Soft when raw; firm and tight-grained once cooked

AROMA Light, sweetly oceanic, with notes of green seaweed

FLAVOUR Mild, light, almost chicken-like, with an aftertaste of driftwood saltiness

APPEARANCE Delicate pink when raw; opaque grey once cooked

YIELD Flesh 55–60% of whole weight

SUBSTITUTES Albacore tuna, blue mackerel, yellowfin tuna

Bonito sashimi with seaweed tempura

Make a simple marinade by heating the soy sauce, mirin and sugar together in a small saucepan over high heat. Bring to the boil, then remove from the heat and set aside to cool to room temperature.

To make a wasabi mayonnaise, mix the mayonnaise, wasabi paste, diced shallot and extra soy sauce in a small bowl until well combined. Pour into a squeeze bottle and refrigerate until ready to use.

Place the bonito fillets on a baking tray. Pour boiling water gently and evenly over the fillets to seal the flesh. Transfer the fillets to a medium bowl and pour the marinade over. Leave at room temperature for 30 minutes.

Meanwhile, combine 1½ tablespoons of water with the seaweed powder and flour in a bowl, mixing gently to form a dough.

Heat the vegetable oil in a small deep saucepan over high heat. As the oil begins to smoke (see note), drop in pieces of dough and fry for about 1 minute, or until golden. Carefully remove the seaweed tempura from the oil and set aside on paper towel to drain.

To serve, slice the bonito, aiming for 32–40 thin slices. Arrange the sliced fish on four serving plates. Place a tiny drop of wasabi mayonnaise on each piece of fish, scatter pieces of seaweed tempura on each plate and finish with the sliced shallots and shiso.

NOTE: It's okay to judge the smoke point of the oil by eye. Depending on the oil used, the temperature will vary from 205 to 230°C (400 to 450°F), tested using an oil thermometer.

SERVES 4–6 AS AN ENTRÉE

400 ml (14 fl oz) light Japanese soy sauce, plus extra 1 teaspoon for mayonnaise

200 ml (7 fl oz) mirin

½ teaspoon caster (superfine) sugar

2 tablespoons Mayonnaise (page 455)

1 teaspoon wasabi paste

1 teaspoon very finely diced red Asian shallot, plus extra, sliced, to serve

1 whole bonito, about 800 g (1 lb 12 oz), cleaned, skin removed, pin-boned, cut into 4 loin fillets

boiling water, as required

1 tablespoon seaweed powder

1 tablespoon tempura flour

125 ml (4 fl oz/½ cup) vegetable oil

baby shiso leaves, to serve

Bonito tataki

SERVES 4–6 AS AN ENTRÉE

½ side fresh bonito, about 500 g (1 lb 2 oz)
sea salt, to taste
1 heaped teaspoon grated ginger
2 tablespoons thinly sliced green spring onion (scallion) tops
125 ml (4 fl oz/½ cup) Ponzu Sauce (page 455)
lemon oil, to serve (see note page 25)

Lay the bonito on a clean work surface, skin side up, and sprinkle with a little sea salt. Using a blowtorch, flame the skin until it turns dark. Turn the fish over and flame the flesh until it begins to turn opaque. (You could also sear the fish under a hot grill/broiler or in a heavy-based frying pan over high heat.)

Cut the seared bonito into slices 1 cm (½ in) thick. Serve on a platter with the ginger and spring onion. Put the ponzu sauce in a serving jug or bowl, drizzle lemon oil into it and serve on the side.

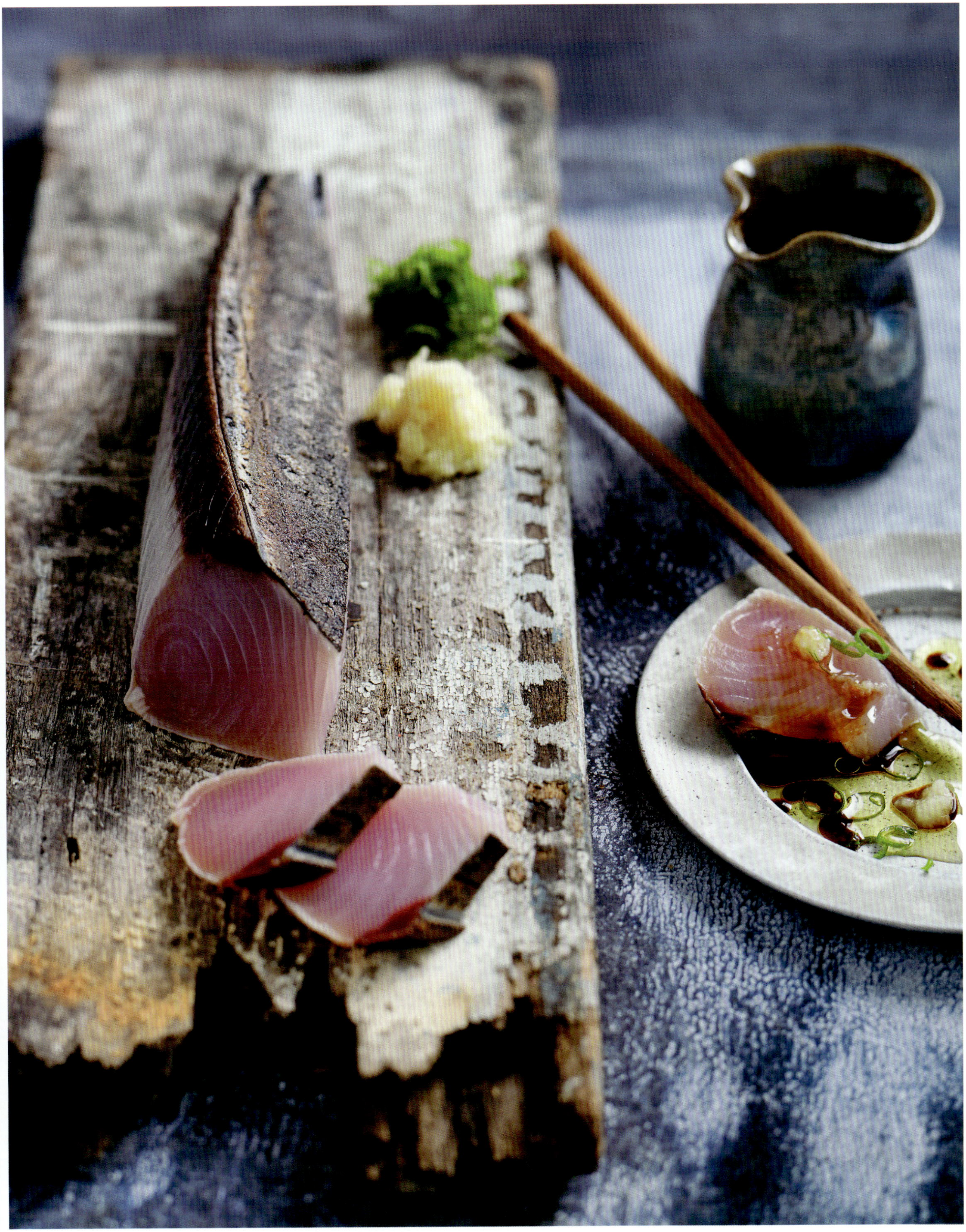

Yellowfin bream

BREAM

Many fish are generically labelled bream, but chefs tend to seek out the delicious inshore and estuary black bream (*Acanthopagrus butcheri*), pikey bream (*Acanthopagrus berda*) and yellowfin bream (*Acanthopagrus australis*). These fish inhabit inshore and estuarine environments, scavenging for cunjevoi (sea squirts), small fish, molluscs and worms. This produces their firm flaky flesh, luscious fat content and a certain grassy flavour.

The colour of bream can vary according to the water in which they're living. In the lakes and estuaries of southern Australia, the water is often discoloured by flood waters, which means 'black' bream is often olive green to golden bronze. In the waters of the surf or outside river mouths, say in the mid-north of Western Australia, where the 'black' bream feed over clean sand, they are bright silver.

The three species are caught around the entire Australian coast, but are sometimes confused with deep-sea bream or morwong (see page 51), which are caught in deeper waters.

SEASONALITY Year round, with a peak in NSW and Vic. from late summer to early winter

CATCHING METHODS Gillnet, purse seine, trap, some hook and line trolling

COMMON LENGTH 25–45 cm (10–18 in)

COMMON WEIGHT 350 g – 1 kg (12 oz – 2 lb 4 oz)

IDENTIFIABLE FEATURES Black: upper body silvery–olive brown or bronzy black, even greenish at times, with small black spots along the shoulder, fins brownish black; pikey and yellowfin: commonly confused with the black bream, although both have bold yellow pectoral and dorsal fins

SUSTAINABILITY Stock status good

BREAM IN THE KITCHEN

Black and yellowfin bream are both typically fattier than snapper or deep-sea bream. Often, you'll find thick deposits of fat inside their belly cavity, but more importantly there is also fat throughout the flesh. This fat delivers a delicious eating experience with both raw and cooked fish.

Fresh bream is good raw, but can be cooked on the bone, pot-roasted in the oven, or filleted and pan-fried. Always leave the skin on to intensify the flavours. With a simple, accentuated bone structure, it's an easy fish to eat both on the bone and filleted. You'll need to score the whole fish to cook it evenly. When pot-roasting in stock, add complementary tastes, such as butter, ginger and parsley; or butter, ginger, caramelised garlic, French shallots, black pepper and stock. Tomatoes and other lightly acidic fruit go well with bream, thanks to its fat content. Pour the sauce over it.

It's great barbecued, but make sure you fill the cavity with herbs, lemon and seasoning. Slather in butter, wrap in foil, then cook. If pan-frying with crisp skin (see page 437), pair it with Asian greens such as bok choy (pak choy).

SPECIAL STORAGE AND HANDLING Buy whole; remove gut and gills as soon as possible – they can rot quickly, discolouring the belly flesh and spoiling the flavour. Store as usual. Leave filleting until just before cooking.

BEST COOKING METHODS Pot-roasted on the bone, pan-fried with crisp skin (fillets, see page 437)

TEXTURE Firm when raw; moist and soft with a small tight flake once cooked

AROMA Zesty notes of green seaweed with hints of fresh river water

FLAVOUR Mildly sweet, with notes of tidal rock pool and fresh oyster

APPEARANCE Flesh light pinkish grey when raw, arctic white once cooked

YIELD Boneless fillets about 40% of whole weight

SUBSTITUTES Deep-sea bream, pink snapper, silver warehou, tropical snapper

Black bream

Bream with bok choy, parsley root and salted red chilli

SERVES 4

2 parsley roots (Hamburg or turnip-rooted parsley), trimmed if preferred, peeled and cut in half lengthways (see note)
iced water, as required, to refresh
2 bok choy (pak choy), well rinsed, cut in half lengthways
4 × 200 g (7 oz) bream fillets
2 tablespoons rice flour
80 ml (2½ fl oz/⅓ cup) ghee (see note page 26)
40 g (1½ oz) butter
sea salt and freshly ground black pepper, to taste
2 tablespoons salted red chilli (see note page 247), to serve
1 tablespoon lemon oil, to serve (see note page 25)

Heat a medium saucepan of salted water over high heat and bring to the boil. Add the parsley root and blanch for 3–4 minutes, or until just soft but still slightly firm. Remove and plunge into a bowl of iced water to refresh. Drain and set aside.

Return the saucepan to the heat and bring the water back to the boil. Blanch the bok choy for 30 seconds, or until just soft. Remove and plunge into a bowl of iced water to refresh. Drain and set aside.

To prepare bream fillets for pan-frying with crisp skin, lay them on a work surface and dust the skin sides with the rice flour. Place each fillet, flesh side down, on a sheet of baking paper large enough to cover the fillet.

Heat a cast-iron or heavy-based frying pan (or two smaller pans – it's essential that the fish is not overcrowded in the pan; see note) over medium–high heat and add the ghee. When the pan is hot and the ghee translucent, place the fillets in the pan, skin side down, leaving the paper on the flesh side. Place a 1 kg (2 lb 4 oz) weight – such as a heavy pot or another pan – on top of the fillets and cook for 4 minutes, lifting the weight once or twice then moving the fillets gently around the pan so they don't burn. Reduce the heat to low. Remove the weight and the paper, then, using a spatula, gently flip each fillet to quickly seal the other side. (Cooking times may vary depending on the size of the fish from which the fillets were cut; for more information, see page 437.)

Meanwhile, heat the butter in a frying pan over medium heat. When the butter is bubbling, add the blanched parsley root and bok choy, stir through, then season with a little salt and pepper.

Place a bream fillet on each plate, skin side up, then add the parsley root and bok choy, together with any butter from the pan. Garnish with salted red chilli and finish with a splash of lemon oil.

NOTES: If parsley roots are unavailable, use parsnips, turnips or any root vegetable you prefer.

If you don't have a pan large enough for all the fillets, or two smaller pans, cook the fish in two batches. Keep the first batch warm while you cook the second.

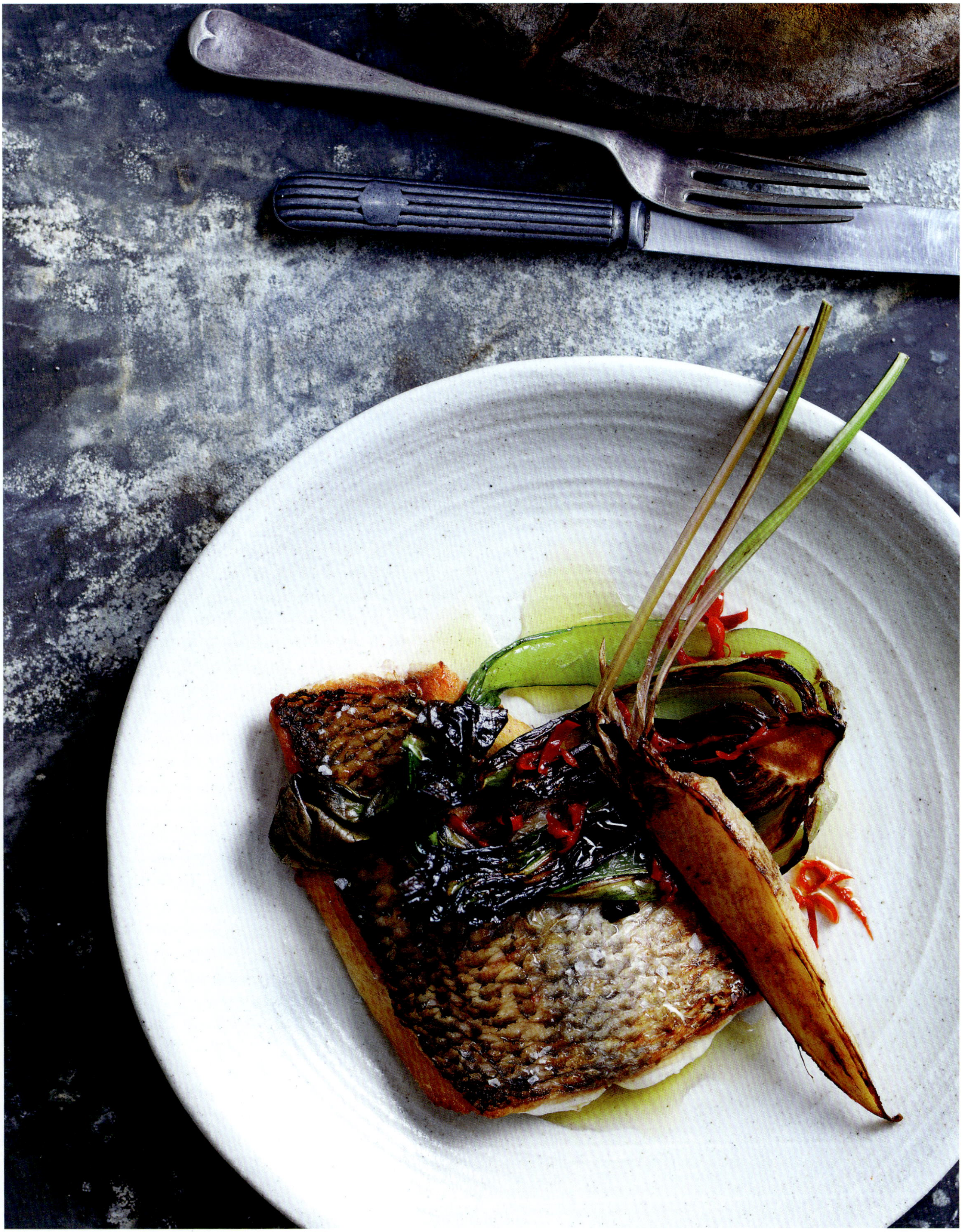

Grey morwong

BREAM, DEEP-SEA

Sea bream is a general name for the grey morwong (*Nemadactylus douglasii*), blue morwong or queen snapper (*Nemadactylus valenciennesi*), jackass morwong or tarahiki (*Nemadactylus macropterus*) and red or banded morwong (*Cheilodactylus fuscus*), not to be confused with estuarine bream species (see Bream, page 45). Historically, the trawl fisheries of south-eastern Australia and northern New Zealand produced bream of variable quality, but sea bream caught using hook and line trolling is outstanding.

Sea bream live at 50–200 m (160–650 ft) and feed on squid, molluscs, prawns (shrimp) and other crustaceans. This yields a high fat content that makes them highly versatile and premium eating, but also means they spoil quickly if poorly handled. The layer of fat under the skin can often taint the flesh with a strong rotten-vegetable flavour.

Red morwong, often found live in the tanks of fishmongers and Chinese restaurants, are valued as highly for their appearance and shape as for their delicate sweet flavour, ideally suited to the Cantonese technique of steaming with ginger and shallots. Hunt out line-caught fish, or inspect the whole fish from which fillets will be cut.

SEASONALITY Year round, with peaks in NZ, NSW and Vic. from late summer to early winter
CATCHING METHODS Hook and line trolling (for the best fish), purse seine, bottom otter trawl
COMMON LENGTH 25–60 cm (10–24 in)
COMMON WEIGHT 550 g – 3 kg (1 lb 4 oz – 6 lb 12 oz)
IDENTIFIABLE FEATURES Large eyes, small mouth and a central extended ray on the pectoral fin
SUSTAINABILITY Stock status good

DEEP-SEA BREAM IN THE KITCHEN

Bream has a sweet flavour coupled with a deep, sometimes grassy umami savouriness. This makes it best eaten with simple flavours, such as citrus, capers, olives and tomatoes. It's good raw, and is used in many Asian dishes and steamed whole. The firm flesh can withstand pan-frying or deep-frying. Try deep-frying it whole then garnishing with citrus or a soy sauce and chilli dressing.

Skinless, boneless tarahiki fillets are a fish and chips staple in New Zealand and Victoria, but they can spoil quickly and become very intense, with an almost acrid back palate.

BEST COOKING METHODS Fried, steamed
TEXTURE Firm when raw; creamy, moist and soft with a small tight flake once cooked
AROMA Zesty notes of green seaweed, a little funky if the fish is not well handled
FLAVOUR Mildly sweet, with grassy notes and a finish of shiitake mushroom
APPEARANCE Flesh light grey with a pink hue when raw, arctic white once cooked
YIELD Boneless fillets about 40% of whole weight
SUBSTITUTES Blue warehou, pink snapper, tropical snapper

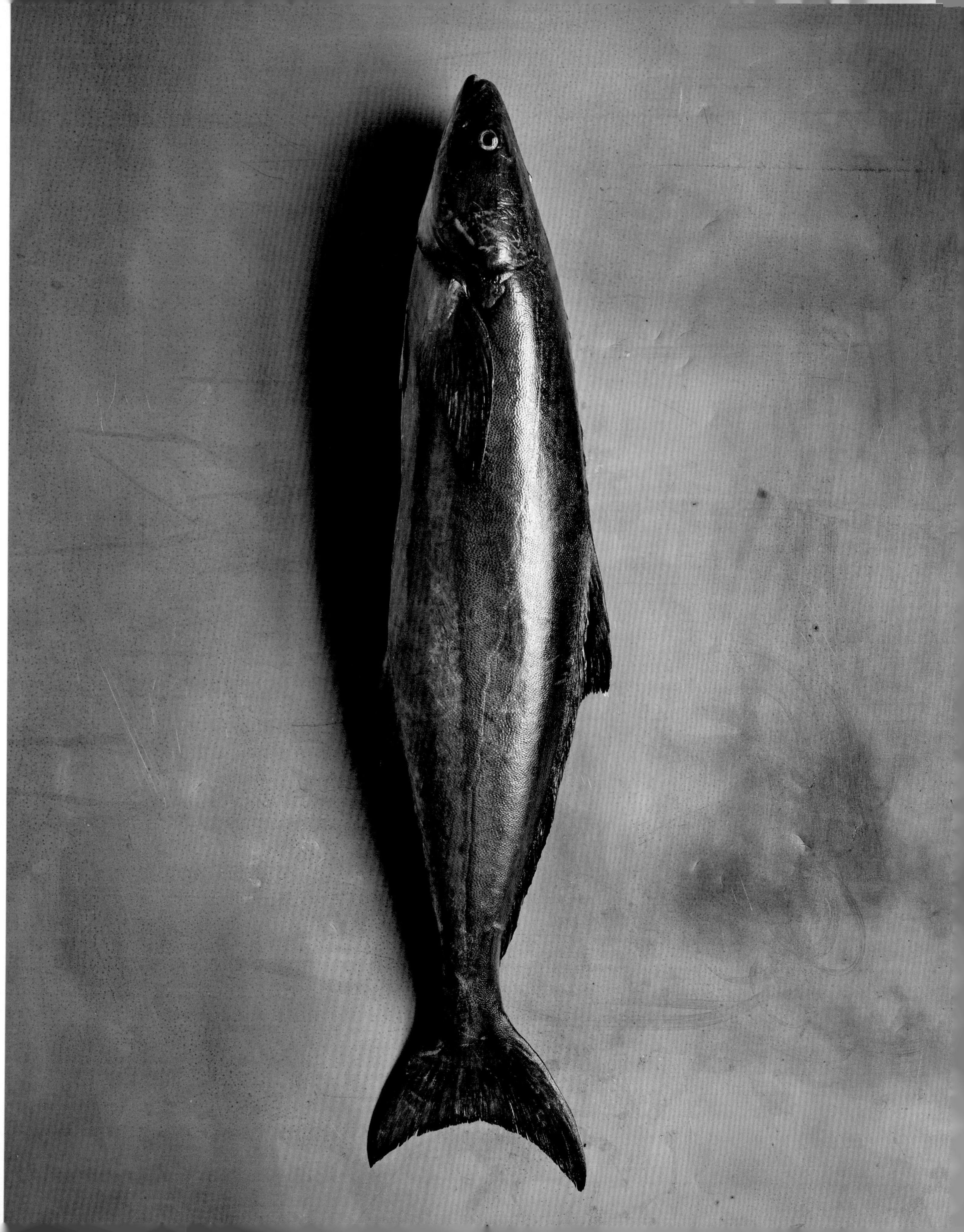

COBIA

The cobia (*Rachycentron canadum*), or black kingfish, is found in the tropical and subtropical waters of northern Australia, and other tropical zones throughout the world. It's a beautiful fish, with a large, broad, flattened head, piercing eyes and tapering body. It moves through the water with the style and grace of a stealth bomber. Fast-growing and fast-moving, this species of the open ocean has long been revered by anglers as a terrific catch, but its marvellous culinary characteristics have been largely overlooked.

The flesh of this high-yielding fish is broad-flaked, firm and sweet. It can be sliced for raw preparations, or steamed, roasted, pan-fried, wok-fried or grilled (broiled). It has a high fat content, so unlike most other white-fleshed fish, it retains moisture. It also has a thin layer of fat just under the skin, which renders during cooking, adding moisture to the flesh and crisping up the skin like pork crackling.

Cobia is now farmed, mostly as a winter crop in Far North Queensland by savvy prawn (shrimp) farmers. It has adapted well to domestication and is a standout Australian farmed fish, some say superior even to its wild equivalent. Like many tropical species, it tends to spawn during the warmer months, at which time its flesh will often lose its firm texture and natural sweetness. This soft flesh is not prevalent in farmed cobia, however.

SEASONALITY Wild: peak in summer but best in winter; farmed: February–November
CATCHING METHODS Longline, trap, hook and line trolling, handline
COMMON LENGTH 30–150 cm (12–60 in)
COMMON WEIGHT Up to 30 kg (66 lb)
IDENTIFIABLE FEATURES Dark brown on back grading to white on belly, with two darker brown horizontal bands on flanks
SUSTAINABILITY Farmed and wild: very sustainable – fast-growing, highly productive and highly managed

John dory

DORY

To many, the john dory (*Zeus faber*) is the king of table fish, which perhaps makes the mirror dory (*Zenopsis nebulosa*) the lost prince. Both are extraordinary-looking fish, with a flat, dinner-plate shape, a dorsal fin resembling a mohawk and a small head with a quizzical downward-facing mouth that gives them the appearance of a questioning judge. The john dory is readily identifiable from the golden-ringed, black 'thumbprint of St Peter' on both sides. The mirror dory looks similar, but is silver all over (with a pale spot). Both have smooth skin that appears to be scale-less.

Dories spend most of the year in very deep water, around 700–1500 m (2300–5000 ft), where they prey upon smaller fish in darkness. They're not fast swimmers, relying instead on stealth and their expanding jaw to catch their prey. They're especially fussy eaters, preferring live young fish, which undoubtedly accounts for their delicious flavour. During June and July they congregate around coastal underwater mountains just 300 m (1000 ft) from the surface, which means they're easier to catch. At this time their winter fat makes them spectacular eating.

John dory are found along the southern coast from southern Queensland to the central coast of Western Australia, but most available for sale are caught off New Zealand. Mirror dory are found in similar waters but more commonly in south-eastern Australia.

John dory is highly regarded for its sweet, delicate flesh, but mirror dory tastes similar at around a third the price. All dories are relatively expensive, however, due to their low fillet yield. Whereas many fish will return around 60 per cent of their landed weight as edible fillet, you're lucky to get 30 per cent from dories, and filleting raw can be quite tricky.

SEASONALITY John dory: year round, with a peak in winter; mirror dory: late autumn to mid-spring
CATCHING METHOD Mid-water trawl
COMMON LENGTH 30–60 cm (12–24 in)
COMMON WEIGHT 500–800 g (1 lb 2 oz – 1 lb 12 oz)
IDENTIFIABLE FEATURES John dory: thin, flat body, smooth golden-olive skin, dark-ringed black mark on sides; mirror dory: thin, flat body, smooth mirror-like silver skin, pale spots on sides
SUSTAINABILITY Not subject to quotas; not considered overfished

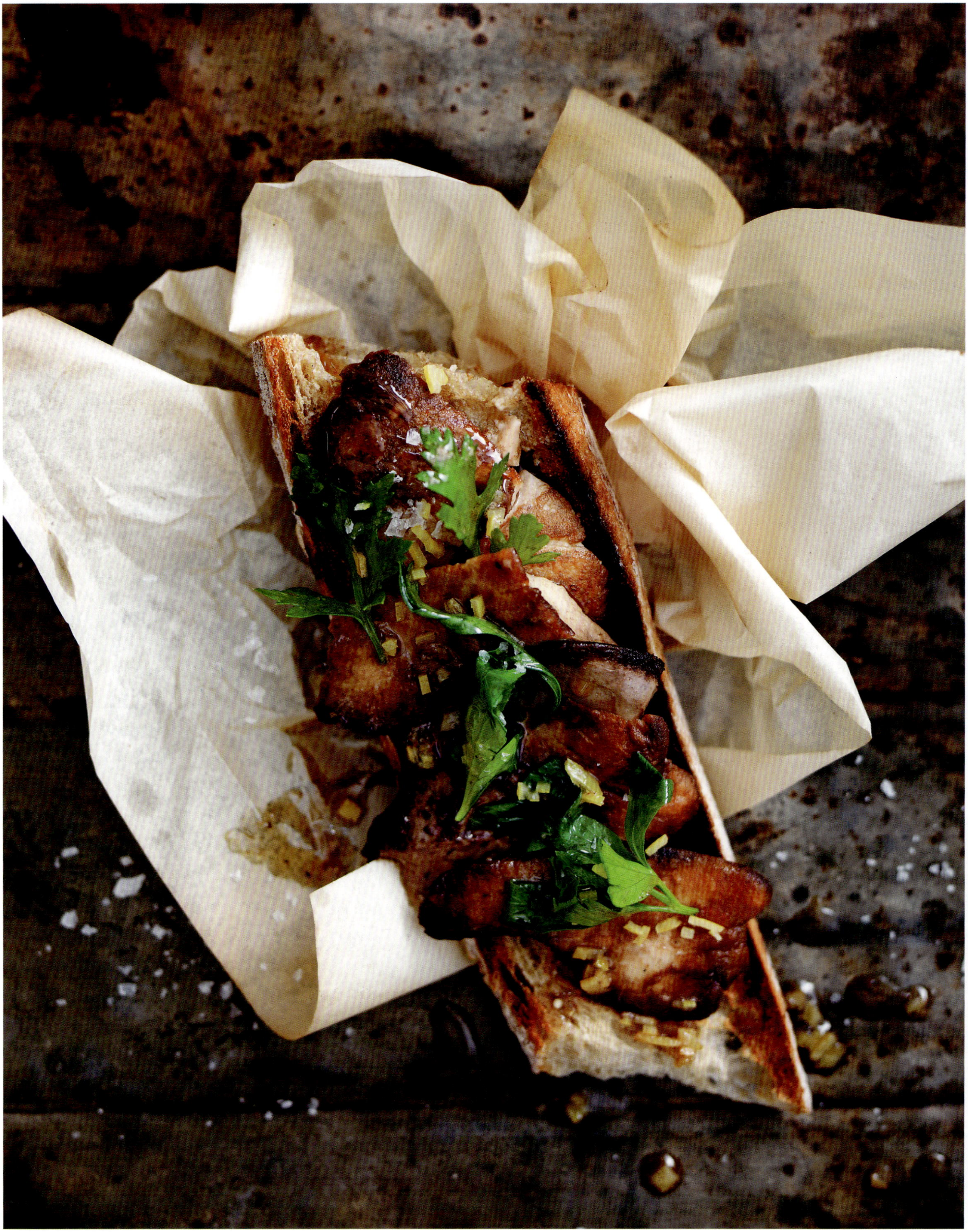

Pan-fried john dory liver on toast

In a medium bowl, dissolve the 2 tablespoons of salt in 1 litre (35 fl oz/4 cups) of water. Soak the livers in the salt solution overnight. The next day, remove the livers and carefully trim off the veiny sections.

Heat the ghee in a large heavy-based frying pan over medium–high heat. When the ghee begins to smoke, add the livers. Fry for 1 minute, then add the fresh butter and turn the livers gently using a spatula. Remove the livers from the pan and drain on paper towel.

Add the preserved lemon to the same pan, off the heat, with a pinch of salt, the lemon juice and the parsley, then stir well to combine.

Cut the livers into 1 cm (½ in) thick slices. Arrange the toasted baguette on serving plates and top with slices of liver. Spoon the lemon butter over and serve immediately.

SERVES 4

2 tablespoons sea salt, plus a good pinch extra

4 whole john dory livers

2 tablespoons ghee or clarified butter (see note page 26)

10 g (¼ oz) butter

½ Preserved Lemon (page 461), rind only, pith removed, cut into very fine dice

juice of ½ lemon

1 small handful flat-leaf (Italian) parsley leaves

baguette, cut in half lengthways, then sliced and toasted, to serve

Mirror dory fillet with chips and salad

SERVES 4

1 tablespoon lemon juice

80 ml (2½ fl oz/⅓ cup) extra virgin olive oil

sea salt and freshly ground black pepper, to taste

4 mirror dory fillets (from 2 whole fish; see note), skin on, ribcage removed (see page 431)

2 tablespoons rice flour

80 ml (2½ fl oz/⅓ cup) ghee (see note page 26)

2 large vine-ripened tomatoes, each cut into 8 wedges

4 large radicchio leaves, torn

1 large handful watercress

½ iceberg lettuce, torn

Chips (page 459), to serve

1 lemon, cut in quarters, to serve

tomato sauce (ketchup), to serve (optional)

Make a dressing by whisking together the lemon juice and olive oil with a little salt and pepper in a small bowl. Set aside.

To prepare the dory fillets for pan-frying with crisp skin, lay them on a work surface and dust the skin sides with the rice flour. Place each fillet, flesh side down, on a sheet of baking paper large enough to cover the fillet.

Heat two large cast-iron or heavy-based frying pans (these are large fillets and it's essential that the fish is not overcrowded in the pan) over medium–high heat and divide the ghee between the two pans. When the pans are hot and the ghee is translucent, place the fillets in the pans, skin side down, leaving the paper on the flesh side. Place 1 kg (2 lb 4 oz) weights – such as a heavy pot or another pan – on top of the fillets and cook for 2 minutes, lifting the weights once or twice then moving the fillets gently around the pans so they don't burn.

Remove the paper, gently flip the fillets using a spatula and quickly seal the flesh side. Mirror fillets are thin and become dry if overcooked, so remove them from the pans once sealed and immediately transfer to serving plates. (Cooking times may vary depending on the size of the fish from which the fillets were cut; for more information, see page 437.)

Quickly toss the tomato, radicchio, watercress and lettuce in a bowl with the dressing. Serve the dory fillets with the chips and salad, with lemon quarters and tomato sauce (if using) on the side.

NOTES: This recipe works well with any dory.
   If you only have one large pan, cook the fillets in two batches. Keep the first batch warm while you cook the second.

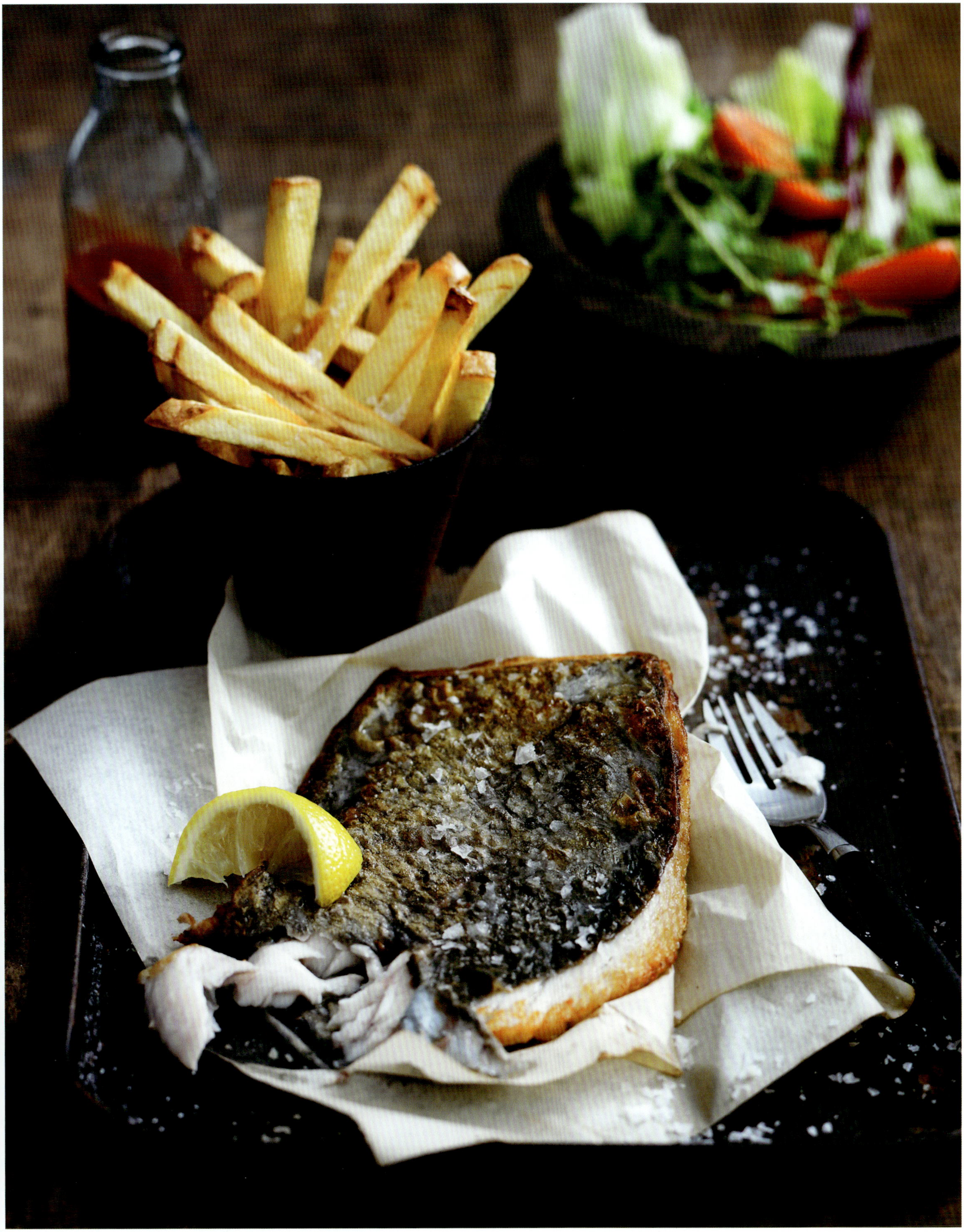

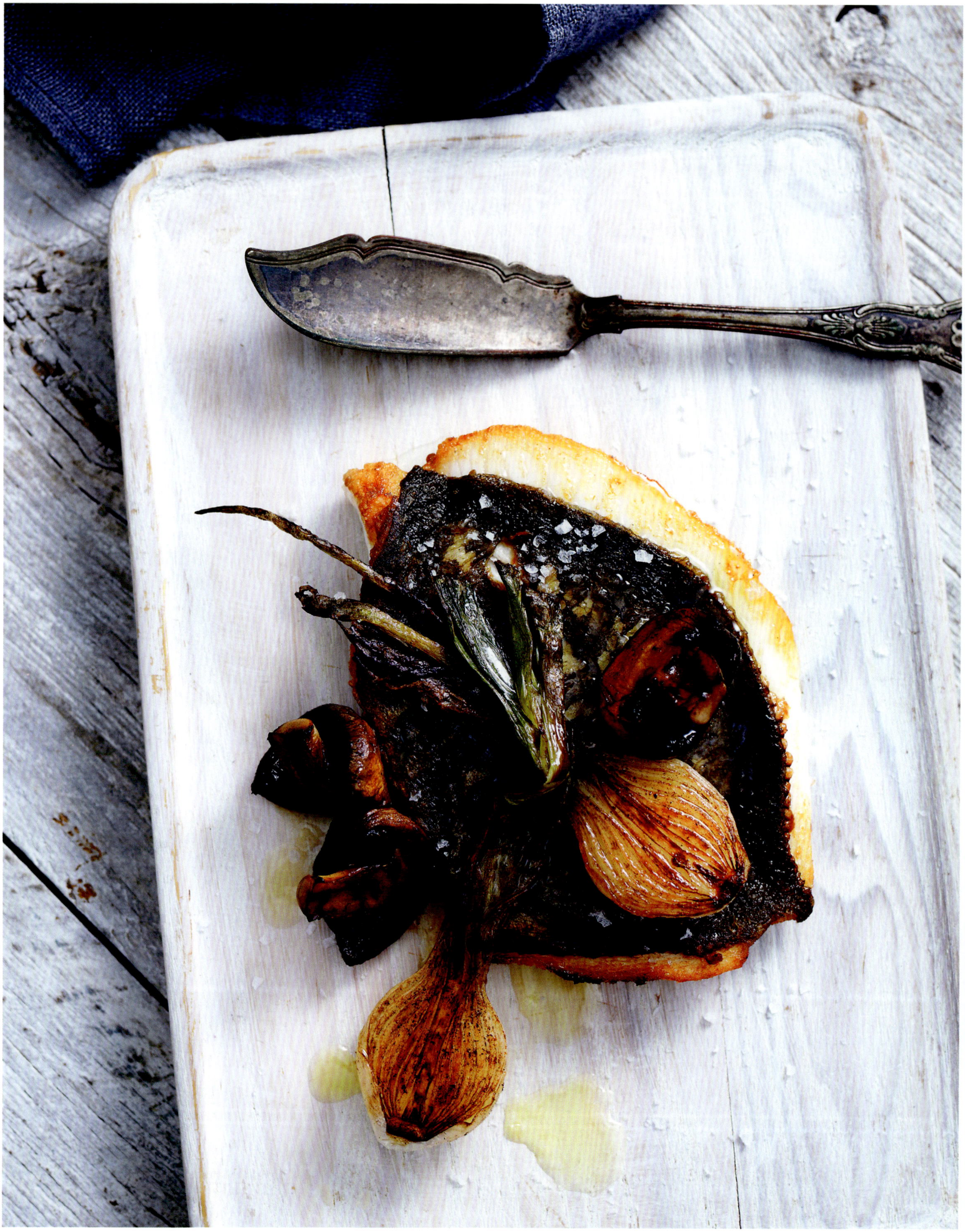

John dory with caramelised spring onions

Heat a small saucepan of salted water over high heat and bring to the boil. Add the spring onions and blanch for about 3 minutes, until just soft. Remove and plunge into a bowl of iced water to refresh, then drain.

Cut the spring onions in half lengthways. Melt the butter in a small heavy-based frying pan over medium–high heat until bubbling. Add the spring onion and mushrooms, season with salt and pepper, then caramelise on the cut side for 3–4 minutes. Set aside in a warm spot.

To prepare the john dory fillets for pan-frying with crisp skin, lay them on a work surface and dust the skin sides with the rice flour. Place each fillet, flesh side down, on a sheet of baking paper large enough to cover the fillet.

Heat a large cast-iron or heavy-based frying pan (or two smaller pans – it's essential that the fish is not overcrowded in the pan; see note) over medium–high heat and add the ghee. When the pan is hot and the ghee translucent, place the fillets in the pan, skin side down, leaving the paper on the flesh side. Place a 1 kg (2 lb 4 oz) weight – such as a heavy pot or another pan – on top of the fillets and cook for 4 minutes, lifting the weight once or twice then moving the fillets gently around the pan so they don't burn. Reduce the heat to low. Remove the weight and the paper, then, using a spatula, gently flip each fillet to quickly seal the other side. (Cooking times may vary depending on the size of the fish from which the fillets were cut; for more information, see page 437.)

Lay a john dory fillet on each of four plates, skin side up, and sprinkle a little sea salt over the skin. Add two spring onion halves and two mushrooms to each plate. In a small cup, combine the chardonnay vinegar and lemon juice. Splash the vinegar mixture over the fish and serve.

NOTES: This recipe works well with any dory.
If you don't have a pan large enough for all the fillets, or two smaller pans, cook the fish in two batches. Keep the first batch warm while you cook the second.

SERVES 4

4 bulb spring onions (scallions), peeled, stems intact
iced water, as required, to refresh
80 g (2¾ oz) butter
8 Swiss brown mushrooms, halved
sea salt and freshly ground black pepper, to taste
4 × 200 g (7 oz) john dory fillets (for the best fillets use a 1.2 kg/ 2 lb 10 oz whole fish; see note)
2 tablespoons rice flour
80 ml (2½ fl oz/⅓ cup) ghee (see note page 26)
60 ml (2 fl oz/¼ cup) chardonnay vinegar
1 tablespoon lemon juice

Pot-roasted whole john dory with wild garlic

SERVES 1–2

1 × 1 kg (2 lb 4 oz) whole john dory, cleaned
1 wild garlic bulb with stem (see note)
iced water, as required, to refresh
40 g (1½ oz) butter
pinch of sea salt
2 tablespoons whole blanched almonds, lightly roasted
1 tablespoon roughly crushed black peppercorns, plus extra to taste
60 ml (2 fl oz/¼ cup) Fish Stock (page 457)

Trim the tail and fins from the john dory using a pair of scissors or a sharp knife then discard. Leave the head on.

Heat a small saucepan of salted water over high heat until boiling. Place the garlic bulb in the water to blanch for about 2 minutes, until soft. Remove the garlic and plunge it into a bowl of iced water to refresh. Cut the garlic bulb into quarters lengthways and set aside.

Heat a large frying pan with a lid over medium–low heat then add the butter and the salt. When the butter starts to bubble, lay the fish in the pan. Coat it in butter on one side, then lift and turn, using a spatula. Add the almonds, pepper and fish stock, then cook, covered, for 3 minutes.

Remove the lid, carefully turn the fish again, then cover and cook for a further 3–4 minutes, until just cooked through.

Toss the garlic through the broth to warm quickly. Serve the fish in the broth, scoop the almonds from the broth to spoon over, and top with the garlic and extra pepper.

NOTE: Wild garlic is in season in spring to early summer (October to December in Australia). If it's not readily available, use French shallots, spring onions (scallions) or pearl onions.

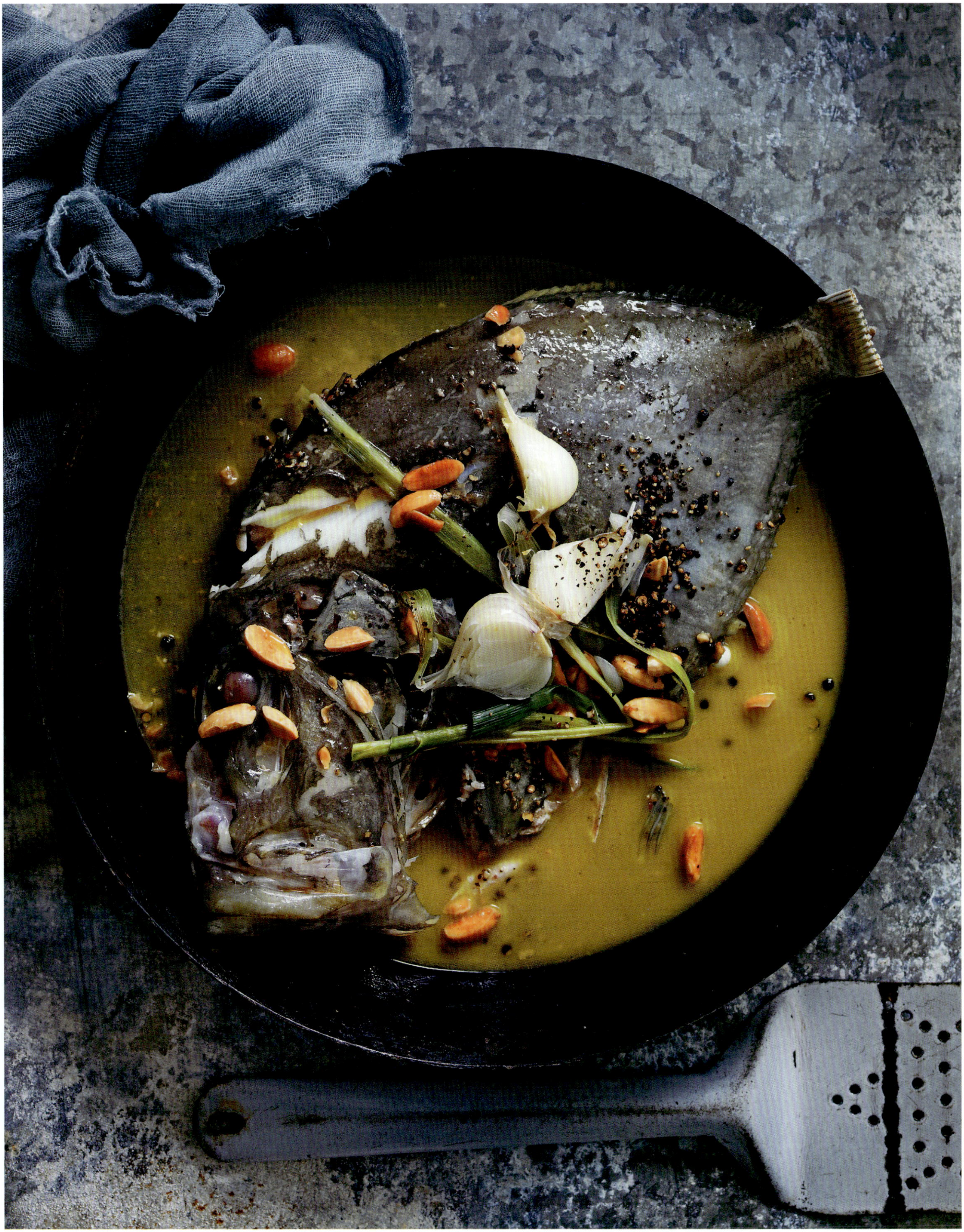

Shortfin eel

EEL

The eel, with its long, snake-like body, small head, pin-like eyes and slippery thick skin, looks like the gangster of the sea. But this sinister appearance belies the fact that it's one of the more delicious fish, often revered more by export buyers in Germany and Japan than here in Australia.

Here we have two main species: the longfin eel (*Anguilla reinhardtii*) and the shortfin eel (*Anguilla australis*). Although they breed in salt water somewhere in the central Pacific Ocean, eels spend most of their lives in fresh water, preferring the still water of coastal swamps and lagoons, farm dams and rivers in eastern and southern Australia. The European conger eel (*Conger conger*), remains in salt water and can grow as long as 2.5 m (8 ft).

Shortfin eels are among our most tolerant native fish species. They survive environmental hazards such as high water temperatures or low dissolved oxygen concentrations, which makes them a species we should favour from an environmental perspective.

Eels are caught year round, although they eat more frogs, crustaceans and other fish during winter and spring, when they become deliciously fatty. Be sure when buying wild eels to insist on them having been purged for a minimum of three days in fresh water. As a rule, the smaller the eel, the sweeter the taste.

SEASONALITY Year round, but mainly in winter in NSW, mainly spring in Vic. and Tas.
CATCHING METHODS 50% grown from wild-caught fingerlings, 50% trapped from the wild
COMMON LENGTH Up to 1 m (39½ in)
COMMON WEIGHT 1–3 kg (2 lb 4 oz – 6 lb 12 oz)
IDENTIFIABLE FEATURES Long and thin, with a dark green–black skin
SUSTAINABILITY Sustainable; increased 'farming' will continue to improve stock

EEL IN THE KITCHEN

The shortfin eel is the preferred eel for barbecuing and sushi. It can be tricky to work with, but it seems to hold its firm texture, whereas the rarer saltwater eels have much softer flesh.

Live eels are quite tricky to handle, so you're better off purchasing processed fish. Eel is best smoked, barbecued or braised. It's the sort of fish that needs to be cooked right through and even caramelised on the outside to give it a real nuttiness – crisp on the outside and soft in the middle. Smoked eel is the most amazing eating experience, and is great for salads, pâtés, sushi and on its own. The smoked eel you buy at the fish market is an excellent product, especially when fresh rather than frozen.

After filleting fresh eel, plunge the fillets into iced water to set the protein. Remove from the water and cook under a grill (broiler) on high until soft and tender, then baste with a teriyaki or Japanese soy sauce and finish on the barbecue.

Smoked eel is mostly prepared using a hot-smoking technique, where the eel is cooked at a temperature of 75–90°C (170–190°F), rather than cold smoking, which is done at 30–35°C (90–95°F). To smoke 600–800 g (1 lb 5 oz – 1 lb 12 oz) eel, wearing rubber gloves, rub the freshly dispatched and gutted eel with table salt to remove the natural slime. Make a brine of 12 litres (25 pt/ 48 cups) of water, 1.3 kg (3 lb) of table salt, 300 g (10½ oz) of raw (demerara) sugar and 1 tablespoon of molasses, stirred together warm to dissolve the sugar and salt, then cooled. Soak the whole eel in this brine for 24 hours. Drain and dry the eel, then refrigerate, uncovered, for 3–4 hours.

Preheat the oven to 240°C (475°F) and spread 2 cups of hardwood smoking chips (available in hardware stores) over the base of a large roasting tin. Place a wire rack over the chips, sit the eel on the rack and cover the tin with foil. Bake for 30–35 minutes then remove the tin from the oven but leave the eel covered for a further hour. Use the eel immediately to enjoy its soft, juicy texture, or refrigerate for later use.

BEST COOKING METHODS Grilled (broiled), smoked, barbecued
TEXTURE Flesh meaty, firm and tight-grained
AROMA A pork-like, sweet meatiness once cooked
FLAVOUR Deep, rich, umami-filled, with a pork-belly sweetness
APPEARANCE Flesh dark when raw; grey-white once cooked
YIELD Flesh about 40% of whole weight
SUBSTITUTES None

Longfin eel

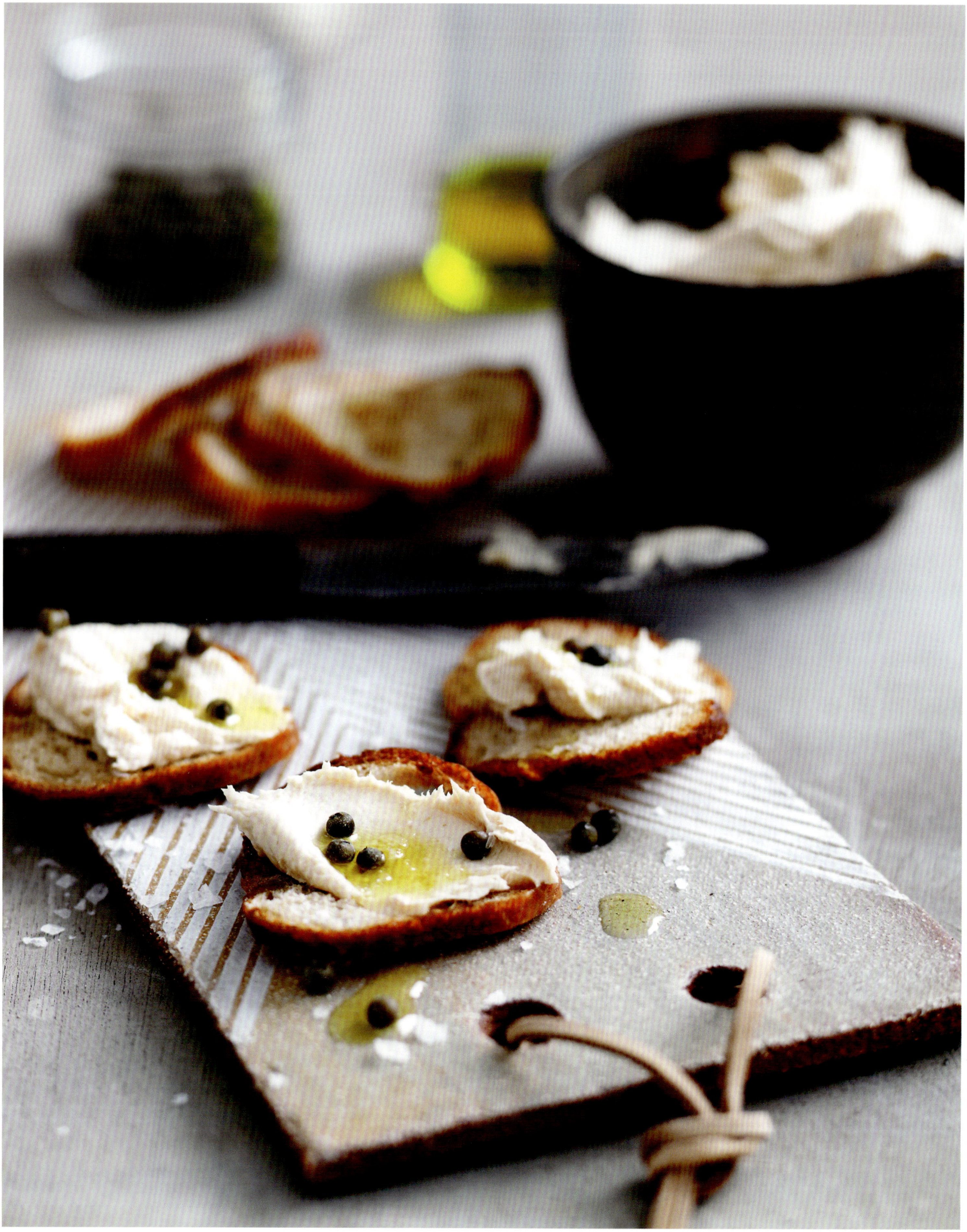

Smoked eel and green peppercorn pâté

Using a food processor, purée the eel with the peppercorns until smooth. Add the wine and salt then the butter, a little at a time, until smooth. Add the cream and blend to mix, taking care not to process too long or the mixture will split.

Serve on crostini, with a splash of olive oil and garnished with a few extra peppercorns.

NOTES: For instructions on smoking eel, see page 72.

This recipe works with most hot-smoked fish, including salmon and trout.

Tinned green peppercorns are available from gourmet grocery stores and some supermarkets.

SERVES 4

300 g (10½ oz) smoked eel, skin off and bones removed, roughly shredded (see note)

½ teaspoon tinned green peppercorns (see note), drained, plus extra to serve

2 tablespoons dry white wine

pinch of sea salt

100 g (3½ oz) butter, softened

2 tablespoons thin (pouring) cream

crostini, to serve

extra virgin olive oil, to serve

Pan-fried eel with tomatoes and garlic

SERVES 4

100 g (3½ oz) butter
2 teaspoons caster (superfine) sugar
75 g (2¾ oz/½ cup) whole peeled garlic cloves (15–20 cloves)
60 ml (2 fl oz/¼ cup) chicken stock
1 whole eel, cut through the bone into 2 cm (¾ in) cutlets
150 g (5½ oz/1 cup) assorted cherry and small roma (plum) tomatoes (see note)
sea salt and freshly ground black pepper, to taste

Preheat the oven to 180°C (350°F).

Place a small ovenproof frying pan over medium–high heat. Add 40 g (1½ oz) of the butter and the sugar, then cook until the butter has melted and the sugar dissolved. Add the garlic cloves and toss to coat, then add the stock. Bring gently to the boil, then reduce the heat to low and simmer until the liquid has reduced and the garlic cloves are soft and golden. Remove from the pan and set aside.

Heat a large heavy-based frying pan over medium heat. Add the remaining butter then, as it melts and begins to foam, add the eel cutlets. Toss well in the butter, then reduce the heat to medium–low and pan-fry the cutlets for 2 minutes on each side.

Add the tomatoes and pan-roasted garlic cloves, then season well with salt and pepper. Transfer the pan to the oven to cook the eel for a further 5 minutes.

Serve at the table in the pan to share, or transfer to a serving platter or individual plates.

NOTES: Any whole small tomatoes can be used in this dish, as long as they are sweet and delicious.
   Basil leaves are an excellent addition to this recipe – try stirring them through just before serving, or add as a garnish.

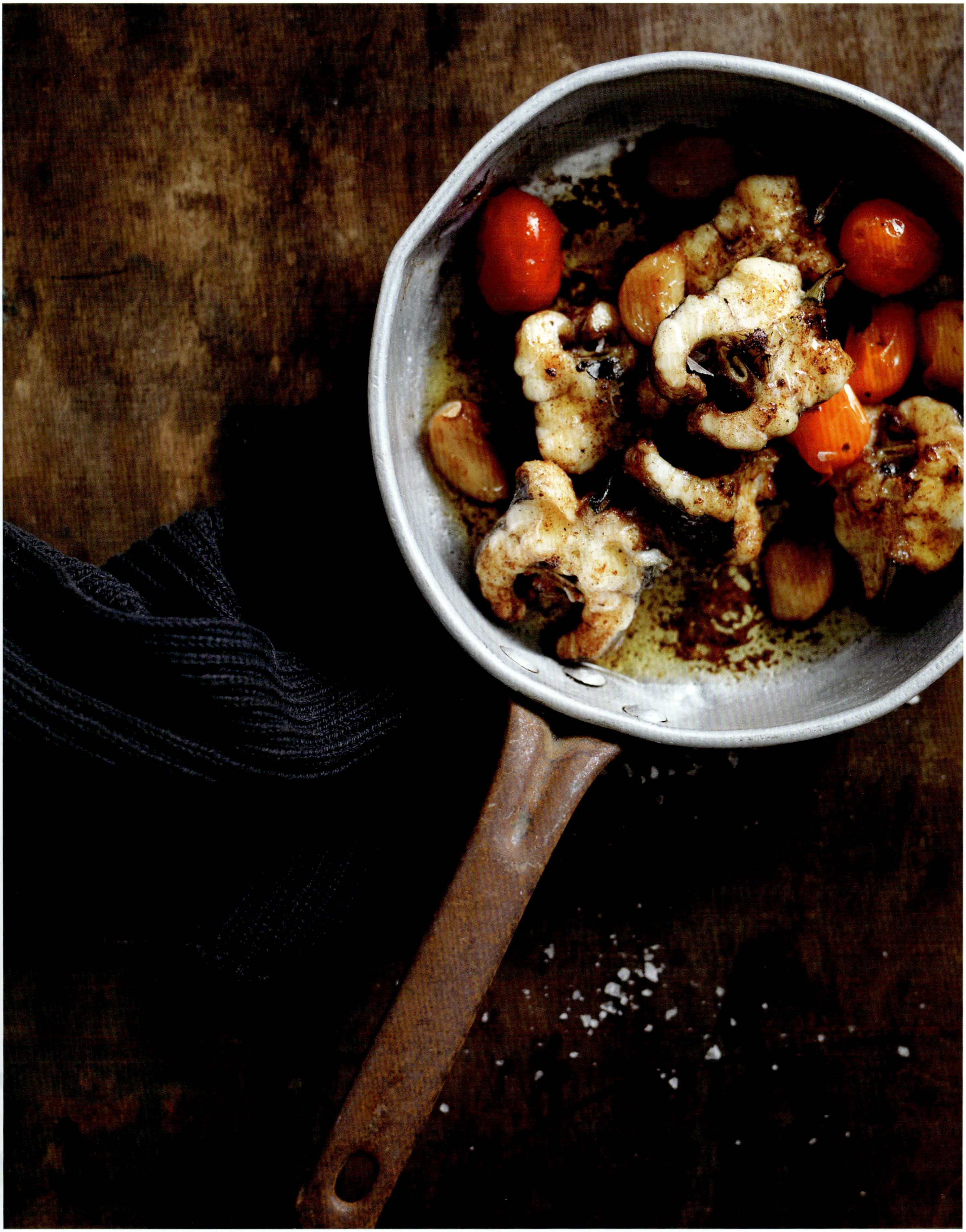

Tiger flathead

FLATHEAD

Few fish better reflect the range, variety and quality of Australian seafood than the humble flathead. In less than 30 years, it has gone from lowly bycatch to one of the most important and high-value table fish in Australia. There's no mistaking these fish, with their distinctive shape – literally a flat, triangular head with flounder-like eyes on top, an extremely large mouth and a long round tail. They're affectionately known as flatties, lizards and even crocs by anglers Australia-wide.

Although the flathead is sold generically as a single fish, there are more than 40 different species in Australian waters, the majority of the 68 species found throughout the world. Flatheads inhabit various coastal waters around Australia, both estuarine and inshore, as well as the deep open waters along and off the continental shelf.

Most flatheads lack the swim bladder other fish use to stay buoyant, so they lie camouflaged and partially buried in the sand or mud of the seabed, waiting for prey to swim or walk by. They feed opportunistically on small fish, squid and crustaceans; this produces their characteristic sweet, moist flesh with a broad flake. Flathead don't eat plants or mud, so their flesh has a clean, mild flavour.

SEASONALITY March–December in NSW, Vic. and Tas.
CATCHING METHODS Bottom otter trawl, Danish seine
COMMON LENGTH 40–50 cm (16–20 in)
COMMON WEIGHT 500 g – 1.5 kg (1 lb 2 oz – 3 lb 5 oz)
IDENTIFIABLE FEATURES Flat triangular head, large mouth
SUSTAINABILITY Strictly managed by quota

COMMON FLATHEAD SPECIES

Blue-spotted flathead
Platycephalus caeruleopunctatus
Covered in small pale blue or red spots. Typically smaller than tiger flathead, it's caught quite close to shore, off southern Queensland, New South Wales and eastern Victoria.

Deepwater flathead
Neoplatycephalus conatus
Closely related to tiger flathead, but without its distinctive stripes and spots. It's caught in the Great Australian Bight on the upper levels of the continental shelf off South Australia by commercial trawlers at depths of 100–500 m (330–1640 ft).

Dusky flathead
Platycephalus fuscus
The largest of the flatheads, and readily identified by its dark olive–brown back and white belly. It's found in the tidal rivers, estuaries, lakes, bays and inshore shallows of the east coast of Australia, from Cairns to Lakes Entrance.

Grassy flathead
Platycephalus laevigatus
A close cousin of the dusky flathead, but with a portlier shape and lighter, translucent grey flesh. It's found around southern New South Wales and Victoria, where it's often referred to as black or rock flathead.

Sand flathead
Platycephalus bassensis
Quite similar to blue-spotted flathead and the paler deepwater flathead, with a pale khaki skin that often has a light green tinge. It's found mainly in bays and estuaries along the south-eastern coast of Australia.

Tiger flathead
Neoplatycephalus richardsoni
Easily identified by its tiger-like dark stripes on pale khaki skin that's also covered in bright orange–red spots. This fish is unusual among flatheads in having a swim bladder that allows it to move up and down in the water, which means anglers search for it further out to sea. It's caught all around southern New South Wales, Victoria and Tasmania.

FLATHEAD IN THE KITCHEN

Although flathead is mostly sold in skinless, boneless fillets, seek out whole fish, ideally with a good cover of fresh sea slime and a full complement of scales. A freshly filleted flathead will deliver a far superior eating experience than one that has been industrially filleted and soaked in water (flathead fillets absorb water readily, which not only reduces their shelf life but rips out fat and flavour). The flesh should be resilient to the touch and neither soft nor floppy. If you can't or don't want to fillet it yourself, ask your fishmonger to *dry*-fillet it for you, leaving the skin on. The flesh of the dusky and blue-spotted flathead is especially firm, making them ideal for both raw and cooked preparations.

Ideally, like other whole fish, flathead should be stored in a still environment free from circulating air – in other words, the vegetable crisper in the fridge. Flathead is quite a lean fish, with a low to medium fat content. Lean fish generally have a higher water content and so tend to weep when you cook them. A lot of water will run out of overcooked flathead, and this will cause the protein to split. Overcooking it in a stock or a curry over high heat will result in dry fish.

When cooking fillets, always cook with the skin on – all the good oils and flavours are in the skin. Flathead shines when grilled (broiled), crumbed, pan-fried with crisp skin, deep-fried or baked whole. When pan-frying, heat oil or ghee in the pan until a haze forms across the top of the pan indicating it's very hot. Gently place the fish in the pan, skin side down, dropping it in away from you so you don't splash yourself with oil. Place a weight on the fish (another small pan will do the trick) to allow the flesh to poach and the skin to crisp up. Never cook fish on the flesh side or you'll damage it.

Because flathead weeps naturally as it's cooked, one neat trick is to flour the skin lightly – not to add a crust but to soak up all the surface moisture.

SPECIAL STORAGE AND HANDLING
Try to buy whole fish, then ask your fishmonger to fillet them for you, or at least gill, gut and scale them. Wrap in muslin (cheesecloth) or freezer film, then store as usual. If your fishmonger fillets, ask them to dry-fillet and wrap tightly in freezer film, then store as usual. Always avoid using plastic wrap because it will sweat. Store at 1–2°C (34–36°F) and bring to room temperature before cooking.

BEST COOKING METHODS Grilled (broiled), fried, crumbed, baked whole

TEXTURE Firm when raw; soft once cooked

AROMA Clean ocean, starchy vegetable, mushy peas and roasted nuts

FLAVOUR Sweet ocean with savoury, nutty notes of buttered vegetables

APPEARANCE Flesh opalescent, with clear blood lines

YIELD Flesh 25–30% of whole weight

SUBSTITUTES Blue cod, gurnard, latchet, mirror dory

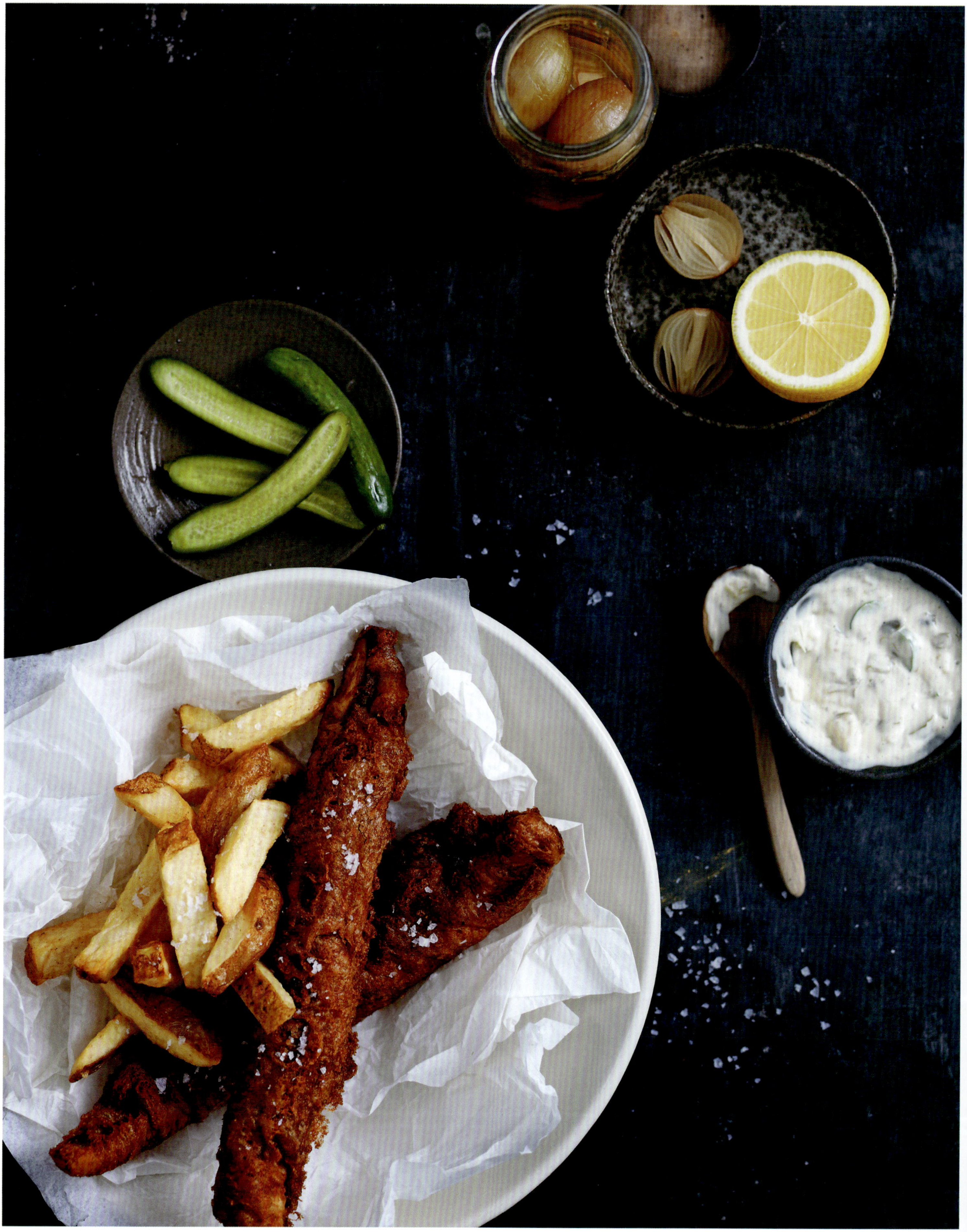

Deep-fried flathead and chips with home-made tartare sauce

For the tartare sauce, place the mayonnaise, shallot, gherkin and capers in a medium bowl and stir to combine. Check the seasoning and add salt and pepper to taste. Add a squeeze of lemon juice (if desired). Transfer the tartare sauce to a sealed airtight container and refrigerate. (It will keep in the fridge for 3 days.)

Preheat the oven to very low, about 130°C (250°F).

Half-fill a 6 litre (203 fl oz/24 cup) saucepan with vegetable oil and place over high heat (see note). Heat the oil to 180°C (350°C) – check with an oil thermometer. (For a guide to testing the oil temperature without a thermometer, see note page 109.)

For maximum freshness, begin the beer batter only when ready to cook the flathead. Combine the self-raising flour, rice flour and baking powder in a large bowl. Mix the honey and vodka together in a small bowl, then pour into the flour mixture, stirring to mix well. Add the beer and whisk the mixture – a little more beer can be added if the batter is too thick. (The greater the carbonation from the beer in the mixture, the crisper the batter will be.)

Place the rice flour for dusting in a large bowl. Dust each fillet in the rice flour, then dip into the batter. Gently drag the fillets against the inside of the bowl to remove any excess batter, then drop them carefully into the hot oil. (You may need to cook the fish in batches so you don't overcrowd the pan and lose heat.) Deep-fry for 2 minutes, or until crisp and golden, then remove and place on a baking tray lined with paper towel to drain. Keep the fish warm in the oven while you cook the remaining fillets.

Place the fish on serving plates with the chips. Serve the tartare sauce, gherkins, pickled onions and lemon on the side.

NOTES: The vodka keeps the batter crisp for longer.
When deep-frying in a saucepan, it's advisable to keep the oil level a good 10 cm (4 in) below the rim of the pan. The other option for deep-frying is, of course, an electric deep-fryer. The used oil can be strained, cooled and refrigerated for later use.

SERVES 4

vegetable oil, for deep-frying
160 g (5¾ oz/1 cup) rice flour, for dusting
4 × 150 g (5½ oz) flathead fillets, skin on, pin-boned
1 quantity Chips (page 459)
8 gherkins (pickles), cut in half lengthways
8 pickled baby onions
2 lemons, cut in half, seeds removed

TARTARE SAUCE
(Makes about 250 ml/9 fl oz/1 cup)
235 g (8½ oz/1 cup) Mayonnaise (see page 455)
1 French shallot, peeled and finely diced
½ large gherkin (pickle), about 35 g (1¼ oz), roughly chopped
35 g (1¼ oz) capers in vinegar, drained, well rinsed and roughly chopped
sea salt and freshly ground black pepper, to taste
lemon juice, to taste (optional)

BEER BATTER
200 g (7 oz/1⅓ cups) self-raising flour
400 g (14 oz/2½ cups) rice flour
1 tablespoon baking powder
55 g (2 oz) honey
350 ml (12 fl oz) vodka, preferably 37% (see note)
550 ml (19 fl oz) beer, or as required

Flathead with sauce gribiche

SERVES 4

4 × 200 g (7 oz) flathead fillets, skin on, pin-boned
2 tablespoons rice flour
80 ml (2½ fl oz/⅓ cup) ghee (see note page 26)
sea salt, to serve

SAUCE GRIBICHE
235 g (8½ oz/1 cup) Mayonnaise (see page 455)
2 hard-boiled eggs, peeled and roughly chopped
50 g (1¾ oz/¼ cup) capers in vinegar, drained and well rinsed
1 small handful flat-leaf (Italian) parsley leaves, roughly chopped
1 large gherkin (pickle), chopped
sea salt and freshly ground black pepper, to taste

To make the sauce gribiche, combine all the ingredients and season to taste. The sauce can be made creamier by adding a little warm water, if desired. (It will keep in a sealed container in the fridge for 3 days.)

To prepare the flathead fillets for pan-frying with crisp skin, lay them on a work surface and dust the skin sides with the rice flour. Place each fillet, flesh side down, on a sheet of baking paper large enough to cover the fillet.

Heat a large cast-iron or heavy-based frying pan (or two smaller pans – it's essential that the fish is not overcrowded in the pan; see note) over medium–high heat and add the ghee. When the pan is hot and the ghee translucent, place the fillets in the pan, skin side down, leaving the paper on the flesh side. Place a 1 kg (2 lb 4 oz) weight – such as a heavy pot or another pan – on top of the fillets and cook for 4 minutes, lifting the weight once or twice and moving the fillets gently around the pan so they don't burn. Reduce the heat to low. Remove the weight and the paper then, using a spatula, gently flip each fillet to quickly seal the other side. (Cooking times may vary depending on the size of the fish from which the fillets were cut; for more information, see page 437.)

Serve the flathead immediately, skin side up, with a liberal pinch of sea salt on the skin and the sauce gribiche on the side.

NOTE: If you don't have a pan large enough for all the fillets, or two smaller pans, cook the fish in two batches. Keep the first batch warm while you cook the second.

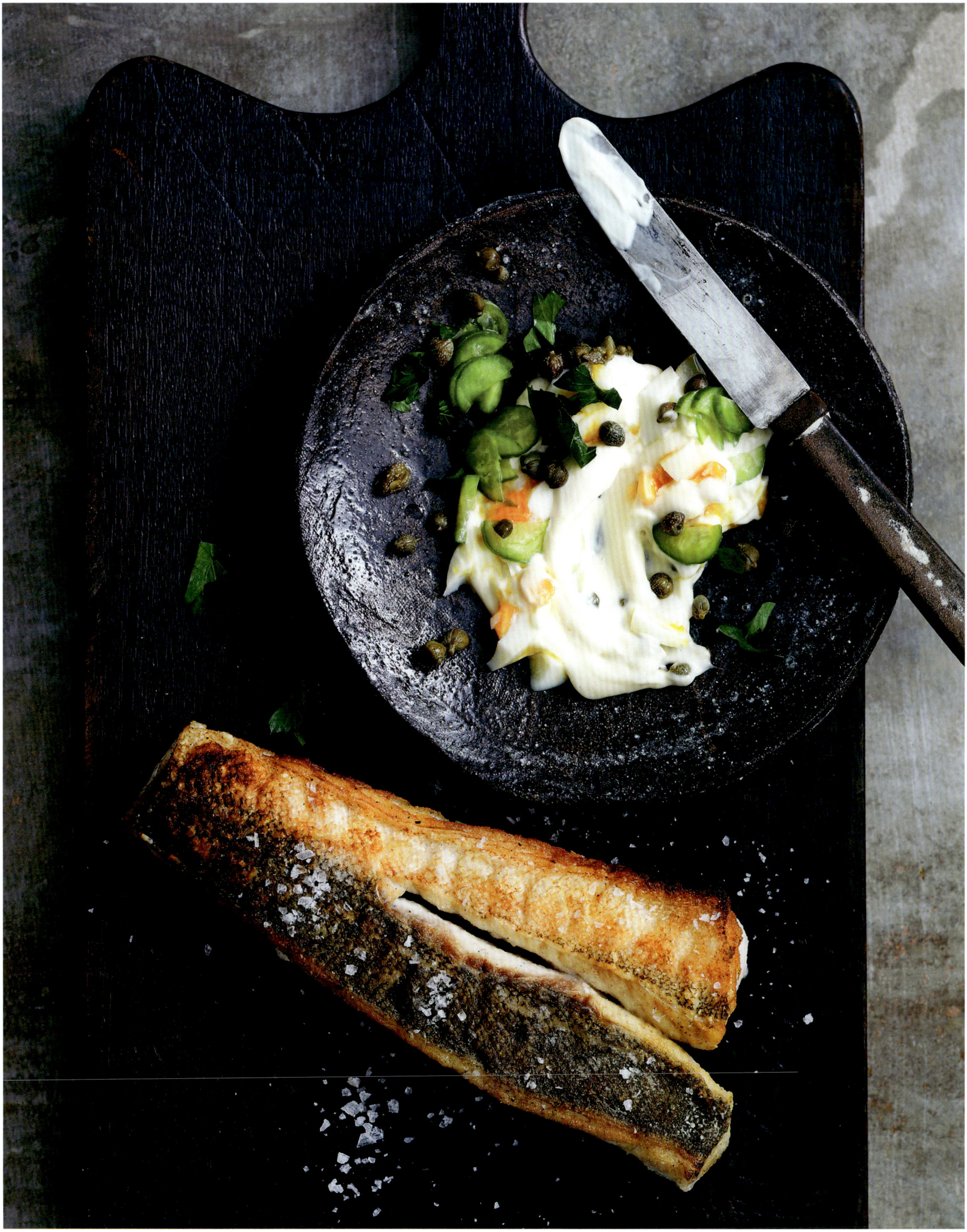

Pot-roasted whole flounder with togarashi

SERVES 2

30 g (1 oz) togarashi (see note)
1 whole flounder (about 600 g/ 1 lb 5 oz), head on, tail and fins trimmed
40 g (1½ oz) butter
8 slow-roasted tomatoes (see note)
1 handful mixed fresh herb leaves of choice, for a salad
lemon oil, to serve (see note page 25)
sea salt, to taste

Preheat an oven grill (broiler) to high.

Spread the togarashi on a tray and coat the flounder liberally on both sides.

Heat a large ovenproof frying pan over medium heat. Add the butter and, when it begins to bubble, add the flounder. Cook for 2 minutes on one side, then gently turn using a spatula and cook for 2 minutes on the other side, or until the fish is just cooked.

Remove the pan from the heat and place under the hot grill for 1–2 minutes to crisp up the skin. (This will also help confine the chilli heat of the togarashi to the skin of the fish.)

Transfer the fish from the pan to a serving platter. Place the roasted tomatoes on top and serve a small herb salad on the side, dressed lightly with lemon oil and salt.

NOTES: Togarashi is a Japanese 'seven spice' mix. Pepper and chilli are the main ingredients, and although the spice mixture can differ, it tends to include nori and sesame. Togarashi can be found in Asian supermarkets.

To slow-roast tomatoes, cut roma (plum) tomatoes in half lengthways, place on a baking tray and cook at 100°C (200°F) for about 30 minutes. Drying the tomatoes this way adds an intensity of flavour. As a variation, try roasting them with very finely shaved garlic scattered over the top.

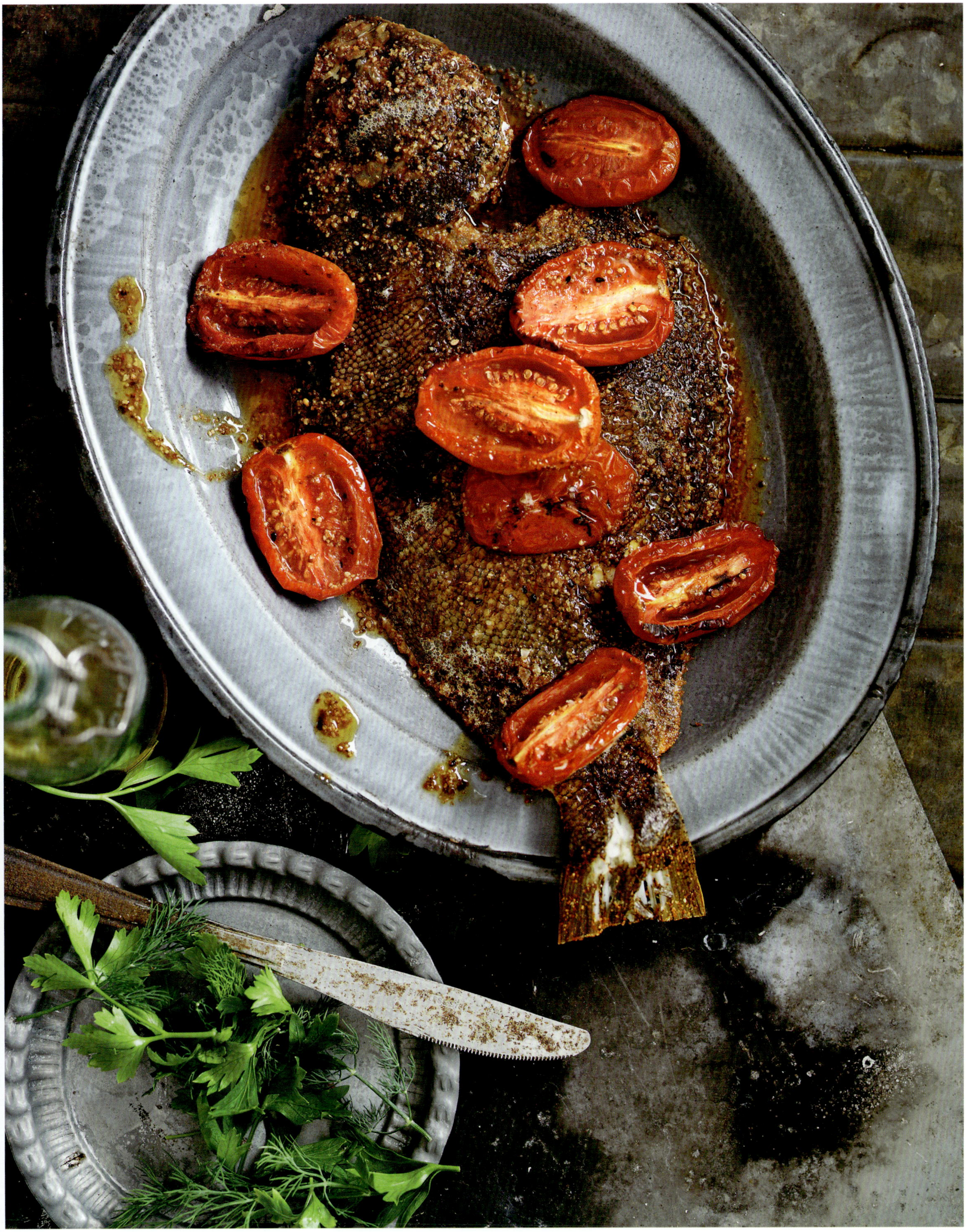

Southern sea garfish

GARFISH

There are many species of garfish, but the most common found in restaurants and retail outlets in Australia are the eastern sea garfish (*Hyporhamphus australis*) and the southern sea garfish (*Hyporhamphus melanochir*). Both are fast-growing, abundant and found around most of the Australian coast, usually at depths of 1–5 m (3–16 ft) in shallow bays and estuaries with large, healthy seaweed beds.

The southern sea garfish, silvery with a dark stripe on the sides and a fluorescent-green back, is found off the eastern, southern and western coasts.

The eastern sea garfish has three narrow brown lines along the back, coarser scales and a slightly larger mouth. It lives off the southern coast from New South Wales to South Australia.

Available seasonally are the shortnose or snubnose garfish (*Arrhamphus sclerolepis*) and the three-by-two garfish (*Hemiramphus robustus*).

SEASONALITY Year round, with peaks in WA and Qld in summer; in NSW, Vic. and Tas. in winter; and in SA in autumn–spring
CATCHING METHODS Some line, mostly beach seine and Danish seine
COMMON LENGTH 20–45 cm (8–18 in)
COMMON WEIGHT 100–300 g (3½–10½ oz)
IDENTIFIABLE FEATURES Long and slender, with a long, pencil-like beak
SUSTAINABILITY Stock status good

GARFISH IN THE KITCHEN

Garfish deteriorates quickly, so it must be super-fresh and given close attention when cooking. Larger specimens are relatively easy to fillet, but the fillets are very fragile and thin.

A really fresh garfish makes amazing sashimi – simply peel the skin back. Or paint it with butter and cook it slowly at the bottom of the oven under a grill (broiler). It's too small for pan-frying, but you can cook it in a warm pan with just-frothing soft butter, off the direct heat. It should remain translucent and soft. You can cook garfish whole, but it will dry out very quickly.

The sweet, lean flesh goes well with simple flavours that won't dominate – butter, preserved lemon, capers, parsley, celery salt, cucumber salsa, vinaigrette and rice (i.e. as sushi).

BEST COOKING METHODS Raw, grilled (broiled), tempura/deep-fried
TEXTURE Firm, with a tight grain
AROMA Bright, clean, with an iodine zing and notes of fresh asparagus and cut grass
FLAVOUR Sweet, with a delicious iodine spritz
APPEARANCE Fillets opaque grey when raw; snow white once cooked
YIELD Flesh about 40% of whole weight
SUBSTITUTES Whiting

Sicilian-style garfish

SERVES 4 AS AN ENTRÉE

1 garlic clove, peeled
2 tablespoons lemon juice
160 ml (5¼ fl oz) extra virgin olive oil
4 tablespoons chopped oregano
sea salt and freshly ground black pepper, to taste
8 whole garfish, scored on the diagonal
1 tablespoon melted butter

Preheat an oven grill (broiler) to high.

To make the Sicilian-style dressing, rub the garlic clove around the inside of a stainless-steel bowl. Whisk the lemon juice and olive oil in the bowl, then add the oregano and season with salt and pepper. Set aside.

Lay four of the garfish side by side on a baking tray. Insert three skewers through the fish to join in one piece. Repeat with the remaining garfish.

Brush the garfish with a little butter. Place under the hot grill and cook for 90 seconds. Turn and cook for a further 90 seconds.

Transfer the grilled garfish to a serving platter. Serve drizzled with the Sicilian-style dressing.

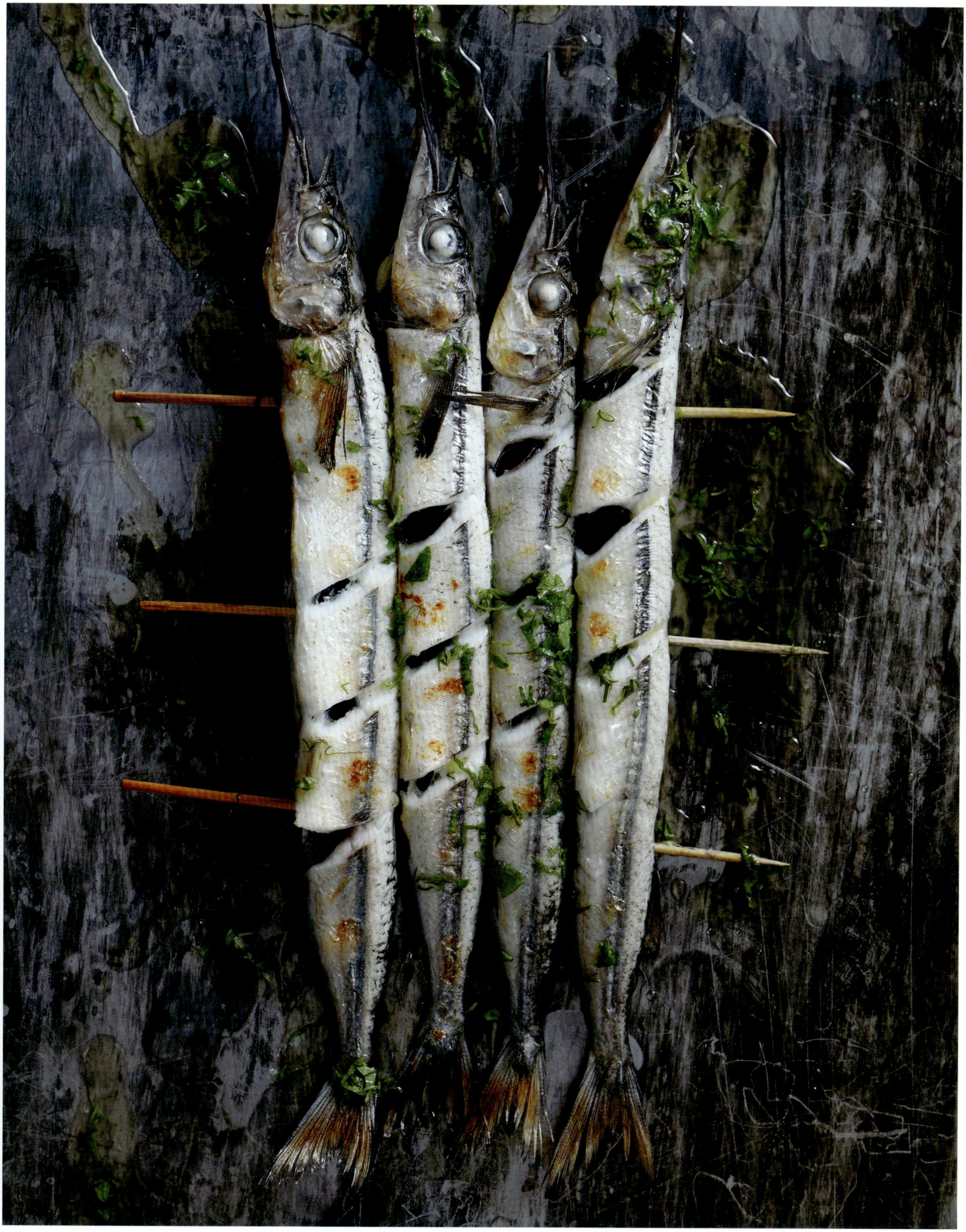

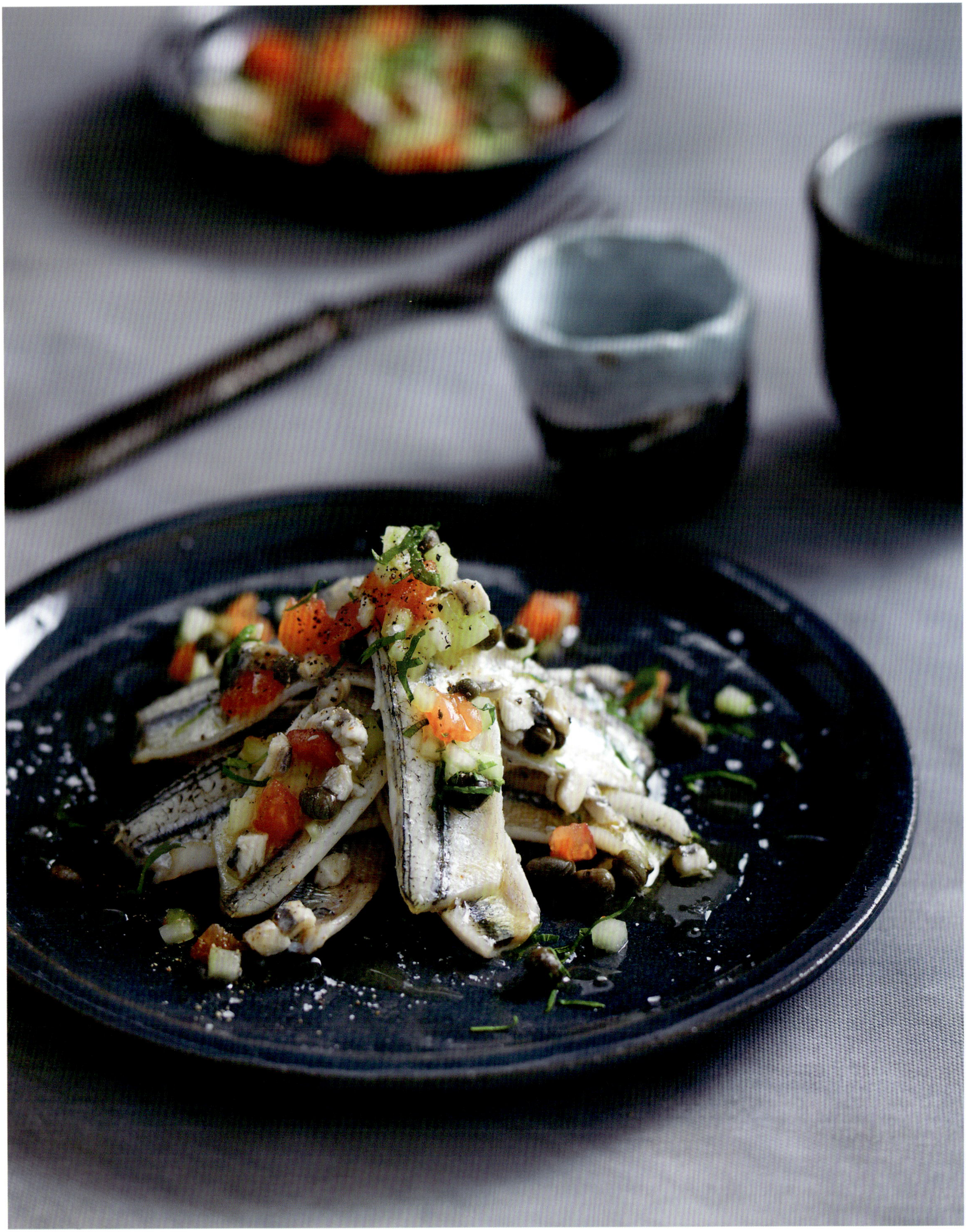

Grilled garfish fillets with cucumber and anchovy salsa

To make the salsa, combine the cucumber, tomato, capers, anchovies and parsley in a bowl, then mix thoroughly. Add a good splash of lemon oil and the salt, then toss gently.

Preheat an oven grill (broiler) to high.

Lay the garfish fillets on a baking tray, skin side up. Brush the fillets with the butter. Place under the hot grill and cook for 1 minute.

Transfer the fillets to serving plates, arranging them in a star pattern layered one on top of another. Spoon the salsa over the top and serve.

NOTE: To blanch a large tomato, cut a small cross in the base. Using a spoon, lower it carefully into boiling salted water for just 10 seconds. Remove and plunge into iced water for 20 seconds, then gently remove from the iced water and peel – the skin should come off easily.

SERVES 4

12 whole garfish, filleted (about 100 g/3½ oz fish per person)
40 g (1½ oz) butter, melted

CUCUMBER & ANCHOVY SALSA

1 large Lebanese (short) cucumber, peeled, seeds removed, very finely diced
1 large vine-ripened tomato, blanched, peeled, seeds removed, very finely diced (see note)
1 tablespoon drained baby capers in vinegar
2 white anchovies, diced
1 tablespoon finely shredded flat-leaf (Italian) parsley
lemon oil, as required (see note page 25)
good pinch of sea salt

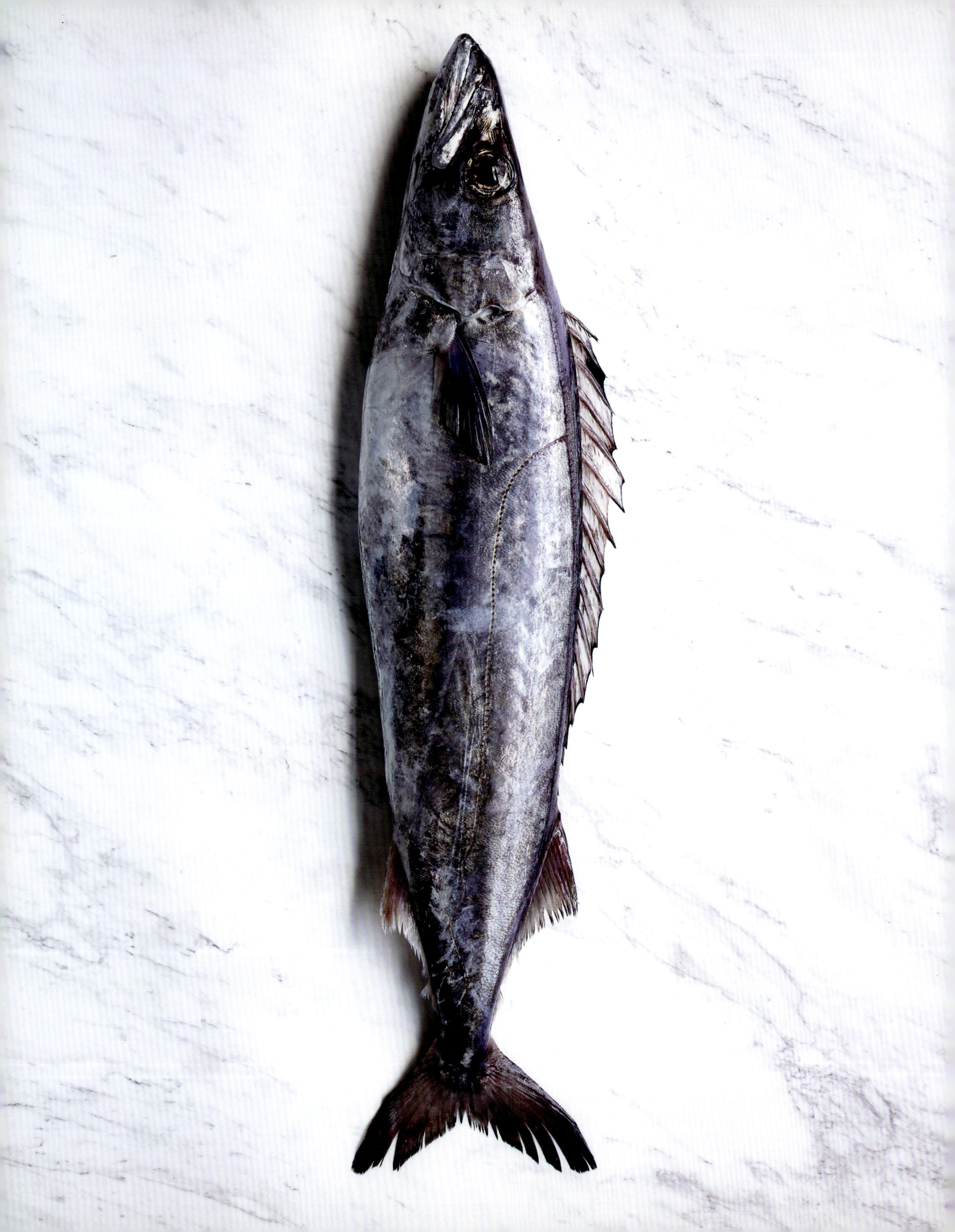

GEMFISH

Gemfish (*Rexea solandri*) was once the king of fish and chip shops, especially in New South Wales. Overenthusiastic fishing greatly damaged stocks of this excellent eating fish, causing the fishery to collapse by the mid-1980s. Through good fishing management since then, this species has become one of the poster boys of recovery, now landed commercially for all to enjoy, albeit in much smaller numbers than before.

The gemfish comes from the same family as barracouta, and is sometimes referred to as king couta. It's also known as hake, even though true hake isn't in the same family. Gemfish are generally silvery, darkening to a bluish or purplish tinge after capture.

They live in deep water off the coasts of New South Wales, Victoria, South Australia and Tasmania. They're generally found in large schools at depths of 100–800 m (330–2600 ft). Although most are trawl-caught, line-caught fish is superb.

SEASONALITY Year round, with a peak in winter
CATCHING METHODS Mid-water trawl, some bottom longline and dropline
COMMON LENGTH 60–90 cm (24–35½ in)
COMMON WEIGHT 2–5 kg (4 lb 8 oz – 11 oz)
IDENTIFIABLE FEATURES Smooth silver skin, protruding lower jaw, menacing-looking teeth, large dark eye
SUSTAINABILITY Recovering

GEMFISH IN THE KITCHEN

Although gemfish are generally caught in the range of 2–5 kg (4 lb 8 oz – 11 lb), they can grow to 15 kg (33 lb). Anything up to 7 kg (15 lb) tastes grassy because the younger fish feed off seagrass, and the flesh can be a bit soft as well. Larger fish eat other fish, so they taste so dramatically different you'd almost think they were a different fish – they have a firm texture with sweet flesh.

When caught and handled properly, gemfish is amazing to eat. It's best filleted and pan-fried with crisp skin, without other strong flavours. It's great with green vegetables, especially peas or broccoli. You can also use Asian techniques and flavours; when cooked Asian sweet-and-sour style, its flavour can easily resemble pork.

Gemfish is excellent well battered and fried. It's also lovely when smoked.

BEST COOKING METHODS Pan-fried with crisp skin (fillets, see page 437), roasted, steamed, smoked, battered and fried
TEXTURE Medium–soft, with a broad, scalloping flesh that, if fresh and well handled, cooks firm
AROMA Deep fresh fish, with a note of fresh grass
FLAVOUR Mild to medium, deep, rich, with a long-lasting umami back palate
APPEARANCE Flesh pinkish white to opaque grey when raw; clean white once cooked
YIELD Flesh 55–60% of whole weight
SUBSTITUTES Most large white fish (e.g. warehou)

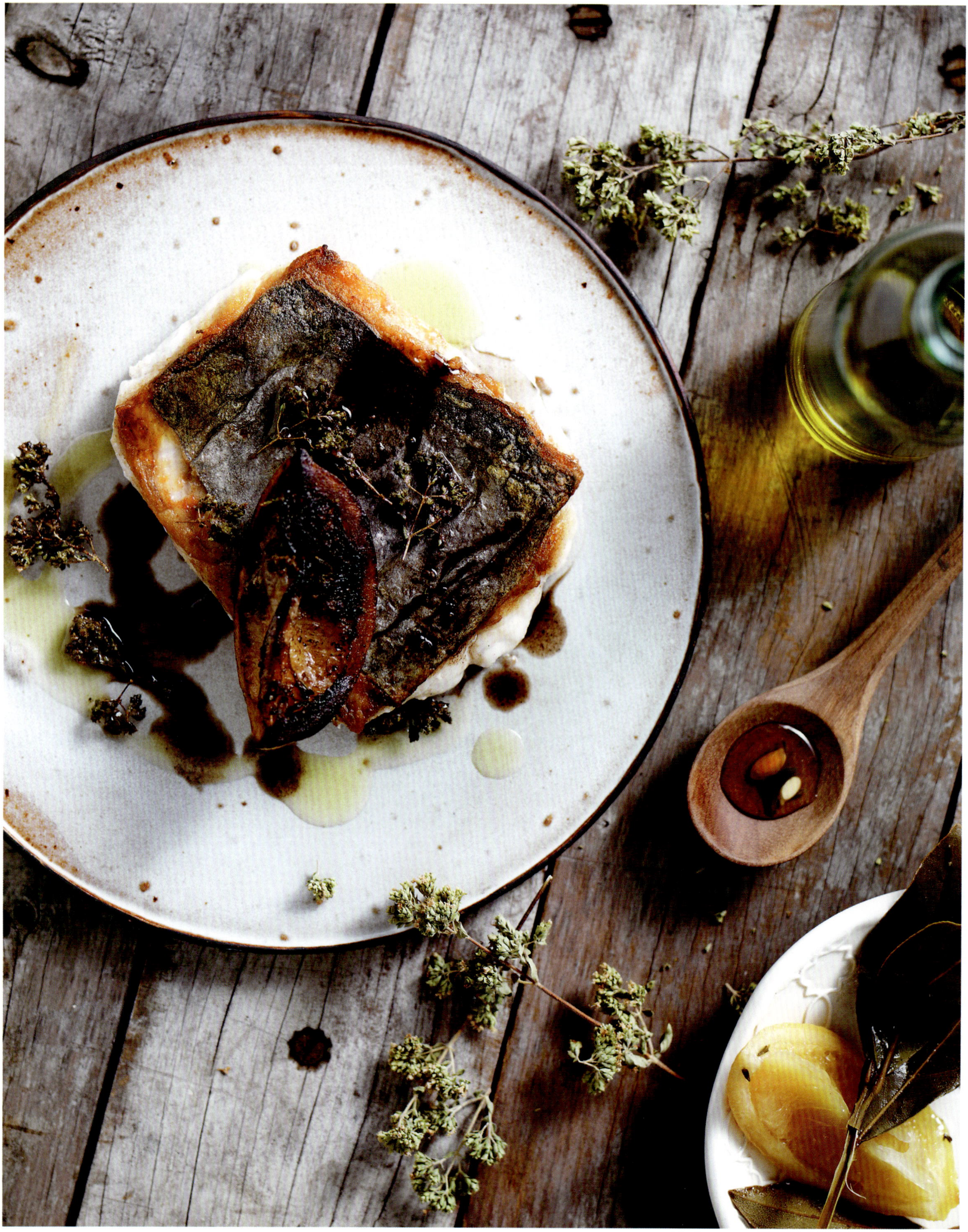

Gemfish with preserved lemon and oregano

To prepare the gemfish fillets for pan-frying with crisp skin, lay them on a work surface and dust the skin sides with the rice flour. Place each fillet, flesh side down, on a sheet of baking paper large enough to cover the fillet.

Heat a large cast-iron or heavy-based frying pan (or two smaller pans – it's essential that the fish is not overcrowded in the pan) over medium–high heat and add the ghee. When the pan is hot and the ghee translucent, place the fillets in the pan, skin side down, leaving the paper on the flesh side. Place a 1 kg (2 lb 4 oz) weight – such as a heavy pot or another pan – on top of the fillets and cook for 4 minutes, lifting the weight once or twice then moving the fillets gently around the pan so they don't burn. Reduce the heat to low. Remove the weight and the paper then, using a spatula, gently flip each fillet to quickly seal the other side. Remove the fish from the heat and set aside in a warm place to rest. (Cooking times may vary depending on the size of the fish from which the fillets were cut; for more information, see page 437.)

Heat a small heavy-based frying pan over medium heat and add the butter. When the butter is starting to turn golden and bubbly, add the preserved lemon and cook, turning, for 5 minutes, or until well caramelised. Add the oregano and season with a little pepper (there's no need for salt – the preserved lemon is salty enough).

Place the rested gemfish fillets on serving plates. Top each fillet with a preserved lemon quarter, then spoon over the oregano and butter. Finish each with a dash of lemon oil and serve.

NOTES: If you don't have a pan large enough for all the fillets, or two smaller pans, cook the fish in two batches. Keep the first batch warm while you cook the second.

If you find the preserved lemon too salty, soak the cut quarters in a bowl of cold water for 1 hour. Pat dry before caramelising.

SERVES 4

4 × 200 g (7 oz) gemfish fillets, skin on, pin-boned
2 tablespoons rice flour
80 ml (2½ fl oz/⅓ cup) ghee (see note page 26)
80 g (2¾ oz) butter
1 Preserved Lemon (page 461), cut into quarters (see note)
4 dried Greek oregano sprigs
freshly ground black pepper, to taste
lemon oil, to serve (see note page 25)

Brandade

SERVES 4 AS AN ENTRÉE

270 g (9½ oz) Salted Fish (page 462) made with gemfish (see note)
600 ml (21 fl oz) milk
130 g (4½ oz) boiled all-purpose potatoes, dried (see note)
16 cornichons
1 small handful watercress
2 teaspoons drained and well-rinsed capers in vinegar
lemon oil, to serve (see note page 25)
freshly ground black pepper, to serve
½ baguette or long bread roll, cut in half lengthways and toasted

To prepare the salted fish for cooking, gently rinse off the salt under cold running water, without thoroughly washing it. Pour the milk into a deep frying pan and bring to the boil over high heat. Remove the pan from the heat and add the fish. Leave to poach for 2 minutes, then remove using a slotted spoon, reserving the milk.

Flake the fish roughly and place in a small saucepan over low heat. Add the dried potatoes and, using a wooden spoon, work them into the fish. Warm the mixture through, adding a little of the reserved milk if a wetter brandade is preferred.

Spoon the brandade onto serving plates and serve with the cornichons, watercress and capers. Top with a little lemon oil and pepper to finish, and the toasted baguette for spreading.

NOTES: Other fish that work well in this recipe include ling and blue-eye trevalla.
    To 'dry' boiled potatoes, drain them well, remove the skin and return them to the saucepan over low heat until any moisture on the potatoes has evaporated.

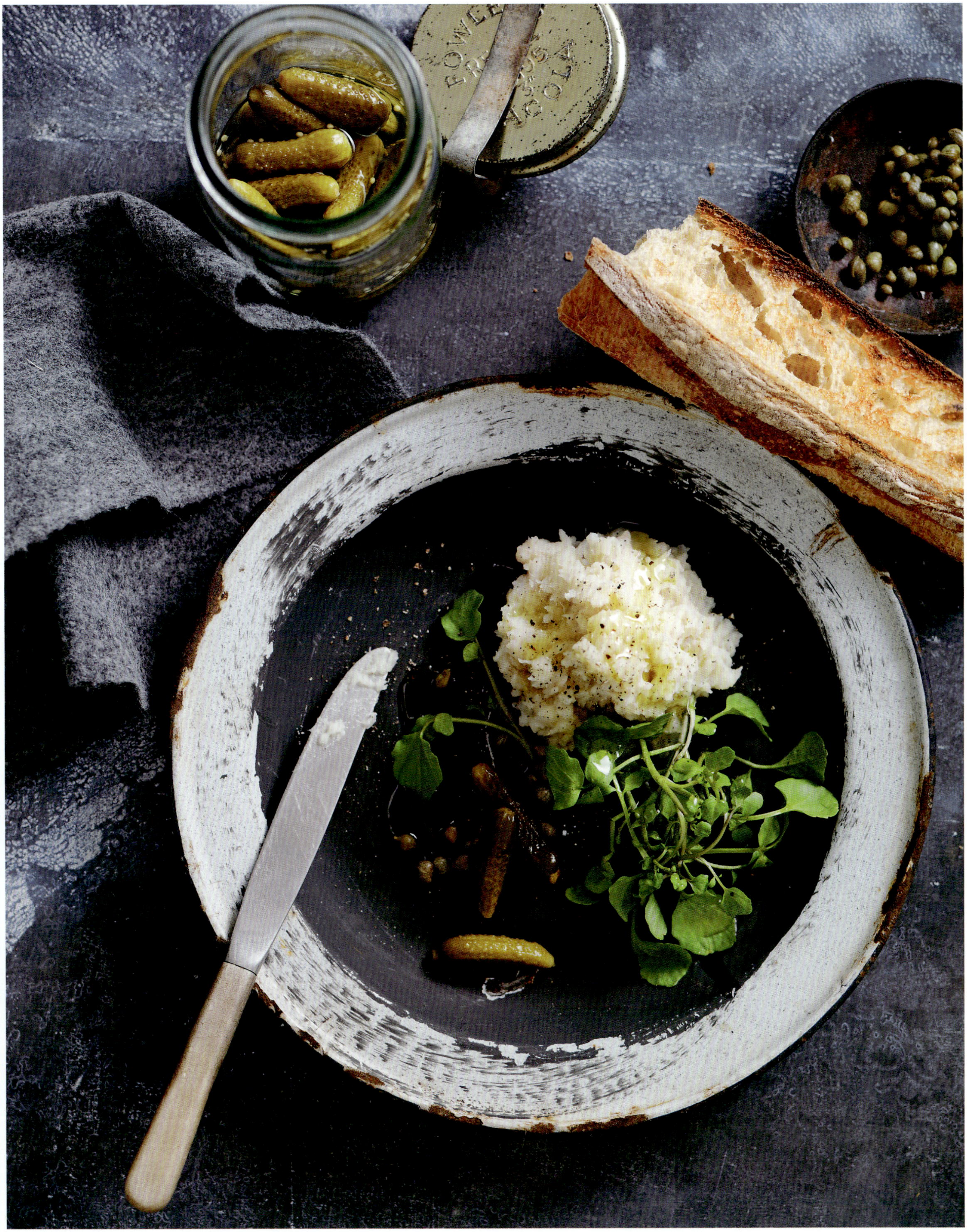

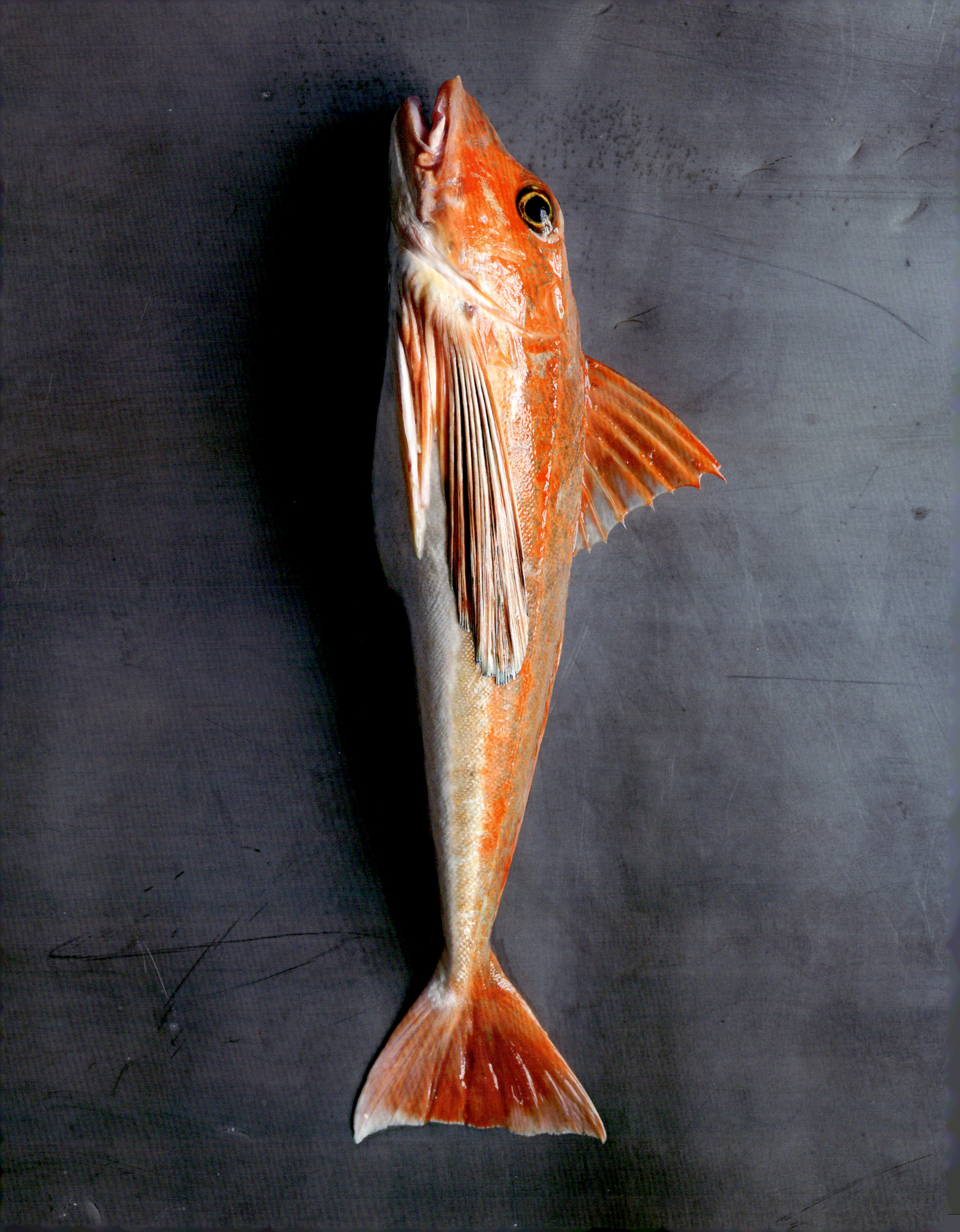

GURNARD

The red gurnard (*Chelidonichthys kumu*) is a blunt-snouted, prehistoric-looking fish found off southern and eastern Australia. Its lean, firm white flesh is prized in Italy and Japan but mostly disregarded here. The name gurnard or gurnet is derived from the French verb *grogner*, 'to grunt', a reference to the sound made by the swim bladder when the fish is taken from the water. New Zealanders call it New Zealand flathead.

Gurnards are a burnt-orange sandy colour, with reddish bands and blotches that can vary from bright to dull, depending on where the fish has been swimming. The round pectoral fins are greenish with bright blue margins and covered in bright blue spots; towards the back of the fin is a roundish black blotch that has a bright blue margin and white spots scattered inside.

Gurnards use their fins to search the seabed for their favourite foods – crabs, fish and shrimp; their diet produces a delicious rich and firm flesh that holds together well during cooking. As their fat is predominantly immediately under the skin, however, the flesh has very low oil content and can readily dry out if not handled with care.

The gurnard is often confused with another dramatic-looking fish from the same family, the latchet (*Pterygotrigla polyommata*). The latchet is also reddish on top but has a silvery belly. Its pectoral fins are blue to purplish with bands of yellow to green spots, and the blotches at the back are black with a white margin. The latchet also has two distinctive spines on the snout. It has a much leaner diet than the gurnard, which means a lower fat content and an even greater capacity to dry out if not well handled.

SEASONALITY Year round, with a peak in spring–summer
CATCHING METHODS Mid-water trawl, some handline
COMMON LENGTH 30–50 cm (12–20 in)
COMMON WEIGHT 600 g – 2 kg (1 lb 5 oz – 4 lb 8 oz)
IDENTIFIABLE FEATURES Red body with round, blue- or yellow-spotted pectoral fins
SUSTAINABILITY Stock status good

GURNARD IN THE KITCHEN

It's important that whatever the cooking method, gurnard (and latchet) always be cooked with the skin on. Gurnard has a slightly higher fat content than latchet, which means that whether cooked whole or as a fillet, latchet really needs the protection of its skin to retain moisture in the cooked flesh.

Gurnard are fantastic fish cooked whole – the gelatinous moisture from the bones adds plenty to the flesh. Deep-frying whole brings out the fats and also makes it really crisp. Gut it, scale it, score the sides, coat it in flour and drop it straight into the fryer (a 700 g/1 lb 9 oz fish will need 2–3 minutes). It tastes completely different this way from fried fillets. Dress it with soy sauce, dried shallots and chilli – beautiful!

When cooking fish in a deep-fryer, you need to score the skin to an even distance from the bones – nice and deep at the shoulder and shallower towards the tail. As you move along the fish, space the cuts more widely – one finger apart, two fingers, three fingers.

Latchet is fantastic as sushi and sashimi, and also grills (broils) well. Some people like to use gurnard for fish and chips, but it's not the best as a skin-off, stand-alone fillet.

SPECIAL STORAGE AND HANDLING
Try to buy whole fish, then ask your fishmonger to fillet them, or at least gill, gut and scale them for you. Wrap in muslin (cheesecloth) or freezer film, then store as usual. If your fishmonger fillets, ask them to dry-fillet and wrap tightly in freezer film, then store as usual. Always avoid using plastic wrap because it will sweat. Store at 1–2°C (34–36°F) and bring to room temperature before cooking.

BEST COOKING METHODS Steamed, pan-fried, roasted, deep-fried; always cook with skin on

TEXTURE Firm with small, tight flakes (latchet is much firmer and drier)

AROMA Sweet, almost spicy, with light almond notes

FLAVOUR Complex, savoury, with oceanic, nutty notes of buttered zucchini (courgette)

APPEARANCE Flesh white–pink when raw; arctic white once cooked

YIELD Boneless fillet about 33% of whole weight

SUBSTITUTES Flathead

Fried whole gurnard with chilli jam

For the chilli jam, heat the sesame oil in a medium saucepan over medium heat. Add the onion and cook, stirring constantly, for about 6 minutes, or until well caramelised. Add the red and green chillies then cook, stirring frequently, for 4 minutes. Add the sugar and cook for a further 4 minutes. Add the sherry vinegar and 100 ml (3½ fl oz) of water, then keep cooking over medium heat for about 15 minutes, until the mixture has a jam-like consistency. Add the lime zest and juice, reduce the heat to low and simmer for 5 minutes. Remove from the heat and cool to room temperature. If not using immediately, seal in an airtight container and refrigerate (see note overleaf).

Half-fill a saucepan wide enough to hold the whole fish with vegetable oil and place over high heat (see note overleaf). Heat the oil to 180°C (350°C) – check with an oil thermometer. (For a guide to testing the oil temperature without a thermometer, see note overleaf.)

Score the fish to the bone, spacing the cuts about one finger-width apart near the head and further apart as the fillet gets thinner, closer to the tail. Dust the fish lightly with plain flour.

Carefully submerge the fish completely in the hot oil and fry for about 3 minutes, then carefully turn it over and cook for a further 2–3 minutes, until crisp and cooked through. Remove and drain well on a baking tray lined with paper towel.

RECIPE CONTINUED OVERLEAF >

SERVES 4

vegetable oil, for deep-frying
1 whole gurnard, about 900 g (2 lb), gutted, scaled and cleaned
plain (all-purpose) flour, for dusting
2 tablespoons fried red Asian shallots (see note overleaf)
1 spring onion (scallion), trimmed, outer layer removed, thinly sliced on the diagonal
½ teaspoon crushed dried red chilli (see note overleaf)
1 small handful coriander (cilantro) sprigs
1 tablespoon finely diced Preserved Lemon rind (page 461)

CHILLI JAM
(Makes about 700 g/1 lb 9 oz/4 cups)
100 ml (3½ fl oz) sesame oil
1 kg (2 lb 4 oz) peeled and very thinly sliced red onion (about 9 onions)
6–8 long red chillies, seeds removed, julienned (to yield 60 g/2¼ oz)
about 20 small green chillies, seeds removed, julienned (to yield 40 g/1½ oz)
150 g (5½ oz/¾ cup) lightly packed light brown sugar
200 ml (7 fl oz) sherry vinegar
finely grated zest and juice of 4 limes

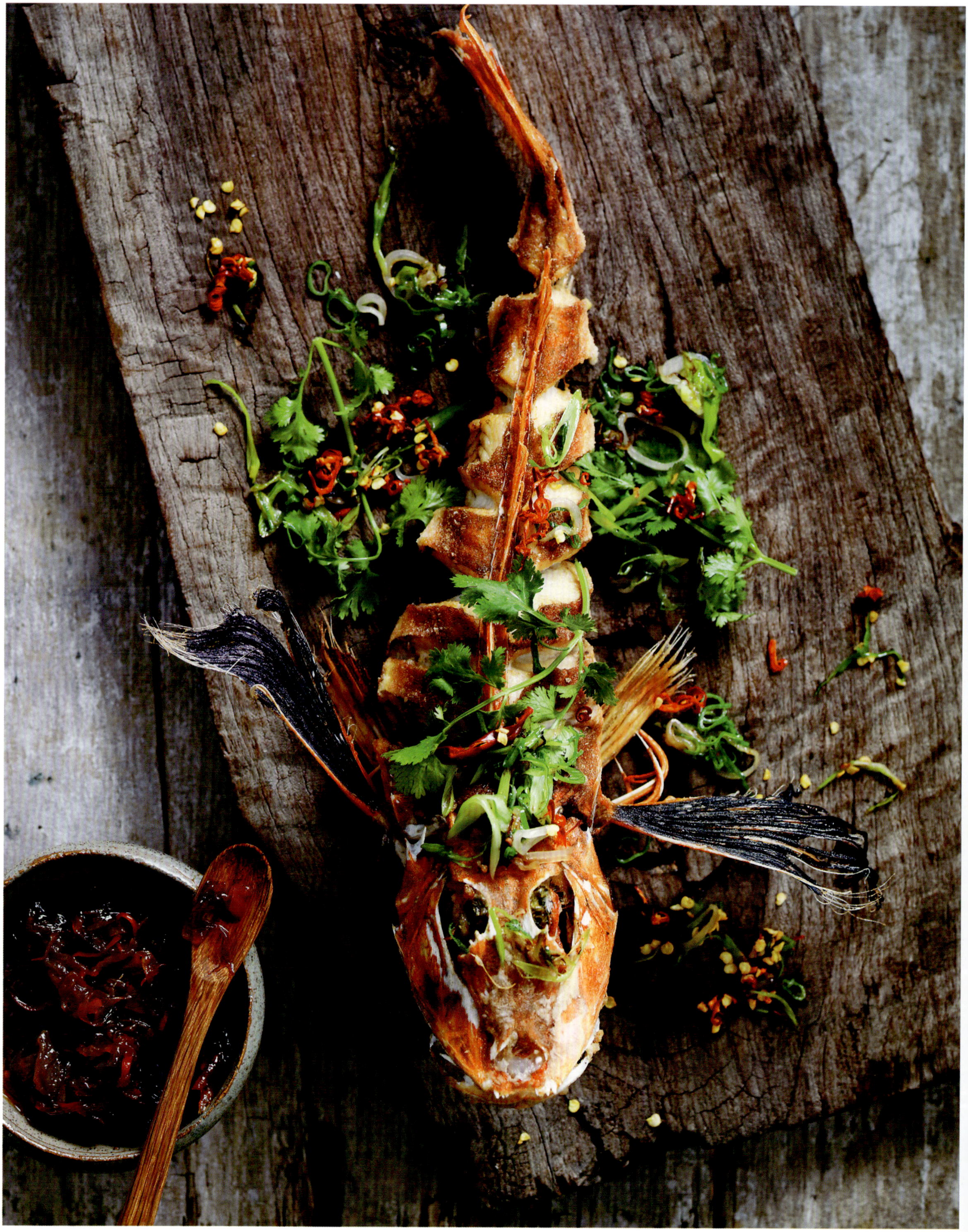

<< **RECIPE CONTINUED FROM PREVIOUS PAGE**

Place the fish on a serving platter and scatter over the fried shallots, spring onion, dried chilli, coriander and preserved lemon. Serve with the chilli jam on the side.

NOTES: Fried red Asian shallots are available in Asian supermarkets. To make your own, slice shallots very thinly and fry over low heat, being careful not to over- or undercook them. Drain well on paper towel. They will keep for several days in an airtight container in the pantry, but are best used within 2 days.

To make dried red chillies, dry fresh chillies overnight on a baking tray in a 110°C (225°F) oven. They will crumble easily.

The chilli jam is best made about a week ahead. It will keep in an airtight container in the fridge for 3 months.

When deep-frying in a saucepan, it's advisable to keep the oil level a good 10 cm (4 in) below the rim of the pan. The other option for deep-frying is, of course, an electric deep-fryer. The used oil can be strained, cooled and refrigerated for later use.

To test the temperature of the oil without a thermometer, drop a cube of bread into the saucepan. If the bread turns golden in 15 seconds, the temperature is sitting perfectly on 180°C (350°F). If the bread only takes 10 seconds to turn golden, then the oil is around 190°C (375°F). If it takes 20–30 seconds to brown, the oil is too cold. Be patient and bring the oil to the correct temperature before proceeding.

HAPUKA IN THE KITCHEN

Although underrated, particularly in comparison to its cousins the blue-eye trevalla, bass groper and bar cod, hapuka is one of the higher value finfish species in Australia and New Zealand, where it's found predominantly in fine-dining and Asian restaurants. It's becoming more common in retail shops, particularly Asian fishmongers, where it's often sold as large cutlets. The heads and wings make excellent eating, and are often sold separately from the fillet.

It's an incredibly versatile fish in the kitchen, with the right fat content and texture to maintain its integrity using a whole suite of culinary methods. Its broad scalloping flesh, intramuscular fat and rich sweet flavour make it perfect in curries and pot roasts, as well as roasted, pan-fried with crisp skin, grilled (broiled), poached and steamed. The only cooking technique that isn't recommended is battering and frying; although it works, it seems a waste when all the other methods show it off in such a beautiful light.

Baby hapuka are fabulous raw, such as in sashimi, sushi and ceviche. It shines when pan-fried with crisp skin – the fat under the skin helps it crisp up nicely without affecting the flesh. Its firm flake stands up to the robust flavour profile and heat of curries – unlike many white fish, which turn to mush. Nevertheless, it's best to cook the fish gently first, then add it to the broth, soup or curry to serve. The integrity of the fish is paramount.

Hapuka isn't as sweet as bass groper or blue-eye trevalla, so you can use more savoury accompaniments. Mushrooms are hapuka's best friend – especially pine mushrooms. It works well paired with sweeter green vegetables but much better with savoury ones, such as salt-roasted celeriac (see page 463), or roast vegetables, such as pumpkin (winter squash) and beetroot (beets). It's also lovely with a horseradish cream.

BEST COOKING METHODS Roasted, grilled (broiled), pan-fried with crisp skin (fillets, see page 437), poached, steamed

TEXTURE Broad scalloping flesh, unctuous and soft to firm, depending on the season and the size of the fish

AROMA Sweet, clean, with a rich creamy note

FLAVOUR Rich, with notes of seaweed and iodine, and a cream-like finish

APPEARANCE Flesh translucent grey–white when raw; bright white once cooked

YIELD Flesh about 40% of whole weight

SUBSTITUTES Bass groper and bar cod, blue-eye trevalla, pink snapper, striped trumpeter, tropical snapper

Steamed hapuka with mushrooms, soy and baby bok choy

Fill a Chinese steamer, wok or saucepan with water and bring to the boil over high heat.

Line two metal or bamboo steamer baskets with baking paper to prevent sticking. Place the bok choy in one steamer basket and the hapuka fillets in the other. Set aside.

Heat the vegetable oil in a medium saucepan over medium–high heat and add the onion. Cook for 1 minute, stirring constantly then add the garlic and ginger. Continue cooking for another minute, until the vegetables are softened and starting to colour. Add the mushrooms and toss well to coat. Increase the heat to high and cook the mushrooms for a further minute, tossing well. Add the rice wine, sugar and mushroom soy sauce. Stir until the sugar has dissolved, then add the stock and bring to the boil. Reduce the heat and simmer for about 10 minutes. Taste the mushrooms to ensure they are balanced and well seasoned, then adjust if necessary with more sugar and/or soy sauce.

While the mushrooms are simmering, set the steamer baskets over the boiling water, with the fish on the bottom, and cover with a tight-fitting lid. Steam the bok choy for 1 minute, or until wilted and soft. Remove from the steamer and keep warm. Cover and leave the hapuka to cook for a further 4 minutes (see note).

To serve, place the bok choy on four serving plates and lay the hapuka fillets on top. Spoon the mushrooms and sauce over the fish. Season each serve with a drop or two of sesame oil and top with coriander leaves.

NOTE: Cooking times may vary according to the size of the fish and the thickness of the fillets, and whether you use a Chinese steamer or a double boiler, so take care not to overcook the fish.

SERVES 4

4 heads baby bok choy (pak choy), well rinsed and cut in half lengthways

4 × 200 g (7 oz) pieces hapuka fillet, skin off, pin-boned

60 ml (2 fl oz/¼ cup) vegetable oil

1 small red onion, peeled, cut in half and thinly sliced

4 garlic cloves, peeled and thinly sliced

3 cm (1¼ in) piece ginger, peeled and julienned

35 g (1¼ oz/½ cup) sliced fresh shiitake mushrooms

75 g (2¾ oz/½ cup) sliced oyster mushrooms

5 g (⅛ oz/¼ cup) roughly torn wood ear fungus

15 g (½ oz/¼ cup) enoki mushrooms, ends trimmed

2 tablespoons Chinese rice wine (shaoxing)

1 tablespoon soft brown sugar, or as needed

2 tablespoons mushroom soy sauce, or as needed

250 ml (9 fl oz/1 cup) chicken stock

½ teaspoon sesame oil

coriander (cilantro) leaves, to serve

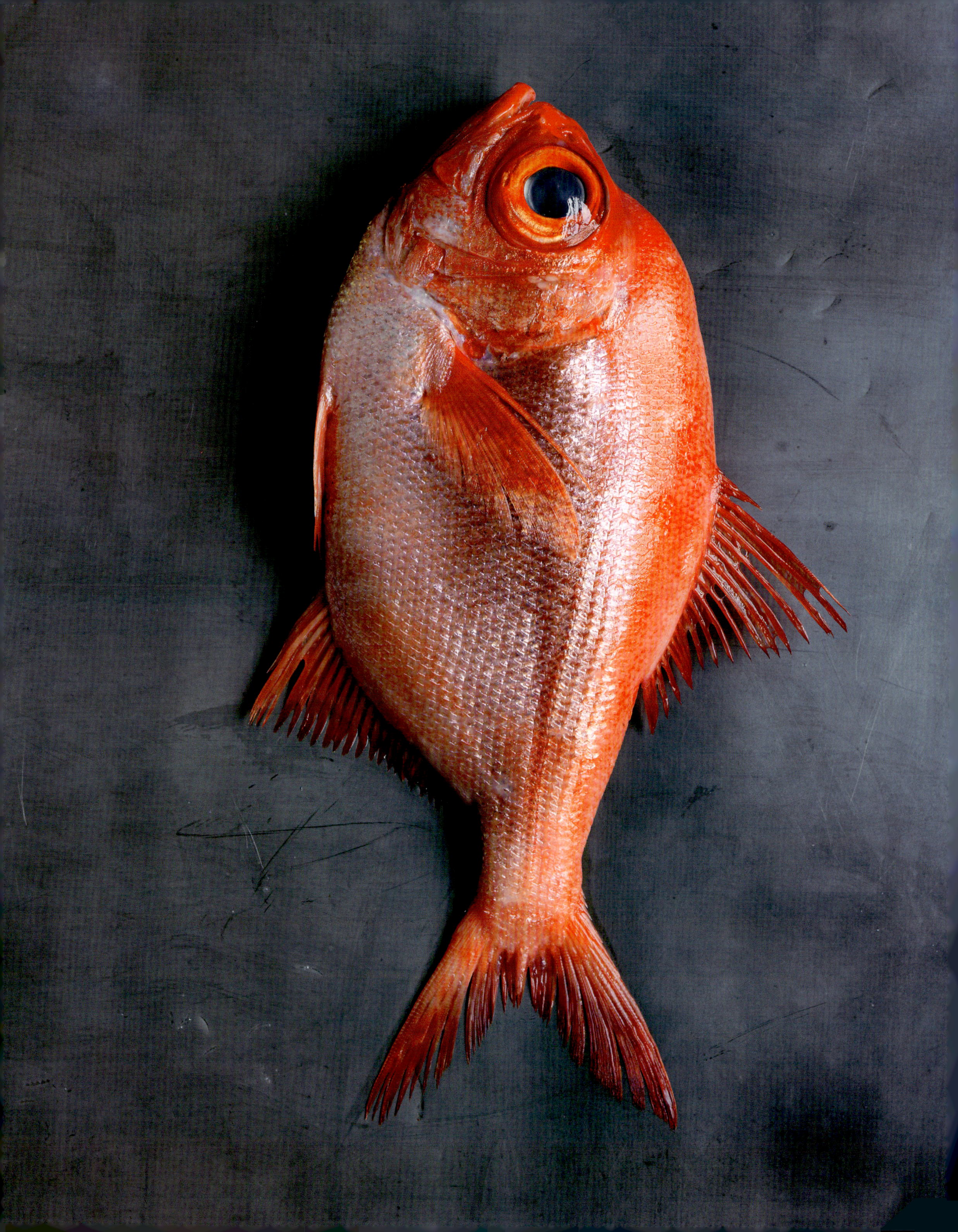

IMPERADOR

The name imperador (*Beryx decadactylus*) is Portuguese for emperor and signals the regal nature of this fish, which is often confused with alfonsino. It has a deep, thick body, bright red back, bright orange fins and belly, and silvery pink sides. The eyes are large, with a blood-red iris. Although purists use the name imperador for *Beryx decadactylus* and alfonsino for the closely related species *Beryx splendens*, they're often mistaken for each other in the market and both are highly prized for their great eating qualities.

Imperador generally live near the sea floor at depths of 200–400 m (650–1300 ft), although they can be found as deep as 1300 m (4250 ft). Found all around the south coast of Australia and off the eastern coast of New Zealand, they're predominantly caught using longlines and mid-water trawls at night, when they move up from the sea floor to search for prey.

Their distinctive colouring and large eyes make them perfect night-time stalkers of fish, crustaceans, squid and other molluscs. This exotic diet is directly reflected in the tasty flesh, which is particularly highly regarded by chefs in Japan, where it's called kinmedai. It's often used as the hero fish in a nigiri selection or braised in hotpots.

SEASONALITY Year round, with a peak in summer–autumn

CATCHING METHODS Bottom longline, dropline, mid-water trawl

COMMON LENGTH 30–80 cm (12–31½ in)

COMMON WEIGHT 800 g – 3 kg (1 lb 12 oz – 6 lb 12 oz)

IDENTIFIABLE FEATURES Impressive, bright red, with a long, rangy tail and a large, dark round eye; it truly looks like an emperor

SUSTAINABILITY Considered sustainable

IMPERADOR IN THE KITCHEN

When a chef says 'fat is flavour', this delicious sashimi fish is what they're talking about. You can pan-fry fillets with crisp skin (see page 437), and it works well braised in a pot, marinated and grilled (broiled), or roasted. Chefs will tell you it's a bit of a waste not to eat it raw. It's bold enough to take on vinegars, and is therefore well suited to carpaccio, with ponzu sauce (page 455) the ideal accompaniment. Not only can you taste the fat, you can see the marbling of the fat in the flesh – it's a textural treat.

BEST COOKING METHODS Raw (sushi, sashimi, carpaccio), braised, roasted, steamed, pan-fried

TEXTURE Medium–firm; broad scalloping flake

AROMA Intense, full, with bright notes of seaweed and egg white

FLAVOUR Rich, sweet, with lingering umami and notes of omelette

APPEARANCE Flesh pink–white when raw; white once cooked

YIELD Flesh about 40% of whole weight

SUBSTITUTES Bass groper and bar cod

One-pot imperador with fig and verjuice

SERVES 4 AS AN ENTRÉE

4 × 120 g (4¼ oz) imperador fillets, skin on, pin-boned
sea salt, to taste
160 ml (5¼ fl oz) boiling water
2 tablespoons ghee (see note page 26)
2 figs, carefully torn in half lengthways
80 ml (2½ fl oz/⅓ cup) verjuice
freshly ground black pepper, to taste

Place the imperador fillets on a work surface and score the skin. Rub a little salt into the skin and leave for 10 minutes. Rinse the salt off under cold running water and place the fish on a wire rack set over a baking tin, skin side up. Pour 2 tablespoons of the boiling water over the skin of each fillet to set the proteins and fats – this makes the skin delicious to eat.

To prepare the imperador fillets for pan-frying with crisp skin, lay them, flesh side down, on a sheet of baking paper large enough to cover the fillet.

Place a large heavy-based frying pan over medium–high heat and add the ghee. When a thin blue haze rises from the surface of the ghee, add the fish, skin side down, leaving the paper on the flesh side. Place a 1 kg (2 lb 4 oz) weight – such as a heavy pot or another pan – on top of the fillets and cook for 2 minutes.

Remove the weight, add the figs to the pan, flesh side down, and cook for a further 1 minute. Remove the paper from the fish and turn to seal. (Cooking times may vary depending on the size of the fish from which the fillets were cut; for more information, see page 437.) Remove the fish and figs from the pan, increase the heat to high, add the verjuice and toss well to deglaze the pan.

Place the imperador and figs on serving plates. Pour the pan juices over the fish, then season with salt and pepper to finish.

NOTE: Imperador is a very rich fish. It works beautifully in an entrée as a small portion.

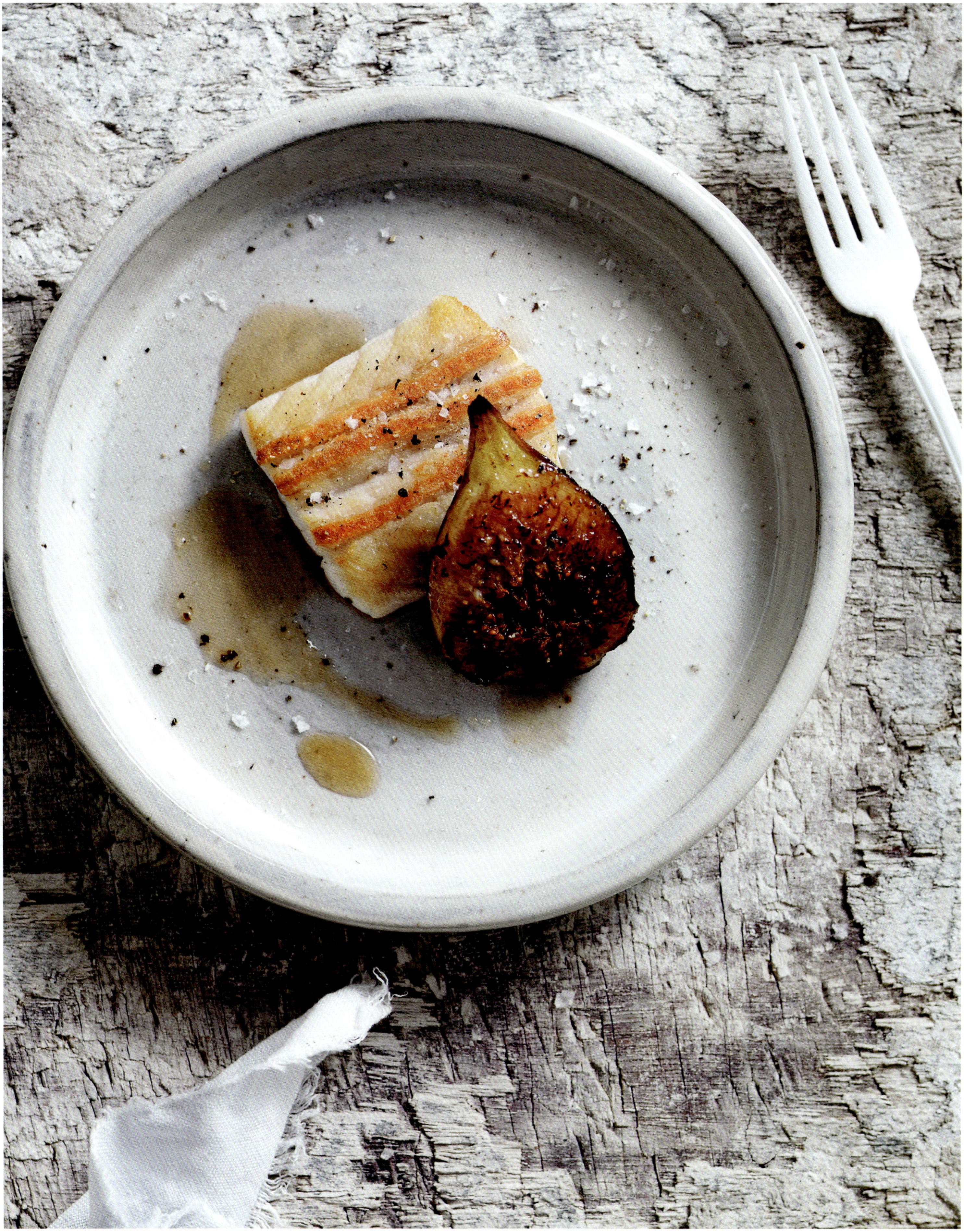

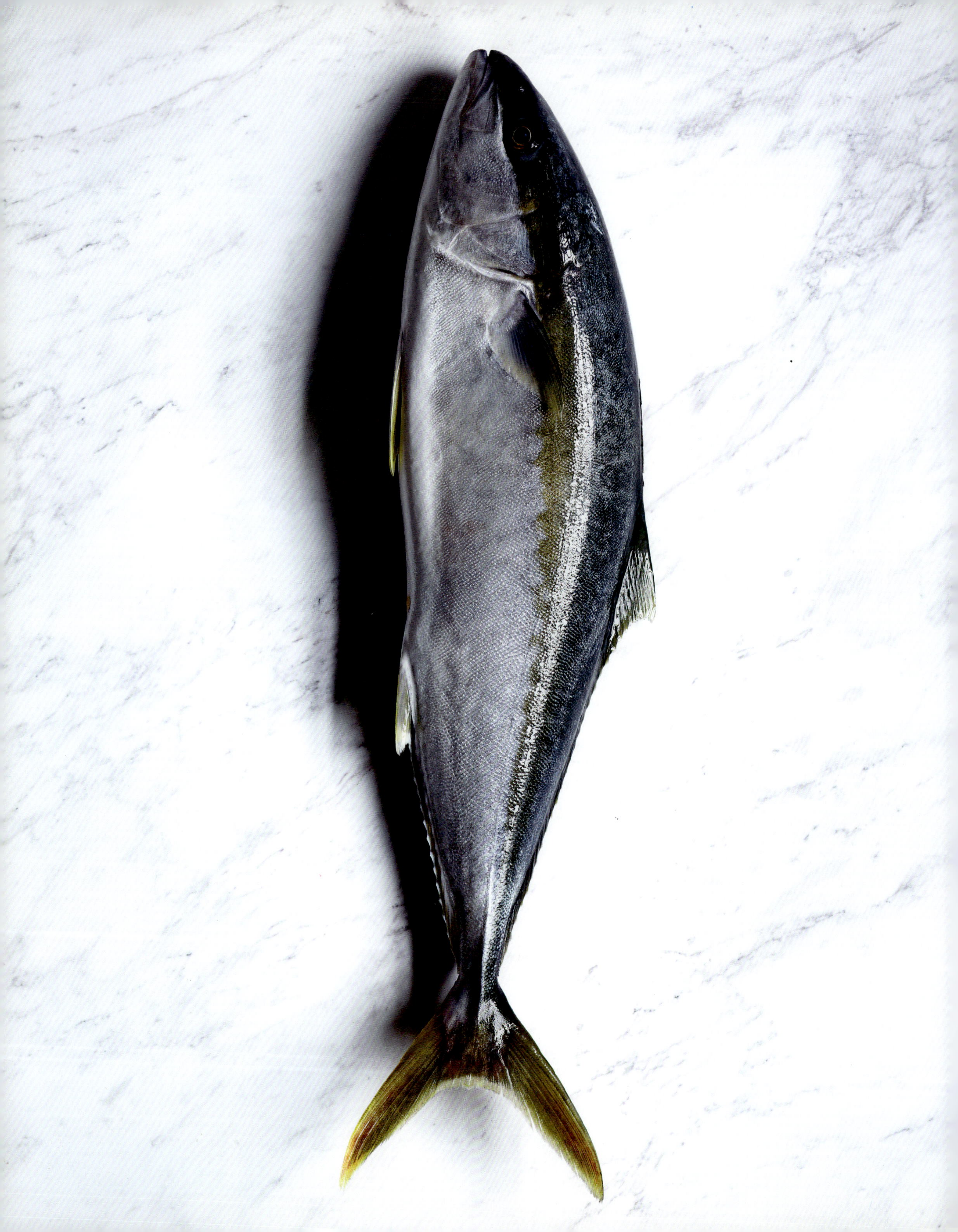

KINGFISH, YELLOWTAIL

The southern subspecies of the yellowtail kingfish (*Seriola lalandi lalandi*) is endemic to the subtropical and temperate waters surrounding Australia and New Zealand. It's been a popular table fish in Australia for close to a century, but overfishing in the 1940s saw stocks so depleted that the wild catch on the east coast has been small, seasonal and unpredictable ever since. Wild fish from the east coast, especially north of Sydney, are also subject to a naturally occurring myxosporea parasite that can make the flesh of a perfect-looking fish turn to paste when cooked.

The yellowtail kingfish is a powerful swimmer with an elongated body shaped like a torpedo and small, smooth scales. The fact that it's a more or less docile opportunistic feeder made it a good candidate for farming, but it took some serious science from the South Australian fishery developers to get there. It means, however, that premium-quality farmed and wild kingfish are now available pretty much year round. This farmed fish goes by the Japanese name for the species, hiramasa, to differentiate it from wild-caught fish. The Asian subspecies, *Seriola lalandi aureovitta*, is found in southern Japanese waters around Okinawa.

Several subspecies of yellowtail kingfish are found around the world, where it's known variously as amberjack, gelbschwanz, magiatiko and charuteiro. In Japan, it's regarded as a premium sashimi fish.

SEASONALITY Wild: year round, best from autumn to spring; farmed: year round, with highest fat content in late autumn to winter
CATCHING METHODS Wild: trap, hook and line trolling
COMMON LENGTH Wild and farmed: 60–250 cm (24–98½ in)
COMMON WEIGHT Wild and farmed: 3–5 kg (6 lb 12 oz – 11 lb)
IDENTIFIABLE FEATURES Sleek torpedo-shaped body, dark green back, silver belly, brilliant gold stripe above pectoral fin line
SUSTAINABILITY Wild: stock status good; farmed: certified by Friend of the Sea

YELLOWTAIL KINGFISH IN THE KITCHEN

In late autumn, the fat content of kingfish flesh is more than 15 per cent, which gives it a beautiful unctuous texture raw (as sashimi, sushi, carpaccio or ceviche) and provides great versatility cooked. The clean, naturally sweet flavour of the flesh suits both Eastern and Western techniques. It's an amazing fish raw, but just as exciting pan-fried with crisp skin. You could cook it on the bone, but it's at its best raw or as fillets.

It's one of the hardest fish to cook and get right. Despite its high fat content, it doesn't do well with a high oven heat, as different parts of the fish cook at different rates and it can dry out. To be successful, you need to cook it medium–rare or rare, then rest it before serving.

Kingfish can handle big Mediterranean flavours – tomato, olives, onion, mushrooms, capsicum (pepper) and chilli. You shouldn't need to add any fat because it has such a high natural fat content.

There's a vast difference between wild-caught and farmed fish, although both are excellent in their own way. The wild fish has a more obvious savoury flavour and tends to cook more evenly, although it will also readily dry out if overcooked.

SPECIAL STORAGE AND HANDLING Extraordinary shelf life; gill and gut whole fish, wrap in freezer film and store in the coolest part of the fridge. Fillet immediately before use; otherwise, wrap fillets in paper towel, then freezer film, then tightly in plastic wrap to minimise oxidisation.

BEST COOKING METHODS Wild: sashimi, seared, pan-fried with crisp skin (fillets; see page 437); farmed: sashimi

TEXTURE Soft and buttery when raw; firm, with a tight grain, once cooked

AROMA Soft, clean and starchy, with riesling-like kerosene hints, more pronounced once cooked

FLAVOUR Sweet artichoke notes when raw; robust and intense with a more pronounced oiliness once cooked

APPEARANCE Wild: flesh light to dark pink when raw, brilliant white once cooked; farmed: flesh buttermilk white when raw, brilliant white once cooked

YIELD Boneless fillet about 55% of whole weight

SUBSTITUTES Cobia, mahi mahi, Spanish mackerel, trevally

Escabeche of yellowtail kingfish

Season the kingfish with salt on both sides.

Heat a large heavy-based frying pan over high heat and add 100 ml (3½ fl oz) of the olive oil. Sear the fish for 90 seconds on each side, then transfer to a small deep non-reactive dish.

To make the escabeche, add the remaining oil to the same frying pan and reduce the heat to medium–low. Add the carrot, onion and garlic, then cook, stirring occasionally, for about 5 minutes, until soft. Add the thyme sprigs, bay leaves, fennel seeds, white peppercorns, saffron with its soaking liquid, vinegar and 250 ml (9 fl oz/1 cup) of water. Increase the heat to high and bring to the boil. Check the seasoning and adjust if necessary, then reduce the heat to low and simmer for 5 minutes. Remove the frying pan from the heat and leave to cool for 30 minutes.

Spoon the cooled escabeche over the fish, cover with plastic wrap and refrigerate for 2 hours (see note).

To serve, thinly slice or gently flake the fish and arrange on a serving platter. Spoon the escabeche over and top with the mixed herbs. Serve with fresh bread and aioli on the side.

NOTES: This dish can be prepared a day ahead. If refrigerating overnight, let the fish come to room temperature before serving.

You can also serve this dish warm. Remove the hot escabeche from the heat, pour it over the fish and cover with foil. Leave to marinate for 1 hour at room temperature, then slice and serve straight away.

SERVES 4

500 g (1 lb 2 oz) yellowtail kingfish fillets, skin off, blood line removed
sea salt and freshly ground white pepper, to taste
160 ml (5¼ fl oz) extra virgin olive oil
1 small carrot, peeled and sliced into thin rounds
1 small red onion, peeled, cut in half and thinly sliced
4 garlic cloves, peeled and thinly sliced
6 thyme sprigs
2 fresh bay leaves
2 teaspoons fennel seeds, crushed
2 teaspoons white peppercorns
good pinch of saffron threads, soaked in 1 tablespoon hot water for 15–30 minutes
60 ml (2 fl oz/¼ cup) sherry vinegar
1 small handful mixed herbs (such as coriander/cilantro, mint, parsley, oregano), to serve
bread, to serve
Aioli (page 393), to serve

Wild kingfish with barbecued leek and pickled beetroot

SERVES 4

8 baby beetroot (beets), thinly sliced with a mandoline
pickling liquid (as for Pickled Green Chilli, page 281)
1 leek, white part only, well washed
4 × 200 g (7 oz) wild kingfish fillets, skin on, pin-boned
2 tablespoons rice flour
80 ml (2½ fl oz/⅓ cup) ghee (see note page 26)
lemon oil, to serve (see note page 25)
sea salt and freshly ground black pepper, to taste

Place the sliced beetroot in a small bowl with enough pickling liquid to cover. Set aside to pickle lightly.

Preheat a barbecue grill to hot, or heat a stovetop grill pan over high heat.

Place a small saucepan of salted water over high heat and bring to the boil. Add the leek and blanch for 3 minutes, or until soft. (If the leek is too long for the pot, cut it in half on the diagonal.) Remove the leek and set aside to cool at room temperature.

To prepare the kingfish fillets for pan-frying with crisp skin, lay them on a work surface and dust the skin sides with the rice flour. Place each fillet, flesh side down, on a sheet of baking paper large enough to cover the fillet.

Heat a large cast-iron frying pan over medium–high heat (or two smaller pans – it's essential that the fish is not overcrowded in the pan; see note). Add the ghee to the pan. When the pan is hot and the ghee translucent, place the fish in the pan, skin side down, leaving the paper on the flesh side. Place a 1 kg (2 lb 4 oz) weight – such as a heavy pot or another pan – on top of the fillets and cook for 4 minutes, lifting the weight once or twice then moving the fillets gently around the pan so they don't burn. (Cooking times may vary depending on the size of the fish from which the fillets were cut; for more information, see page 437.)

Reduce the heat to low. Remove the weights and the paper then, using a spatula, gently flip each fillet and cook for 1 minute more. Remove the pan from the heat and set aside to rest for 4 minutes.

While the fish is cooking, char the leek on the barbecue or grill pan on all sides. Slice on the diagonal into eight long pieces. Slice each rested kingfish fillet in half lengthways. Place the fish on serving plates with the barbecued leek and strained pickled beetroot. Finish with a little lemon oil, salt and pepper.

NOTE: If you don't have a pan large enough for all the fillets, or two smaller pans, cook the fish in two batches. Keep the first batch warm while you cook the second.

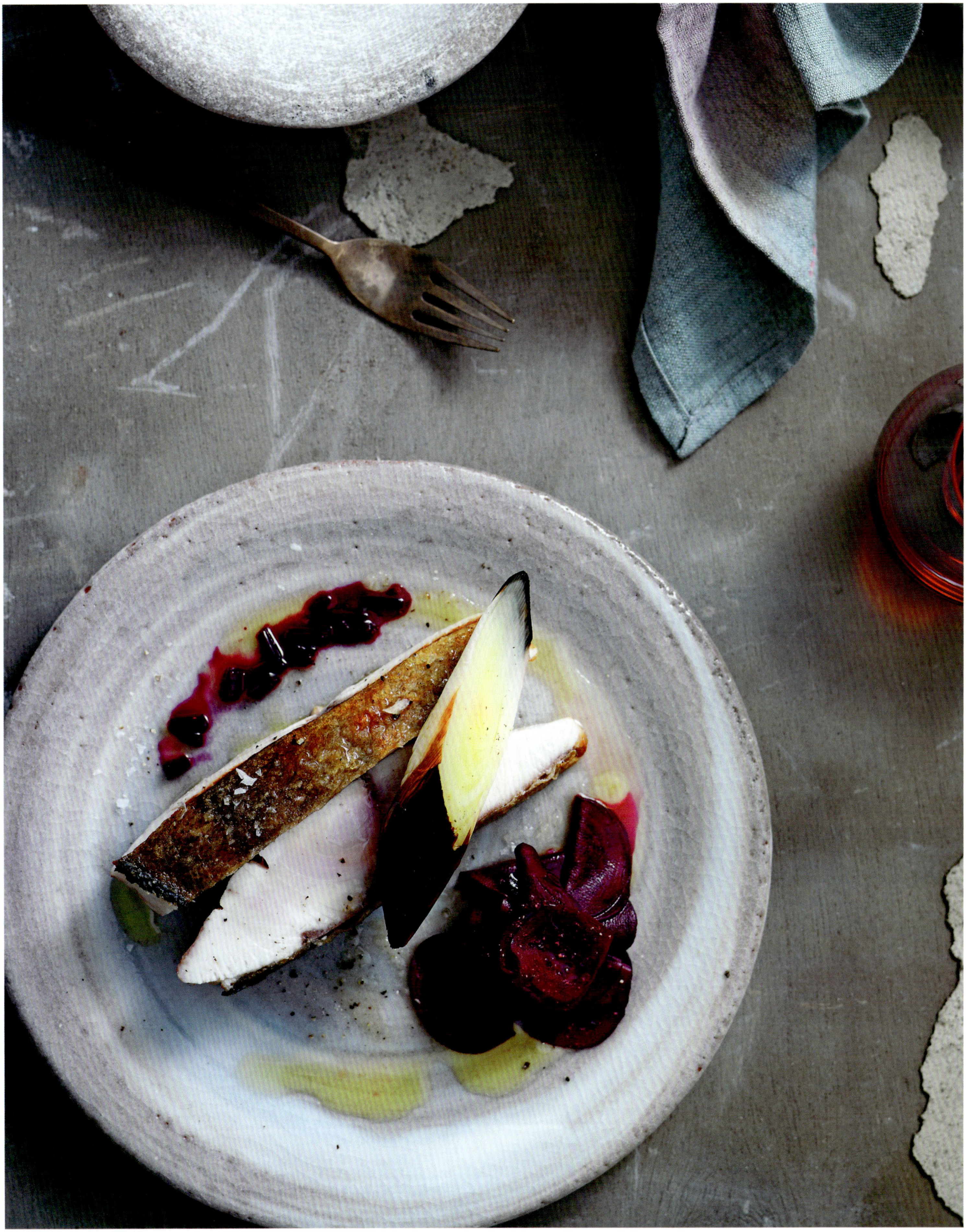

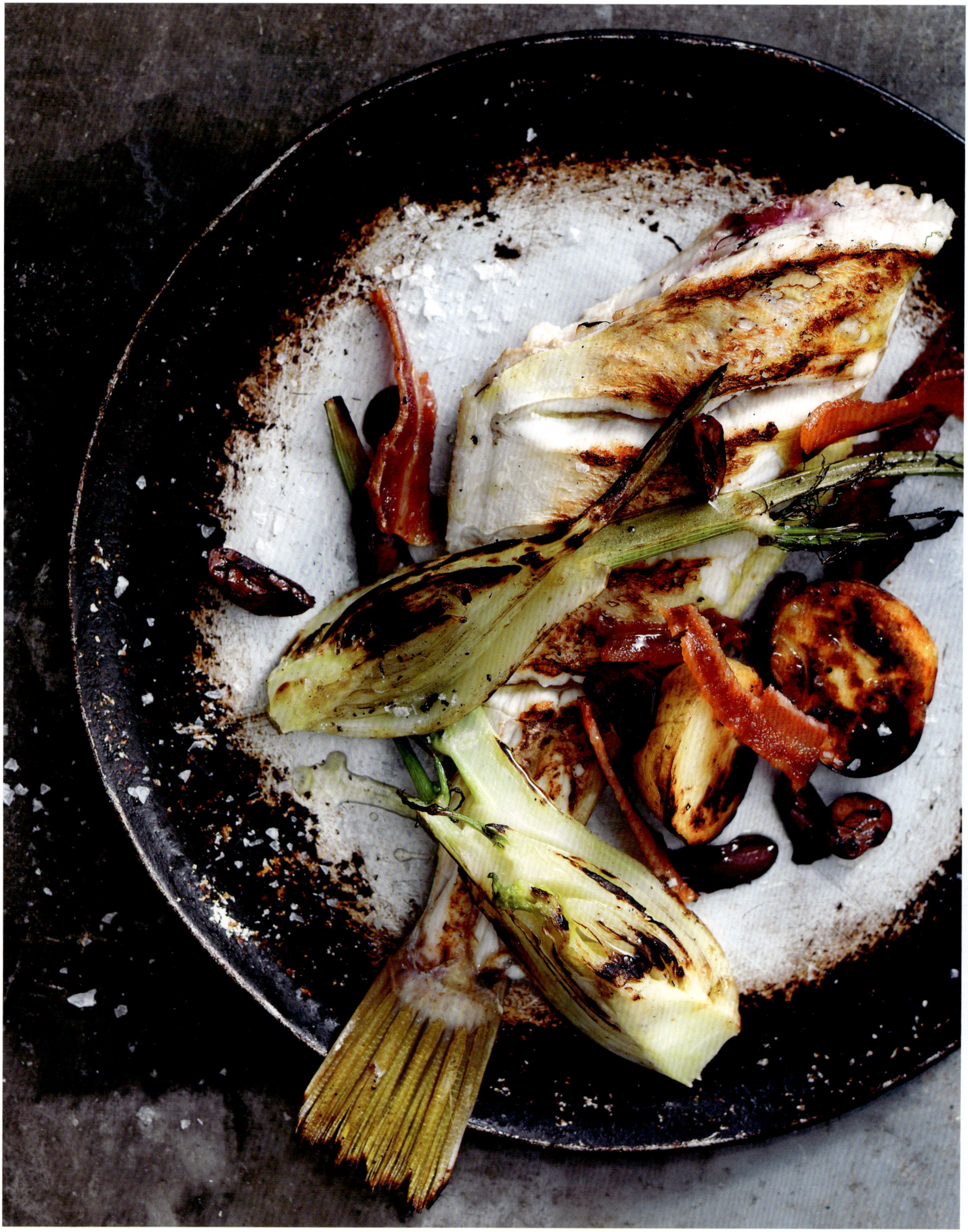

Leatherjacket with potato, fennel, olives and pancetta

Preheat a flat-top barbecue hotplate to high, or heat a flat stovetop grill pan over high heat.

Place the potato and fennel in a small saucepan and cover with the cold stock and olive oil. Bring to the boil over high heat. Reduce the heat to medium, then simmer for 10–15 minutes until the vegetables are tender. Remove the vegetables from the stock and set aside.

Place the leatherjackets directly on the hot grill plate. Cook for about 2 minutes, then carefully turn the fish using a spatula. Add the potato, fennel, olives and pancetta to the grill plate at this stage, to heat through and caramelise a little while the fish is cooking. Cook the fish for a further 2–4 minutes, until just cooked through.

Remove all the ingredients from the barbecue and serve on a platter. Finish with a splash of lemon oil and a good sprinkling of sea salt.

SERVES 4

2 waxy potatoes (such as kipfler/fingerling), cut in half

1 whole fennel bulb, trimmed and cut into quarters

750 ml (26 fl oz/3 cups) Fish Stock (page 457)

250 ml (9 fl oz/1 cup) extra virgin olive oil

2 whole leatherjackets, about 400 g (14 oz) each, heads and skin removed, skinned, fins trimmed

2 tablespoons pitted kalamata olives

120 g (4¼ oz) pancetta, cut into lardons

lemon oil, to serve (see note page 25)

sea salt, to taste

Pink ling

LING

Ling are as close as we get in our part of the world to the fabled Atlantic cod – both are eel-like fish with a long, tapering body and small, snake-like head. The ling is the largest of the cod family, with the characteristic sensitive barbell dangling under its chin (but folded away in the photo).

Pink ling (*Genypterus blacodes*) is caught abundantly around southern Australia and New Zealand year round, while rock ling (*Genypterus tigerinus*) is caught mostly around south-eastern Australia. They are caught on the continental shelf and slopes at depths of 20–800 m (60–2600 ft), where they are ferocious hunters of squid and small fish.

Ling are mostly caught by bottom otter trawl and Danish seine, which makes them a reliable, consistent and versatile fish.

SEASONALITY Year round, with a peak in winter and spring
CATCHING METHODS Bottom otter trawl, Danish seine
COMMON LENGTH 50–90 cm (20–35½ in)
COMMON WEIGHT 500 g – 5 kg (1 lb 2 oz – 11 lb)
IDENTIFIABLE FEATURES Pink ling: long, eel-like, pink skin mottled with brown spots; rock ling: darker, with mottled grey skin
SUSTAINABILITY Managed by quota

LING IN THE KITCHEN

Crumbed ling will deliver the best fish burger you could ever imagine – so much so, that it's startling people don't do it all the time. It could be because most ling is so large it's generally sold already gutted, skinned and filleted, but if you can get it whole and fillet it yourself, you'll find that the quality of the fish is so much better.

It's not great in a curry or pan-fried with crisp skin, but it's at its best coated in panko breadcrumbs or batter then cooked in the deep-fryer or slowly grilled (at the bottom of the oven under a grill/broiler). It's also delicious simply grilled or steamed. Served with salad, lemon, chips and a nice mayonnaise, nothing competes with it. Try crumbed ling with gherkin and mayonnaise in a bun (see overleaf) – it'll change your life.

SPECIAL STORAGE AND HANDLING
Buy whole; remove gut and gills immediately. Store as usual. Fillet only just before cooking.
BEST COOKING METHODS Crumbed or battered and deep-fried, pan-fried, steamed, grilled (broiled), roasted
TEXTURE A broad flake with a soft–medium marshmallow-like lightness
AROMA Light, clean, brightly vinegary
FLAVOUR Mild, sweet, with a light honeyed note and a mild, clean, round aftertaste
APPEARANCE Flesh grey–white when raw; bright white once cooked
YIELD Flesh 45–50% of whole weight
SUBSTITUTES Blue cod, deep-sea bream, hapuka

Ling burger

SERVES 4

vegetable oil, for deep-frying
1 egg
2 teaspoons milk
80 g (2¾ oz/½ cup) rice flour
25 g (1 oz) panko (Japanese-style) breadcrumbs
4 × 120 g (4¼ oz) ling fillets, skin removed, pin-boned
4 brioche buns, cut in half horizontally
8 baby cos (romaine) lettuce leaves
2 whole pickled onions, sliced into rings
2 Pickled Cucumbers (page 460), thinly sliced lengthways
100 g (3½ oz) Tartare Sauce (page 83)

Half-fill a 6 litre (203 fl oz/24 cup) saucepan with vegetable oil and place over high heat (see note). Heat the oil to 180°C (350°C) – check with an oil thermometer. (For a guide to testing the oil temperature without a thermometer, see note.)

In a large, shallow bowl, whisk the egg and milk together to make an egg wash. Place the rice flour in another bowl and the panko breadcrumbs in a third. Dust each ling fillet in the rice flour first, then dip it in the egg wash and, lastly, the breadcrumbs.

Tap off any excess crumbs and lower the ling fillets carefully into the hot oil. Fry the ling for about 2 minutes, or until crisp and golden. Remove from the saucepan and drain on a baking tray lined with paper towel.

Place the bottom half of each brioche bun on a tray. Add two lettuce leaves to each and top with the fried fish. Add the pickled onion rings, pickled cucumber and tartare sauce, then place the other brioche half on top and serve.

NOTES: When deep-frying in a saucepan, it's advisable to keep the oil level a good 10 cm (4 in) below the rim of the pan. The other option for deep-frying is, of course, an electric deep-fryer. The used oil can be strained, cooled and refrigerated for later use.

To test the temperature of the oil, drop a cube of bread into it. If it turns golden in 15 seconds, it's sitting perfectly on 180°C (350°F). If the bread takes only 10 seconds to turn golden, then the oil is around 190°C (375°F). If it takes 20–30 seconds to brown, the oil is too cold. Be patient and get the oil to the correct temperature before proceeding.

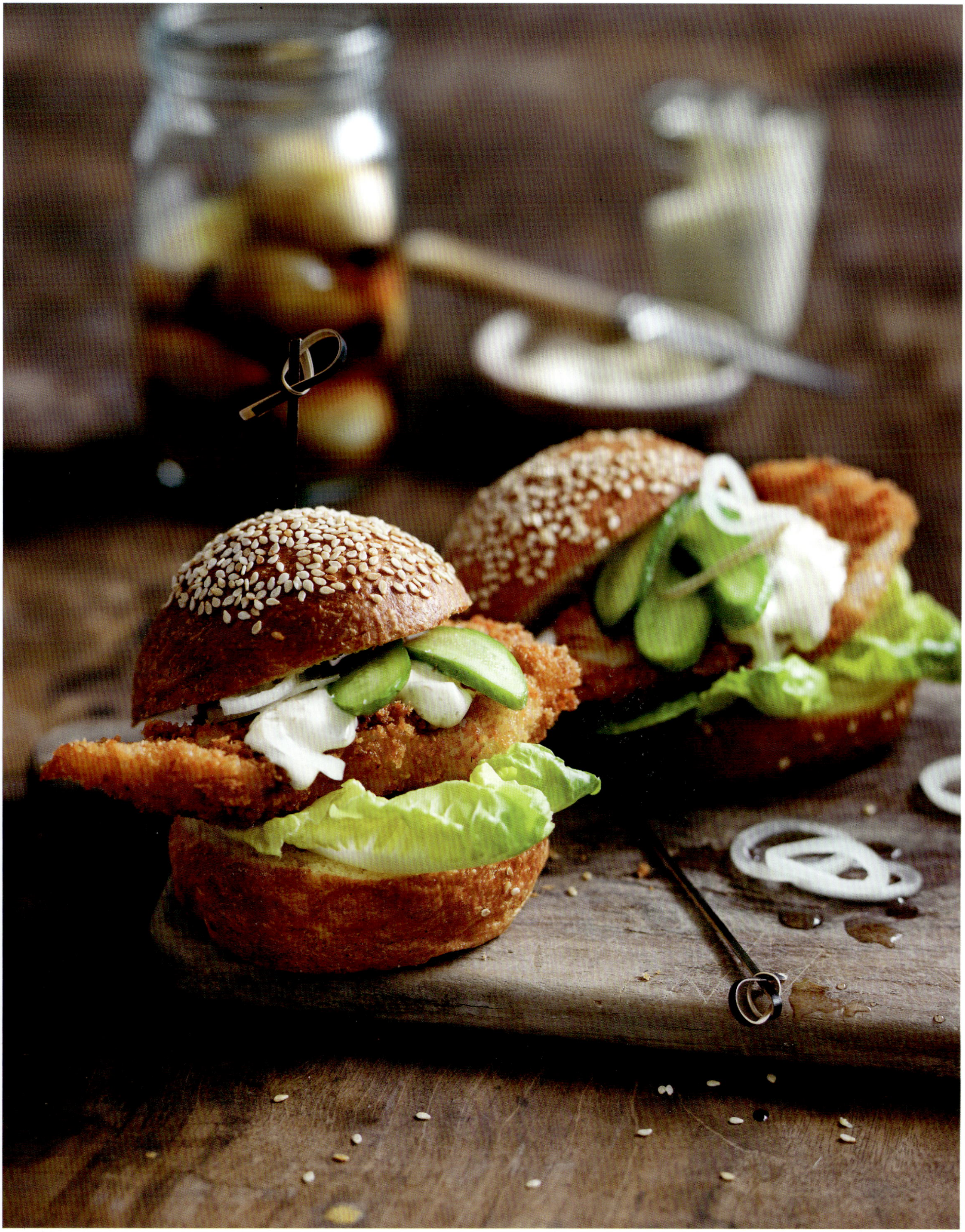

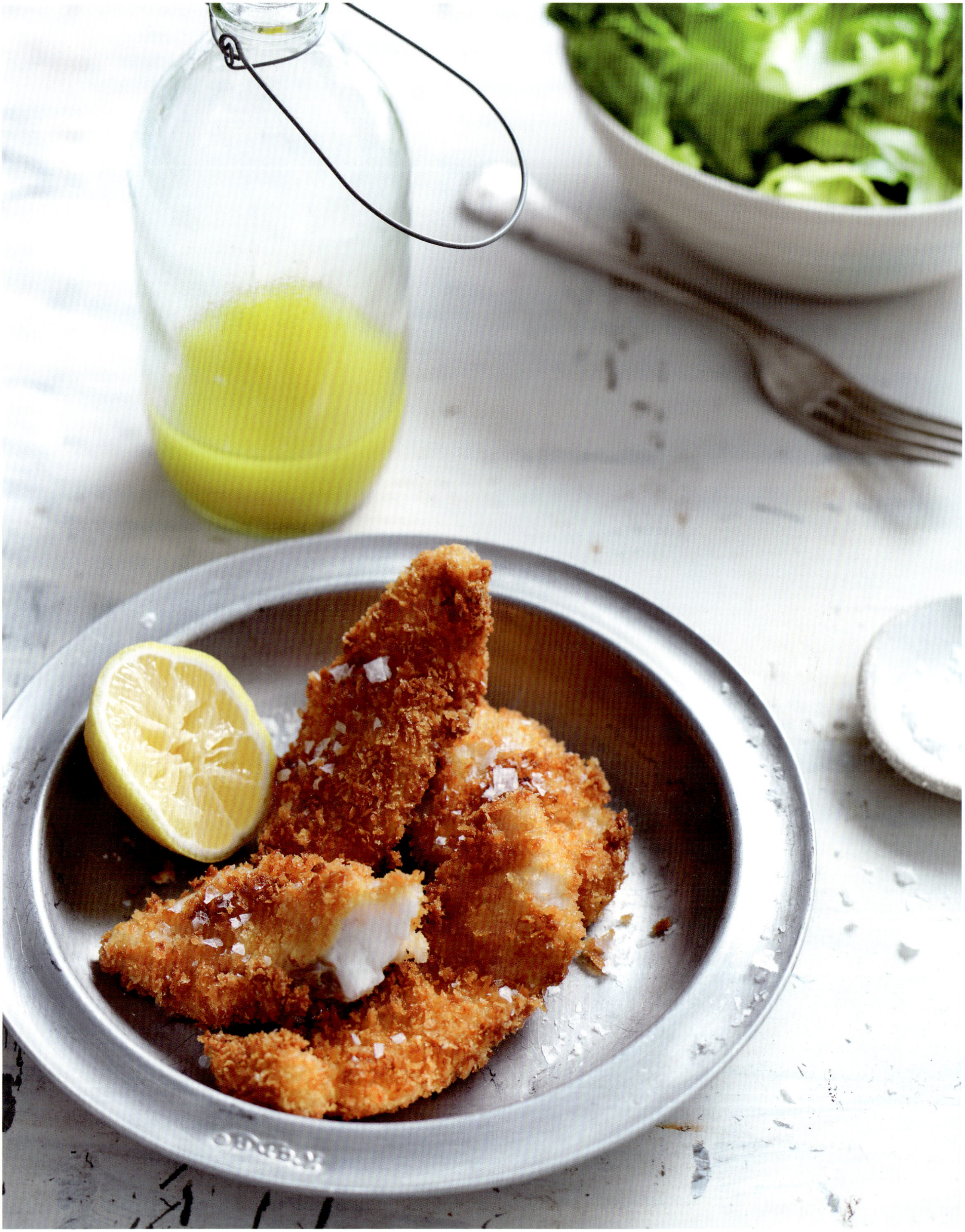

Crumbed ling with salad greens and lemon dressing

Preheat the oven to 130°C (250°F).

Make a lemon dressing by whisking the olive oil in a bowl with the lemon juice and a pinch each of salt and pepper. Set aside.

Half-fill a 6 litre (203 fl oz/24 cup) saucepan with vegetable oil and place over high heat (see note). Heat the oil to 180°C (350°C) – check with an oil thermometer. (For a guide to testing the oil temperature without a thermometer, see note.)

In a large shallow bowl, beat the eggs and milk together to make an egg wash. Place the rice flour in another bowl and the panko breadcrumbs in a third. Dust each piece of ling in the rice flour first, then dip it in the egg wash and, lastly, the breadcrumbs.

Tap off any excess crumbs and carefully lower the ling pieces into the hot oil. You may need to cook the fish in a few batches to avoid overcrowding the pan. Fry for about 2 minutes, or until crisp and golden. Remove from the saucepan and place on a baking tray lined with paper towel to drain. Keep the cooked fish in the oven to stay warm while you fry the remaining pieces.

Serve the ling with a squeeze of lemon and a pinch of salt. On the side, add your favourite salad greens in a serving bowl, drizzled with the lemon dressing, and a little tartare sauce, if using.

NOTES: When deep-frying in a saucepan, it's advisable to keep the oil level a good 10 cm (4 in) below the rim of the pan. The other option for deep-frying is, of course, an electric deep-fryer. The used oil can be strained, cooled and refrigerated for later use.

To test the temperature of the oil without a thermometer, drop a cube of bread into the saucepan. If the bread turns golden in 15 seconds, the temperature is sitting perfectly on 180°C (350°F). If the bread only takes 10 seconds to turn golden, then the oil is around 190°C (375°F). If it takes 20–30 seconds to brown, the oil is too cold. Be patient and bring the oil to the correct temperature before proceeding.

SERVES 4

125 ml (4 fl oz/½ cup) extra virgin olive oil

juice of 1 lemon, plus extra to serve

sea salt and freshly ground black pepper, to taste

vegetable oil, for deep-frying

2 eggs

1 tablespoon milk

160 g (5¾ oz/1 cup) rice flour

50 g (1¾ oz) panko (Japanese-style) breadcrumbs

800 g (1 lb 12 oz) ling fillet, skin removed, pin-boned, sliced into four 2 cm (¾ in) thick steaks

salad greens, to serve

Tartare Sauce (page 83), to serve (optional)

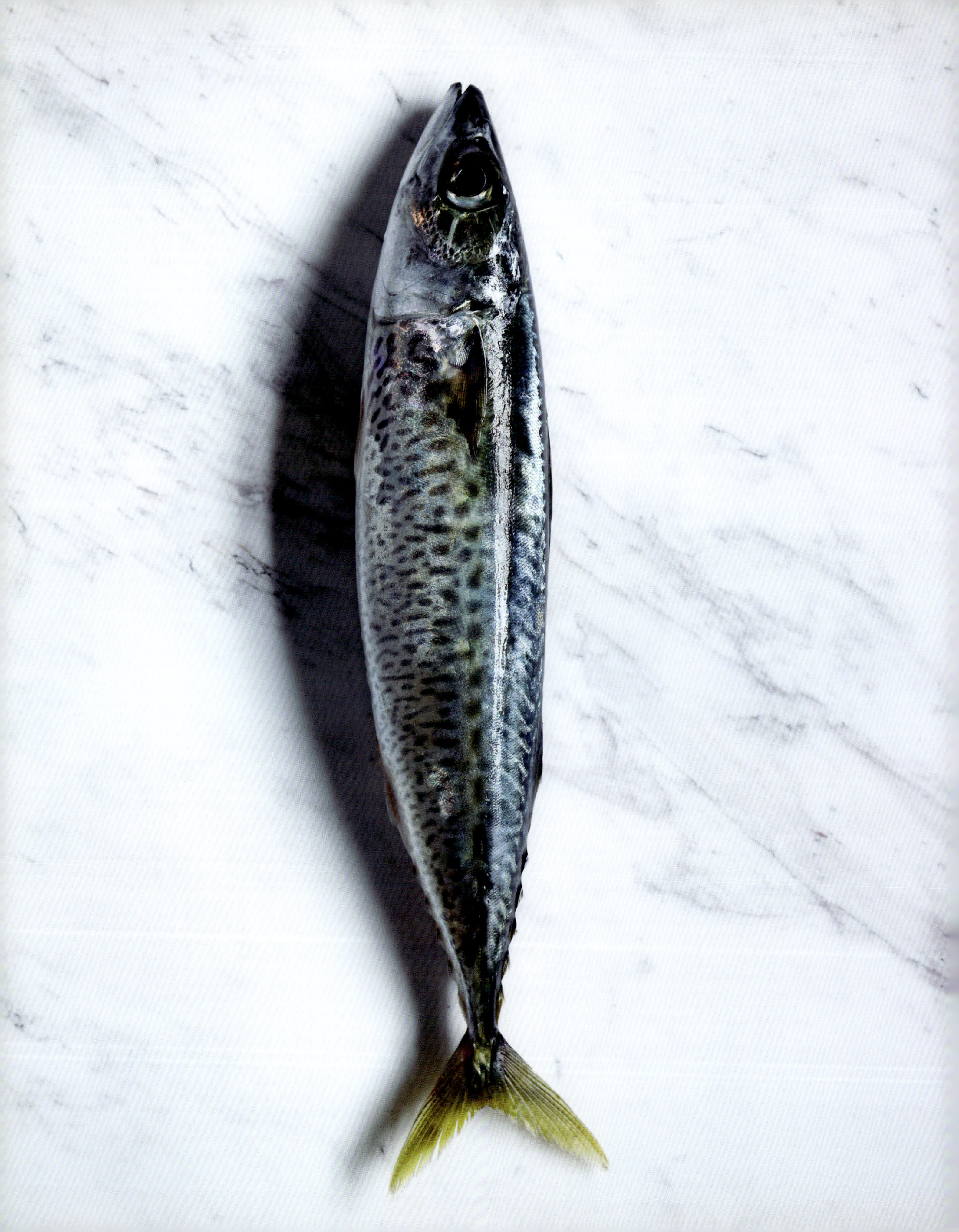

MACKEREL, BLUE

The little blue or slimy mackerel (*Scomber australasicus*) tends to be taken for granted. They're often a kid's first keeper catch – they're easy to hook on simple handline jigs, and they themselves make first-class bait for other fish. They are, in fact, important as bait in commercial fisheries – many of the tuna, lobster, crab and even other mackerel fisheries depend heavily on blue mackerel as bait.

Fast-breeding and abundant throughout Australia, the blue mackerel has been largely overlooked as a table fish due to its dark, often soft flesh, and its propensity to spoil quickly if not carefully handled at and after catch.

SEASONALITY Year round, with a peak in autumn to early winter
CATCHING METHODS Purse seine, beach seine, trawl
COMMON LENGTH 10–25 cm (4–10 in)
COMMON WEIGHT 100–400 g (3½–14 oz)
IDENTIFIABLE FEATURES Simple torpedo shape, smooth snout, large dark eyes, sleek dark-blue back with black stripes, spotted silver belly
SUSTAINABILITY Stock status very good

BLUE MACKEREL IN THE KITCHEN

Blue mackerel is a fantastic option for a range of uses, from sousing to pickling, curing or cooking, but it must be fresh, whatever you do with it. Buy it whole – it's much easier to tell if it's fresh. It's also a great fish for practising filleting, thanks to its soft flesh and simple bone structure.

Blue mackerel has a wonderfully high fat content, which is why it's so popular in Japanese and Scandinavian cuisines, but this also makes it ideal for smoking.

When raw, it can sometimes be almost too fatty, so it's best to set the protein by curing or pickling, or by pouring boiling water over the fillets before slicing and serving.

BEST COOKING METHODS Salted, cured, soused, grilled (broiled), barbecued
TEXTURE Soft when raw; medium firmness once cooked
AROMA Intense, oily, with a slight mineral or iodine note
FLAVOUR Juicy roast meat, with notes of green seaweed and iodine
APPEARANCE Flesh deep pink with grey hues when raw; dull white once cooked
YIELD Boneless fillet about 65% of whole weight
SUBSTITUTES Bonito, trevally

Pickled mackerel

SERVES 4 AS AN ENTRÉE

Japanese table salt, as required
4 × 75–150 g (2½–5½ oz) mackerel fillets, skin on, pin-boned
250 ml (9 fl oz/1 cup) Japanese rice vinegar
light Japanese soy sauce, to serve

Sprinkle a layer of salt over the base of a deep stainless-steel tray. Lay the mackerel fillets on top, ensuring the side touching the salt is coated liberally, then turn and salt the other side, adding more salt as required. Cover the tray with plastic wrap and refrigerate for 2 hours. Remove the fish from the fridge and rinse the salt off quickly under cold running water.

Place the fillets in a non-reactive dish and add the rice vinegar. Cover once again with plastic wrap and leave the fish at room temperature for 20 minutes to pickle. Remove the fish from the pickling liquid.

Place the first fillet on a cutting board and, using a tissue, wipe off the thin membrane (known as the 'second skin'). Repeat with the second fillet.

Cut the mackerel into 1 cm (½ in) thick slices – you should get around 32 slices. Lay the slices on a serving platter or across four serving plates.

Serve with the soy sauce on the side.

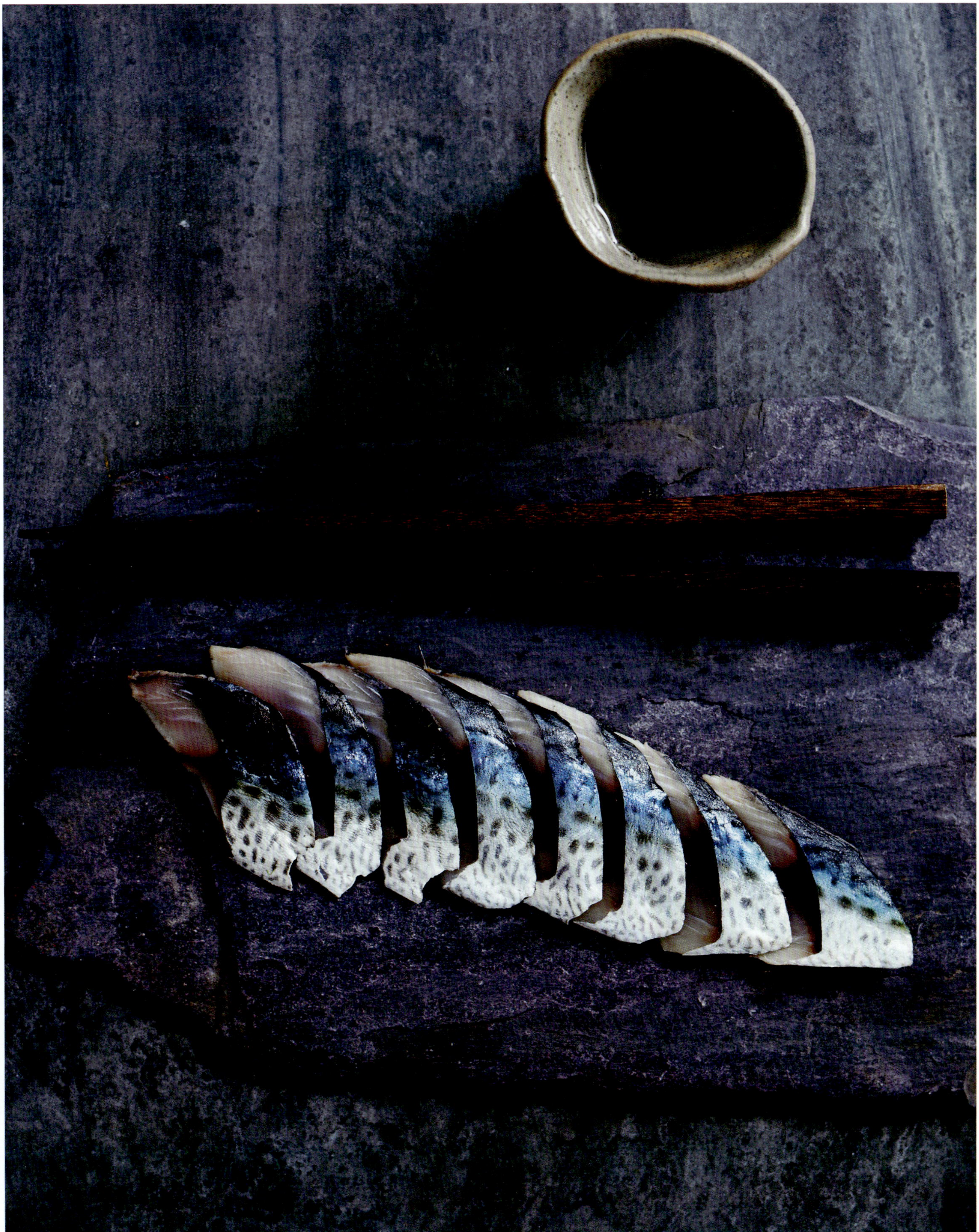

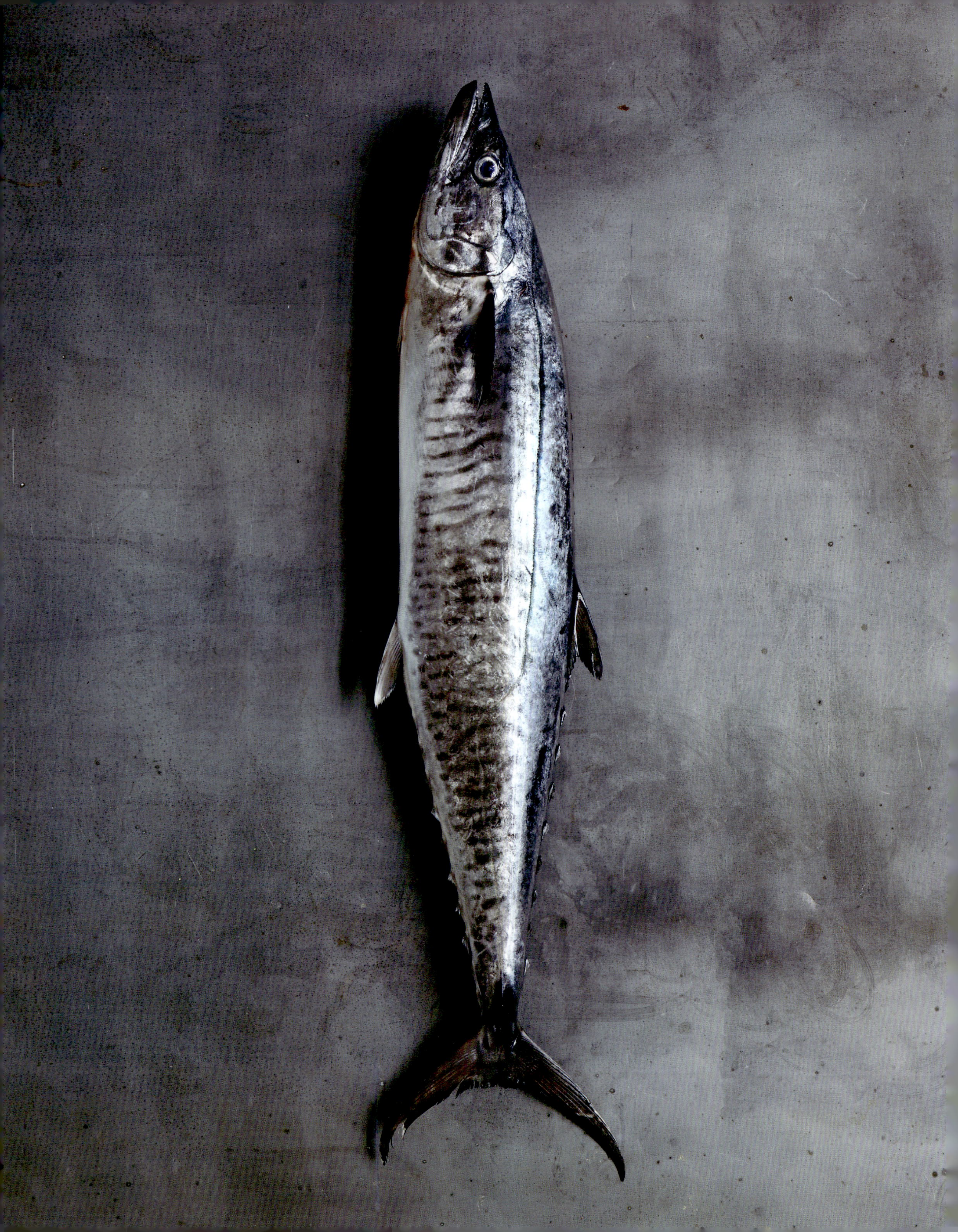

MACKEREL, SPANISH

Apart from being a highly sought-after recreational species, the Spanish mackerel (*Scomberomorus commerson*) – and its close cousins the spotted (*Scomberomorus munroi*), school (*Scomberomorus queenslandicus*) and grey (*Scomberomorus semifasciatus*) mackerels – makes excellent eating. It's caught abundantly in northern Australia during spring and summer, and in lower numbers in autumn and early winter.

The fast-swimming Spanish mackerel, one of the fish at the top of the food chain, can be an aggressive feeder. It's caught using hook and line trolling techniques, and its quality is generally excellent as a result. This, combined with its high oil content, facilitates a vast range of culinary options, from simple preparations to complex Japanese techniques. The thin skin, thick rounded trunk and simple bone structure also offer a broad range of cut options, from fillets to cutlets.

Mackerel fishers are among the most colourful on Australian waters. They track schools of these hardy fish for weeks on end, spending long hours under the searing sun in humid conditions. Their thirsts are understandably legendary.

Mackerel can sometimes be responsible for ciguatera poisoning, a type of food poisoning caused by a toxin whose effects can persist for many years. It's best to avoid fish (or fillets from fish) that are more than 10 kg (22 lb).

SEASONALITY Year round, with a peak from late winter to spring
CATCHING METHOD Hook and line trolling
COMMON LENGTH 55–125 cm (22–49 in)
COMMON WEIGHT 2–15 kg (4 lb 8 oz – 33 lb)
IDENTIFIABLE FEATURES Rounded thin spear shape, horizontal stripes
SUSTAINABILITY Stock status good

SPANISH MACKEREL IN THE KITCHEN

Most fish don't need to be rested after cooking (although it never hurts and can enhance the flavour), but mackerel is best after resting. Sear it nicely all over for a crisp skin, then rest it and keep it rare or even medium-rare in the middle. Cook for 2 minutes with a weight on top, pop it in the oven for 4 minutes, then give it 2 minutes' rest.

Big flavours work – beetroot, salted chilli, roast vegetables, yoghurt – as does sweetness. This highly versatile fish, with its meat-like flesh, is suited to both raw and cooked preparations.

BEST COOKING METHOD Seared then rested
TEXTURE Firm, with a tight grain
AROMA Intense umami character of caramelised meat, with a sweet oceanic zing
FLAVOUR Juicy taste of baked meat, with notes of sweet avocado, roasted nut and toasted bread
APPEARANCE Deep pink with a grey hue when raw; dull white once cooked
YIELD Boneless fillet about 75% of trunk weight
SUBSTITUTES Mahi mahi, trevally, yellowtail kingfish

Mackerel with beetroot and chilli relish

SERVES 4

2 teaspoons lemon juice
1½ tablespoons extra virgin olive oil
4 × 200 g (7 oz) mackerel fillets, skin on, pin-boned
2 tablespoons rice flour
80 ml (2½ fl oz/⅓ cup) ghee (see note page 26)
sea salt, to serve
1 tablespoon salted red chilli (see note page 247), to serve
Potato Crisp (page 461), to serve
pinch of crushed chilli flakes, to serve

BEETROOT AND CHILLI RELISH

250 ml (9 fl oz/1 cup) red wine vinegar
2 tablespoons light brown sugar
75 g (2¾ oz/½ cup) currants
1 long red chilli, split lengthways, seeds removed, finely chopped
280 g (10 oz/2 cups) grated beetroot (beet), from 2 whole beetroot
ice, for cooling

Preheat the oven to 200°C (400°F).

For the relish, combine the vinegar, sugar, currants and chilli in a small saucepan, then bring to the boil over high heat. Reduce the heat to medium–high and simmer for 6–7 minutes, until the liquid has reduced in volume by a third. Add the grated beetroot and stir constantly for 12–14 minutes, until the beetroot is tender and sticky. Remove from the heat, transfer to a bowl, sit it over a larger bowl filled with ice and continue stirring until it is cool (the ice will arrest the cooking process, helping the relish retain its vibrant colour).

Combine the lemon juice and olive oil in a small bowl and set aside.

To prepare the mackerel fillets for pan-frying with crisp skin, lay them on a work surface and dust the skin sides with the rice flour. Place each fillet, flesh side down, on a sheet of baking paper large enough to cover the fillet.

Heat a medium heavy-based, ovenproof frying pan (or two smaller pans – it's essential that the fish is not overcrowded in the pan) over medium–high heat and add the ghee. When the pan is hot and the ghee translucent, place the fillets in the pan, skin side down, leaving the paper on the flesh side. Place a 1 kg (2 lb 4 oz) weight – such as a heavy pot or another pan – on top of the fillets and cook for 2 minutes, lifting the weight once or twice and moving the fillets gently around the pan so they don't burn. Remove the weight and transfer the pan to the oven for 4 minutes. Take the fish from the oven and remove the paper. Using a spatula, gently turn the fillets over and rest for 2 minutes. (Cooking times may vary depending on the size of the fish from which the fillets were cut; for more information, see page 437.)

Remove the fish from the pan and place it on a cutting board. Cut each fillet into three clean medallions and place on serving plates. Add a pinch of salt to the fish skin and drizzle over the lemon dressing. Serve with the beetroot and chilli relish, topped with a little salted red chilli and potato crisp seasoned with salt and crushed chilli flakes.

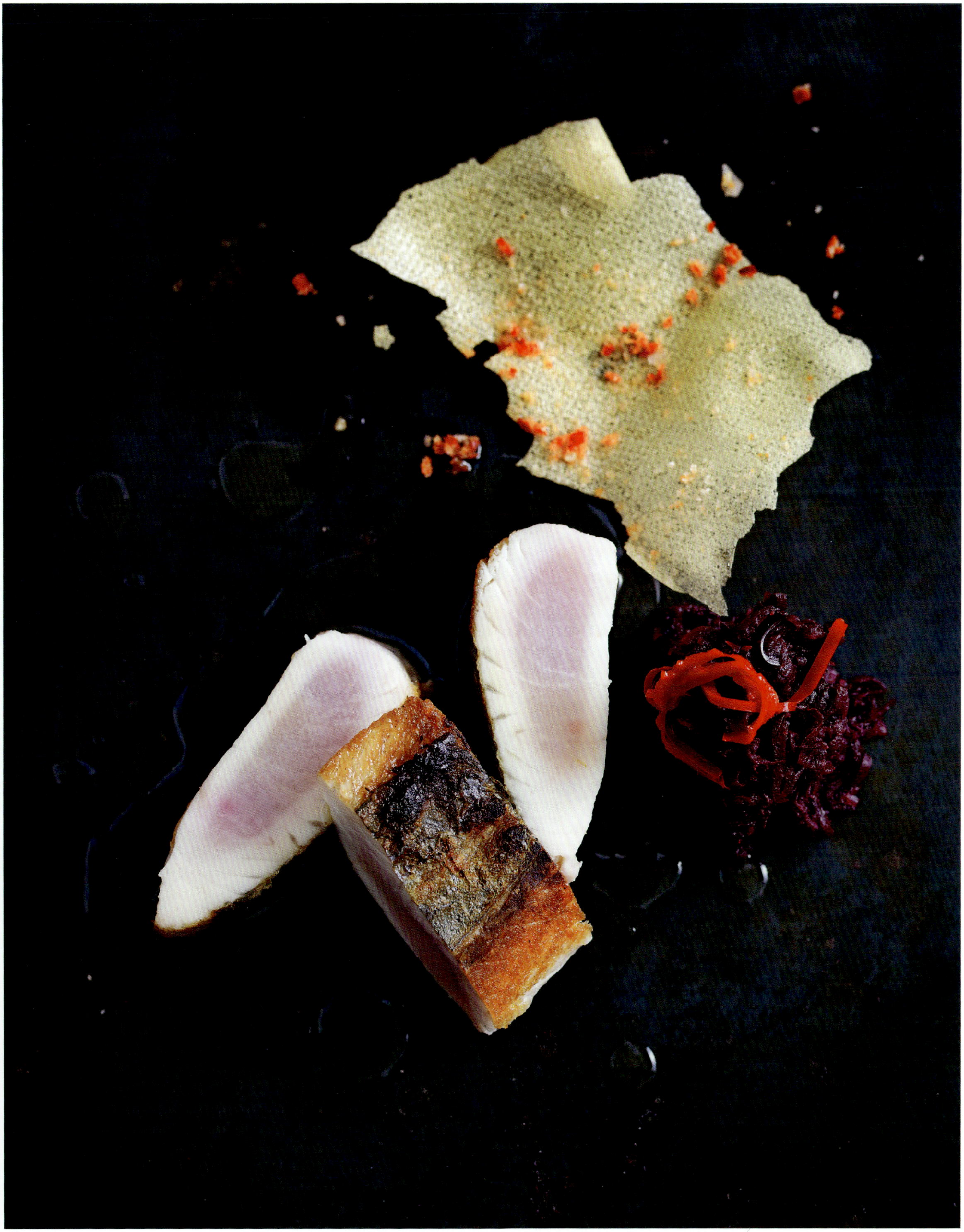

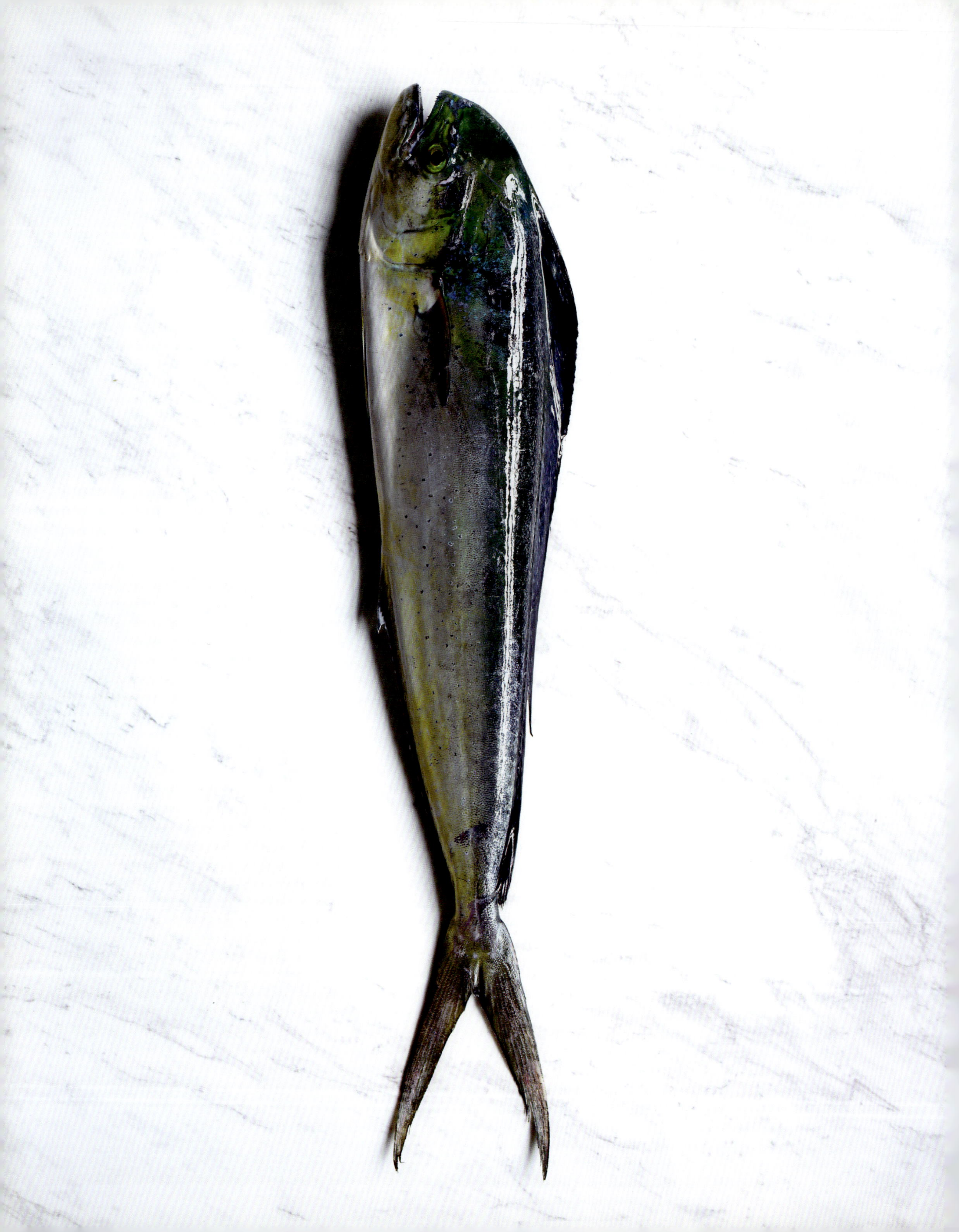

MAHI MAHI

The fish so good they named it twice – well at least the Hawaiians did. The name means 'very strong fish', in honour of its power in the water. It's certainly less confusing than its other names: dolphinfish or dorado.

Mahi mahi (*Coryphaena hippurus*) roam the temperate and tropical oceans, feeding voraciously and growing quickly. They travel in large schools so can offer a prolific catch. Like the famous ocean 'hunters' – tuna, swordfish, marlin – mahi mahi eat pilchards, mackerel and squid, but also scavenge for scallops, crabs and prawns (shrimp). Mahi mahi are mostly a bycatch of the tuna longline fleet off the east coast of Australia.

SEASONALITY Year round, with a peak in summer in WA and the north-east
CATCHING METHOD Pelagic longline
COMMON LENGTH 100–250 cm (39½–98½ in)
COMMON WEIGHT 2–30 kg (4 lb 8 oz – 66 lb)
IDENTIFIABLE FEATURES Brilliant metallic blue–green back, silver–gold sides with rows of dark spots
SUSTAINABILITY Regarded as sustainable; fast-growing and a prolific breeder

MAHI MAHI IN THE KITCHEN

The scalloping flesh of the thin-skinned mahi mahi has a sweet, clean and mild flavour. During summer, the fat content is high, making the cooked flesh moist and juicy. Known as shiira in Japan, it's a popular species for tempura, and the wings and head are often used in robatayaki grills.

When small (around 50 cm/20 in), the flesh is still very soft and oily, so it's ideal for sashimi. Larger fish have firmer flesh, making them better when cooked. Don't cook mahi mahi any more than rare or medium-rare. It must be scaled, but the skin is well worth eating, especially pan-fried crisp. Skin on, it can take bolder flavours, such as pumpkin, celeriac and baked root vegetables. It can also work in a subtle curry or a tomato broth, and with stronger flavours such as lemongrass.

SPECIAL STORAGE AND HANDLING
To avoid rapid oxidisation, wrap fillets tightly in freezer film, then tightly in plastic wrap, and store as usual
BEST COOKING METHODS Raw when small, pan-fried with crisp skin (fillets, see page 437) when large
TEXTURE Soft when small, firm when large
AROMA Robust, grassy, with a clean, light note of seaweed
FLAVOUR Clean, sweet, fresh, with notes of rock pool and seaweed
APPEARANCE Fillet dull white with a pinkish hue when raw; arctic white once cooked
YIELD Skinless, boneless fillet about 65% of whole weight
SUBSTITUTES Tropical snapper

Mahi mahi with caramelised onion and tahini

SERVES 4

40 g (1½ oz) butter
2 brown onions, skin on, cut in half lengthways
60 ml (2 fl oz/¼ cup) Fish Stock (page 457), or as required
4 × 200 g (7 oz) mahi mahi fillets, skin on, pin-boned
2 tablespoons rice flour
80 ml (2½ fl oz/⅓ cup) ghee (see note page 26)
95 g (3¼ oz/⅓ cup) plain yoghurt
2 tablespoons tahini
1 teaspoon sesame seeds
1 teaspoon lemon oil (see note page 25)
generous pinch of sea salt
4 lemon cheeks (see note)

Preheat the oven to 180°C (350°F).

Heat the butter in a small saucepan over low heat. Add the onion halves, cut side down, and cook gently to caramelise. When the butter begins to colour, add a splash of stock. Continue adding a little stock as needed so the onions don't stick. Cook for about 20 minutes, watching to ensure they caramelise without burning.

To prepare the mahi mahi fillets for pan-frying with crisp skin, lay them on a work surface and dust the skin sides with the rice flour. Place each fillet, flesh side down, on a sheet of baking paper large enough to cover the fillet.

Heat a large ovenproof frying pan (or two smaller pans – it's essential that the fish is not overcrowded in the pan; see note) over medium–high heat and add the ghee. When the pan is hot and the ghee translucent, place the fillets in the pan, skin side down, leaving the paper on the flesh side. Place a 1 kg (2 lb 4 oz) weight – such as a heavy pot or another pan – on top of the fillets and cook for 2 minutes, lifting the weight once or twice then moving the fillets gently around the pan so they don't burn. Remove the weight, transfer the pan to the oven and cook for a further 4 minutes. Remove from the oven and discard the paper. Using a spatula, gently flip the fillets and rest for 2 minutes. (Cooking times may vary depending on the size of the fish from which the fillets were cut; for more information, see page 437.)

Meanwhile, thoroughly mix the yoghurt and tahini then transfer to four small side dishes. Top with sesame seeds and lemon oil.

Transfer the mahi mahi from the pan to a chopping board. Cut the fillets carefully through the centre. Place two fish pieces on each plate and sprinkle the salt over. Serve each with a caramelised onion half, a lemon cheek and a bowl of the tahini mix.

NOTES: For lemon cheeks, slice the two sides off a lemon to get two very sharp, clean cheek-shaped pieces with no seeds.

If you don't have a pan large enough for all the fillets, or two smaller pans, cook the fish in two batches. Keep the first batch warm while you cook the second.

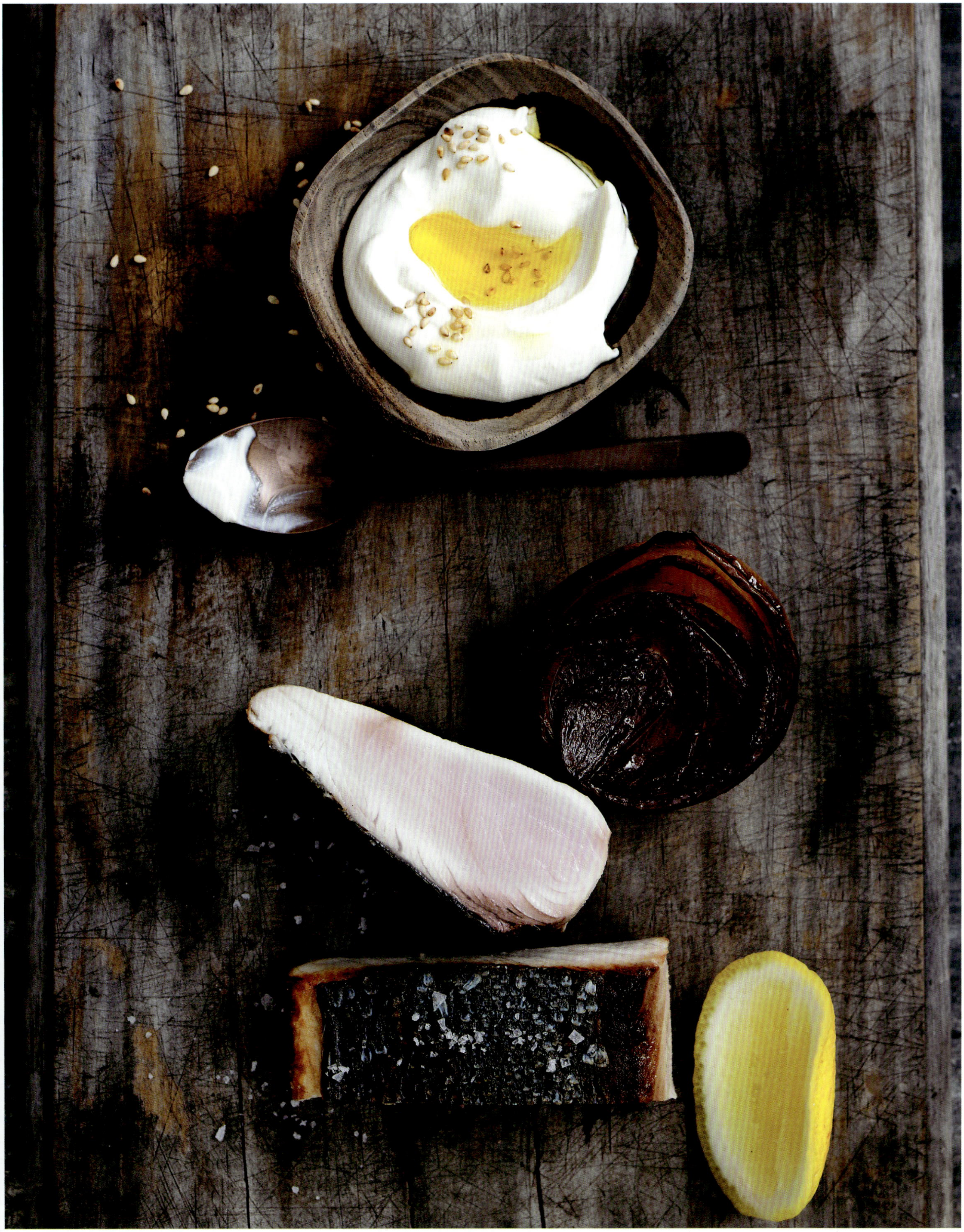

Blue-spotted goatfish (red mullet)

MULLET, RED

Despite its name, the red mullet is only a very distant cousin of the much-maligned fish often offered by fishmongers under the same name. It can be either of two common species: the blue-spotted goatfish (*Upeneichthys vlamingii*) or the blue-striped goatfish (*Upeneichthys lineatus*). They're found inshore around estuaries and rocky bays, the blue-spotted in our southern seas and the blue-striped in northern temperate waters.

They have distinctive eyes with a brilliant-red iris surrounding a dark pupil. The vivid body colouring can vary from almost iridescent red to rose pink, with azure-blue stripes and spots. The colour fades dramatically after death, but this has no effect on the freshness of the flesh inside. They have two long sensory barbels under their chin (folded away in the photo) that help them find small crustaceans, molluscs and fish eggs. This diet makes their flesh extremely tasty.

The flesh has a deep sweetness but with the intense umami character traditionally associated with lobster or crab. The skin is also delicious, crisping up with a blistered texture reminiscent of roast chicken. The supply of red mullet is inconsistent, and chefs often ask their fishmonger to buy it at any price. It has recently become popular with Asian buyers, especially Vietnamese.

SEASONALITY Year round (in limited numbers), with a peak in summer
CATCHING METHODS Handline, purse seine
COMMON LENGTH 15–30 cm (6–12 in)
COMMON WEIGHT 100–500 g (3½ oz – 1 lb 2 oz)
IDENTIFIABLE FEATURES Red iris around dark pupil, body iridescent red to rose pink, with azure-blue stripes and spots
SUSTAINABILITY Regarded as sustainable

RED MULLET IN THE KITCHEN

Red mullet is particularly wonderful for soup. Roast some vegetables, then add the *whole* fish, gut in, scales on. Add garlic, tomato and water, cook it down and put it *all* through a food mill. It's delicious, especially with croutons.

The fillets aren't large, but they're delicious and perfect for an entrée. Pan-fry with crisp skin, and serve with tomato, olives and basil. Or use smaller fish for sausages or ravioli. It's good roasted, but it's hard to get a fish big enough. It might look like pink snapper, but it would be a waste to eat raw.

BEST COOKING METHODS Whole in soups, pasta fillings, pan-fried with crisp skin (fillets, see page 437)
TEXTURE Firm, oily
AROMA Roasted crustacean shells, with a note of orange peel
FLAVOUR Deep savoury umami character, with long sweet notes
APPEARANCE Flesh rose to dark red when raw; brilliant white once cooked
YIELD Flesh 45–50% of whole fish
SUBSTITUTES None

Red mullet with tomato, onion and basil

SERVES 4 AS AN ENTRÉE, 2 AS A MAIN

2 tablespoons vegetable oil
2 small red onions, skin on, cut in half
16 cherry tomatoes on the vine
4 × 100 g (3½ oz) red mullet fillets, skin on, pin-boned
2 tablespoons rice flour
2 tablespoons ghee (see note page 26)
sea salt, to taste
8 basil leaves, to serve

Heat the vegetable oil in a medium heavy-based frying pan over medium–low heat. Add the onion halves, cut side down, and cook, without moving them, for 15–20 minutes, until very caramelised and blackened. Remove the onions from the pan, peel off and discard the skin, then set aside in a warm place.

Return the pan to the heat without cleaning it. When very hot, add the tomatoes. Toss well in any remaining oil and cook over high heat for 2–3 minutes, until they blister. Remove from the heat and set aside in a warm place.

To prepare the mullet fillets for pan-frying with crisp skin, lay them on a work surface and dust the skin sides with the rice flour. Place each fillet, flesh side down, on a sheet of baking paper large enough to cover the fillet.

Heat a medium cast-iron frying pan (or two smaller pans – it's essential that the fish is not overcrowded in the pan; see note) over medium–high heat, then add the ghee. When the pan is hot and the ghee translucent, place the fillets in the pan, skin side down, leaving the paper on the flesh side. Place a 1 kg (2 lb 4 oz) weight – such as a heavy pot or another pan – on top of the fillets and cook for 90 seconds, lifting the weight once or twice and moving the fillets gently around the pan so they don't burn. Remove the weight and the paper then, using a spatula, gently flip the fillets to seal the other side for 10 seconds. (Cooking times may vary depending on the size of the fish from which the fillets were cut; for more information, see page 437.)

Serve the red mullet with a sprinkle of sea salt on the skin, and the onion and tomatoes on the side. Garnish with the basil leaves.

NOTE: If you don't have a pan large enough for all the fillets, or two smaller pans, cook the fish in two batches. Keep the first batch warm while you cook the second.

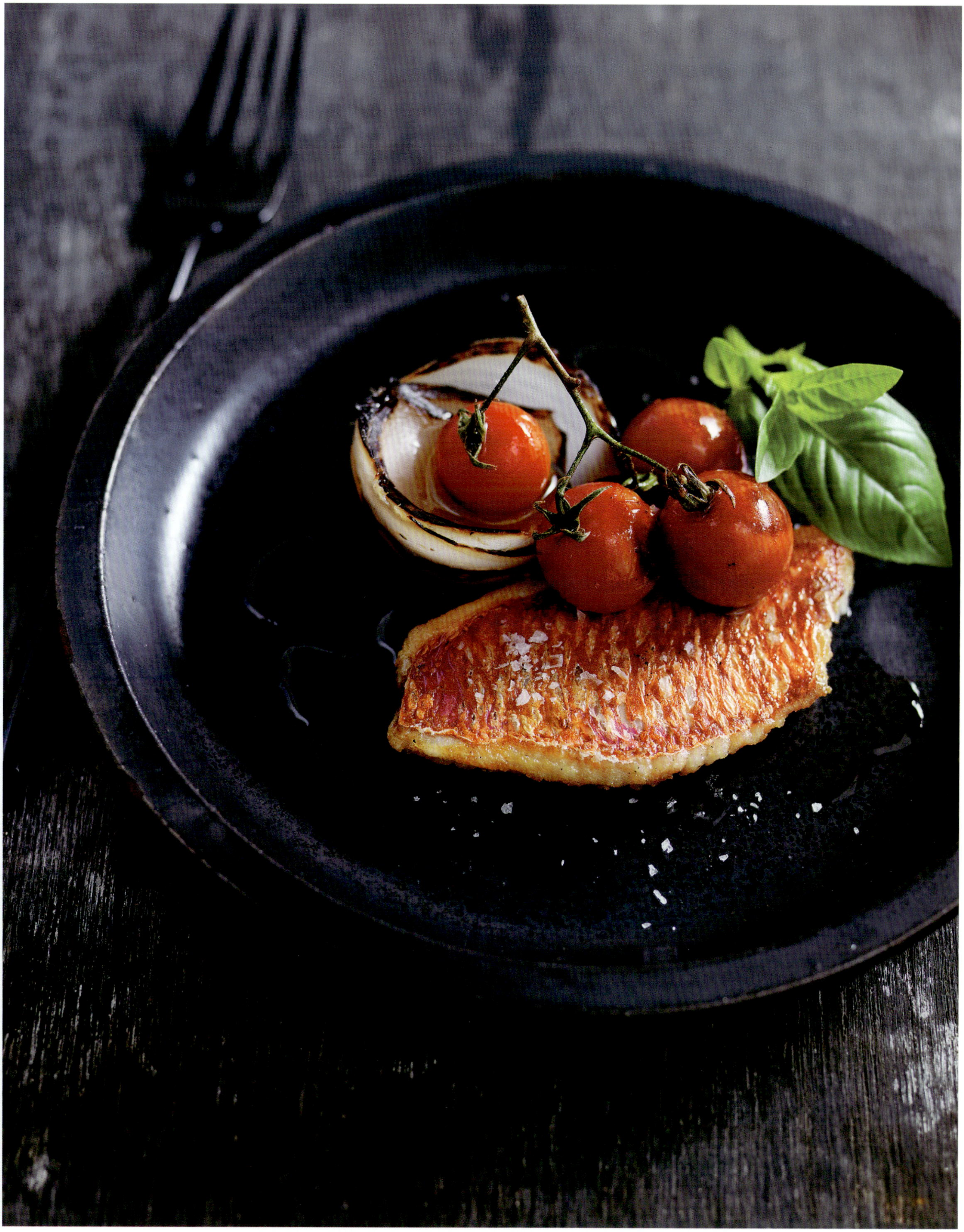

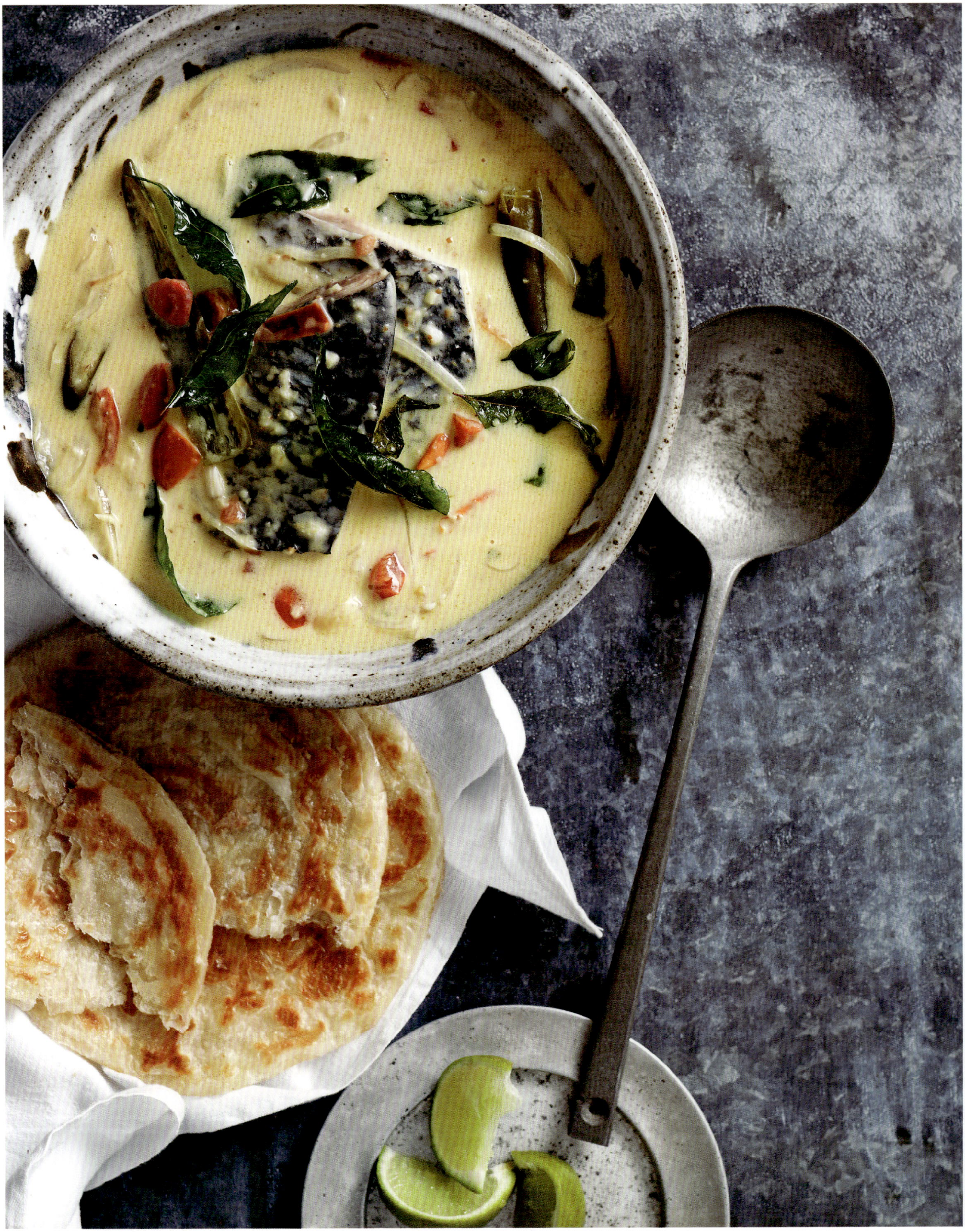

South Indian curry of mullet

To make the curry paste, blend all the ingredients in a food processor until smooth. If necessary, add a couple of teaspoons of water to get the paste moving.

Heat 2 tablespoons of the vegetable oil in a medium–large saucepan over medium heat. When the oil is hot but not smoking, add the onion and fry for 3 minutes, or until soft and golden. Stir in the curry paste and fry for a few minutes more, still stirring.

Add the tomato, tamarind water and sugar, increase the heat to medium–high, then cook until most of the liquid has evaporated. Add the coconut milk, chillies and 100 ml (3½ fl oz) of water. Bring to the boil, then reduce the heat to medium–low and simmer for 5–10 minutes. Taste for balance: if the curry needs a little more sourness or sharpness, add a touch more tamarind; if it needs sweetness, add caster sugar – just a little at a time to avoid over-seasoning.

Meanwhile, heat the remaining oil in a small frying pan over medium–high heat until smoking, then add half the curry leaves. Toss for 30 seconds, or until crisp. Remove from the oil using a slotted spoon and set aside on paper towel to drain for serving. With the pan still on the heat, add the mustard seeds and remaining curry leaves. Fry for 30 seconds, or until the mustard seeds start to pop, then remove the pan from the heat and add these leaves, the seeds and the oil to the curry sauce.

Remove the curry sauce from the heat and add the mullet to the saucepan. Poach off the heat for 1–2 minutes, or until just cooked.

Serve immediately, from the saucepan or a serving bowl. Top with the reserved fried curry leaves, and serve with roti and lime wedges on the side.

NOTE: Tamarind water is available in Asian supermarkets. Or make your own by soaking tamarind pulp in boiling water until cool. Mash with a fork, then strain out the pulp.

SERVES 2–4

80 ml (2½ fl oz/⅓ cup) vegetable oil
1 brown onion, peeled and thinly sliced
1 large tomato, roughly chopped
60 ml (2 fl oz/¼ cup) tamarind water (see note), plus extra as required
2 teaspoons caster (superfine) sugar, plus extra as required
400 ml (14 fl oz) tinned coconut milk
2 long green chillies, split lengthways, seeds removed
20 fresh curry leaves
½ teaspoon black mustard seeds
1 × 400–500 g (14 oz – 1 lb 2 oz) whole mullet, filleted, each fillet (about 200 g/7 oz each) cut into 2 large pieces
roti, to serve
lime wedges, to serve

CURRY PASTE

3 cm (1¼ in) piece ginger, peeled
5 garlic cloves, peeled
2 teaspoons chilli powder
½ teaspoon ground turmeric
pinch of ground fenugreek
½ teaspoon salt
1 tablespoon coriander seeds, toasted and ground
1 teaspoon cumin seeds, toasted and ground

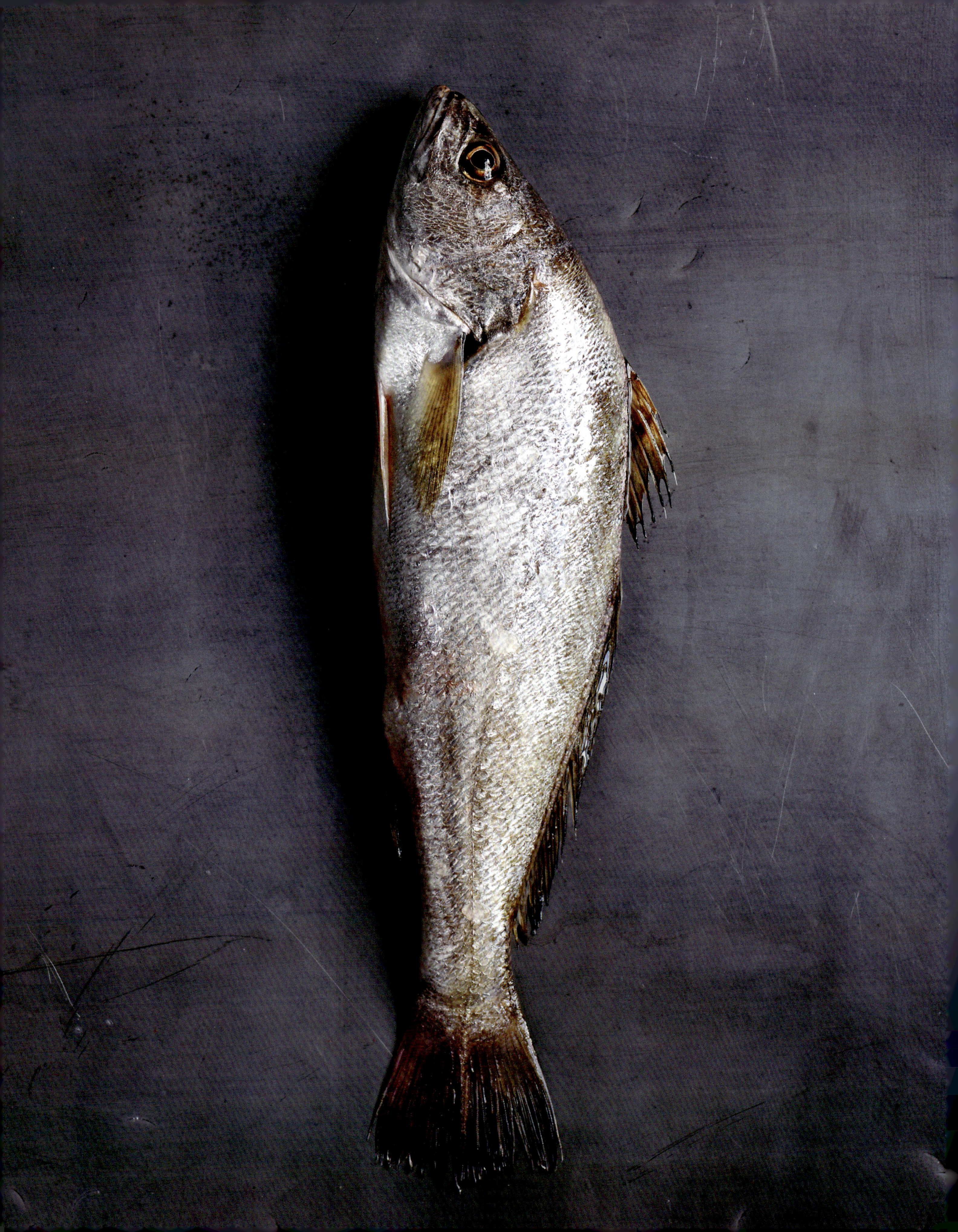

MULLOWAY

Mulloway (*Argyrosomus japonicus*) is the largest and most prized of Australia's estuarine species. This member of the jewfish family has a more defined, scalloping flesh and a sweeter flavour than the northern or black jewfish (*Protonibea diacanthus*). It's a close cousin of the culinarily famed northern hemisphere sea bass.

Wild mulloway has a unique iodine zing from feeding in the seagrass beds and muddy banks of estuaries, where it lies lazily in wait for passing prey. It grows slowly, but once the fat is on, it's hard to shift. Small mulloway are called 'soapies' because their flesh is especially soft and fatty.

Called suzuki in Japan, it's highly regarded as a sashimi fish, but is also used by tempura and robatayaki chefs. Its large belly cavity means a low yield, but it makes superb eating.

SEASONALITY Year round; best in May–June
CATCHING METHODS Beach seine, hook and line trolling
COMMON LENGTH Up to 150 cm (60 in)
COMMON WEIGHT Up to 35 kg (77 lb)
IDENTIFIABLE FEATURES Large scales, large mouth, black spot above pectoral fin, convex tail fin
SUSTAINABILITY Stock status good

MULLOWAY IN THE KITCHEN

Farmed fish are quite small, selling at 3–4 kg (6 lb 12 oz – 8 lb 13 oz), but you can buy wild fish up to 9 kg (20 lb), and the texture is quite different. Under 6–7 kg (13–15 lb) it could be a 'soapie'. The bigger the fish, the firmer the texture.

Wild mulloway has a big flavour and big texture. It's white, but it's so meaty it resembles a red fish such as tuna or salmon. It's great skin on, especially when pan-fried.

Farmed fish at around 2 kg (4 lb 8 oz) are best raw, especially as carpaccio, with a hearty flavour added – preserved lemon (page 461) or ponzu sauce (page 455). You could put larger farmed fish in a curry, but it can tense up. It's great cooked on the bone. Don't be afraid to put it in a pizza oven whole without covering it, or even on a spit – the large muscles stay together when cooked.

SPECIAL STORAGE AND HANDLING
Scale, gut and gill small fish to remove bacteria, wipe belly cavity dry, wrap whole fish tightly in freezer film and keep in the vegetable crisper in the fridge. Fillet as close to use as possible; store fillets as usual.
BEST COOKING METHODS Pan-fried, roasted whole
TEXTURE Soft (especially when small) and moist
AROMA Bright, fresh, with notes of cabbage and zesty seaweed
FLAVOUR Iodine zing, notes of green melon and cucumber, long-lasting mineral aftertaste
APPEARANCE Flesh greenish light grey when raw; grey–white once cooked
YIELD Boneless fillet about 40% of whole weight
SUBSTITUTES Barramundi, blue-eye trevalla, jewfish, mangrove jack, warehou

Mulloway with pan-fried brussels sprouts, bacon and sage

SERVES 4

12 brussels sprouts
iced water, as required, to refresh
4 × 200 g (7 oz) mulloway fillets, skin on, pin-boned
2 tablespoons rice flour
80 ml (2½ fl oz/⅓ cup) ghee (see note page 26)
2 tablespoons vegetable oil
2 bacon rashers, cut into 2 cm (¾ in) pieces
1 handful sage leaves
125 ml (4 fl oz/½ cup) lemon oil (see note page 25)
60 ml (2 fl oz/¼ cup) cabernet vinegar
sea salt and freshly ground black pepper, to taste

Preheat the oven to 200° (400°F).

Bring a medium saucepan of salted water to the boil over high heat. Cut a reasonably deep cross in the top of each brussels sprout and add to the boiling water. Simmer for 5 minutes, or until the sprouts are tender but still a little firm. Remove and plunge into a bowl of iced water for 20 seconds. Cut each sprout in half lengthways. Set aside.

Lay the mulloway fillets on a work surface and dust the skin side of each fillet with the rice flour.

Heat a large cast-iron frying pan over medium–high heat (or two smaller pans – it's essential that the fish is not overcrowded in the pan; see note). Add the ghee to the pan. When the pan is hot and the ghee translucent, place the fillets in the pan, skin side down, and cook for 1 minute. Transfer to the oven and cook for a further 3 minutes. Remove from the oven, flip the fish carefully using a spatula, then leave to rest for 2 minutes in a warm place. (Cooking times may vary depending on the size of the fish from which the fillets were cut; for more information, see page 437.)

While the fish is cooking, heat the vegetable oil in a deep-sided frying pan over high heat for 1 minute, or until it begins to smoke. Add the brussels sprouts, bacon and sage, then fry for 2 minutes, or until all are golden brown and crisp. Remove using a slotted spoon and transfer to a medium bowl. Add the lemon oil, vinegar and a good pinch each of salt and pepper, then toss well.

Place each mulloway fillet on a serving plate and sprinkle a little salt over the skin. Spoon the brussels sprouts mixture on top and serve immediately.

NOTE: If you don't have a pan large enough for all the fillets, or two smaller pans, cook the fish in two batches. Keep the first batch warm while you cook the second.

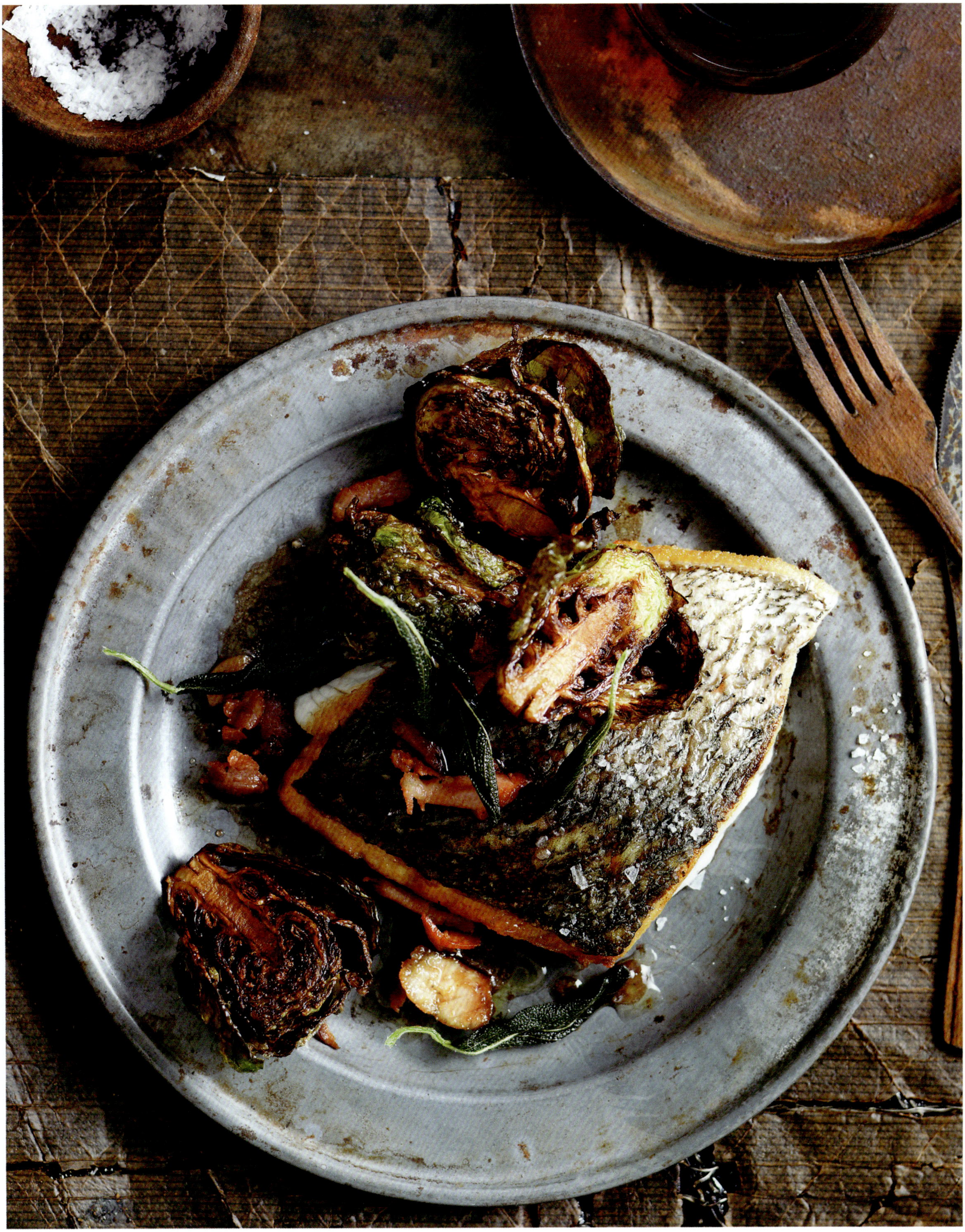

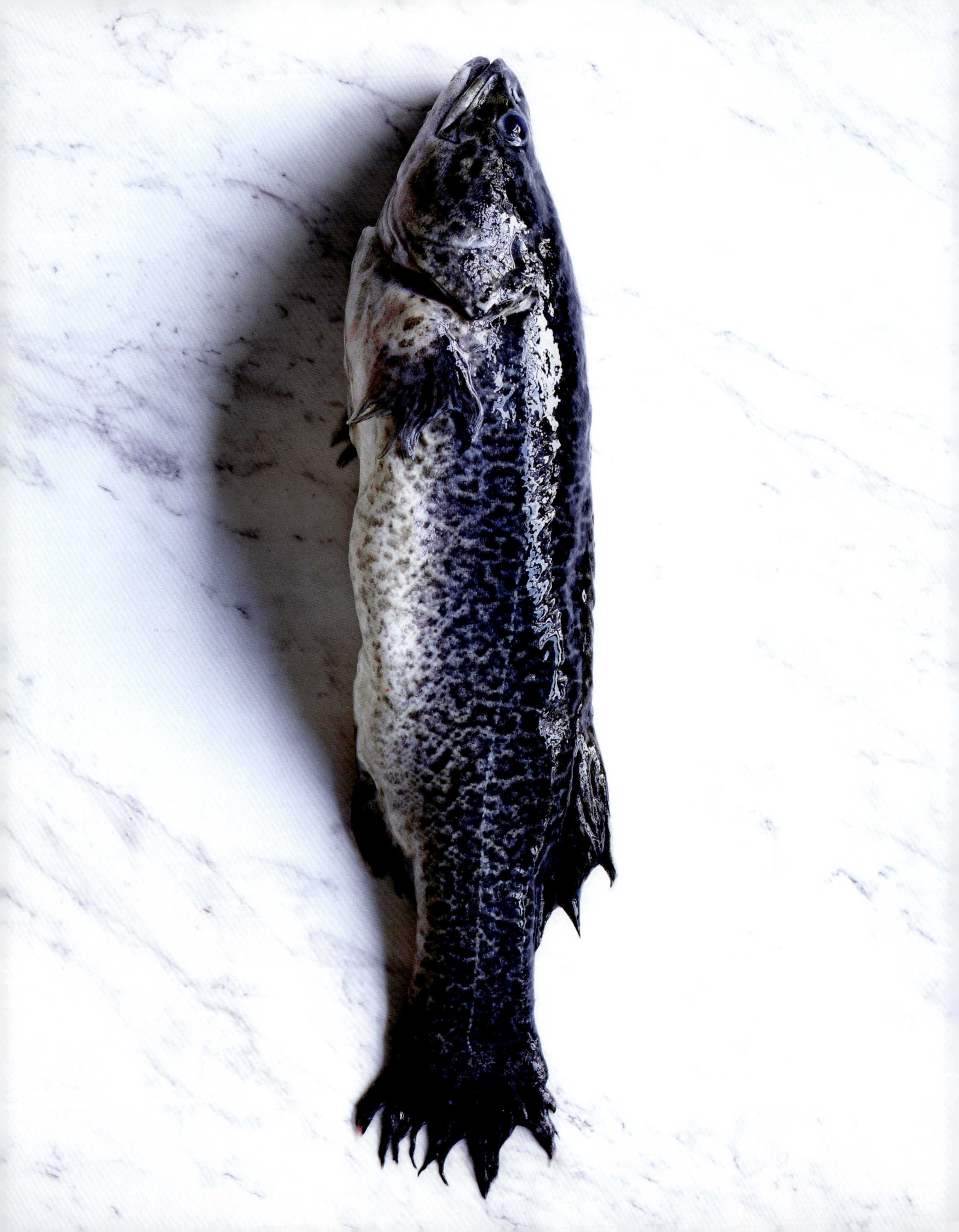

MURRAY COD

The Murray cod (*Maccullochella peelii peelii*) is a fish without peer. No one knows why we call it cod – it bears no resemblance or relationship to either the famed Atlantic cod or the various tropical cod found in Australia. Native to Australia and endemic to the waters of the Murray Darling Basin, it's among the world's largest exclusively freshwater finfish species. Some specimens have been recorded at more than 1.8 m (6 ft) long and weighing a massive 115 kg (250 lb).

Early last century, the Murray cod was fished almost to extinction, and it still remains on the endangered species list. The expansion early in the twentieth century of dryland irrigation for water-thirsty crops contributed to major degradation of the natural Murray cod habitat, reducing the size of its backyard and, more importantly, bedroom. In 2003, the Federal Government listed the Murray cod as vulnerable, and in October that year the International Union for Conservation of Nature declared it critically endangered. This is only one step away from extinction in the wild, which puts it in the same category as Africa's western gorilla. This means that the species can no longer be commercially fished, and the catch of recreational anglers has been massively restricted. Murray cod are now exclusively farmed, mostly in recirculating water systems, and are often available live. Most of these fish are sold in the 600 g to 1 kg (1 lb 5 oz to 2 lb 4 oz) range.

The raw flesh is pale grey–white, often with dark or pink capillaries running through the muscle and a thick layer of creamy fat lining the belly. This high fat content makes it unlike any other freshwater fish. When cooked, the flesh is brilliant white, juicy and rich, with a broad flake and a complex creamy, umami-packed yet mildly earthy flavour.

SEASONALITY Year round
CATCHING METHOD Farmed
COMMON LENGTH 30–70 cm (12–27½ in)
COMMON WEIGHT 500 g – 3 kg (1 lb 2 oz – 6 lb 12 oz)
IDENTIFIABLE FEATURES Mottled green, gold and brown back, clean white belly, small dark eyes on top of a small head
SUSTAINABILITY Excellent (farmed)

MURRAY COD IN THE KITCHEN

This mighty river fish has an incredible fat content, retained as much through the flesh as in the belly and skin. This provides a broad platform for robust and aggressive flavours, and pairs well with big sweet and salty tastes, such as tomatoes, basil, olives and even anchovies. If you want to cook it whole, it's best roasted rather than poached in foil like a snapper. Fry it with the skin on, then roast it in the oven. It's not a fish you want to undercook, as its fat renders through the flesh as it heats, distributing both moisture and flavour.

The skin is arguably the most amazing of any Australian fish. The layer of fat between the skin and the flesh means it cooks up like pork crackling. With the skin on, the Murray cod works very well cooked directly over a fire or in a pizza oven. The robustness of the skin and the extraordinary fat content ensure the flesh retains its moisture.

SPECIAL STORAGE AND HANDLING
Whole live fish should be dispatched at purchase, buried in ice, gilled, gutted and scaled immediately, then stored as usual. Fillet just before cooking, as the flesh will oxidise quickly; store fillets as usual.

BEST COOKING METHODS Roasted whole, pan-fried

TEXTURE Firm when raw; soft or medium flake once cooked

AROMA Clean, with a hint of mushrooms and fresh hay

FLAVOUR Lightly cooked fresh cabbage, with hints of buttered mushrooms and potatoes

APPEARANCE Pale grey–white when raw; arctic white once cooked

YIELD Boneless fillet about 40% of whole weight

SUBSTITUTES Bass groper and bar cod, coral trout, hapuka

Harissa-painted Murray cod

Soak the chillies in warm water for 45 minutes, or until soft. Drain and squeeze out the excess water, then transfer to a blender with the garlic, salt, coriander and cumin. Process until smooth.

Lay the cod fillets on a tray. Using a pastry brush, paint a generous layer of harissa on the skin of each fillet (see note).

Heat a large cast-iron or heavy-based frying pan (or two smaller pans – it's essential that the fish is not overcrowded in the pan; see note) over medium–high heat, then add the olive oil. When a thin blue haze rises from the surface of the oil, place the fillets in the pan, skin side down. Reduce the heat to medium and cook for 2 minutes. Turn the cod using a spatula and cook for a further 2 minutes. Remove the fillets from the pan and set aside in a warm place to rest for 2 minutes. (Cooking times may vary depending on the size of the fish from which the fillets were cut; for more information, see page 437.)

Serve the cod with the lemon cheeks and a simple green salad.

NOTES: Spoon any unused harissa into a jar and cover with a thin layer of olive oil. It will keep in the fridge for up to 1 month and is great for many uses.

If you don't have a pan large enough for all the fillets, or two smaller pans, cook the fish in two batches. Keep the first batch warm while you cook the second.

SERVES 4

8 small dried red chillies
(see note page 109)
2 garlic cloves, peeled
½ teaspoon sea salt
½ teaspoon ground coriander
1 teaspoon ground cumin
4 × 200 g (7 oz) Murray cod fillets, skin on, pin-boned
80 ml (2½ fl oz/⅓ cup) extra virgin olive oil
lemon cheeks, to serve
(see note page 144)
green salad, to serve

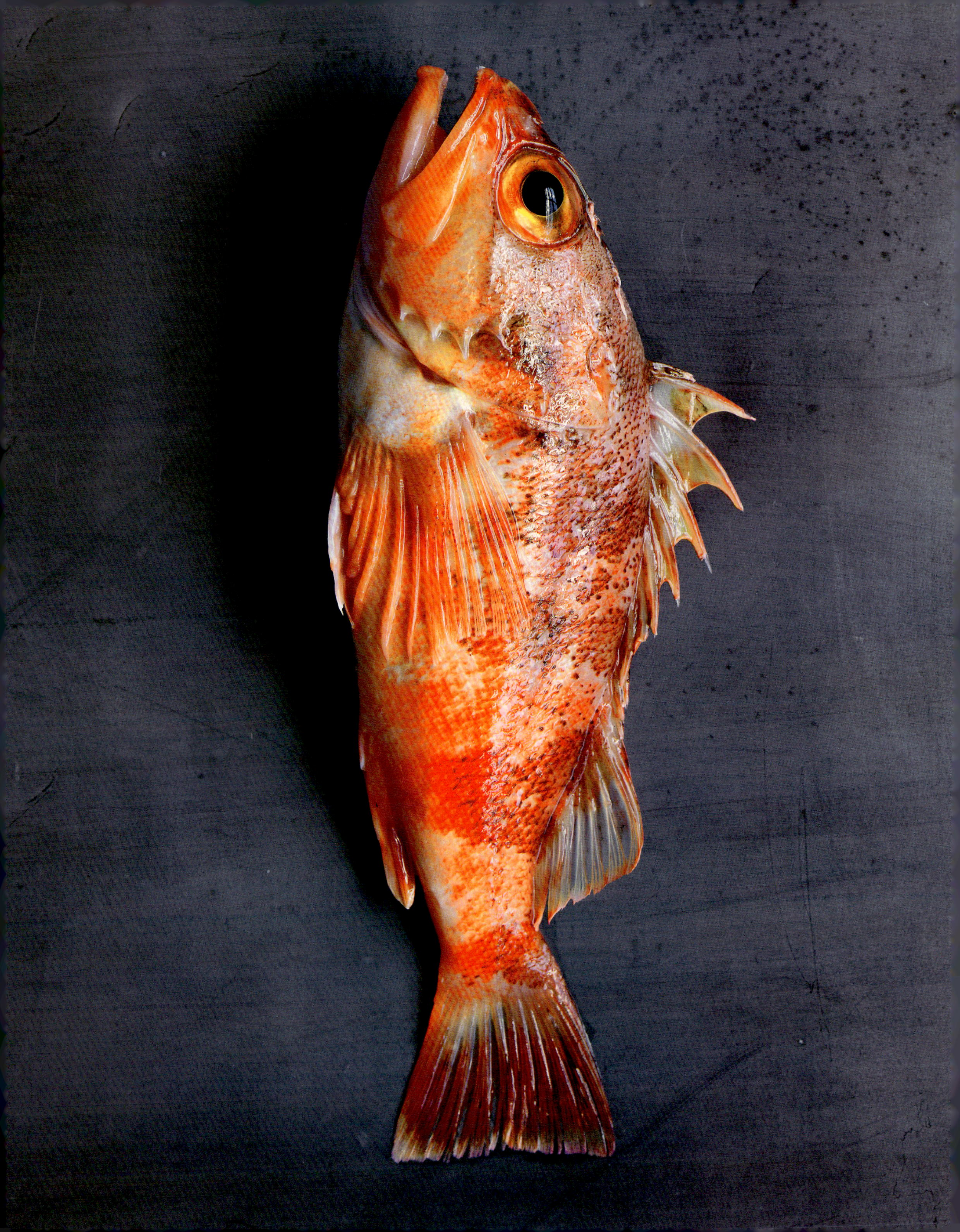

PERCH, BIG-EYE OCEAN

Variously known as sea perch or scorpion fish, the big-eye ocean perch (*Helicolenus barathri*) has a look that defies its clean, mild flavour. It lives in the deep sea, where its bright red skin keeps it hidden from predators and it disappears into the black abyss. Its bulbous eyes ensure it can see, and just for good measure it's covered in large spikes.

Living mainly in the trenches of the continental shelf and slope to about 600 m (2000 ft), it's found off New Zealand; off southern New South Wales, Victoria and Tasmania; and in the Great Australian Bight off South Australia. It has a large mouth and a long-based dorsal fin. The skin has vague brown bars and the scales have greenish flecks.

The smaller reef ocean perch (*Helicolenus percoides*), lives off New South Wales at 80–350 m (260–1150 ft). Growing to 30 cm (12 in), it's orange, with dark spots and bars on the head and body.

SEASONALITY Mainly June–November
CATCHING METHODS Mid-water trawl but increasingly line-caught, particularly in NZ
COMMON LENGTH 35–50 cm (14–20 in)
COMMON WEIGHT 800 g – 2 kg (1 lb 12 oz – 4 lb 8 oz)
IDENTIFIABLE FEATURES Red body with green flecks and faint bars, large mouth, large eyes
SUSTAINABILITY Managed by quota

BIG-EYE OCEAN PERCH IN THE KITCHEN

This is a beautiful fish, but it's best not to eat it raw. Fry or steam it whole, or grill (broil) or poach it lightly with the skin off and painted with butter. If the heat is too high, the protein will split and white liquid will come out, so to grill in the oven, sit it at the bottom for 2–3 minutes.

Try classic sauces of lemon, parsley and butter, or salsas – cucumber, capers and anchovy. It pairs well with eggplant (aubergine), mushrooms or leek, and always benefits from butter, which delivers the fat missing in the fish and greater roundness. If frying whole, Asian ingredients are great. Avoid frying it in batter – the fish just goes watery.

BEST COOKING METHODS Fried whole, steamed whole with Asian flavours, or skinned, painted with butter and grilled (broiled)
TEXTURE Flesh soft, with a broad flake
AROMA Light, clean iodine, with hints of egg white
FLAVOUR Mild, sweet, with notes of light umami and cooked egg white
APPEARANCE Fillets bright white with red central band
YIELD Boneless flesh 30–35% of whole weight
SUBSTITUTES Redfish, red rock cod

Steamed whole big-eye ocean perch with coconut, chilli and lime broth

SERVES 2–4

1 litre (35 fl oz/4 cups) tinned coconut milk
5 cm (2 in) piece ginger, scrubbed
1 lemongrass stem, white part only, bruised
4 kaffir lime leaves, lightly crushed to release the oils
2 small red chillies
½ teaspoon caster (superfine) sugar, or as required
1 tablespoon fish sauce, or as required
juice of 1 lime, or as required
1 whole big-eye ocean perch, about 1 kg (2 lb 4 oz)
chilli oil, to serve (optional)
steamed rice, to serve

In a medium saucepan, heat 500 ml (17 fl oz/2 cups) of water with the coconut milk, ginger, lemongrass, lime leaves, chillies, sugar and fish sauce over medium heat. Bring the mixture to a gentle boil, then reduce the heat to medium–low and simmer until it has reduced by about a third.

Remove the broth from the heat, season with the lime juice and taste for balance. Adjust as necessary with additional sugar, fish sauce and/or lime juice, as desired. Leave the aromatics in the broth to continue infusing while cooking the fish.

Score the perch to the bone, spacing the cuts about a finger-width apart near the head and progressively further apart moving down towards the tail. Place it in a stovetop steamer or a double boiler. Steam for 10–12 minutes on a moderate steam setting or over medium heat.

Gently remove the perch from the steamer and place on a platter. Either pour the hot coconut broth into a serving bowl and serve on the side, or spoon about 200 ml (7 fl oz) of the broth over the fish (see note).

Serve with a dash of chilli oil in the broth (if desired) and steamed rice.

NOTE: This recipe will make about 1 litre (35 fl oz/4 cups) of broth. Feel free to use all of it for a soupy dish. Otherwise, refrigerate any left-over broth in a sealed container for later use – it will keep well for 3 days. It's equally delicious poured over noodles with crabmeat or prawns (shrimp).

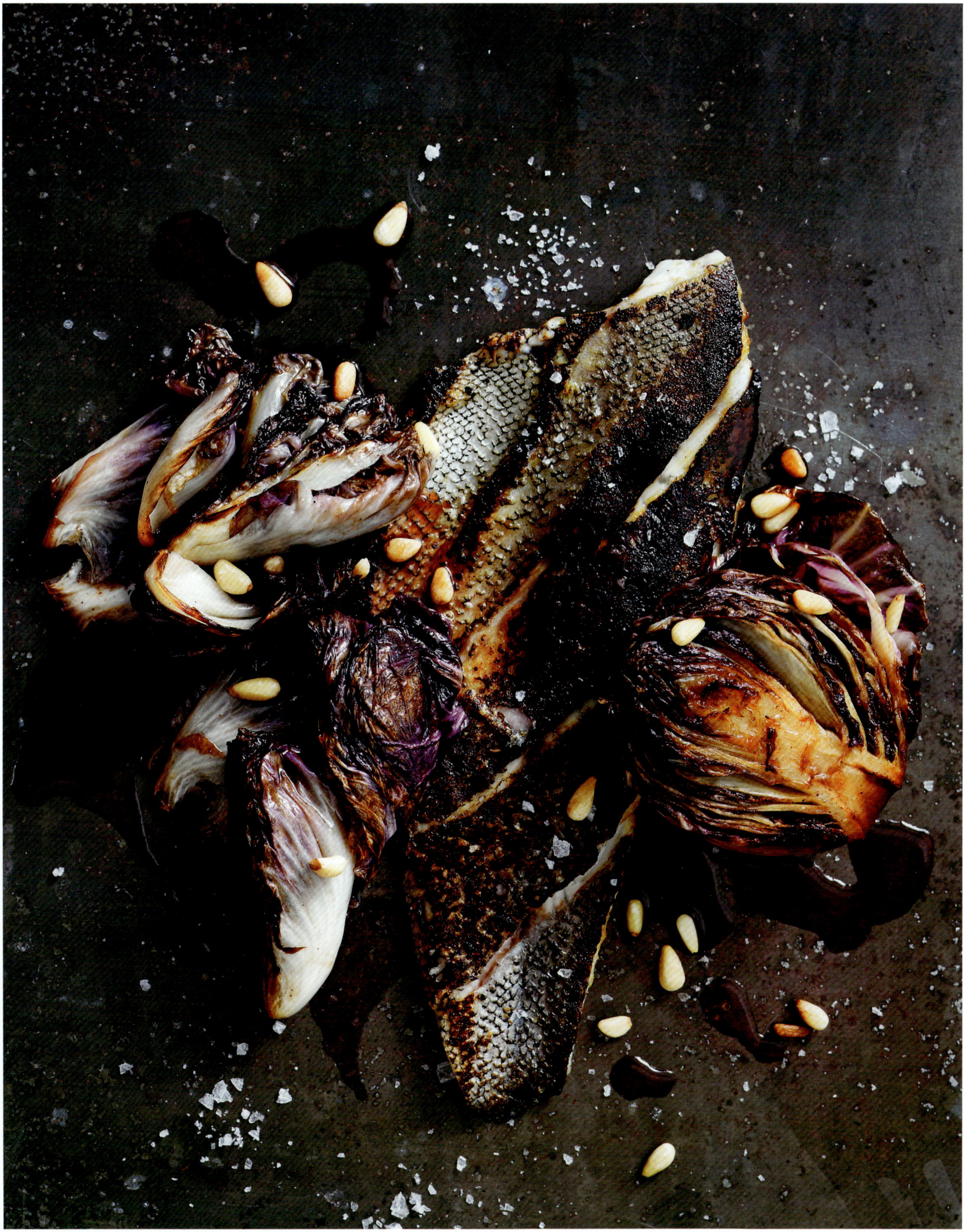

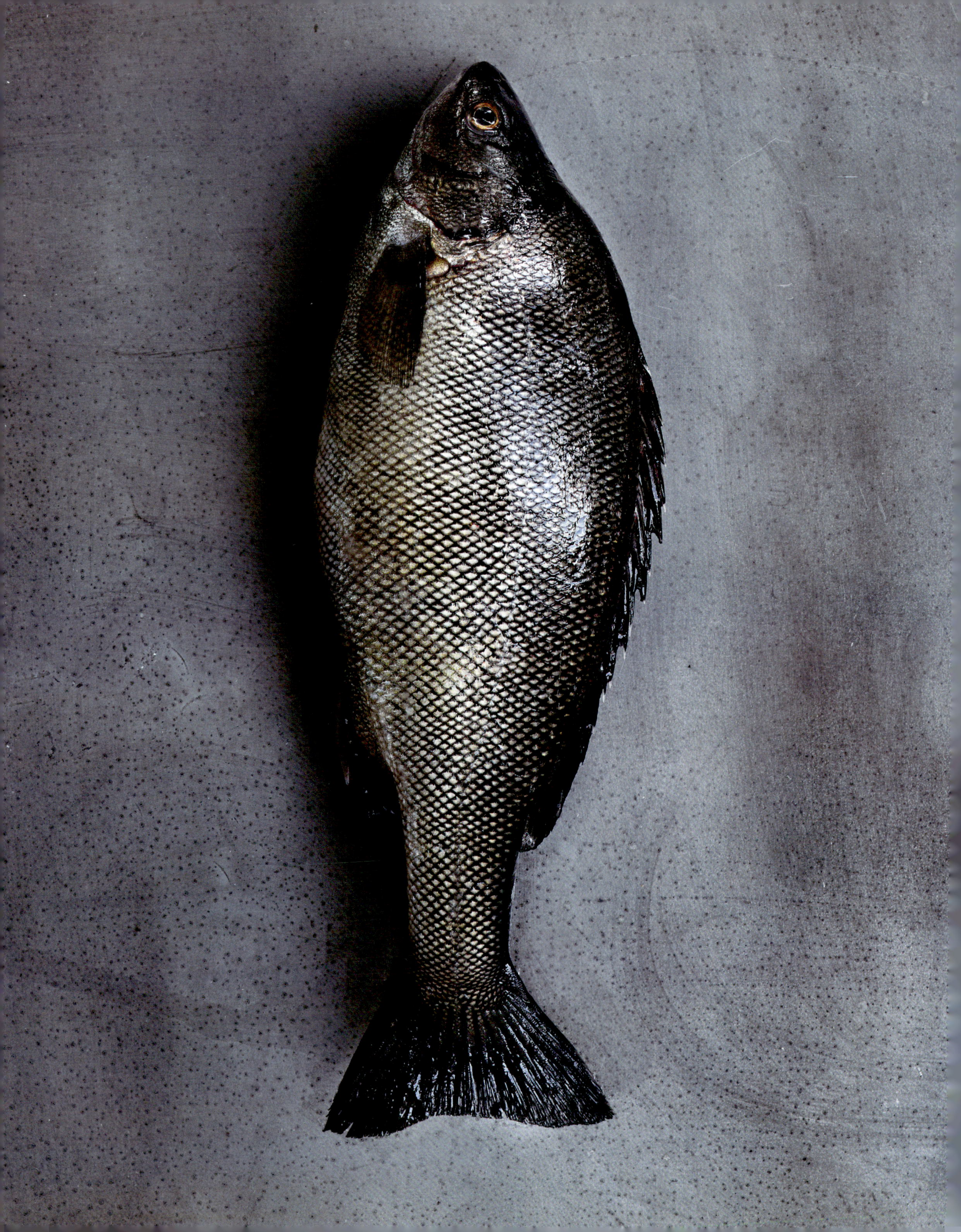

PERCH, SILVER

The silver perch (*Bidyanus bidyanus*), also known as bidyan, black bream and simply silver, is a native freshwater fish found throughout the inland waterways of southern Queensland, New South Wales, Victoria and South Australia. It's dark silver to grey, has quite a small mouth and small scales edged in black.

This hardy fish lives in a multitude of habitats, from the cool clear waters of the highlands to the turbid slow-flowing rivers of the Murray–Darling Basin. Within these environments, it tolerates a wide range of water qualities and eats pretty much anything, including insects, small crustaceans and vegetation. This means that the flavour and texture of wild-caught fish can vary widely.

It has recently become a popular fish for freshwater aquaculture, driven mostly by demand from the Asian community for a freshwater white-fleshed fish of consistent quality. Almost all of the silver perch now available is farmed.

Several other freshwater perch are highly regarded in their local regions, including the golden or yellowfin perch (*Macquaria ambigua*), the Macquarie perch (*Macquaria australasica*), and the European pest species the redfin perch (*Perca fluviatilis*).

SEASONALITY Year round
CATCHING METHOD Farmed
COMMON LENGTH 25–50 cm (10–20 in)
COMMON WEIGHT 450 g – 1.5 kg (1 lb – 3 lb 5 oz)
IDENTIFIABLE FEATURES Dark grey on top, silvery on the sides and belly; small mouth
SUSTAINABILITY Considered one of the most sustainable farmed species; wild populations are greatly reduced; the Macquarie perch is protected in NSW

SILVER PERCH IN THE KITCHEN

Silver perch makes excellent eating, especially at around 1 kg (2 lb 4 oz). Larger fish carry a fair amount of fat, but this appears in bands along the belly and back, and can be easily removed either before or after cooking.

It responds well to simple cooking methods, particularly dipping a fillet in flour and then gently pan-frying, or baking a smaller fish whole. It's especially valued in Asian (particularly Cantonese) cuisine. Its soft to medium flesh and high fat content mean it carries flavours well. It's particularly well suited to steaming whole, and can be found that way in many Chinese and Vietnamese restaurants.

BEST COOKING METHODS Pan-fried (fillets), baked whole, steamed whole

TEXTURE Medium to firm, with a tight flake

AROMA Clean, with a light note of freshly cut grass

FLAVOUR Mild, with a light sweet character and mushroomy back palate

APPEARANCE Translucent grey–white when raw; pearl white once cooked

YIELD Flesh about 45% of whole weight

SUBSTITUTES Barramundi, deep-sea bream

Vietnamese-style whole fried silver perch

Using a mortar and pestle, pound the lemongrass as finely as possible. Crush in the peppercorns, garlic and coriander, then the chilli. Add the palm sugar and fish sauce and pound until the sugar has dissolved, then stir in the turmeric. Taste for balance and adjust if necessary with more fish sauce and/or palm sugar.

Score the perch to the bone, spacing the cuts about a finger-width apart at the thickest part near the head and progressively further apart moving down to the tail. Place the fish in a deep tray and rub the marinade well into both sides of the fish. Cover and leave in the fridge to marinate for 2 hours.

Half-fill a large saucepan with vegetable oil and place over high heat (see note). Heat the oil to 180°C (350°C) – check with an oil thermometer. (For a guide to testing the oil temperature without a thermometer, see note.)

Remove the perch from the marinade and pat dry with paper towel. Dust lightly with rice flour.

Carefully lower the perch into the hot oil and fry for 4 minutes on each side, or until crisp and just cooked through. The flesh should be separating from the bone – check by carefully pulling the flesh away at the deepest score line. Remove the perch and drain well on a tray lined with paper towel.

Serve the perch on a platter with the fried shallots, spring onion and coriander leaves scattered over and lime cheeks on the side.

NOTES: When deep-frying in a saucepan, it is advisable to keep the oil level a good 10 cm (4 in) below the rim of the pan. The other option is to use an electric deep-fryer. The used oil can be strained, cooled and refrigerated for later use.

To test the temperature of the oil without a thermometer, drop a cube of bread into the saucepan. If the bread turns golden in 15 seconds, the temperature is sitting perfectly on 180°C (350°F). If the bread only takes 10 seconds to turn golden, then the oil is around 190°C (375°F). If it takes 20–30 seconds to brown, the oil is too cold. Be patient and bring the oil to the correct temperature before proceeding.

SERVES 4

2 lemongrass stems, white part only, finely chopped

¼ teaspoon white peppercorns

3 garlic cloves, peeled and roughly chopped

4 coriander (cilantro) roots and stems, well washed and roughly chopped

2 long red chillies, split lengthways, seeds removed, roughly chopped

1 tablespoon grated palm sugar (jaggery), or as required

1 tablespoon fish sauce, or as required

½ teaspoon ground turmeric

1 whole silver perch (about 800 g – 1 kg/1 lb 12 oz – 2 lb 4 oz)

vegetable oil, for deep-frying

rice flour, for dusting

fried red Asian shallots (see note page 109), to serve

1 spring onion (scallion), thinly sliced on the diagonal

coriander (cilantro) leaves, to serve

lime cheeks (see note page 144), to serve

Red emperor with mushrooms and yoghurt

SERVES 4

40 g (1½ oz) butter
1½ tablespoons plain yoghurt
4 × 200 g (7 oz) red emperor fillets, skin on, pin-boned
2 tablespoons rice flour
80 ml (2½ fl oz/⅓ cup) ghee (see note page 26)
vegetable oil, for cooking
8 Swiss brown mushrooms, cut in half
sea salt and freshly ground black pepper, to taste
1 teaspoon finely chopped chives
lemon oil, to serve (see note page 25)

To make a beurre noisette (nut-coloured butter), heat a small heavy-based frying pan over high heat. Add the butter – it will quickly melt and turn a golden, nut-brown colour. Remove from the heat and pour immediately into a cold bowl. Put the yoghurt in a small bowl. Gently fold through the cooled butter, then set aside at room temperature.

Preheat a cast-iron grill pan or heavy-based frying pan over high heat.

To prepare the red emperor fillets for pan-frying with crisp skin, lay them on a work surface and dust the skin sides with the rice flour. Place each fillet, flesh side down, on a sheet of baking paper large enough to cover the fillet.

Heat a separate large cast-iron or heavy-based frying pan (or two smaller pans – it's essential that the fish is not overcrowded in the pan; see note page 154) over medium–high heat and add the ghee. When the pan is hot and the ghee translucent, place the fillets in the pan, skin side down, leaving the paper on the flesh side. Place a 1 kg (2 lb 4 oz) weight – such as a heavy pot or another pan – on top of the fillets and cook for 4 minutes, lifting the weight once or twice then moving the fillets gently around the pan so they don't burn. Reduce the heat to low. Remove the weight and the paper then, using a spatula, gently flip each fillet to quickly seal the other side. Remove the pan from the heat and set aside for the fish to rest for 1 minute. (Cooking times may vary depending on the size of the fish from which the fillets were cut; for more information, see page 437.)

When the fish is nearly cooked, add a splash of vegetable oil to the hot grill pan. Cook the mushrooms on both sides for 3–4 minutes, until golden and soft but still firm. Transfer to a bowl and season well with salt and pepper.

Place the fillets on serving plates. Top each with a quenelle of yoghurt and sprinkle with chives. Add the mushrooms, then finish with a few drops of lemon oil and a little salt and pepper.

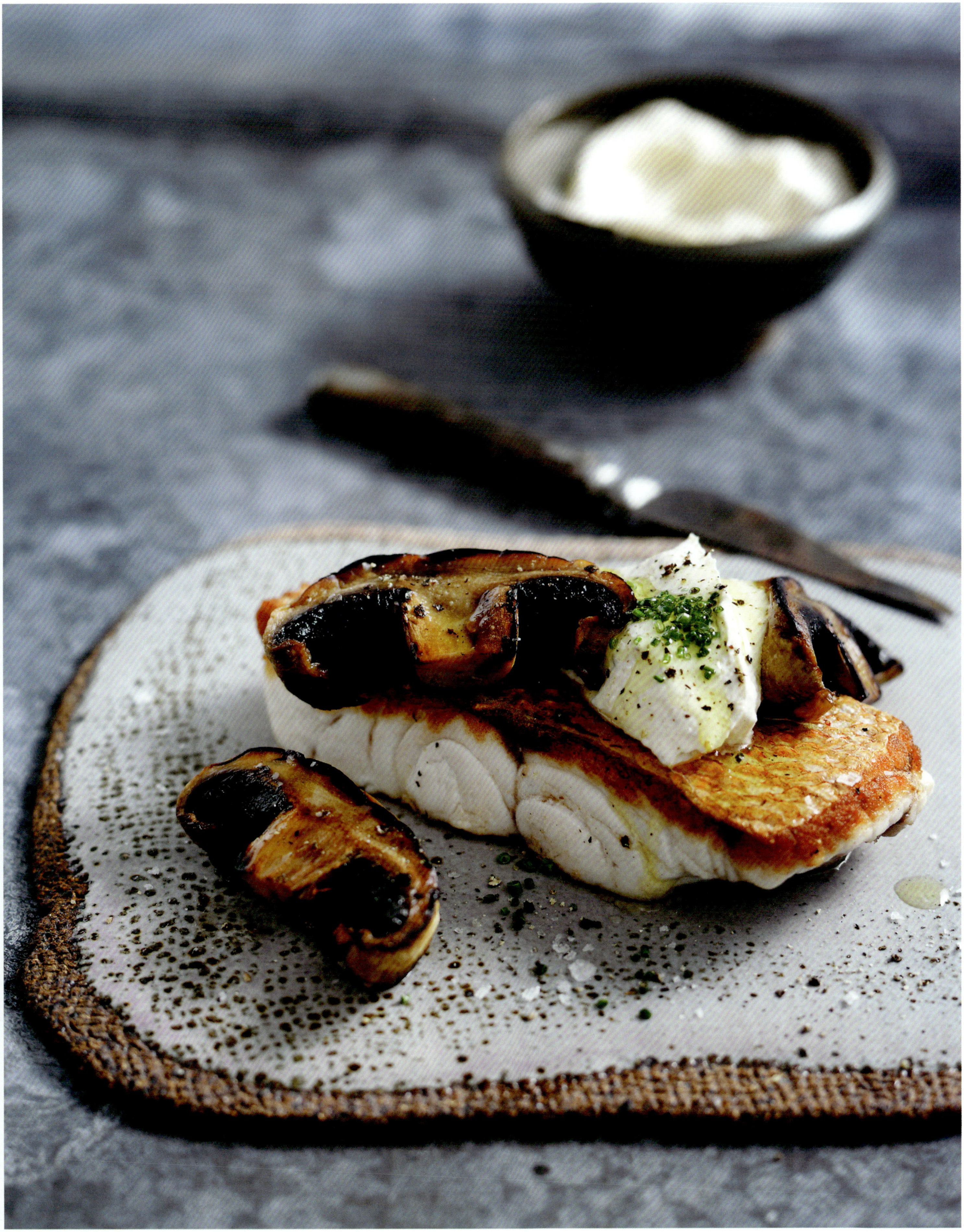

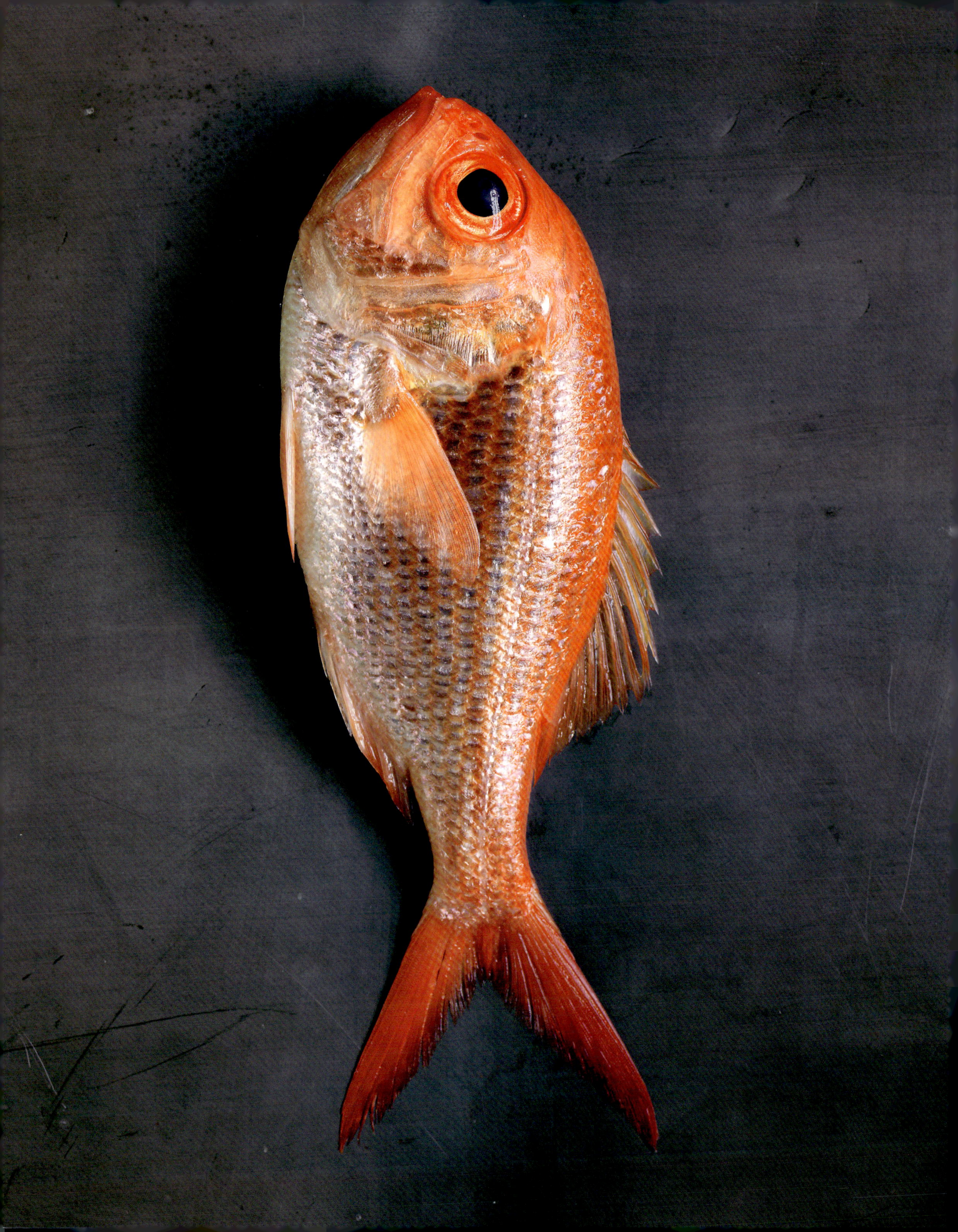

REDFISH

The clownish look of the redfish (*Centroberyx affinis*), with its big eyes, large sad mouth and brilliant colour, somewhat belies its delicious taste. Perhaps its other common name, nannygai, is more suited to its rather comic appearance.

Endemic to the temperate waters of Australia's eastern and southern coasts, from Jervis Bay in New South Wales to Lancelin in Western Australia, the redfish is a deepwater species often found at 100–250 m (330–820 ft). The fish from the east coast of Australia are typically smaller than those from South Australia.

Because of its tough scales and sharp spikes, the redfish is often sold skinned and boned. Recently, fishers have been targeting larger fish, which are line-caught, ike jime spiked (see page 15) and gill-bled, rendering them some of the most delicious sashimi fish available.

SEASONALITY Year round, with peaks in winter and spring
CATCHING METHODS Mid-water trawl, Danish seine, trap, pelagic longline
COMMON LENGTH 20–50 cm (8–20 in)
COMMON WEIGHT 200 g – 2 kg (7 oz – 4 lb 8 oz)
IDENTIFIABLE FEATURES Big eyes, large downturned mouth, tough red skin
SUSTAINABILITY Sustainably managed by state and federal fishing agencies

REDFISH IN THE KITCHEN

This is a great fish to serve raw, in sashimi, sushi and carpaccio. It's better in these dishes, however, if given a little heat first – scored, salted and doused in hot water. This helps set the protein and lighten the texture a little. It holds up well to all cooking methods – pan-fried in butter, grilled (broiled) or deep-fried – but it must be skinned first. Most chefs will tell you, though, that the flavour is too strong and a bit dirty when cooked; they prefer it raw.

Its delicate flesh is as mild as snapper, and its gelatinous nature makes it ideal for fishcakes, particularly Thai or Vietnamese fishcakes, which rely on the binding properties of the minced (ground) flesh.

BEST COOKING METHODS Raw, pan-fried, fishcakes

TEXTURE Soft and yielding when raw; firm once cooked

AROMA Sweet, clean seaweed character

FLAVOUR Mild, clean and sweet, with light notes of melon

APPEARANCE Flesh pink to white when raw; pearl white once cooked

YIELD Flesh about 30% of whole weight

SUBSTITUTES Big-eye ocean perch, blue cod, red rock cod

Vietnamese-style fishcakes with nuoc cham

To make the nuoc cham, use a mortar and pestle to pound the chilli and garlic to a rough paste. Stir in the sugar, then the tamarind water, fish sauce, vinegar and 2 tablespoons of water. Taste and adjust if necessary. Transfer to a bowl and set aside.

Use a mortar and pestle to pound the lemongrass and ginger to as fine a paste as possible. Add the garlic, coriander stem and white peppercorns, then pound again to form a rough paste. Set aside.

Place the fish pieces, fish sauce and salt in a food processor and blend for about 30 seconds. Add the paste and spring onion, then pulse for about 10 seconds, just to combine. Roll the mixture into 12–16 small balls and flatten just slightly using the palm of your hand (see note).

Half-fill a wok or large, deep frying pan with vegetable oil and heat over medium–high heat, or fill a deep-fryer with oil. When the oil reaches 180°C (350°F) – check with an oil thermometer (for a guide to testing the oil temperature without a thermometer, see note) – carefully lower the fishcakes into the wok, in batches. Fry each batch for about 4 minutes or until golden, turning the cakes once and taking care not to overcook them or they will be rubbery.

Using a slotted spoon, remove each batch of fishcakes from the oil and drain well on paper towel. Place on a serving platter. Serve with lettuce leaves for wrapping and the nuoc cham on the side.

NOTES: You could also use snapper or Spanish mackerel.

These fishcakes can be rounder than the Thai version (the flavours of which are a little stronger). You can pan-fry them if preferred.

To test the temperature of the oil, drop a cube of bread into it. If it turns golden in 15 seconds, it's sitting perfectly on 180°C (350°F). If the bread takes only 10 seconds to turn golden, then the oil is around 190°C (375°F). If it takes 20–30 seconds to brown, the oil is too cold. Be patient and get the oil to the correct temperature before proceeding.

SERVES 4

½ lemongrass stem, white part only, finely chopped

1 cm (½ in) piece young ginger, peeled and finely chopped

2 garlic cloves, peeled and finely chopped

4 coriander (cilantro) stems, well washed and finely chopped

1 teaspoon white peppercorns

500 g (1 lb 2 oz) redfish fillets, skin removed, pin-boned and cut into small pieces (see note)

1 tablespoon fish sauce

½ teaspoon sea salt

2 spring onions (scallions), outer layer removed, thinly sliced

vegetable oil, for deep-frying

iceberg lettuce leaves, to serve

NUOC CHAM

2 long red chillies, split lengthways, seeds removed, roughly chopped

1 garlic clove, peeled

1 tablespoon caster (superfine) sugar

1 tablespoon tamarind water (see note page 151)

2 tablespoons fish sauce

1 tablespoon rice wine vinegar

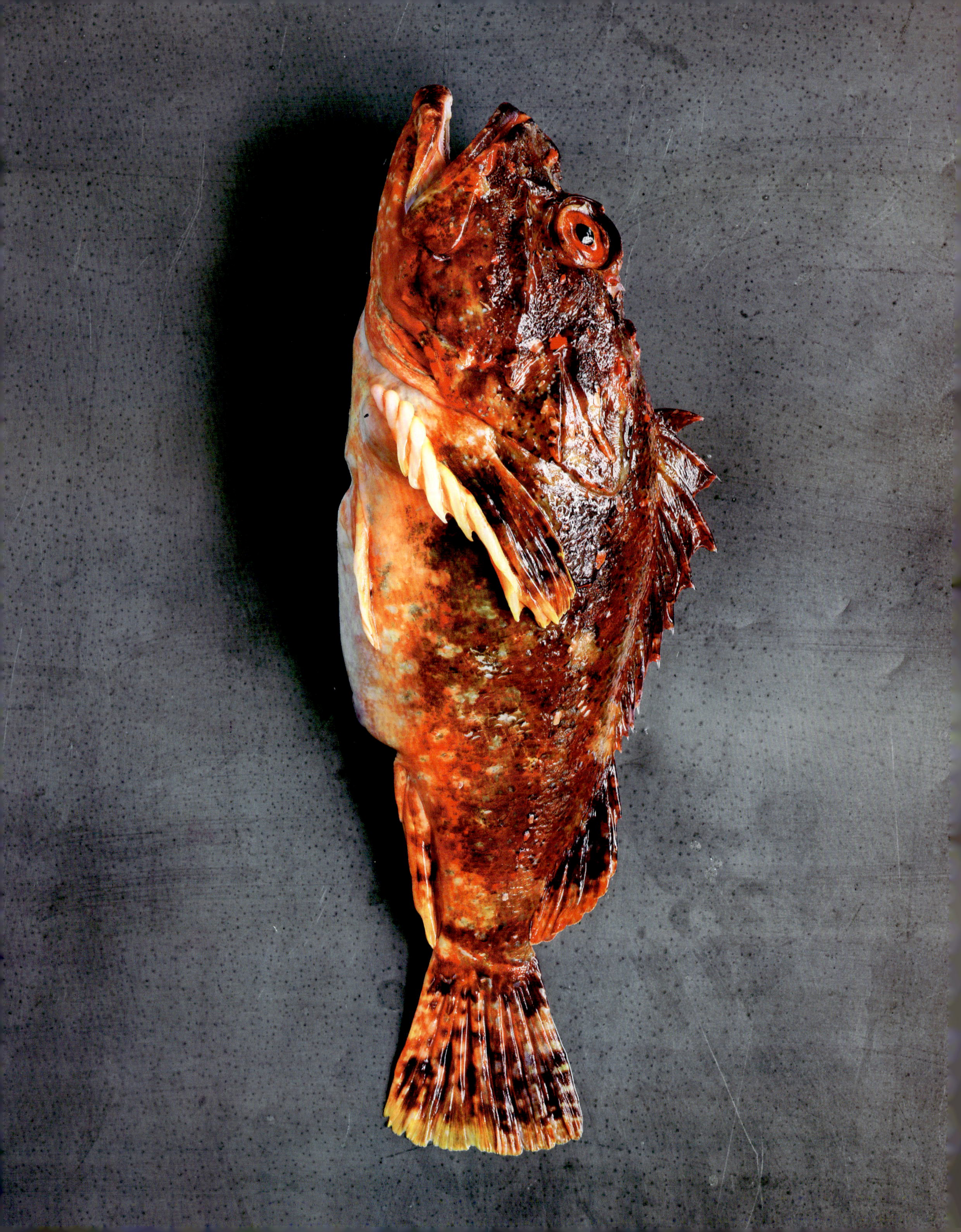

RED ROCK COD

There are some 35 common species of Australian scorpion fish, but the eastern red rock cod (*Scorpaena cardinalis*) is the most sought after for its culinary qualities. This chunky, brightly coloured rock cod has a wild, almost prehistoric appearance: sharp, poisonous spines; and feathery fins that help it camouflage itself in surrounding coral. Its colours and markings also help it hide.

Rock cod are nocturnal predators and spend their daylight hours resting in hidden crevices in the reefs. From this position they ambush their prey, including small fish, squid, octopus, prawns (shrimp) and crabs. Rock cod can use their venomous spines both to stun their prey and fend off predators. Spiking yourself can be very painful.

Although reasonably plentiful, the fish is only sporadically available in Australian fish markets, as many catchers and processors export it directly to France, Italy or Japan, where its lobster-like flesh is highly regarded. This makes it one of the more expensive species.

SEASONALITY Year round, with a peak in autumn
CATCHING METHODS Trap, dropline, bottom otter trawl
COMMON LENGTH 20–30 cm (8–12 in)
COMMON WEIGHT 500 g – 2 kg (1 lb 2 oz – 4 lb 8 oz)
IDENTIFIABLE FEATURES Bright red, rock-like, protruding eyes, a row of twelve venomous spines
SUSTAINABILITY Managed to a strict quota

RED ROCK COD IN THE KITCHEN

Rock cod is a star in soups, chowders, bisques and curries. You can use everything – guts, scales, fins, heads and tails. It's also one of the best fish for sauces and stocks, imparting a real depth of flavour. When super-fresh, it can be battered and fried, and works well with beetroot and greens. If pan-frying, skin it and serve it with ginger, soy sauce or lemon – a lemon butter sauce is perfect.

The rock cod is sometimes referred to as poor man's lobster – if simmered whole in salt water and chilled overnight, the pearly white meat picked from the skin and bones has a lobster-like taste. Given the fish's selective diet of premium live seafood, why wouldn't it be delicious?

SPECIAL STORAGE AND HANDLING
Be careful – the sharp spines contain venom. If handling whole fish, wear gardening gloves.
BEST COOKING METHODS In soups and bisques, pan-fried
TEXTURE Firm, flaky
AROMA Clean, sweet, mild
FLAVOUR Mild, sweet, with a distinct, rich umami character not unlike lobster or crab
APPEARANCE Flesh opaque white when raw; pearl white once cooked
YIELD Flesh about 30% of whole weight
SUBSTITUTES Big-eye ocean perch, redfish

Mixed seafood and vegetable pot with rouille

SERVES 4 (see note)

1 litre (35 fl oz/4 cups) Shellfish Broth (page 458), diluted with 1 litre (35 fl oz/4 cups) water, plus an extra 1 litre (35 fl oz/4 cups) shellfish broth to serve (see note)
1 × 500 g (1 lb 2 oz) red rock cod tail
2 whole prawns (shrimp), heads removed
2 baby (patty pan) squash, cut in half lengthways
2 whole baby green zucchini (courgettes)
2 spring onions (scallions), trimmed
6 clams, steamed open (see page 318; or see note)
crusty bread, to serve

ROUILLE

4 garlic cloves, peeled
small pinch of saffron threads
pinch of sea salt
2 egg yolks
250 ml (9 fl oz/1 cup) olive oil
1 teaspoon red wine vinegar
sea salt and freshly ground black pepper, to taste
35 g (1¼ oz) fresh white breadcrumbs
50 ml (1¾ fl oz) prawn (shrimp) stock

To make the rouille, grind the garlic, saffron, salt and egg yolks to a paste using a mortar and pestle. Transfer the mixture to a bowl.

Gradually drizzle the olive oil into the mixture, stirring vigorously to form a mayonnaise-like emulsion. Stir through the vinegar and taste for seasoning, adding salt and pepper as required. Stir through the breadcrumbs and stock. Cover and reserve in the fridge; it will keep for up to 3 days.

Heat the diluted shellfish broth in a medium saucepan over medium–high heat. When at a strong simmer, remove the pan from the heat, then immediately add the rock cod tail and cover with a tight-fitting lid for 2 minutes.

Add the prawns, cover again and leave for a further 2 minutes.

In a separate saucepan, heat the serving broth over medium–high heat. When at a gentle simmer, add the squash and zucchini, then simmer until just tender. Add the spring onions and clams at the last minute to heat through.

Carefully transfer the cooked seafood to a large serving bowl as soon as it's ready. Add the vegetables, then ladle the serving broth over. Top with a good spoonful of rouille and serve with crusty bread for dipping.

NOTES: This dish serves two comfortably with no fighting over the prawns, but will easily be enough for four. Adjust the variety and quantity of seafood to suit. Mussels, for example, make a delicious addition.

Two separate broths are used in this dish – a lighter, diluted broth to cook the seafood and a serving broth added to the bowls. The seafood cooks better in the lighter style broth, and this keeps the serving broth pure and clean. Fish stock with a little shellfish oil added also makes a delicious cooking broth for the seafood.

Clams from New Zealand are sold par-cooked and pre-packaged in Australia – they can be used straight from the packet.

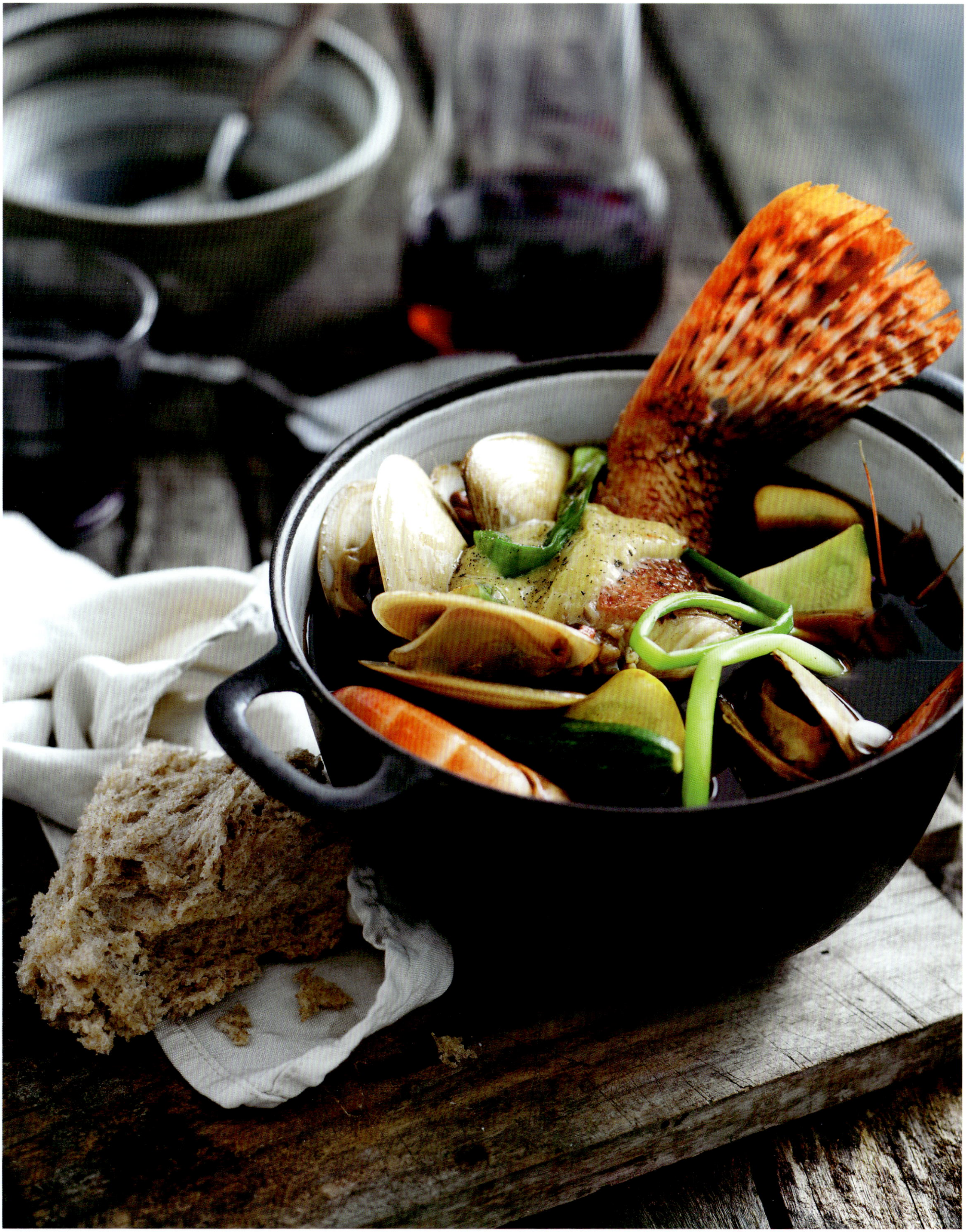

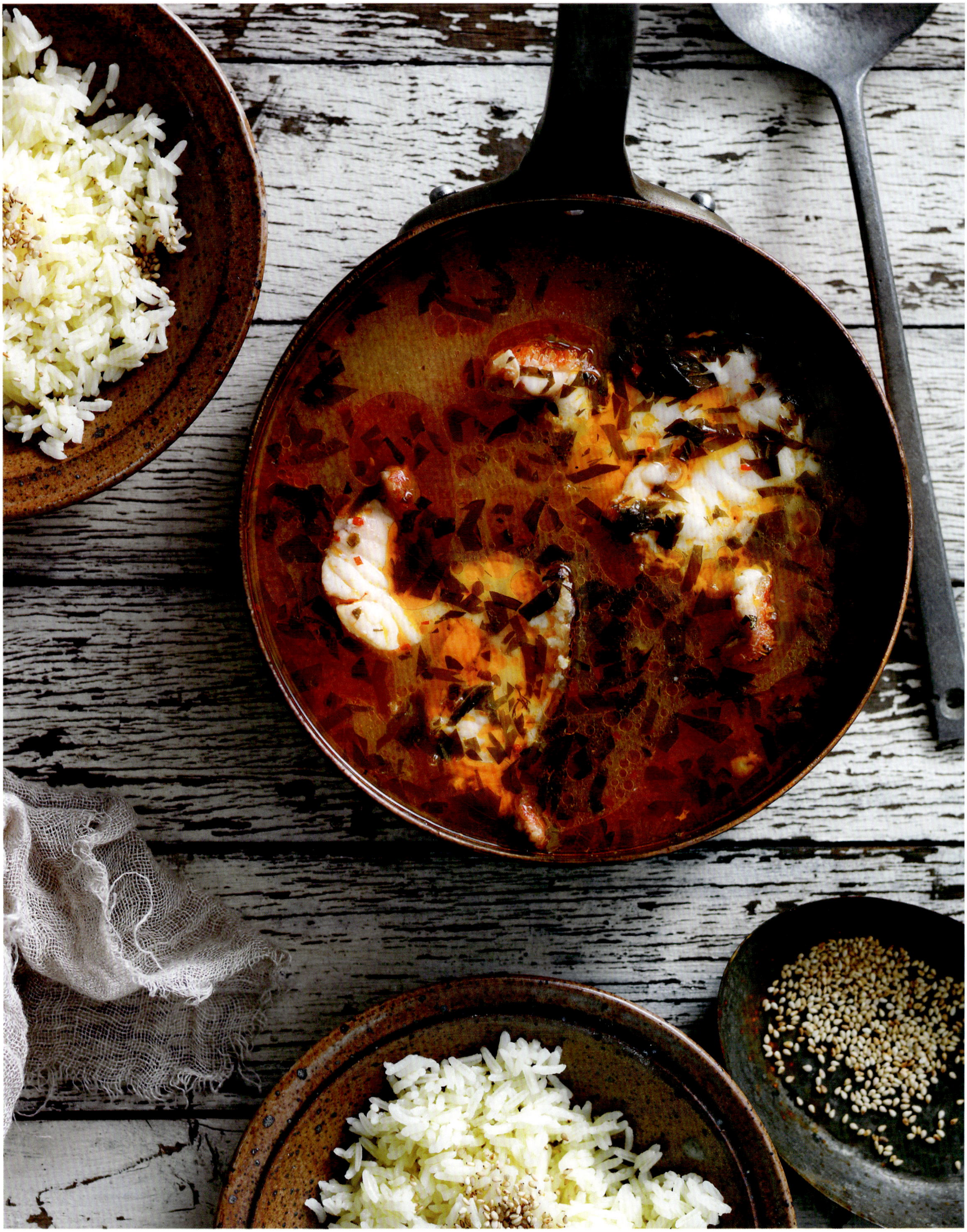

Rock cod cutlets in crazy water

Combine the tomatoes, garlic, parsley, chilli and olive oil with 1.5 litres (52 fl oz/6 cups) of water in a wide, shallow saucepan over high heat. Bring to the boil, then reduce the heat to medium–low and simmer, covered, for 45 minutes, to allow the flavours to develop and reduce the broth by half.

Return the broth to a boil. Remove the pan from the heat, add the rock cod cutlets and cover. Leave the cutlets to poach for 6 minutes, turning them after 3 minutes. Season the broth well with salt and pepper.

Serve the rock cod from the pan, with the buttered rice and lime wedges, if using, on the side.

SERVES 4

600 g (1 lb 5 oz) cherry tomatoes
8 garlic cloves, peeled and thinly shaved using a mandoline
4 tablespoons chopped flat-leaf (Italian) parsley
2 long red chillies, split lengthways, seeds removed, finely chopped
90 ml (3 fl oz) extra virgin olive oil
4 × 250 g (9 oz) rock cod cutlets
sea salt and freshly ground black pepper, to taste
buttered rice topped with toasted sesame seeds, to serve
lime wedges, to serve (optional)

Dried mullet roe (left), salmon roe (top right), trout roe (bottom right)

ROE

The term 'caviar' historically referred to the salt-cured eggs of sturgeon fish but has more recently been appropriated to include the salt-cured eggs of salmon and trout from Australian and New Zealand farms. Salmon 'caviar' is mostly produced as a by-product of salmon farming, but a unique freshwater Atlantic salmon farm in Victoria's Yarra Valley exclusively produces roe for caviar.

Roe from other fish is used to produce a range of cured and dried products, including another popular preparation, bottarga, which is traditionally salted, pressed and dried roe of mullet (bottarga di muggine) or tuna (bottarga di tonno). The best Australian bottarga comes from thin-lipped sea mullet caught off the east coast in early spring. Tuna bottarga is generally imported.

SEASONALITY Year round. New-season salmon and trout roe: autumn; fresh mullet roe: spring

SUSTAINABILITY Farmed caviar is sustainable; mullet and tuna are both regarded as sustainable

ROE IN THE KITCHEN

Sturgeon caviar and cured salmon and trout roe are best used straight, as fresh as possible. Caviars should have a fresh, clean and natural egg-yolk richness combined with a mild seafood flavour.

Caviar is best with crème fraîche, possibly on a blini – the traditional chopped onion, egg and cornichon were used to mask inferior roe.

Good mullet bottarga can at first confuse the palate. The texture initially seems waxy, but then it melts and yields a soft creaminess with a delicate fishy, briny, warm, almost spicy, mouth-filling sensation. A hint of something almost metallic opens up, then the flavour lingers even longer. It's really quite extraordinary.

Bottarga has similar properties to premium dry anchovies, but is much more expensive. It's often served with lemon juice as an appetiser, or used on pasta dishes.

SPECIAL STORAGE AND HANDLING
Caviar: buy fresh and only what you'll eat at once, keep between freezer bricks in the vegetable crisper in the fridge; bottarga: wrap in muslin (cheesecloth) and keep in the fridge for up to 12 months

BEST SERVING METHOD Caviar: simply; bottarga: thinly sliced or grated on pasta or salad

TEXTURE Sturgeon caviar: soft, yielding; salmon and trout roe: crisp, with a pop when bitten

AROMA Caviar: rich, umami-filled, light forest notes, no ammonia, fishy or earthy; bottarga: deep, strong iodine, barbecued-meat umami

FLAVOUR Caviar: mild, sweet, clean iodine, with egg-yolk finish; bottarga: intense, with seaweed snap

APPEARANCE Caviar: translucent, with consistent round pearls and no protective slime; bottarga: full and round lobes, from bright yellow to golden brown

SUBSTITUTES None

Scrambled eggs on brioche with ocean trout roe

SERVES 4

8 eggs
½ teaspoon sea salt
125 ml (4 fl oz/½ cup) thin (pouring) cream
125 ml (4 fl oz/½ cup) milk
40 g (1½ oz) butter, plus extra for spreading on brioche
4 brioche slices
80 g (2¾ oz) ocean trout roe
freshly ground black pepper, to taste

Whisk the eggs, salt, cream and milk together in a medium mixing bowl.

Heat a medium frying pan (a non-stick pan works best for scrambled eggs) over high heat and add the butter. As soon as the butter begins to bubble but not colour, pour in the egg mixture. Cook for 15 seconds, or until the mixture begins to set around the edge of the pan. Do not stir. Instead, fold the mixture in a controlled movement, using a non-stick spatula, moving the cooked mixture from the outside of the pan. This will produce a much silkier texture. Cook for a further 15–20 seconds, then remove from the heat.

While the egg mixture is cooking, toast the brioche slices until golden. Spread them lightly with the extra butter, then place on serving plates. Top each slice with a generous amount of scrambled eggs, then a tablespoon of ocean trout roe. Finish with a grind of pepper and serve immediately.

Bottarga (salted fish roe)

Use a stainless-steel tray large enough to hold the roe. Liberally cover the base of the tray with sea salt. Lay the roe carefully on top, then toss gently to completely cover the roe in salt – the sacs must not be broken. Place another layer of salt over the top, ensuring the roe is snugly packed.

Cover the tray with plastic wrap and refrigerate for 1 month. The salt will draw the moisture from the roe. If liquid builds up in the tray, drain it off and top up the salt.

After 1 month, carefully remove the roe from the salt. Shake off any excess salt.

Using a skewer, poke a hole in each roe sac and tie a long loop of butcher's twine through the hole. Hang the roe in a cool, dry place to air-dry for 10–14 days, until firm.

Wrap the dried roe in plastic wrap and refrigerate until required. It will keep in the fridge for 12 months.

To use, grate or shave the bottarga over pasta or onto crostini.

sea salt, as required

whole fresh fish roe sacs, such as mullet, flathead, mackerel or tuna

King (left) and Atlantic salmon

SALMON

Here in Australia the two common salmon species are the Atlantic salmon (*Salmo salar*), for which Tasmania has become famous, and the chinook or king salmon (*Oncorhynchus tshawytscha*), which is farmed in New Zealand. Atlantic salmon, as its name suggests, is endemic to the northern Atlantic Ocean, and breeds in rivers that flow into it. The king salmon, on the other hand, is the largest of the salmon species found in the northern Pacific Ocean. No wild salmon is commercially available in either Australia or New Zealand.

A defining moment in Australian seafood use was the day in 1985 when the first farmed ocean trout and salmon arrived from Tasmania at the markets in Sydney and Melbourne. Australian chefs suddenly had an *international* ingredient in their kitchens. From a humble harvest of a mere 50 tonnes in the first twelve-week season, Tasmanian salmon became one of the first truly must-have produce lines in Australia, almost overnight. Times have changed – the Tasmanian salmon season now runs for 52 weeks (due to the introduction in the early 1990s of sexless fish that do not spawn) and produces more than 50,000 tonnes.

Salmon farming worldwide has experienced huge growth in the past twenty years. Of the 3 million tonnes farmed worldwide, the king salmon accounts for a mere 1 per cent and the rest is Atlantic salmon. Australia's most famous Atlantic salmon are farmed in the cold, clean waters of Tasmania, but Victoria also has several freshwater farms. New Zealand farms the legendary king salmon, accounting for more than 80 per cent of total world production. Most of this king salmon is ocean-grown, although several small, artisan farms produce fish in the glacial meltwaters of the alpine hydro-canal system of the South Island.

SEASONALITY	Year round; best in winter
CATCHING METHOD	Farmed
COMMON LENGTH	60–90 cm (24–35½ in)
COMMON WEIGHT	3–5 kg (6 lb 12 oz – 11 lb)
IDENTIFIABLE FEATURES	Atlantic: blue–silver sides, sometimes with black dots, white–grey underbelly; king: blue, green, red or purple on back of head, silver sides, black spots on tail
SUSTAINABILITY	Most farms are certified sustainable

SALMON IN THE KITCHEN

The Atlantic salmon is characterised by its firm texture and mild, clean flavour. The king salmon, with its higher fat content, has a luxurious, creamy texture and rich buttery flavour. Both species are beautiful raw but have great versatility in the kitchen. They can be cured, poached, pan-fried with crisp skin, pan-roasted or baked. Both species are a great canvas for flavours, and work well with Eastern or Western spices and sauces.

Salmon is a beautiful fish to cure because of its high fat content and the structure of its flesh – pastrami (see opposite), gravlax, sugar-cured or any other curing method are all great with salmon. It's the most popular fish in Australia to eat pan-fried with crisp skin, smoked, cured, grilled (broiled), poached, roasted whole, in curries and even raw in sashimi and sushi. Poached whole, skinned and garnished with a mousseline sauce (see page 196) – you'd be hard-pressed to find anything better.

BEST COOKING METHODS Grilled (broiled), pan-fried with crisp skin (fillets, see page 437), raw, cured, baked whole

TEXTURE Atlantic: firm, lean; king: soft, buttery

AROMA Clean, with a rich creamy note

FLAVOUR Atlantic: mild, with a distinctive note of nuts and butter; king: fresh, clean, rich, with a hint of double cream

APPEARANCE Flesh orange when raw; pink once cooked

YIELD Flesh about 65% of whole weight

SUBSTITUTES Trout

King salmon pastrami

Using a mortar and pestle, mix the mustard seeds, pepper and coriander seeds together and crush until fine (see page 438). Pass the spices through a fine-mesh sieve, collecting the fine dust. Reserve the rough spice shells that won't pass through the sieve.

Measure the fine spice, then measure out equal amounts of salt and sugar – you should have roughly ⅔ cup of each (spice mix, salt, sugar). Mix all three together in a medium bowl.

Place the salmon on a stainless-steel tray. Rub the spice mixture generously into the flesh on both sides. Cover with plastic wrap and refrigerate for a minimum of 48 hours, turning twice during that time. It's safe to leave the salmon refrigerated in the brine for up to 1 week without risk of over-curing.

To complete the salmon pastrami, remove the fish from the cure and wipe it clean using paper towel. Return the reserved spice husks to the mortar and crush with the pestle as finely as possible. Coat both sides of the salmon in this spice as a crust.

1 LARGE SIDE OF SALMON YIELDS 12–14 PORTIONS

3 tablespoons yellow mustard seeds
3 tablespoons freshly ground black pepper
3 tablespoons coriander seeds, toasted until fragrant
100 g (3½ oz/⅔ cup) fine salt, or as required
150 g (5½ oz/⅔ cup) caster (superfine) sugar, or as required
1 side king salmon fillet, skin removed, pin-boned

King salmon poached in court bouillon with mouseline sauce

SERVES 6–8

3 litres (101 fl oz/12 cups) Court Bouillon (page 457)
1 whole side king salmon, about 1.2 kg (2 lb 10 oz), skin on, pin-boned
a few fennel fronds, to serve
1 teaspoon lemon oil, to serve (see note page 25)
freshly ground black pepper, to serve

MOUSSELINE SAUCE

60 ml (2 fl oz/¼ cup) dry white wine
60 ml (2 fl oz/¼ cup) white wine vinegar
2 red Asian shallots, peeled and finely diced
4 black peppercorns
250 g (9 oz) butter, chilled and cut into 2 cm (¾ in) cubes
juice of 1 lemon
pinch each of sea salt and freshly ground white pepper
150 ml (5 fl oz) thin (pouring) cream, lightly whipped, about halfway to soft peaks

For the mousseline sauce, first make a very buttery, basic beurre blanc (white butter sauce) as follows. Heat the wine, vinegar, shallots and peppercorns in a small saucepan over high heat. Boil, stirring occasionally, for about 3 minutes, until the liquid has reduced to around 2 tablespoons.

Strain the liquid into a bowl through a fine-mesh sieve, discarding the shallots and peppercorns, then return it to the pan over low heat. Add the butter one piece at a time, whisking constantly, adding another piece as soon as the previous one has been incorporated. It's essential that the butter remains chilled throughout the process – if it becomes too warm, the sauce may split. When all the butter has been incorporated (this should take no more than 5 minutes), remove the beurre blanc from the heat and whisk in the lemon juice. Season with the salt and pepper. Transfer the sauce to a bowl and set aside to cool completely.

Gently fold the whipped cream through the cooled beurre blanc. Set aside until ready to serve, but do not refrigerate or the sauce will set like a brick.

Heat the court bouillon in a large shallow saucepan over high heat. Once boiling, remove the pan from the heat and gently lay the salmon in the court bouillon. (You may need to fold the fillet gently in a semicircle around the base of the pan to fit.) Leave the salmon in the court bouillon until the stock cools – the fish should be perfectly cooked.

To serve, gently remove the salmon from the stock and place it on a board or platter. Carefully peel back the skin, top with fennel fronds and serve the mousseline sauce on the side with a splash of lemon oil and a sprinkling of black pepper.

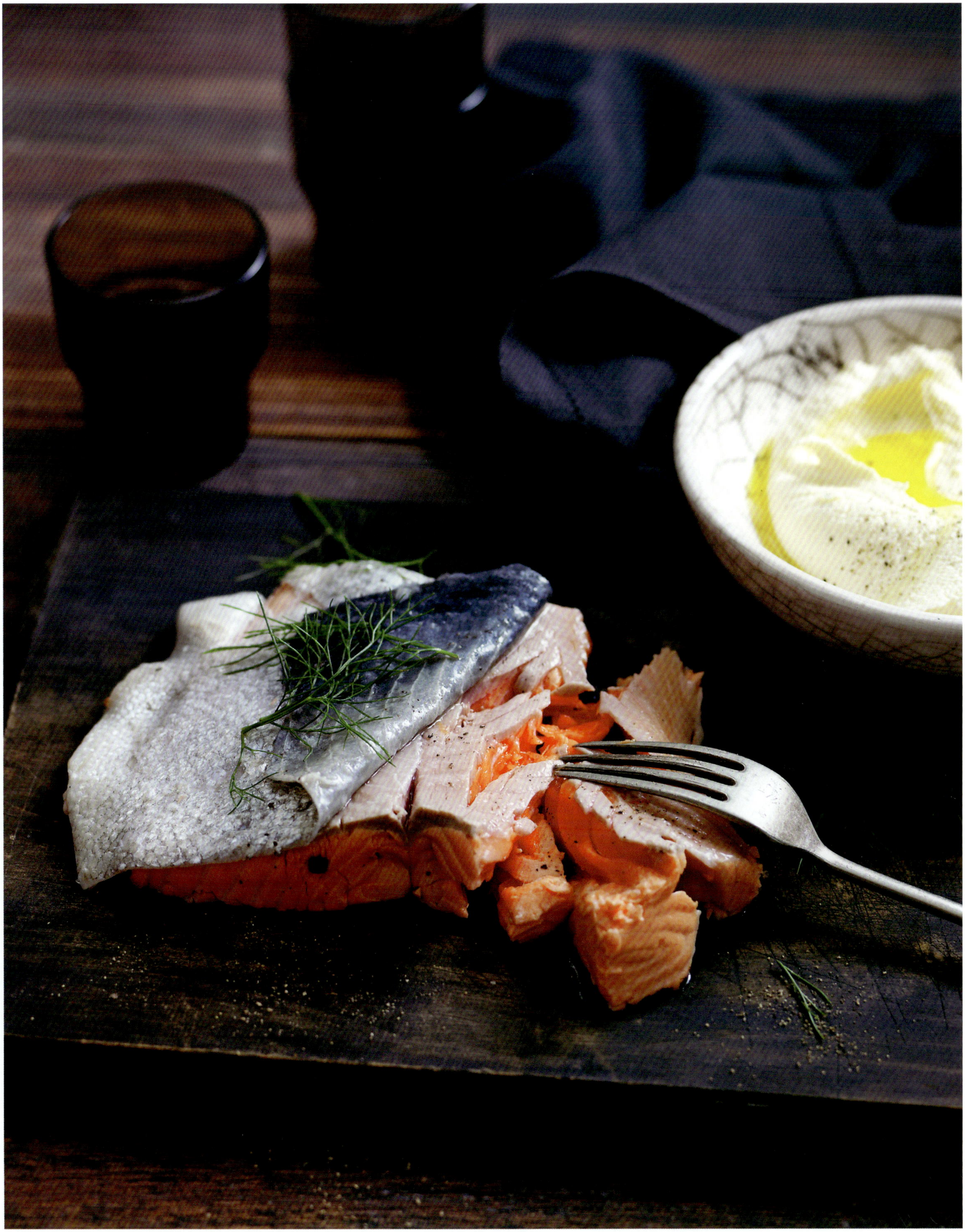

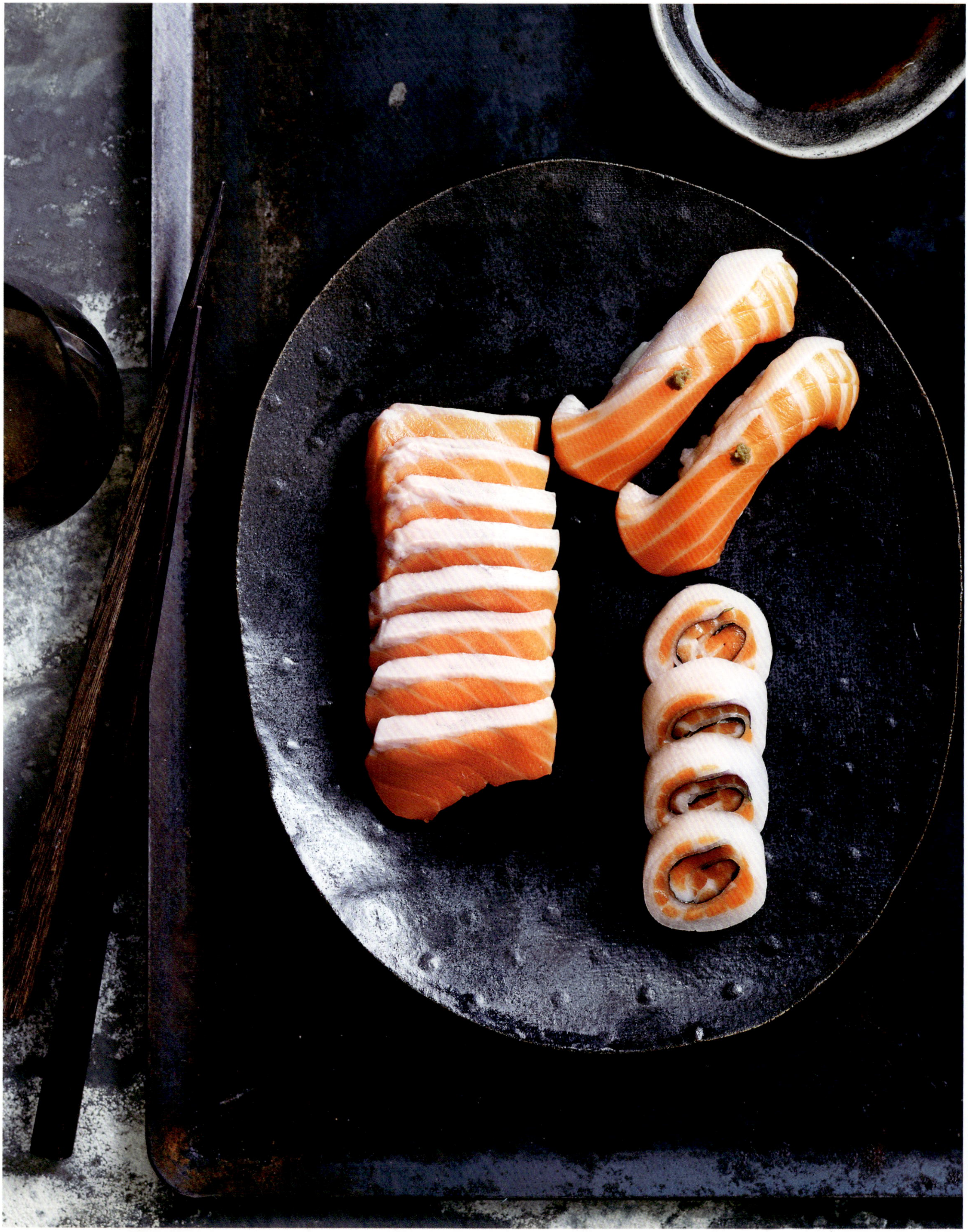

Atlantic salmon sushi and sashimi

To prepare the sushi, mould the sushi rice into four mounds (see page 463). Place a slice of salmon on each and top each with a tiny drop of yuzu paste.

To make the daikon salmon roll, lay the four strips of daikon flat on a clean work surface. Cover each with the salmon and top with the shiso leaf.

Roll each square tightly, trimming the ends of the daikon as the edges meet to create a perfect cylinder. Trim the ends as necessary to neaten. Slice each cylinder into two pieces.

On a platter, arrange the sushi, daikon roll and slices of salmon belly. Serve with Japanese soy sauce.

NOTE: For advice on slicing fish for sashimi, see page 434.

SERVES 2–4

Japanese light soy sauce, to serve

SALMON SUSHI

50 g (1¾ oz) cooked Sushi Rice (see page 463)

4 × 15 g (½ oz) Atlantic salmon shoulder slices

yuzu paste, to garnish

DAIKON SALMON ROLL

4 flat strips of peeled, paper-thin daikon radish, about 4 cm (1½ in) square (use a mandoline for best results)

salmon belly or shoulder, thinly sliced to cover the strips of daikon

2 large shiso leaves, cut in half

SALMON SASHIMI

16 × 20 g (¾ oz) Atlantic salmon belly slices, about 5 mm (¼ in) thick

Salmon with potato and speck salad

SERVES 4 AS AN ENTRÉE

1 tablespoon olive oil

2 speck slices, 5 mm (¼ in) thick, cut into 3 cm (1¼ in) long strips

4 boiled potatoes, skin on, halved

2 French shallots, peeled and very finely diced

½ carrot, peeled and very finely diced

2 tablespoons cabernet vinegar

2 tablespoons lemon oil (see note page 25)

2 tablespoons finely chopped chives

sea salt and freshly ground black pepper, to taste

4 × 100 g (3½ oz) pieces salmon fillet, 2 cm (¾ in) thick, skin on, pin-boned

2 tablespoons rice flour

2 tablespoons ghee (see note page 26)

To make the potato salad, heat the olive oil in a medium frying pan over low heat. Add the speck and cook slowly until the fat has rendered and the speck is golden brown but not crisp. Remove the pan from the heat, then add the potatoes and move them around in the speck and oil to coat without colouring.

Add the shallots and return the pan to a low heat. Cook the shallots for 1 minute, without colouring. Remove the pan from the heat, add the carrot, vinegar, lemon oil and chives, then season with salt and pepper. Set aside in a warm place.

To prepare the salmon pieces for pan-frying with crisp skin, lay them on a work surface and dust the skin sides with the rice flour. Place each piece, flesh side down, on a sheet of baking paper large enough to cover the piece of fish.

Heat a medium cast-iron frying pan (or two smaller pans – it's essential that the fish is not overcrowded in the pan) over medium–high heat and add the ghee. When the pan is hot and the ghee translucent, place the salmon pieces in the pan, skin side down, leaving the paper on the flesh side. Place a 1 kg (2 lb 4 oz) weight – such as a heavy pot or another pan – on top of the salmon pieces (be gentle when using a weight on portions this size). Cook for 2 minutes, lifting the weight once or twice and moving the salmon pieces gently around the pan so they don't burn. Remove the pan from the heat, remove the weight and the paper then, using a spatula, gently flip each piece of salmon. Leave to rest for 1 minute. (Cooking times may vary depending on the size of the fish from which the pieces were cut; for more information, see page 437.)

To serve, spoon the potato salad onto serving plates and add a piece of salmon to each, then sprinkle with sea salt.

NOTE: If you don't have a pan large enough for all the fillets, or two smaller pans, cook the fish in two batches. Keep the first batch warm while you cook the second.

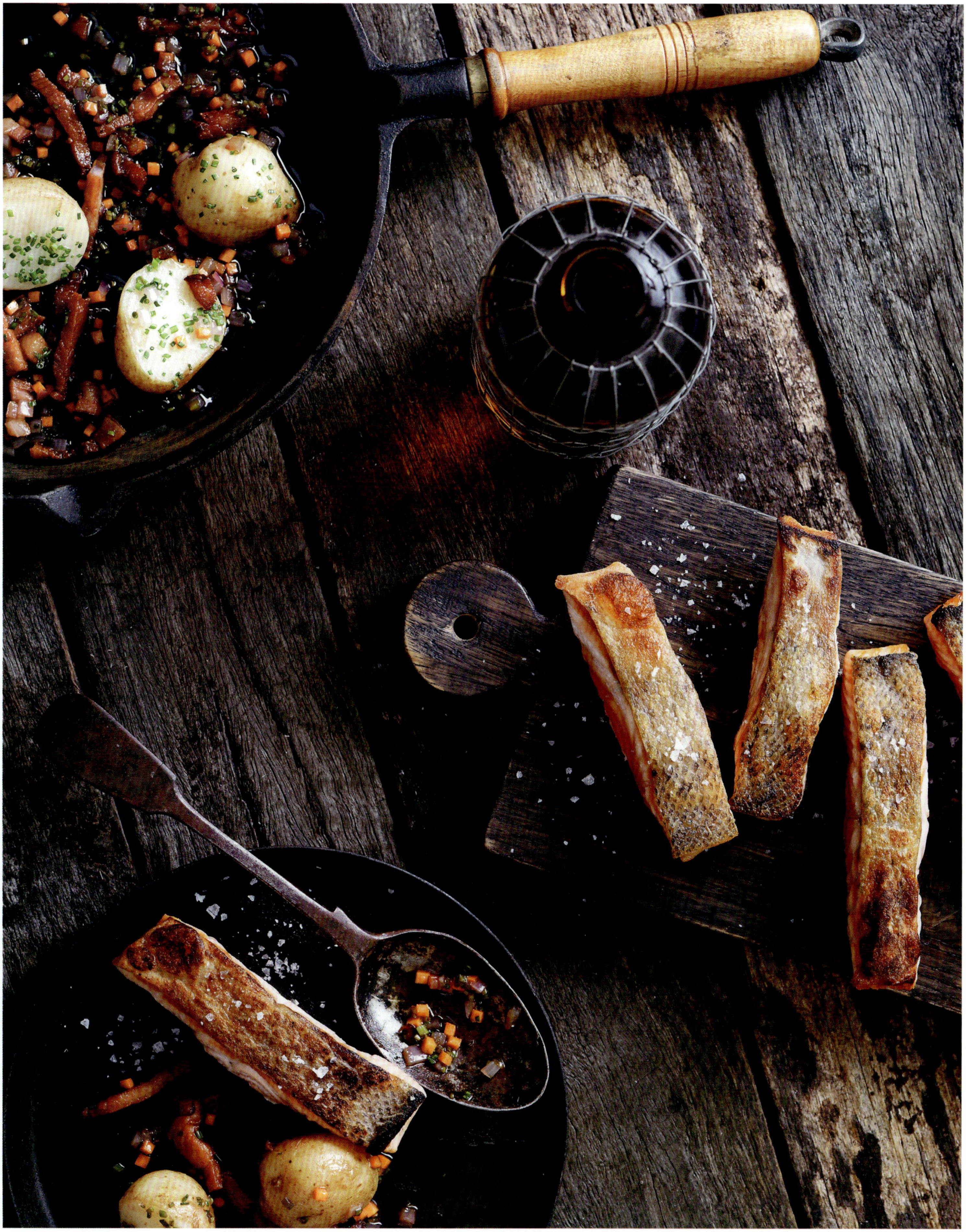

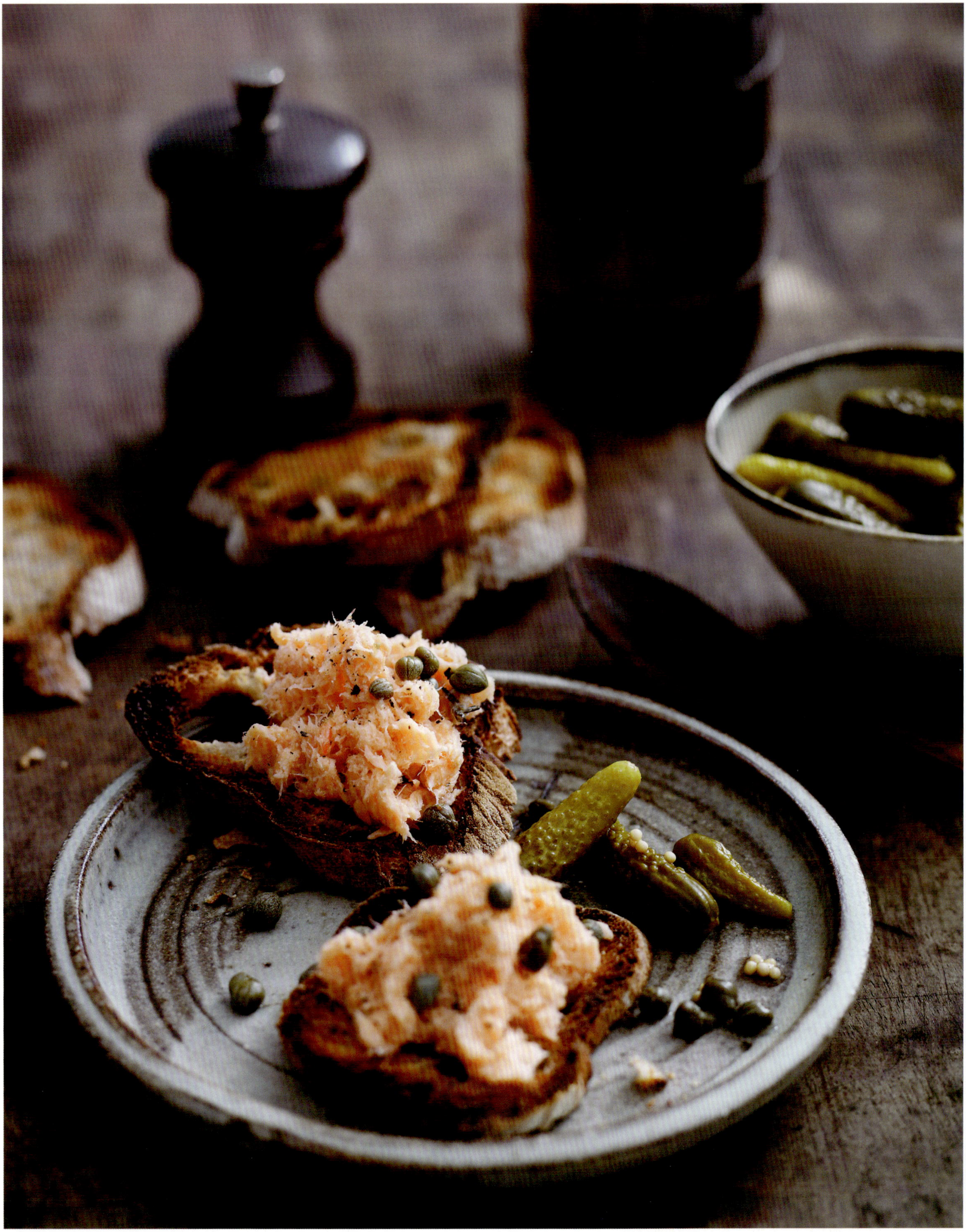

Salmon pâté

Heat the duck fat in a small, deep frying pan over medium heat to 69°C (156°F), measuring the temperature using a thermometer.

Add the salmon scraps, thyme sprigs and garlic to the warm fat. Remove the pan from the heat, cover tightly with foil and leave to cool to room temperature.

Once cooled completely, remove the salmon from the fat and transfer to a bowl. Using two forks, break the salmon apart, adding a little of the duck fat, as necessary, to keep the fish moist. Add the salt and pepper and a squeeze of lemon juice to taste.

Serve the pâté with plain or toasted sliced baguette, cornichons and capers.

NOTES: Salmon pâté also makes a delicious canapé for a dinner party or cocktail soirée.

This dish is a clever way to use left-over scraps of salmon. It can also be made with salmon fillet, cut into thin strips, or a mixture of fillet and other pieces.

SERVES 4 AS AN ENTRÉE

125 ml (4 fl oz/½ cup) melted duck fat, or extra virgin olive oil

400 g (14 oz) salmon scraps (belly, tails, etc.), skin removed, pin-boned (see note)

2 thyme sprigs

1 garlic clove, peeled and finely chopped

pinch each of sea salt and freshly ground black pepper

½ lemon

sliced baguette, to serve

cornichons, to serve

capers, to serve

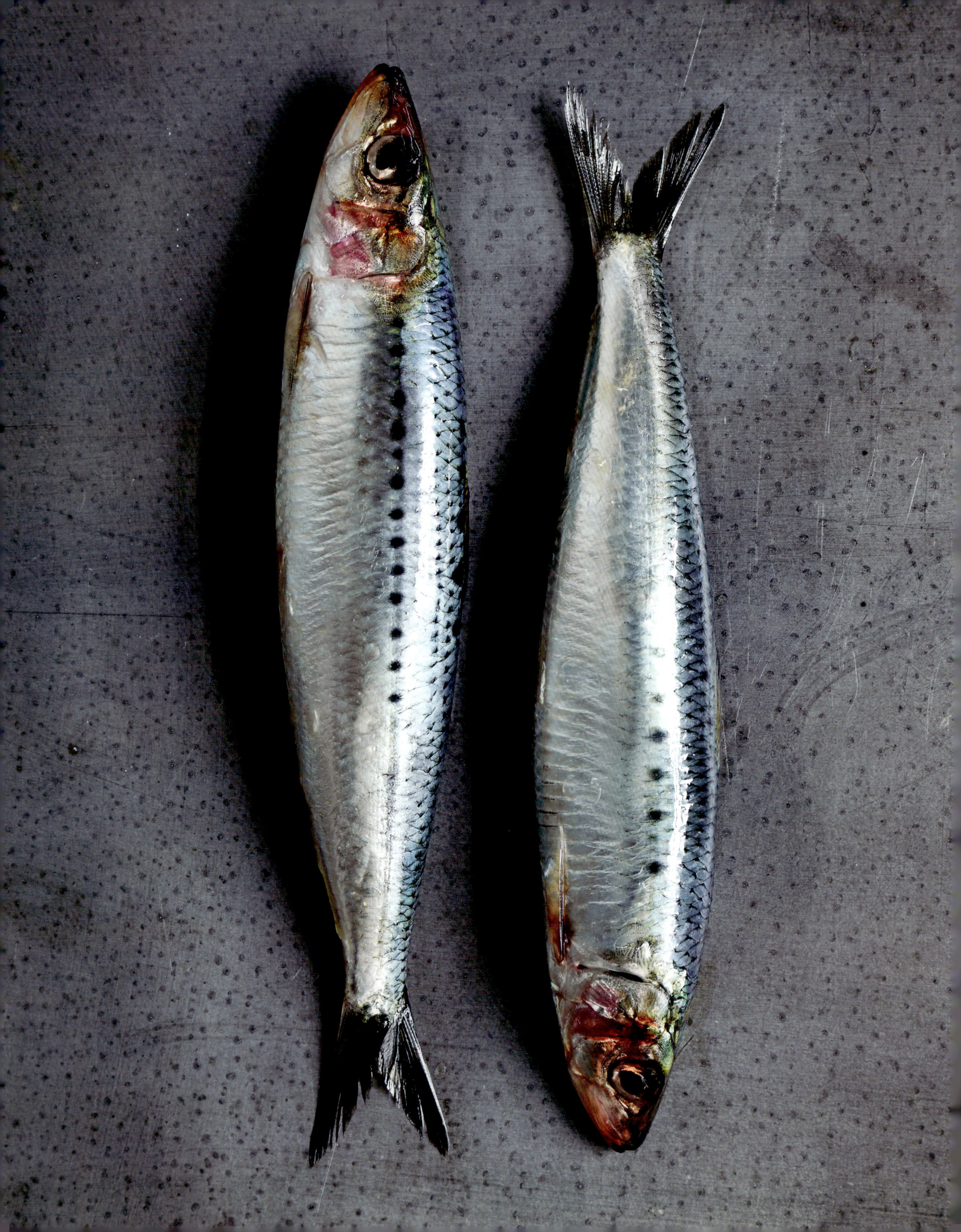

SARDINES

Say sardines and many Australians think of tins packed with greasy, mushy fish in some kind of sauce. Growing up, many of us ate sardines only on camping trips, and then only reluctantly. But fresh sardines can be delectable. Long a favourite fish on Mediterranean menus, they're either grilled (broiled) and then served with lemon and olive oil, mixed with pasta sauces, baked or braised.

Australian sardines (*Sardinops sagax*) are fast-growing fish from the upper waters of the continental shelf surrounding the mainland, making them relatively accessible to the catching fleet. This results in premium quality and great consistency. South Australian waters are particularly abundant in Australian sardines, which are used by Port Lincoln southern bluefin tuna farmers to feed the tuna ranched in the Spencer Gulf from February to September. Specialised processing equipment to produce sardines for human consumption has recently been bought.

A similar commitment was made years ago by Jim 'the Sardine Man' Mendolia in Fremantle, who has been a sardine fisherman since 1980. His father, Francolino, a commercial fisherman from Messina in Sicily, came to Australia for crayfishing but soon noticed lots of sardines in the water. A few Italian families brought anchovy and sardine nets from Italy, and started hanging the nets off the end of their boats then hauling them on board after a day of catching crayfish. They caught too many sardines to use or sell, so in 1988 Francolino bought a factory and began processing the catch under the name Fremantle Sardines.

Inexpensive, consistent and versatile, sardines are also wonderfully sustainable. Australian populations are carefully managed, and current catches are at only 30–35 per cent of the annual sustainable volumes. Local populations have made a comeback in the east, south and west.

SEASONALITY Year round, with a peak in November–July
CATCHING METHODS Purse seine, hoop nets
COMMON LENGTH 14–17 cm (5½–6½ in)
COMMON WEIGHT 80–100 g (2¾–3½ oz)
IDENTIFIABLE FEATURES Underslung lower jaw, silver stripe on side with dark spots below
SUSTAINABILITY Very sustainable

SARDINES IN THE KITCHEN

Sardines are one of the most misunderstood fish in Australia, mainly due to their delicate nature, and to mishandling before they arrive in a commercial kitchen or for public sale. They deteriorate quite quickly, but are glorious when eaten at their optimum. Their high fat content and fine bone structure make them quite fragile, but handled correctly, they offer a unique eating experience.

The Australian sardine is highly versatile. Raw, cured or pickled, the flesh has a soft texture and an abundance of moisture. When cooked it will firm up to be crunchy on the outside. Its high oil content, robust metallic taste and sesame nuttiness make it ideal for pan-frying and grilling (broiling). It's perfectly suited to big, full-flavoured Mediterranean ingredients such as currants, capsicum (pepper) and tomato. To enjoy the fish itself, though, try it cooked on the bone but still slightly translucent in the centre, with a touch of garlic and lemon.

SPECIAL STORAGE AND HANDLING Store fresh sardines on dry paper towel on a drip tray over ice, all sealed in an airtight container; thaw frozen sardines quickly at room temperature and use immediately

BEST COOKING METHODS Pickled, pan-fried, grilled (broiled), but don't overcook

TEXTURE Delicate, soft, moist when raw; firm and crunchy once cooked

AROMA Briny, the sea

FLAVOUR Clean, metallic, with an iodine zing, a sesame nuttiness and a drying, salty finish

APPEARANCE Flesh a brilliant deep red with a translucent sheen

YIELD Flesh 40–45% of whole weight

SUBSTITUTES Anchovies

Sardines on toast

Preheat an oven grill (broiler) to high.

Lay the bread on a baking tray and splash a little olive oil over each slice. Toast on both sides under the grill.

Rub the garlic clove lightly over the oiled side of each slice of toast. Set the toast aside in a warm place.

Place the sardines on a separate baking tray lined with baking paper and drizzle a little olive oil over each fish. Cook under the grill, on the one side only, for 3–4 minutes. Remove and season with salt.

To serve, place two slices of toast on each serving plate and top each with two sardines. Add a dollop of salsa verde on top and serve with a little extra on the side.

SERVES 4

8 bread slices good for toasting (such as baguette, ciabatta or sourdough)
extra virgin olive oil, for cooking
1 garlic clove, peeled
16 fresh sardines, butterflied
sea salt, to taste
2 tablespoons Salsa Verde, plus extra to serve (page 462)

Pan-fried sardines with broccolini, fried bread and capers

SERVES 4 AS AN ENTRÉE, 2 AS A MAIN

150 g (5½ oz) broccolini, ends trimmed

iced water, as required, to refresh

2 tablespoons vegetable oil

2 tablespoons drained and well-rinsed capers in vinegar, dried with paper towel

small pinch of sea salt, plus extra to serve

12 whole sardines, scaled and gutted

2 teaspoons rice flour

60 ml (2 fl oz/¼ cup) ghee (see note page 26)

2 tablespoons fried rye breadcrumbs (see note)

4 lemon cheeks, to serve (see note page 144)

Bring a medium saucepan of salted water to the boil over high heat. Add the broccolini and blanch for 30–60 seconds, or until the stems are just tender but the broccolini is still vibrantly green. Remove immediately and plunge into a bowl of iced water to refresh. Drain well, then tear the broccolini into florets. Set aside.

Heat half the vegetable oil in a medium heavy-based frying pan over high heat. Add the capers and toss for 2 minutes, or until crisp. Remove from the heat, drain off the oil then transfer the capers to a bowl lined with paper towel and set aside – the paper will help keep them crisp.

Return the pan to the heat and add the remaining vegetable oil. After about 1 minute, when the oil is very hot, add the broccolini and salt. Fry, without stirring or tossing, for 1–2 minutes, until dark on one side, leaving the other side fresh and green for added texture and flavour. Remove and set aside in a warm place.

Place the sardines on a work surface and dust lightly with the rice flour.

Heat the ghee in a large heavy-based frying pan over medium heat. When the pan is hot and the ghee translucent, add the sardines and cook for 1 minute on each side. Remove from the pan.

Divide the broccolini and capers among the serving plates. Place the sardines on top, then scatter the fried breadcrumbs over. Serve with lemon cheeks and extra salt on the side.

NOTE: For the fried breadcrumbs, fry slices of rye bread in butter until golden. Chop into rough crumbs, or blitz in a food processor. They will keep in an airtight container in the pantry for 3 days.

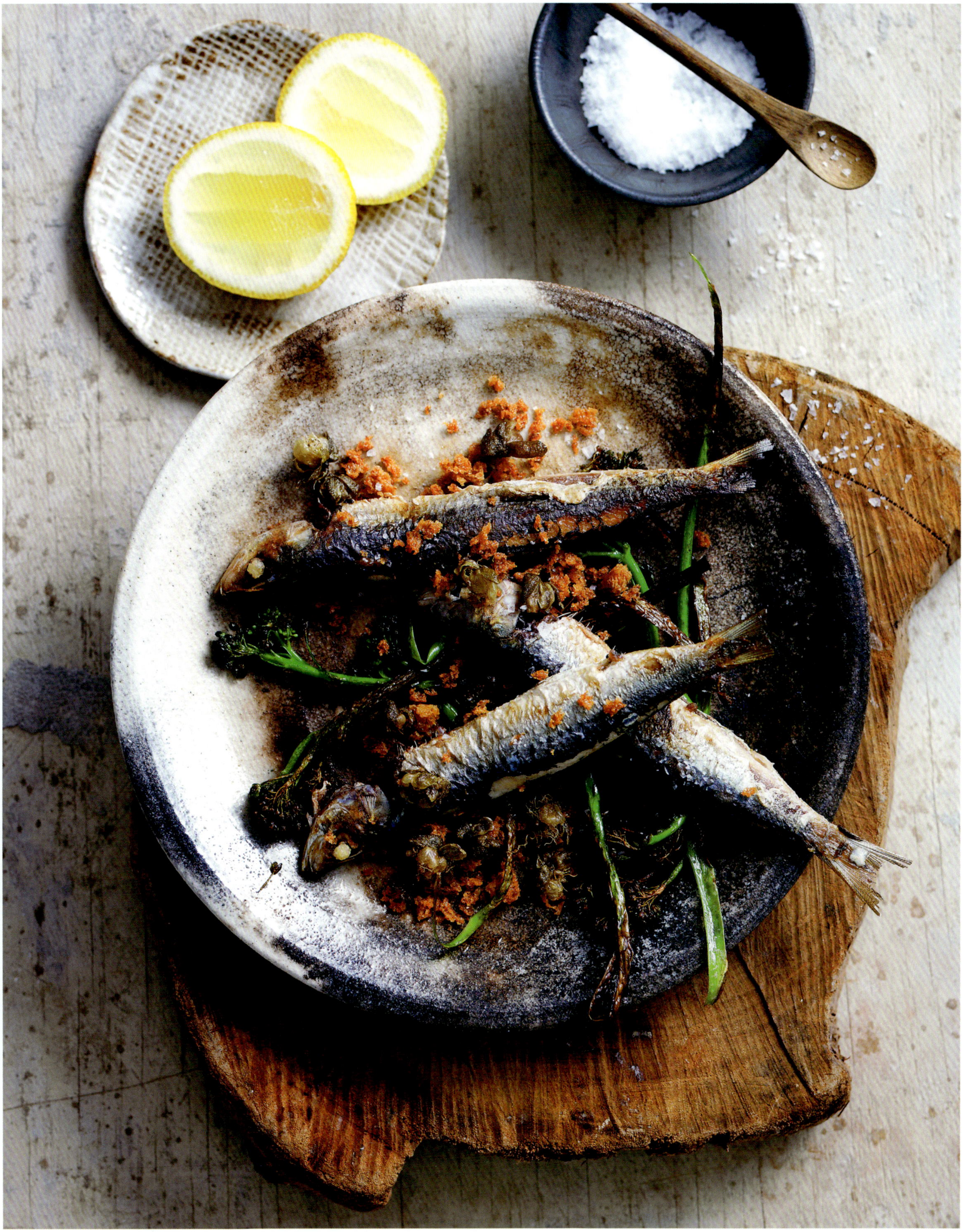

Gummy shark

SHARK

One man's shark is another man's flake – or so it seems. 'Shark' is the common name given to more than 500 different fish whose skeleton is formed from cartilage rather than bone. Skates and rays (see page 215) also fall within this group of cartilaginous fish. Of the many species of shark found in our waters, the most commonly used for cooking are the dusky (*Carcharhinus obscurus*), gummy (*Mustelus antarcticus*), angel (*Squatina australis*), school (*Galeorhinus galeus*), saw (*Pristiophorus cirratus*), whiskery (*Furgaleus macki*), mako (*Isurus oxyrinchus*), blacktip (*Carcharhinus limbatus*) and elephant (*Callorhinchus milii*) sharks, and the roughskin (*Deania calcea*) and spikey (*Squalus megalops*) dogfish.

Sharks, whatever the species, have a universally menacing appearance and ferocious reputation. Some have teeth that are no more likely to cause harm than rough sandpaper, but their smooth skin, evil-looking gill slits on the sides of their head and their way of moving effortlessly through the water gives them the look of a stealth bomber. This scary appearance often belies the tasty, boneless flesh within.

In order to maintain an internal salt concentration similar to that of sea water, sharks retain urea in their blood. While this can assist in effectively 'tenderising' the muscle of the dead fish, if it's not handled well – bled, gutted and chilled quickly – the urea can be converted into ammonia and ruin the flavour and aroma of the flesh.

SEASONALITY Year round
CATCHING METHODS Pelagic longline, gillnet, prawn trawl
COMMON LENGTH Smaller sharks: 100–200 cm (39½–78¾ in); mako: 300–400 cm (118–157½ in)
COMMON WEIGHT Smaller sharks: 3–8 kg (6 lb 12 oz – 17 lb 10 oz); mako: 60–135 kg (132–298 lb)
IDENTIFIABLE FEATURES Streamlined body, smooth skin, obvious gill slits, numerous sharp curving teeth
SUSTAINABILITY School shark: overfished; most species: well managed by state and federal fishing agencies

SHARK IN THE KITCHEN

The popularity of shark in this part of the world is mostly due to its almost universal use as the staple fish in the ubiquitous fish and chips. Commonly referred to as flake, its skinless, boneless form makes it ideal for the batter-and-fry trade. While its texture is soft, it rarely has actual flakes, more a soft but tightly grained flesh.

Despite this common use, shark is a versatile fish, and its mild, sweet flesh and firm texture are suited to a range of preparations, from curries to steaming, roasting and grilling (broiling).

Shark provides a great platform for flavours, but take care that they don't overpower its own mild taste. It's important to marinate it before using high heat, so that it doesn't lose moisture during cooking.

SPECIAL STORAGE AND HANDLING
Buy very fresh and make sure you know which species you're buying, as the flavour and texture can vary. Fillets should have a fresh, vibrant iodine aroma with no traces of ammonia.

BEST COOKING METHODS Grilled (broiled), shallow-fried, pan-fried, deep-fried, barbecued, in curries, steamed

TEXTURE Soft, with a tight-grained flesh

AROMA Mild and sweet, with a clean, bright note of clotted cream

FLAVOUR Mild and sweet, with a clean iodine flavour and light egg-white finish

APPEARANCE Depending on the species, raw fillets pale pink to translucent white when raw; snow white to slightly grey once cooked

YIELD Boneless flesh more than 90% of fillet weight

SUBSTITUTES Flathead, whiting

Fish tacos

For the guacamole, pound the avocado flesh using a large mortar and pestle until it has a rough consistency. Transfer to a bowl, then stir in the spring onion, chilli and coriander. Season with lime juice, olive oil, salt and pepper, cover and refrigerate until required.

For the cabbage salad, combine the cabbage, shallot, coriander and jalapeno in a medium bowl. Toss to combine. Add the lime juice and olive oil, then season with salt and pepper. Cover and refrigerate until required.

Half-fill a 6 litre (203 fl oz/24 cup) saucepan with vegetable oil and place over high heat (see note). Heat the oil to 180°C (350°F) – check with an oil thermometer. (For a guide to testing the oil temperature without a thermometer, see note page 109.) Heat a grill pan over medium heat.

Place the shark strips in a medium bowl. Add the lime juice, salt and olive oil, then toss to combine. Cover and leave in the fridge to marinate for 10 minutes.

Put the rice flour in a medium bowl and the beer batter in a second bowl. Drain the shark pieces from the marinade and toss them through the rice flour. Shake off any excess flour, then dip each piece in the beer batter. Gently drag the shark pieces against the side of the bowl to remove any excess batter, then drop them gently into the hot oil. Cook for 1–2 minutes, until golden and crisp, then remove carefully using a slotted spoon. Drain on paper towel.

Heat the tortillas in the hot grill pan for 1 minute each side.

To assemble, lay a warm tortilla on a clean work surface, add a strip of shark, a spoonful of guacamole and some cabbage salad. Roll the tortilla by first turning up one end, then folding the sides over to form a parcel. Repeat with the remaining ingredients.

NOTE: When deep-frying in a saucepan, it's advisable to keep the oil level a good 10 cm (4 in) below the rim of the pan. The other option for deep-frying is, of course, an electric deep-fryer. The used oil can be strained, cooled and refrigerated for later use.

MAKES 8 TACOS

vegetable oil, for frying
600 g (1 lb 5 oz) gummy shark, skin removed, pin-boned, cut into 8 thick strips
juice of 2 limes
good pinch of sea salt
60 ml (2 fl oz/¼ cup) olive oil
rice flour, for dusting
1 quantity Beer Batter (page 83)
8 flour or corn tortillas
lime wedges and hot sauce, to serve

GUACAMOLE

2 firm, ripe avocados, cut in half, stone removed, flesh scooped out
1 spring onion (scallion), trimmed, outer layer removed, thinly sliced
1 long red chilli, split lengthways, seeds removed, finely chopped
½ bunch coriander (cilantro), roughly chopped
juice of 1 lime, or to taste
1 tablespoon olive oil, or to taste
sea salt and freshly ground black pepper, to taste

CABBAGE SALAD

¼ small white cabbage, very finely sliced with a mandoline
1 French shallot, peeled, thinly sliced
½ bunch coriander (cilantro), roughly chopped
1 jalapeno chilli, split lengthways, seeds removed, thinly sliced
juice of 1 lime
60 ml (2 fl oz/¼ cup) olive oil
sea salt and freshly ground black pepper, to taste

Skate wing

SKATES & RAYS

Skates (Rajidae family) and rays (Dasyatidae family), like their close cousins the sharks (see page 211), have skeletons of cartilage rather than bone. They're flat-bodied and kite-shaped, with broad fleshy pectoral fins or 'wings' – the part most commonly used for food. The main difference between skates and rays is that skates hatch from eggs while rays give birth to live young.

The fish most often sold as 'skate' are the shovelnose and fiddler rays found off southern Australia. The common species are the eastern shovelnose ray (*Aptychotrema rostrata*), the eastern fiddler ray (*Trygonorrhina fasciata*) and the white-spotted guitarfish (*Rhynchobatus australiae*).

SEASONALITY Year round; skate common in spring and summer
CATCHING METHOD Bottom otter trawl
COMMON LENGTH Wings: 15–30 cm (6–12 in)
COMMON WEIGHT Wings: 200–300 g (7–10½ oz)
IDENTIFIABLE FEATURES See below
SUSTAINABILITY Stock status good

SKATES & RAYS IN THE KITCHEN

Many different skates and rays are available in Australia, and although they offer quite different eating characteristics, they're often used in the same culinary applications. Their delicate, mild taste means they can handle many flavours. The wings are a textural delight, and their rippled flesh retains moisture while offering an unctuous, gelatinous eating experience. The wings contain cartilage, which some cultures enjoy eating, so give it a try. If that doesn't take your fancy, try boiling or poaching the wings before removing the flesh from the cartilage, then cooking further using a different method.

The most popular way to cook ray and skate flesh is floured or battered and pan-fried or deep-fried. But it also works well baked, poached and grilled (broiled). Some chefs believe the best method is to crumb and shallow-fry the wings, others like to steam them.

The wings are perfect for Asian curries and big-flavoured Asian sauces – particularly Thai and Malaysian – as the gelatinous nature of the flesh balances the spices well. Try them with black pepper, tamarind and lime, or forget Asian and cook them with butter and parsley.

SPECIAL STORAGE AND HANDLING
Fillet as soon as possible to avoid ammoniation
BEST COOKING METHODS Poached, shallow-fried, grilled (broiled)
TEXTURE Medium, firm, rippled (wing)
AROMA Very sweet, with notes of boiled potato
FLAVOUR Mild, with a sweet, vanilla-like note giving way to fresh steamed cabbage
APPEARANCE Flesh pale pink with distinctive long, linear flakes when raw; pearl white once cooked
YIELD Wings about 70% of whole weight
SUBSTITUTES None

Skate grenobloise

SERVES 4

80 g (2¾ oz/½ cup) rice flour
sea salt and freshly ground black pepper, to taste
4 skate wings, skin removed
80 g (2¾ oz) butter
2 teaspoons drained and well-rinsed capers in vinegar
1 lemon, peeled, pith removed, cut into segments (see note)
1 teaspoon roughly chopped flat-leaf (Italian) parsley

Place the rice flour on a plate and season well with salt and pepper.

Lay each skate wing in the flour to coat one side, then turn and coat the other side – only a light dusting is required, so tap the fish gently to remove any excess flour.

Heat a large cast-iron or heavy-based frying pan (or two smaller pans – it's essential that the fish is not overcrowded in the pan; see note) over medium–high heat and add half the butter. When it begins to bubble, add the skate wings and fry gently for 2 minutes. Using a spatula, turn and cook for a further 1 minute. Remove the skate from the pan, leaving the pan over high heat, and set the fish aside to rest for 1 minute. Transfer the rested skate to serving plates.

To make the grenobloise sauce, add the remaining butter to the hot pan with the capers, lemon segments and parsley. As soon as the butter turns brown and nutty and begins to foam, remove the pan from the heat.

Spoon the grenobloise sauce over the skate and serve.

NOTES: If you don't have a pan large enough for all the wings, or two smaller pans, cook them in two batches. If frying in batches, be sure to undercook the first batch slightly (as the fish will continue to cook when removed from the pan), then leave it to rest in a warm place while you cook the second batch.

As a variation, try replacing the fresh lemon with Preserved Lemon strips (page 461).

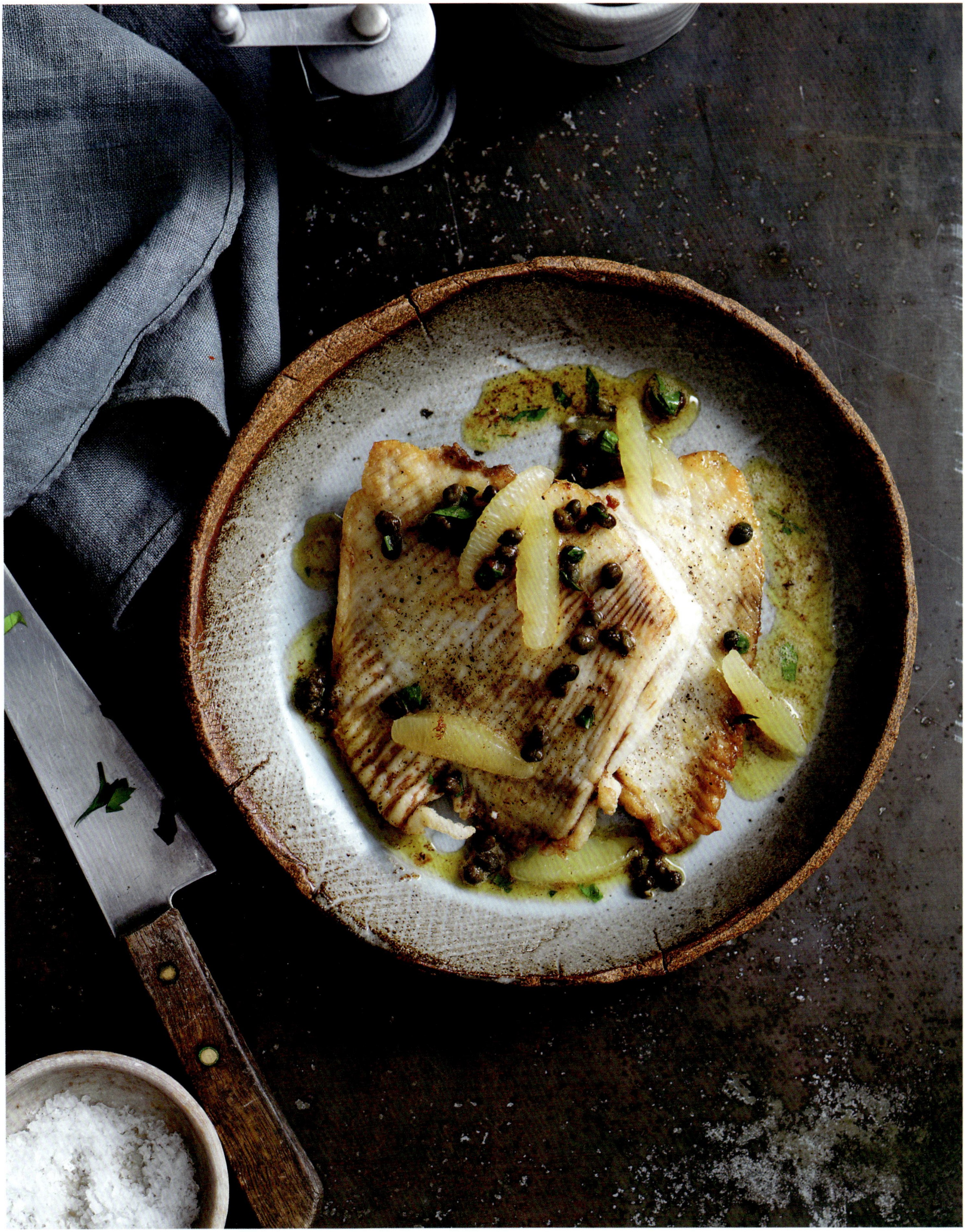

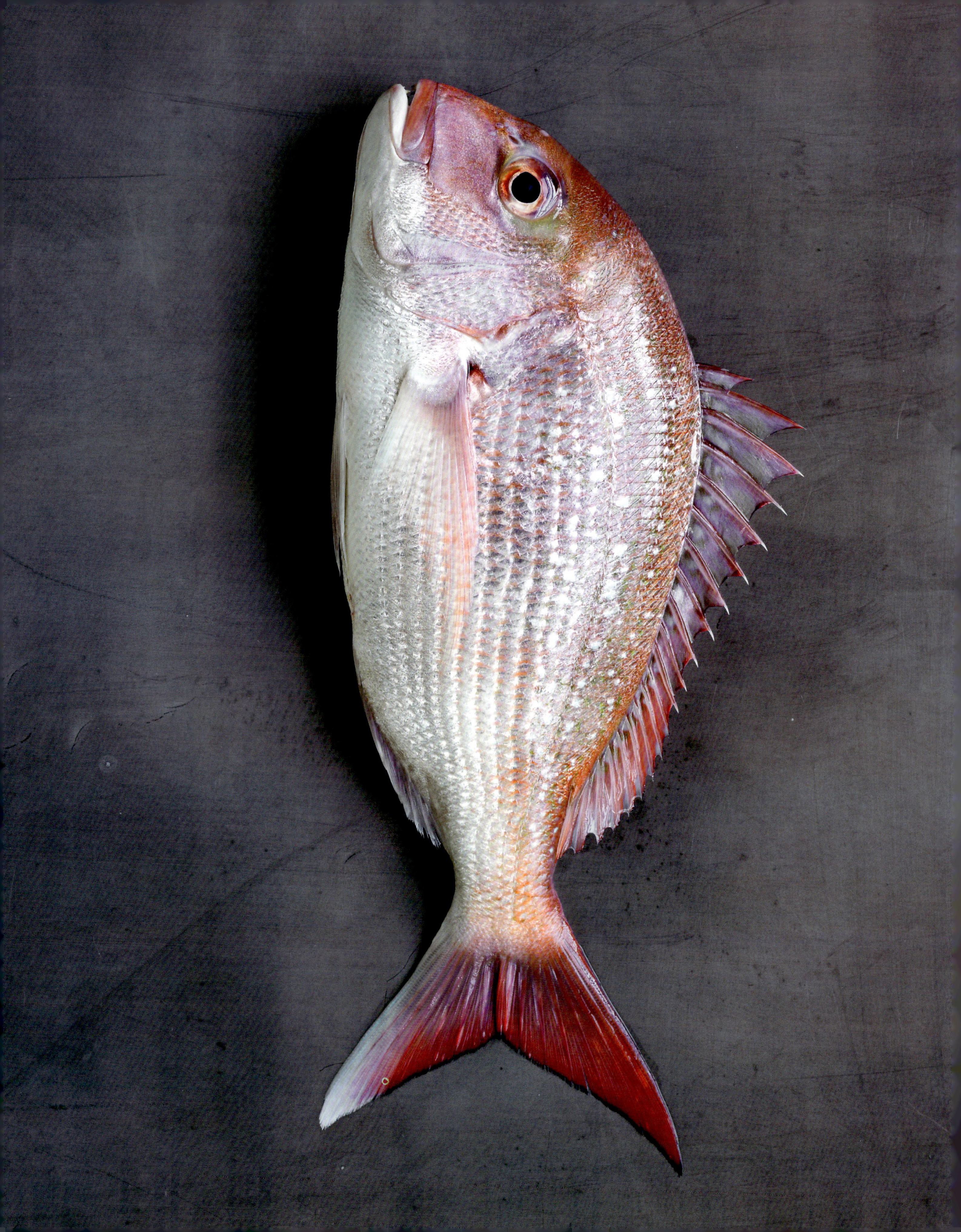

SNAPPER, PINK

Pink snapper (*Pagrus auratus*) is one of Australia's premier table fish and so is highly sought after. Its deliciously tender white flesh and sweet, mild flavour make it one of our most popular and versatile fish.

Despite its name, it belongs to the inshore bream family and is closely related to species such as black bream (see page 45) rather than true snappers, which we usually call tropical snappers (see page 227).

Pink snapper is a schooling fish, and tends to travel in large groups of similar size and age. It's found all around Australia and New Zealand, predominantly in temperate waters to 100 m (330 ft). It's caught year round off southern Australia, but is at its absolute peak in flavour and fat content in winter. The local commercial fisheries in South Australia and Western Australia are closed in November and September respectively.

Interest from Japan in the 1980s and 1990s made snapper fisheries adept at handling the fish for sashimi use, which means the quality is now consistently excellent. They're often ike jime spiked (see page 15) and ice-slurried at catch. Line-caught ike jime fish are especially good.

Pink snapper is a voracious opportunistic feeder with a preference for live fish, shellfish, sea urchins and jellyfish. When the firm raw flesh is cooked, it's moist, with coarse flakes and a mild, sweet, clean flavour.

Some claim the snapper from the south coast of New South Wales and Port Phillip Bay in Victoria to be the fattiest, but try telling that to a fisher from the Hauraki Gulf in New Zealand, the Spencer Gulf in South Australia or Shark Bay in Western Australia.

SEASONALITY WA: winter to summer; SA: peaks in mid-winter and high summer; NSW and Vic.: year round, with a peak in winter to spring; NZ: year round, with a peak in spring to summer

CATCHING METHODS Hook and line trolling, purse seine, mid-water trawl, trap

COMMON LENGTH 30–60 cm (12–24 in)

COMMON WEIGHT 500 g – 5 kg (1 lb 2 oz – 11 lb)

IDENTIFIABLE FEATURES Iridescent pink to burnished copper, with blue spots on back; pink fins; pale pink to creamy white bottom fins; large older males can have a lump on nose

SUSTAINABILITY Stock status good

PINK SNAPPER IN THE KITCHEN

The smaller the snapper, the sweeter its flesh; the larger or older the snapper, the earthier and more brackish its flavour. A small snapper at 800 g – 1 kg (1 lb 12 oz – 2 lb 4 oz) is amazing raw, as sashimi, carpaccio or sushi. The best size for cooking whole is 2–3 kg (4 lb 8 oz – 6 lb 12 oz). To cook on the barbecue, a 3 kg fish is the size you want. When they get to 3–4 kg (6 lb 12 oz – 8 lb 13 oz), the flesh starts to be denser and heavy, almost like a steak, which is ideal for fillets pan-fried with crisp skin. At (13 lb 4 oz), snapper will taste quite different because it's older and its diet is different.

To barbecue whole snapper, stuff it with fragrant herbs and lemon, maybe even fennel, then wrap it in foil or baking paper. Salt-baked snapper is an absolute treat – mix salt and egg whites together, cover the entire fish, bake, then peel the salt back for an intense, beautifully steamed fish. Filleted and pan-fried with crisp skin, it really shines – it can hold a weight until it's cooked all the way through. It's even one of the rare fish that can be a little overcooked. Of course, it's better not to overcook any fish, but if you like your fish a bit beyond opaque, snapper is for you, because the flesh will still stand up to being a bit overdone.

BEST COOKING METHODS Whole, steamed, barbecued, pan-fried with crisp skin (fillets, see page 437), poached, curried

TEXTURE Firm, with coarse flakes when raw; fleshy and moist once cooked

AROMA Clean oceanic aroma, with notes of fresh seaweed and asparagus

FLAVOUR Intensely sweet, with a roast-vegetable savouriness and lasting iodine zing

APPEARANCE Flesh pale white with pink hues when raw; arctic white once cooked

YIELD Boneless fillet about 45% of whole weight

SUBSTITUTES Bream, jackass morwong, morwong, red emperor, tropical snapper

Snapper with buttered greens

Bring a small saucepan of salted water to the boil over high heat.

To prepare the snapper fillets for pan-frying with crisp skin, lay them on a work surface and dust the skin sides with the rice flour. Place each fillet, flesh side down, on a sheet of baking paper large enough to cover the fillet.

Heat a large cast-iron or heavy-based frying pan (or two smaller pans – it's essential that the fish is not overcrowded in the pan; see note) over medium–high heat and add the ghee. When the pan is hot and the ghee translucent, place the fillets in the pan, skin side down, leaving the paper on the flesh side. Place a 1 kg (2 lb 4 oz) weight – such as a heavy pot or another pan – on top of the fillets and cook for 4 minutes, lifting the weight once or twice then moving the fillets gently around the pan so they don't burn. (Cooking times may vary depending on the size of the fish from which the fillets were cut; for more information, see page 437.)

Reduce the heat to low and leave the fish, skin side down, until ready to serve.

Meanwhile, blanch the snow peas and sugarsnaps in the boiling water for about 1 minute, until bright green and just tender. Drain immediately using a colander, then transfer to a small bowl. Add the butter and salt, then toss to coat.

Arrange the buttered greens on serving plates. Pour any remaining butter over the top and garnish with the tarragon.

Remove the weight from the pan and the paper from the fish. Using a spatula, gently flip each fillet over to quickly seal the other side.

Remove the fish from the pan and place on the plates, skin side up, beside the greens, then add a lemon cheek. Sprinkle the snapper skin with extra sea salt and serve immediately.

NOTE: If you don't have a pan large enough for all the fillets, or two smaller pans, cook the fish in two batches. Keep the first batch warm while you cook the second.

SERVES 4

4 × 200 g (7 oz) snapper fillets, skin on, pin-boned

2 tablespoons rice flour

80 ml (2½ fl oz/⅓ cup) ghee (see note page 26)

200 g (7 oz) mixed snow peas (mangetout) and sugarsnap peas, trimmed

40 g (1½ oz) butter

pinch of sea salt, plus extra to serve

4 tarragon sprigs, to garnish

lemon cheeks, to serve (see note page 144)

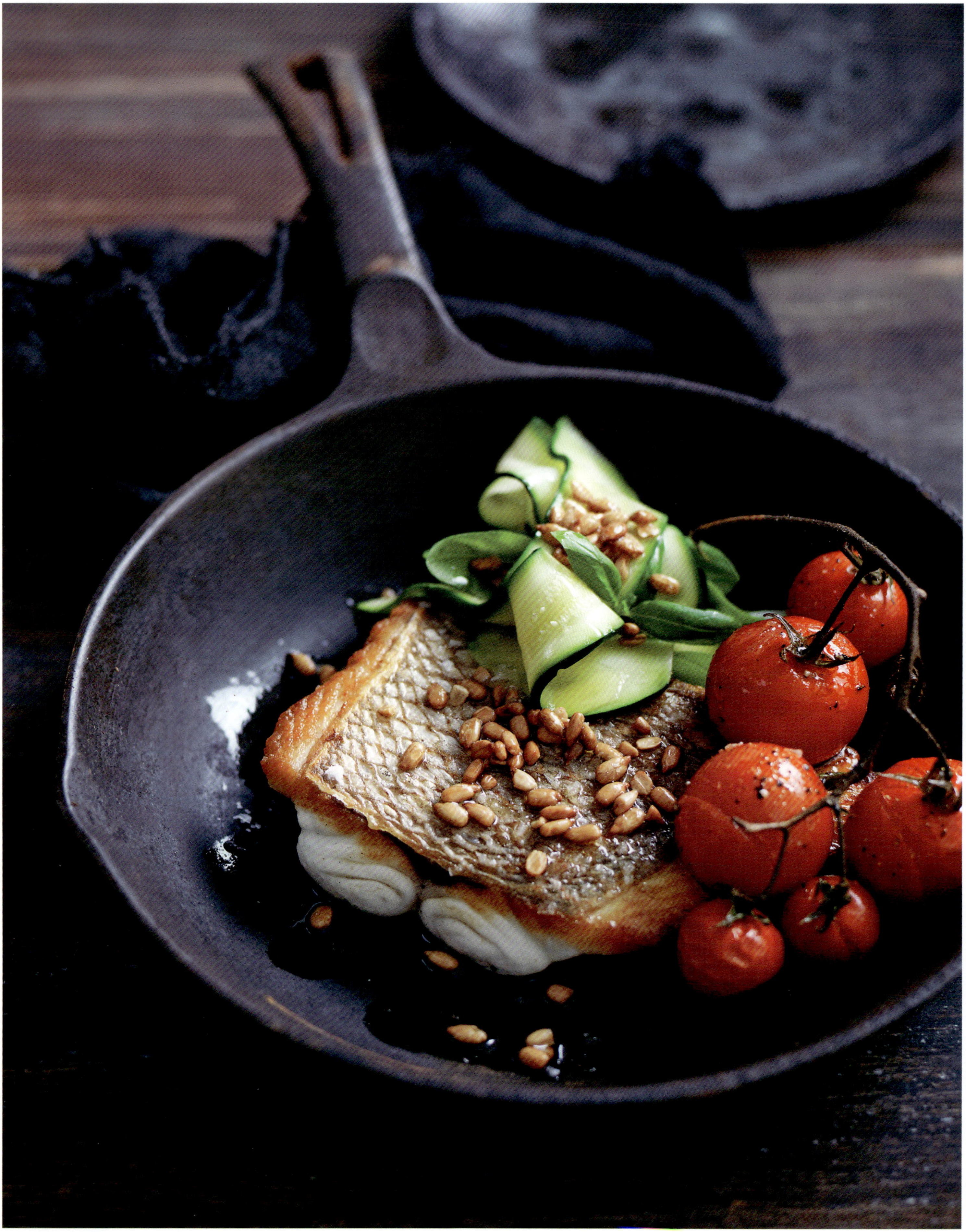

Pan-roasted snapper with cherry tomatoes, zucchini and basil

Preheat the oven to 180°C (350°F).

Heat a large, shallow frying pan over high heat. Add the cherry tomatoes, splash with the lemon oil and sprinkle with sea salt. Pan-fry for 3–4 minutes, until the skins burst, then remove from the heat and set aside.

Lay the snapper fillets on a work surface and dust the skin side of each fillet with the rice flour. Place each fillet, flesh side down, on a sheet of baking paper large enough to cover the fillet.

Heat a large cast-iron or heavy-based ovenproof frying pan (or two smaller pans – it's essential that the fish is not overcrowded in the pan; see note) over medium–high heat, then add the ghee and the butter. When the pan is hot and the butter has melted, place the fillets in the pan, skin side down, leaving the paper on the flesh side. Place a 1 kg (2 lb 4 oz) weight – such as a heavy pot or another pan – on top of the fillets in the pan and cook the fish for 2 minutes. Remove the weight, transfer the pan to the oven and cook the fillets for 4 minutes. Remove from the oven and discard the paper. Using a spatula, gently turn the fillets over and set aside to rest for 2 minutes. (Cooking times may vary depending on the size of the fish from which the fillets were cut; for more information, see page 437.)

Return the tomatoes to the stove over a medium–low heat and add the zucchini and basil. Cook for 2 minutes.

Place each snapper fillet on a serving plate with some tomatoes, zucchini and basil on top of the fish. Scatter over the sunflower seeds and serve immediately.

NOTE: If you don't have a pan large enough for all the fillets, or two smaller pans, cook the fish in two batches. Keep the first batch warm while you cook the second.

SERVES 4

4 bunches cherry tomatoes on the vine, 6–8 tomatoes on each
60 ml (2 fl oz/¼ cup) lemon oil (see note page 25)
sea salt, to taste
4 × 200 g (7 oz) snapper fillets, skin on, pin-boned
rice flour, for dusting
2 tablespoons ghee (see note page 26)
40 g (1½ oz) butter
2 zucchini (courgettes), shaved into ribbons (using a mandoline or vegetable peeler)
1 handful basil leaves
55 g (2 oz/⅓ cup) oven-roasted sunflower seeds

Snapper sushi and sashimi

SERVES 4

Japanese soy sauce, to serve
wasabi paste, to serve

SNAPPER SUSHI
145 g (5¼ oz) cooked Sushi Rice (page 463)
12 × 12 g (½ oz) pieces snapper fillet, scaled
daikon and hot pepper paste, to serve (see note)
2 small shiso leaves, finely shredded

SNAPPER SASHIMI
480 g (1 lb 1 oz) snapper fillet, scaled
sea salt, as required
boiling water, as required

To prepare the sushi, mould the sushi rice into 12 mounds (see page 463). Lay a piece of snapper on each, then top with a tiny drop of daikon and hot pepper paste and a little shiso.

To make the sashimi, use a very sharp knife to lightly score the skin and fat layers of the fillet. Place it on a wire rack over a dish, then lightly salt the skin and leave for 30 minutes. Gently spoon boiling water over the skin, taking care to avoid the flesh.

Slice the fillet into 24 pieces, each about 20 g (¾ oz) and 5 mm (¼ in) thick (see note).

Place the sushi and sashimi pieces on a serving plate and serve with Japanese soy sauce and wasabi.

NOTES: Daikon and hot pepper paste is a bright red paste available in bottles at Japanese or Asian supermarkets.
   For advice on slicing fish for sashimi, see page 434.

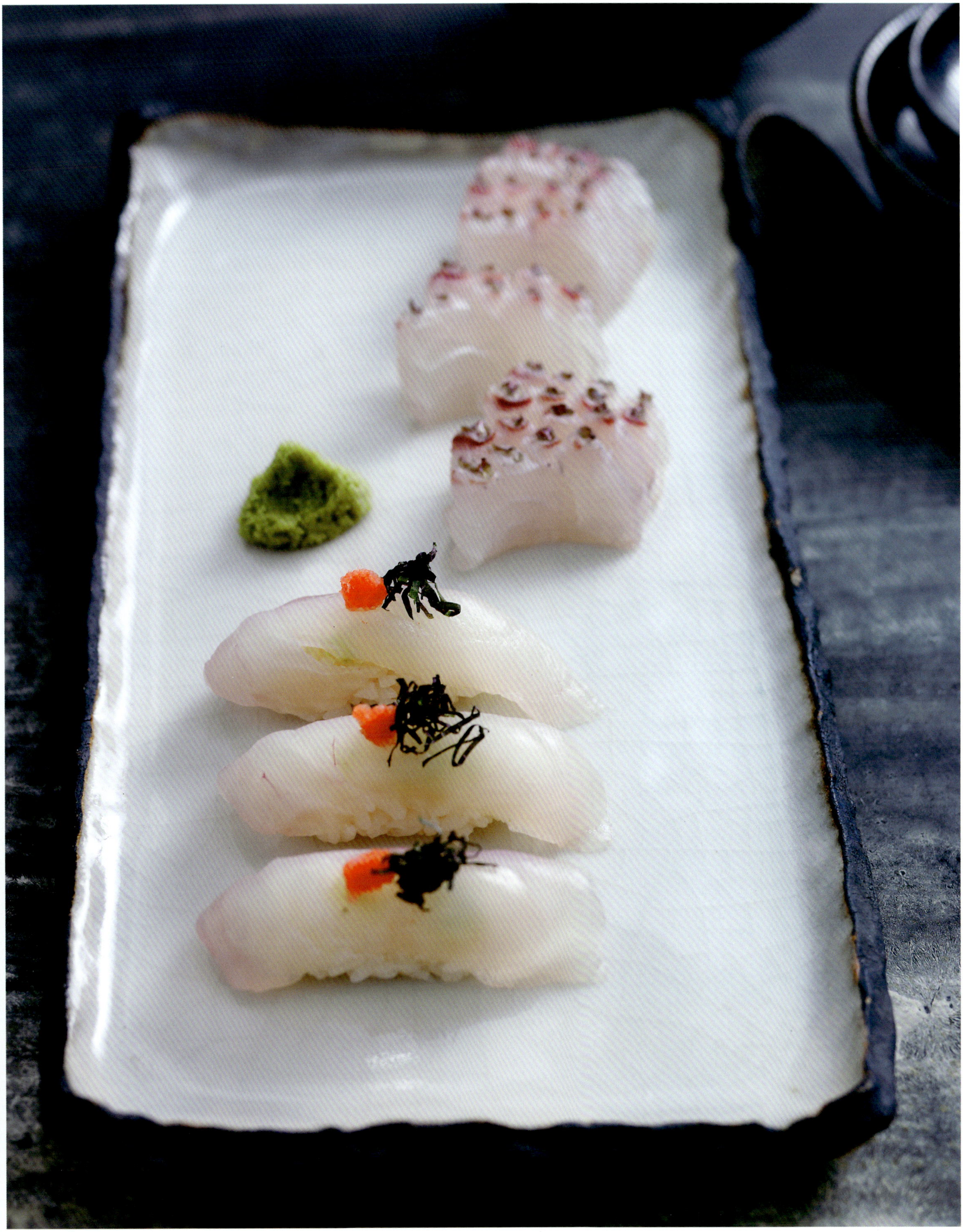

Ruby snapper

SNAPPER, TROPICAL

Tropical snapper is a generic term for a range of sea perches, with approximately 60 different species in Australia. Their flavours and textures are as varied as the numerous species. While some are sweet, clean and mild, others are more robust, sometimes with earthy notes, even of the forest floor. The texture can also range from soft and flaking to firm and almost tough if poorly handled.

The jobfish are typified by their mild sweetness and broad scalloping flesh, while the goldband snapper (*Pristipomoides multidens*) is slightly firmer and the saddletail snapper (*Lutjanus malabaricus*) can be positively tough. It's important to know the provenance and history of the tropical fish you're using – how it was caught, where it's from and how old it is. As a generalisation, line-caught fish will have the best eating qualities, especially raw, where their natural sweetness is most obvious. Other species include ruby snapper (*Etelis carbunculus*), king snapper or rosy jobfish (*Pristipomoides filamentosus*), crimson snapper (*Lutjanus erythropterus*), one-spot snapper (*Lutjanus monostigma*), Spanish-flag jobfish (*Lutjanus carponotatus*) and green jobfish (*Aprion virescens*).

The Australian goldband fishery, based across the northern coastline, is a shining example of a well-managed, sustainable fishery. The majority of the fishing uses traps and balloon trawls, with technology and crews geared to preserving the quality of the fish.

SEASONALITY Year round; more consistent from autumn to late spring
CATCHING METHODS Trap, balloon trawl
COMMON LENGTH Up to 70 cm (27½ in)
COMMON WEIGHT Up to 5 kg (11 lb)
IDENTIFIABLE FEATURES There are two main categories: jobfish types (goldband and king snappers, and green jobfish); and saddletail types (saddletail, crimson, one-spot and Spanish-flag snappers). Jobfish: elongated round body, large forked tail, bright red to dull ochre; saddletail: short, stocky, deep from shoulder to belly, tail smaller and fuller.
SUSTAINABILITY Sustainably managed by quota

Ruby snapper en papillote with zucchini, tomato and garlic

SERVES 4

3 garlic cloves, peeled
20 g (¾ oz) butter
½ teaspoon caster (superfine) sugar
1 tablespoon Fish Stock (page 457)
8 baby zucchini (courgettes), untrimmed, cut in half lengthways
16 slow-roasted roma (plum) tomato halves (see note page 90)
4 × 200 g (7 oz) ruby snapper fillets, skin on, pin-boned
10 g (¼ oz) butter, softened
sea salt and freshly ground black pepper, to taste

Preheat the oven to 200°C (400°F).

Caramelise the garlic by heating a small frying pan over medium–low heat and adding the butter. When the butter melts and begins to froth, add the garlic and toss to coat. Sprinkle with the sugar and keep tossing for 3 minutes, or until the garlic is golden. Add the fish stock, then continue tossing and cooking the garlic for 5–7 minutes, until tender. Cool, then chop finely.

Place four 30 × 50 cm (12 × 20 in) sheets of baking paper side by side on a baking tray.

Layer the vegetables and fish on the centre of each sheet, starting with some zucchini, then tomato and garlic, followed by a snapper fillet, topped with more zucchini and tomato, a little more garlic and ½ teaspoon of butter. Season with salt and pepper.

To make parcels, bring the long sides of the paper together and fold over twice, creating an air pocket. Make small folds to hold the short edges together firmly enough to seal.

Place the tray with the parcels in the oven and bake for 15 minutes.

To serve, place the sealed parcels on plates. Alternatively, undo the parcels and transfer the snapper and vegetables to serving plates, drizzling all the cooking liquids over. Open the parcels with care, as the escaping steam can burn.

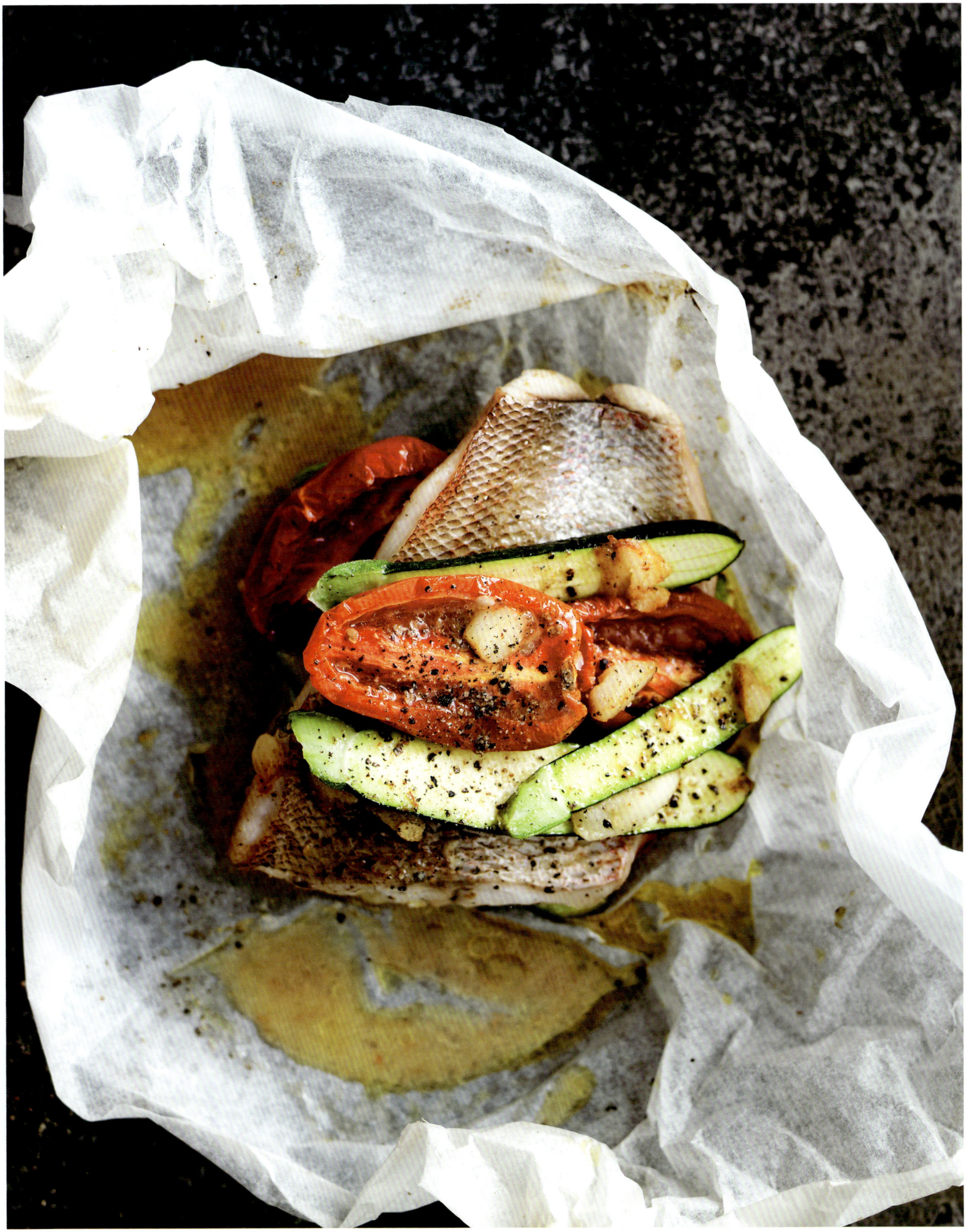

Classic fish pie

SERVES 6–8

800 g (1 lb 12 oz) all-purpose potatoes (such as desiree)

150 g (5½ oz) butter

170 ml (5½ fl oz/⅔ cup) milk

80 ml (2½ fl oz/⅓ cup) thin (pouring) cream

sea salt and freshly ground white pepper, to taste

2 tablespoons extra virgin olive oil

1 leek, white part only, well washed, thinly sliced

3 garlic cloves, peeled and finely chopped

1.2 kg (2 lb 10 oz) tropical snapper fillet, skin removed, pin-boned, cut into large pieces about 40 g (1½ oz) each

125 ml (4 fl oz/½ cup) dry white wine

400 ml (14 fl oz) Fish Stock (page 457)

50 g (1¾ oz/⅓ cup) plain (all-purpose) flour

1 tablespoon dijon mustard

2 tablespoons finely chopped mixed herbs (parsley, chervil and tarragon)

140 g (5 oz/2⅓ cups) panko (Japanese-style) breadcrumbs mixed with 60 g (2¼ oz) melted butter

Preheat the oven to 180°C (350°F).

Fill a steamer or double boiler with water and bring to the boil over high heat. Place the potatoes in the steamer tray and cook until tender (see note).

When the potatoes are nearly cooked, combine one-third of the butter, half the milk and all the cream in a small saucepan and season with salt and white pepper. Place over medium heat and bring to a very gentle simmer without boiling. Reduce the heat to low to keep the mixture warm.

Remove the potatoes from the steamer and peel when comfortable to handle but still hot. Pass the potatoes through a ricer or food mill into a medium bowl. Slowly add the milk mixture and stir to make a well-combined, smooth mash, taking care not to over-mix or the potatoes may become gluey. Set aside.

Heat a large frying pan over medium–low heat with another one-third of the butter and the olive oil. When the butter has melted, add the leek and garlic, then cook, without colouring, for about 5 minutes, stirring constantly, until the leek is sweet and soft. Add the snapper and wine, season with salt and white pepper, stir well and bring to a simmer. Cook for 5 minutes. Remove from the heat and transfer the fish mixture to a colander to drain. Set aside.

Combine the stock and remaining milk in a small saucepan and bring to a gentle simmer over medium–high heat. Reduce the heat to low.

Place a medium saucepan over medium heat and melt the remaining butter. Slowly add the flour, then stir constantly for 2 minutes, or until the paste begins to smell nutty. Gradually add the hot stock mixture and keep stirring until a smooth, thick sauce forms – this is béchamel sauce. Add the mustard and herbs and season with salt and white pepper.

Add the fish mixture to the sauce, stirring gently to combine. Transfer to a medium pie dish and top with the mashed potato. Use a fork to spread the potato evenly over the fish filling. Sprinkle with the breadcrumbs and bake for 15–20 minutes, until the filling is heated through and the topping golden.

NOTE: Steaming the potatoes rather than boiling them will produce a beautifully dry mash that will crisp up wonderfully as a pie top.

Swordfish fillet

SWORDFISH

The swordfish (*Xiphias gladius*), sometimes known as the broadbill, has moist, meaty flesh that's sweet and delicate, mild yet flavoursome – the belly rivals the finest triple cream. Popular in Australia since the early 1990s, swordfish flesh adapts to a range of cooking styles and methods.

Swordfish are found throughout the world's oceans, in temperatures of 5–25°C (40–80°F). They make daily migrations to great depths, from near the surface at night down to more than 1000 m (3300 ft) during the day. They mostly use the cover of darkness and their superior vision to locate and catch their food, which can range from fish to squid, prawns (shrimp) and crabs. Their specific diet can influence the colour of the flesh.

The Australian swordfish fishery is the world's only certified sustainable swordfish fishery. The quality is second to none. Most is caught off the east coast of Australia, from the Coral Sea in the north to southern New South Wales.

SEASONALITY Year round, with a peak on the east coast in spring–summer
CATCHING METHOD Pelagic longline
COMMON LENGTH 200–400 m (78¾–157½ in)
COMMON WEIGHT 10–100 kg (22–220 lb)
IDENTIFIABLE FEATURES Elongated, rounded body, toothless and scaleless in adulthood
SUSTAINABILITY Highly managed by quota; some fisheries certified by Marine Stewardship Council

SWORDFISH IN THE KITCHEN

Swordfish is most commonly available as fillets. If you hold a premium piece of swordfish up to the light, it will look like thick glass. Japanese chefs regard the belly, served raw with ponzu sauce (page 455), as one of the great pleasures of the sea. It has a completely different texture from the rest of the fish – very firm, with a lot of bite.

It can take high heat, so it's perfect barbecued and charred. Drizzle with olive oil and lemon juice, and you have a sensational meal. It's mostly sold as a double loin cut, but it's nicer to have two separate loins and strip off the belly to eat raw. Never eat the skin – it'd make a better handbag.

Because it's meaty, with a high fat content and a mild flavour, the texture is vital. Marinate it in garlic, lemon and olive oil – it soaks up flavours.

It works well roasted with caramelised vegetables – celeriac, carrots – and nuts. Although it's wonderful with ponzu sauce and honey, soy sauce is too salty, drawing the moisture out of the fish and curing it.

BEST COOKING METHODS Raw, grilled (broiled), barbecued
TEXTURE Firm, tightly grained
AROMA Lightly meaty, with notes of egg white
FLAVOUR Rich, deep, with a mild sweet aftertaste
APPEARANCE Flesh pearl white to pink, depending on the season and the fish
YIELD Flesh 100% of loin weight
SUBSTITUTES Warehou

Seared swordfish with caramelised pickled onions and charred eggplant

SERVES 4

1 large or 2 small Japanese eggplants (aubergines)
sea salt and freshly ground black pepper, to taste
80 ml (2½ fl oz/⅓ cup) ghee (see note page 26)
8 pickled onions, cut in half
4 × 200 g (7 oz) swordfish fillets
4 thyme sprigs, to serve
lemon oil, to serve (see note page 25)

Cut the Japanese eggplant lengthways into eight long, thin slices. Sprinkle lightly with salt and set aside for a minimum of 1 hour – this draws moisture from the eggplant and helps it colour and crisp well when cooked.

Preheat the oven to 200°C (400°F).

Heat a medium frying pan over medium heat and add half the ghee. When the ghee begins to smoke, add the pickled onions and eggplant. Allow the vegetables to caramelise on one side only for 1–2 minutes, until golden. Remove from the heat and set aside in a warm place.

Heat a large cast-iron or heavy-based frying pan over medium–high heat (or two smaller pans – it's essential that the fish is not overcrowded in the pan; see note) and add the remaining ghee. When the ghee is smoking, add the swordfish. Reduce the heat to medium and caramelise the fish well on one side. Turn the fish gently using a spatula, then transfer the pan to the oven for 4 minutes. (Cooking times may vary depending on the size of the fish from which the fillets were cut; for more information, see page 437.)

Remove the fish from the oven and rest for 1 minute. Cut each fillet into slices 1 cm (½ in) thick, to make about six slices per portion.

Place the swordfish slices on serving plates with the caramelised vegetables. Top each plate with a thyme sprig, then season with lemon oil, salt and pepper.

NOTE: If you don't have a pan large enough for all the fillets, or two smaller pans, cook the fish in two batches. Keep the first batch warm while you cook the second.

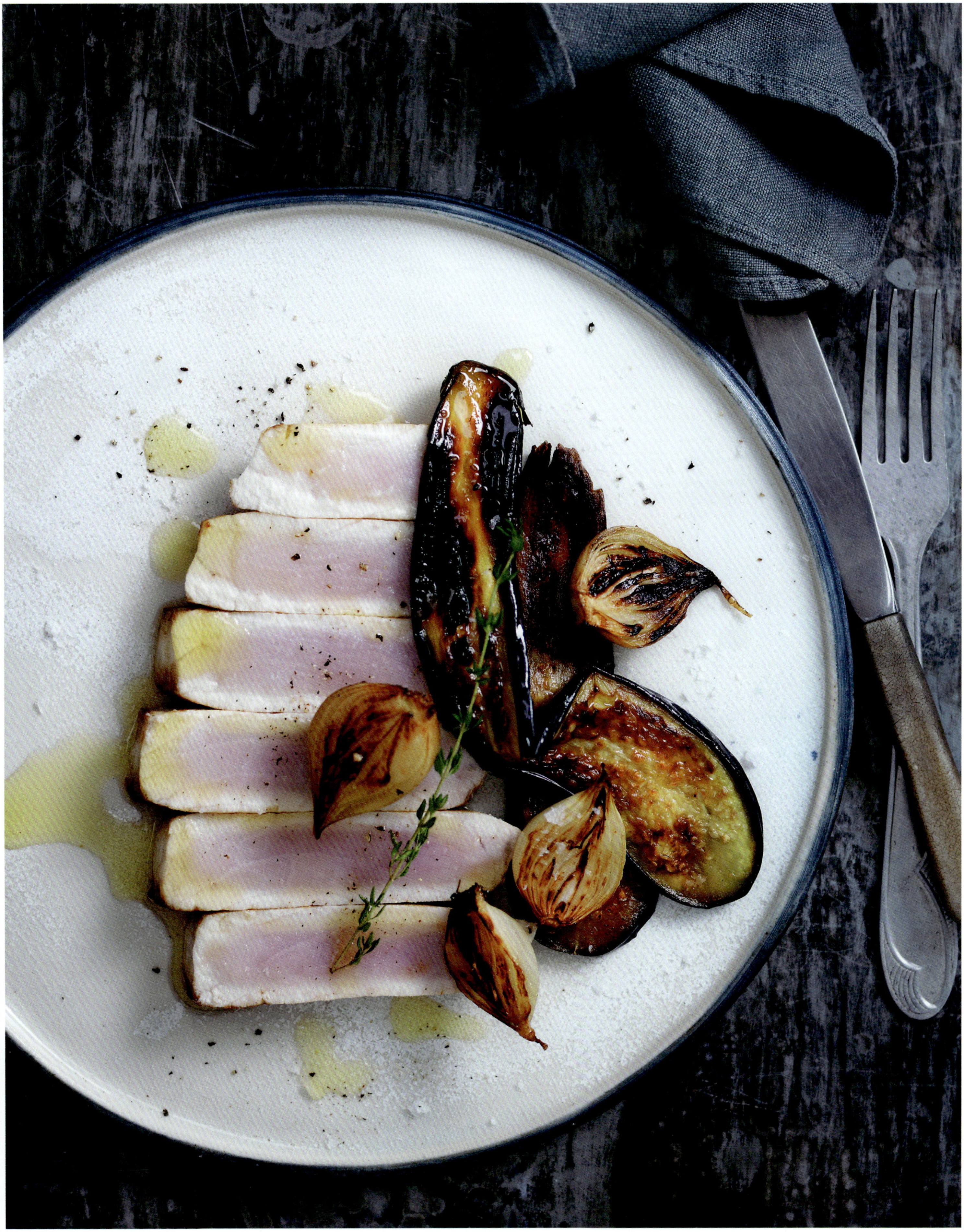

Toothfish fillet

TOOTHFISH

From its home in the freezing 1–5°C (35–40°F) subantarctic waters, the Antarctic toothfish (*Dissostichus mawsoni*) has become one of the true luxury seafoods. It attracts attention – good and bad – wherever and whenever it's served. It's closely related to the sought-after Patagonian toothfish (*Dissostichus eleginoides*), which is known in the United States as Chilean sea bass, in Japan as mero and in Argentina as merluza negra.

It's a mid-water species, generally caught in depths of 70–2000 m (230–6500 ft), but is occasionally found on the sea floor. It ranges throughout the southernmost parts of the Atlantic, Pacific and Indian oceans, mostly at latitudes of 40–60 degrees. The Australian toothfish fishery operates off Heard and McDonald islands in Australian territorial waters at the far south of the Indian Ocean in the subantarctic.

The diet of adult toothfish consists of fish, crustaceans and in particular the Antarctic bay shrimp, which gives them a deliciously rich and tasty flesh. Unlike most other deep- and cold-water fish, the toothfish doesn't have a swim bladder to maintain its buoyancy in the water. Instead, it uses oil. This oil adds to the moisture and flavour of the fish when cooked, and makes it the best natural fish source of omega-3 fatty acids.

The Australian toothfish fishery is highly managed and regarded as the most sustainable in the world. The state-of-the-art boats must report their catch regularly and depart the fishing area when the total allowable catch (TAC) limit is reached.

SEASONALITY May–November
CATCHING METHODS Bottom longline
COMMON LENGTH 100–180 cm (39½–71 in)
COMMON WEIGHT 7–10 kg (15–22 lb)
IDENTIFIABLE FEATURES Elongated body, large scales, ferocious-looking protruding lower jaw
SUSTAINABILITY Highly sustainable and strictly managed by quota; the world's first carbon-neutral fishery

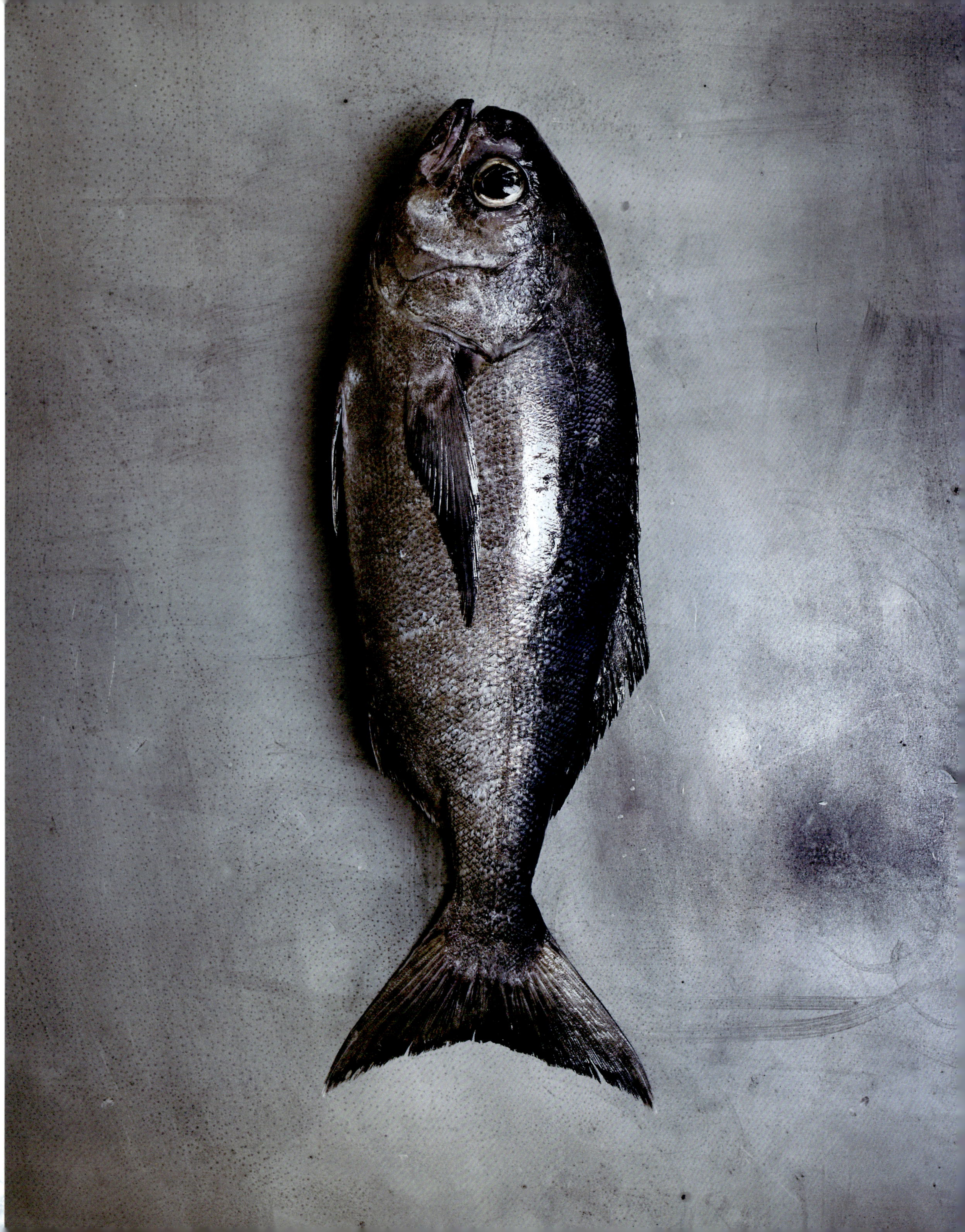

TREVALLA, BLUE-EYE

Also known as big-eye, big-eye trevalla, blue-eye, blue-eye cod, blue-nose, bluenose warehou and even Antarctic butterfish, blue-eye trevalla (*Hyperoglyphe antarctica*) is a big, thick-bodied finfish with a blunt snout, small scales and large, round blue eyes. It's caught in the deep-sea trenches off the continental shelves of Australia and New Zealand. In winter it carries extra fat as protection from the cold Antarctic currents.

Its mild-flavoured flesh makes excellent eating, and it's the darling of the restaurant business. Chefs enjoy it for its versatile broad-flaked flesh, which is firm, white and deliciously sweet.

SEASONALITY Year round; best in winter
CATCHING METHODS Dropline, bottom longline, some mid-water trawl and Danish seine
COMMON LENGTH 30–100 cm (12–39½ in)
COMMON WEIGHT 2–15 kg (4 lb 8 oz – 33 lb)
IDENTIFIABLE FEATURES Silvery with a steel-blue back to pinkish brown with a purplish tinge, eyes deep blue with a golden ring
SUSTAINABILITY Regarded as sustainable; managed by quota in Australia and NZ

BLUE-EYE TREVALLA IN THE KITCHEN

Blue-eye trevalla is often poorly used, but it's great in a curry or grilled (broiled) as medallions. For medallions use a largish fish, of 4–6 kg (8 lb 13 oz – 13 lb). Cut into fillets, then round off the loin. Paint with butter and grill slowly.

It's quite lean, so it's best cooked lightly, even just cooked through. It's not the best fish for pan-frying with crisp skin, but it's good to cook it with the skin and scales on to protect the flesh, then remove the skin before serving. It's ideal for cooking with potato scales (see overleaf), which crisp up and replicate skin and scales. Poach it in a consommé, broth, tomato sauce or curry, or grill it very lightly on its skin under a weight.

It's not great raw; it's better filleted. The tail of a bigger fish is lovely roasted on the bone.

SPECIAL STORAGE AND HANDLING Seek translucent flesh with no tears, gaping or seeping moisture
BEST COOKING METHODS Poached, grilled (broiled), steamed
TEXTURE Soft to medium-firm with a broad flake
AROMA Sweet, fresh, with seaweed notes
FLAVOUR Rich umami, with a long, sweet finish
APPEARANCE Fillets translucent white-grey when raw; pearl white once cooked;
YIELD Flesh about 40% of whole weight
SUBSTITUTES Bass groper and bar cod, blue warehou, hapuka, pink snapper

Blue-eye trevalla roasted on potato scales, with baby beetroot and ricotta

SERVES 4

16 baby beetroot (beets), scrubbed
4 × 200 g (7 oz) blue-eye trevalla fillets, skin on, pin-boned
4 small, all-purpose potatoes (such as desiree), peeled and sliced as thinly as possible (preferably with a mandoline)
100 ml (3½ fl oz) ghee (see note page 26)
80 g (2¾ oz/⅓ cup) ricotta
2 cm (¾ in) piece fresh horseradish
sea salt, to taste
2 tablespoons lemon oil, to serve (see note page 25)

Preheat the oven to 200°C (400°F).

Bring a medium saucepan of salted water to the boil over high heat. Add the beetroot and return to the boil. Reduce the heat to medium and simmer for 30–40 minutes, until the beetroot are just cooked through. Remove from the heat and drain. Peel the beetroot when comfortable to handle, but still hot, discarding the skins, then set the beetroot aside in a warm place.

Place the trevalla fillets on a baking tray, skin side down. Arrange the potato slices on top of each fillet in slightly overlapping layers, to resemble fish scales (see page 437). Turn the fish over, holding the potatoes in place, and press down gently to ensure the 'scales' stick. Trim around each fillet to remove any excess potato.

Heat a large heavy-based, ovenproof frying pan over medium–high heat until a haze appears. Add the ghee. Gently add the fillets, potato side down, and fry until the potato is lightly golden. Transfer the pan to the oven and cook for a further 4 minutes. Remove the pan from the oven and gently remove the skin from each fillet. Turn the fillets over to sear quickly in the still-hot pan, then leave to rest for 1 minute before serving. (Cooking times may vary depending on the size of the fish from which the fillets were cut; for more information, see page 437.)

Serve the fish, potato scales up, with the beetroot on the side. Top the beetroot with a scoop of ricotta then, using a microplane or fine grater, grate fresh horseradish over the ricotta and fish. Season with salt and finish with a splash of lemon oil.

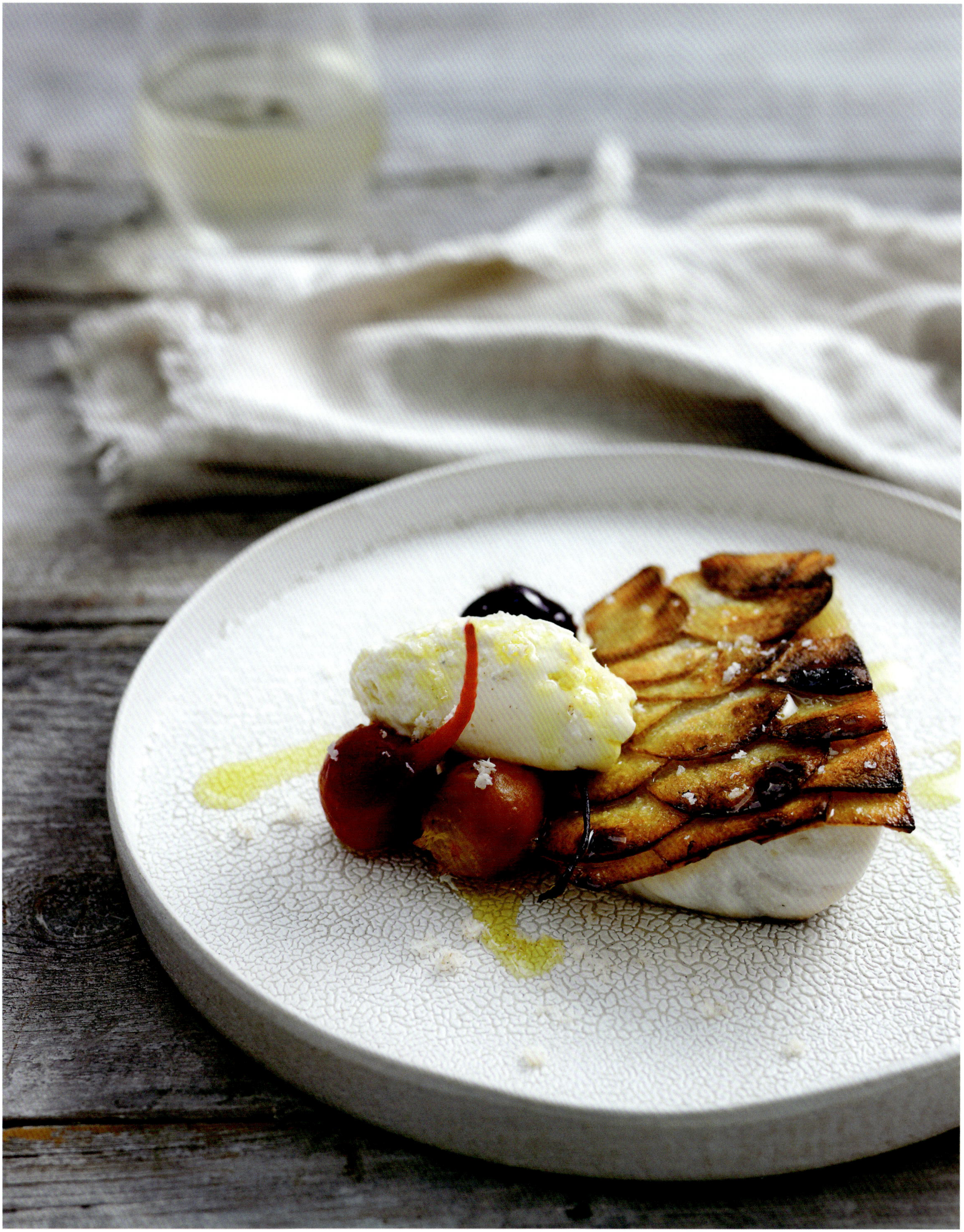

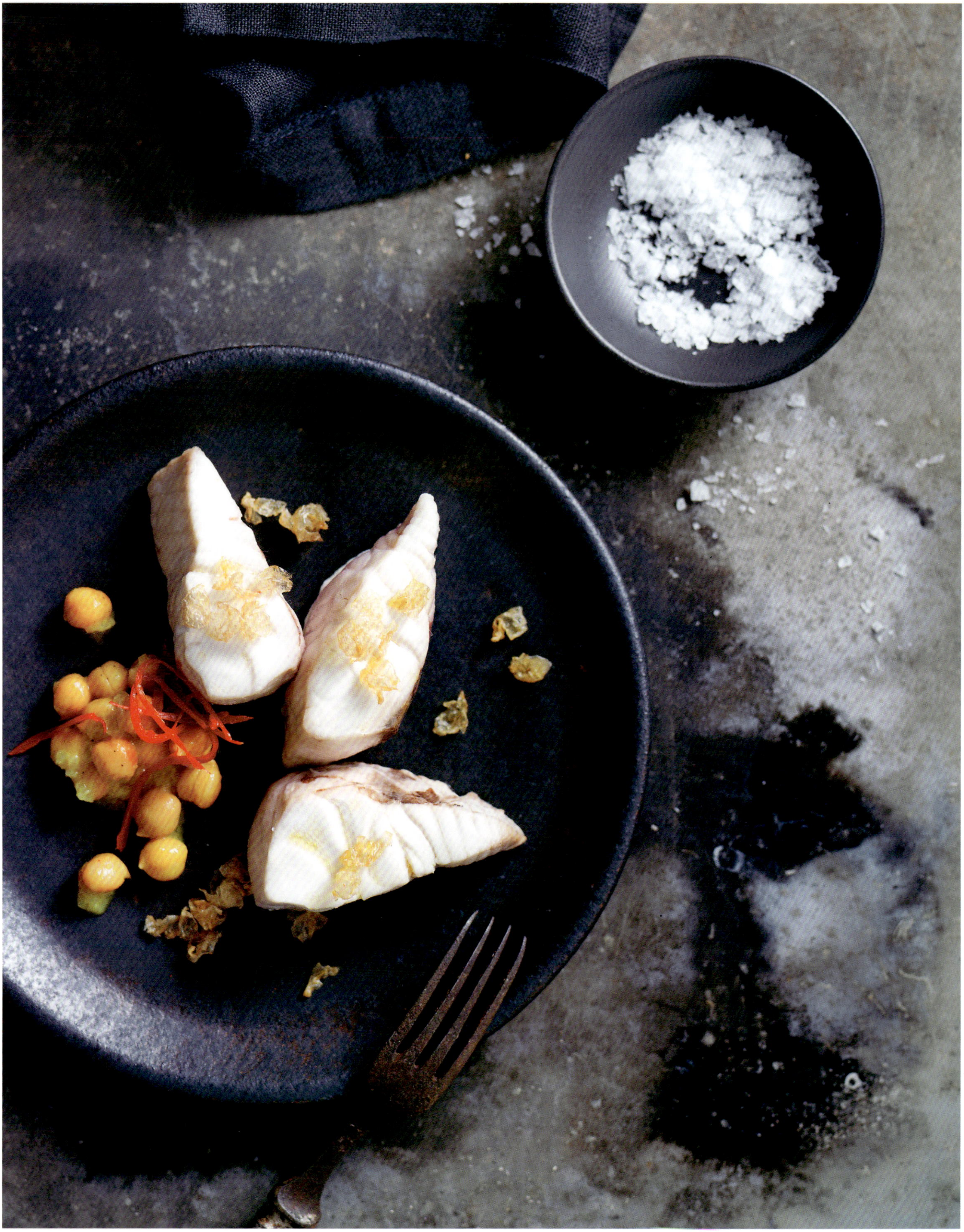

Grilled blue-eye trevalla medallions with curried chickpeas

Preheat an oven grill (broiler) to high.

For the curried chickpeas, drain the chickpeas, taking care to retain any separated husks. Lay the husks on paper towel to dry.

Place the soaked chickpeas in a small saucepan with the quarter onion and the carrot. Cover with cold water and bring to the boil over medium–high heat. Reduce the heat to medium and simmer until cooked and tender, about 1 hour. Drain the chickpeas and discard the cooking liquid.

Heat the 2 tablespoons of vegetable oil in a small saucepan over very low heat. Add the half onion and the garlic, then cover and cook, without colouring, for about 5 minutes, until soft and sweet. Add the curry powder and cook for a further 1 minute. Add the chickpeas then the fish stock and increase the heat to medium. Bring the stock to a gentle boil and simmer for 10 minutes. Season with salt and pepper.

Heat the remaining vegetable oil in a small saucepan over medium–high heat until just smoking. Add the dried chickpea husks and fry until crisp. Using a slotted spoon, transfer the husks to paper towel to drain. Season with sea salt and set aside.

Place the blue-eye medallions on a baking tray and set on the lowest shelf of the oven, as far from the grill element as possible. Grill for 4 minutes, turning at the 2 minute mark. (Cooking times may vary depending on the size of the fish from which the fillets were cut; for more information, see page 437.)

Remove the grilled blue-eye medallions from the oven and transfer to serving plates. Season the fish lightly with sea salt. Spoon the curried chickpeas beside the fish and top with the salted red chilli. Scatter the dried chickpea husks over the fish.

NOTE: To make salted red chilli, split 120 g (4¼ oz) of long red chillies lengthways and remove the seeds. Cut the chillies into a rough julienne, place in a bowl and mix well with 60 g (2¼ oz) of sea salt. (Alternatively, you could blend the seeded chillies to a paste in a food processor with the salt.) Store in a sterilised jar for 2–3 days, then transfer to the fridge.

SERVES 4

200 g (7 oz/1 cup) dried chickpeas, soaked overnight in cold water

¼ brown onion, peeled and roughly chopped, plus extra ½ onion, peeled and finely diced

½ small carrot, peeled and roughly chopped

2 tablespoons vegetable oil, plus extra 250 ml (9 fl oz/1 cup) for frying

½ teaspoon finely crushed garlic

1 tablespoon curry powder

400 ml (14 fl oz) Fish Stock (page 457)

sea salt and freshly ground black pepper, to taste

4 × 200 g (7 oz) blue-eye trevalla fillets, skin removed, pin-boned, each fillet cut into 3 medallions 3–4 cm (1¼–1½ in) thick

2 tablespoons salted red chilli (see note), to serve

Silver trevally

TREVALLY

Dozens of species of trevally are commonly found around the Australian and New Zealand coasts. The more common species include the silver trevally (*Pseudocaranx dentex*), bluefin trevally (*Caranx melampygus*) and bigeye trevally (*Caranx sexfasciatus*). The yellowtail scad (*Trachurus novaezelandiae*) is also a member of the trevally family.

Trevallies are active swimmers, assisted by a streamlined body and very fine scales. Silver trevally are found on inshore reefs and around estuary systems, and can form large schools. The yellowtail scad is found prolifically in bays, harbours and estuary mouths. Silver trevally is mainly caught off south-eastern Australia and all around New Zealand by trawl, purse seine and gillnets. Some premium fish are line-caught and ike jime handled (see page 15) for the sashimi market. It's especially delicious if bled on capture.

An easy fish to fillet, with a simple bone structure, silver trevally is a superb table fish. When very fresh, it makes a spectacular addition to any sashimi plate. Like many oily fish, it has a robust taste and must be handled with care to preserve the integrity of its flavour and texture. The greenish yellowtail scad is plentiful, sustainable and cheap. It's still to be 'discovered' in mainstream Western cuisine, although it's very popular in many Asian cuisines.

SEASONALITY Year round, with a peak in spring and early summer

CATCHING METHODS Purse seine, gillnet, mid-water trawl, handline, setline, dropline

COMMON LENGTH Silver trevally: 20–50 cm (8–20 in); yellowtail scad: 10–20 cm (4–8 in)

COMMON WEIGHT Silver trevally: 300 g – 1.5 kg (10½ oz – 3 lb 5 oz); yellowtail scad: 100–400 g (3½–14 oz)

IDENTIFIABLE FEATURES Silver trevally: smooth skin with small scales, silver with a light yellow horizontal stripe and black spots; yellowtail scad: greenish yellow, with a midline horizontal row of hard scales

SUSTAINABILITY Regarded as sustainable

TREVALLY IN THE KITCHEN

Trevally caught in southern Australia are quite small, while those from northern Australia and New Zealand are much bigger. Whatever its size, it has a strong flavour when cooked. It's simply beautiful raw, with a similar texture to hiramasa kingfish – that firm, glassy, crisp bite. Try it as sashimi, sushi or tartare, served with simple accompaniments such as soy sauce or ponzu sauce (page 455). If soy or ponzu aren't your thing, olive oil, capers, onions, parsley and lemon make great accompaniments. Some Japanese chefs like to wave heat over the fish to release the oils without cooking it.

If you do cook it, either keep it on the bone, in foil on the barbecue, or pot-roast it with oil, lemon, stock and butter, being careful not to overcook it. Serve it with a sweet vegetable such as roasted onion and a roasted lemon for contrast.

Yellowtail scad has a strong flavour that some people find too much, but it's marvellous for the true fish lover. It's at its best when barbecued whole, skin on, then served with Mediterranean accompaniments – ratatouille, eggplant (aubergine), tomato, onions, olives, garlic. Or you can pan-fry it, for 2–3 minutes on each side, to char up the skin like crackling. Use a weight so the fish cooks evenly without curling up.

You can also pot-roast yellowtail scad, or cook it under a gentle grill (broiler). It's not overly sensitive, but it's not enjoyable if overcooked. Asian flavours such as coriander (cilantro), basil, chilli, tamarind and soy sauce make great accompaniments. When super-fresh it responds really well to pickling in salt and vinegar.

BEST COOKING METHODS Raw, pan-fried with crisp skin (fillets, see page 437), whole

TEXTURE Medium to firm

AROMA Rich, with a note of fresh cabbage

FLAVOUR Full, mouth-filling, with a rich sweetness and lingering umami character

APPEARANCE Flesh pale pink to red–brown when raw; pearl white once cooked

YIELD Fillets about 45% of whole weight

SUBSTITUTES Bonito, cobia, yellowtail kingfish

Silver trevally sashimi

Place the sliced trevally on a serving platter, with the top loin or shoulder slices folded in half and the belly slices laid flat in a curving column down the plate.

Serve with the ginger, spring onion, soy sauce and wasabi.

NOTE: For further advice on slicing fish for sashimi, see page 434.

SERVES 4

8 × 20 g (¾ oz) silver trevally top loin or shoulder slices, about 5 mm (¼ in) thick (see note)

16 × 20 g (¾ oz) silver trevally belly slices, about 5 mm (¼ in) thick (see note)

grated ginger, to serve

green spring onion (scallion) tops, thinly sliced, to serve

Japanese light soy sauce, to serve

wasabi, to serve

Barbecued yellowtail scad with peas, lettuce and bacon

SERVES 4 AS AN ENTRÉE

2 × 200 g (7 oz) whole yellowtail scad, tails and fins trimmed
1 tablespoon vegetable oil
40 g (1½ oz) butter
1 small French shallot, peeled and diced
2 tablespoons bacon lardons
80 g (2¾ oz/½ cup) fresh green peas
60 ml (2 fl oz/¼ cup) Fish Stock (page 457)
2 large cos (romaine) lettuce leaves, roughly shredded

Preheat a flat-top barbecue hotplate to high, or heat a flat stovetop grill pan over high heat.

Score the yellowtail on an angle at 2 cm (¾ in) intervals on both sides. Brush the fish with the vegetable oil and place on the barbecue or hot pan. Cook for about 1 minute on each side, or until just cooked through. Remove from the heat and leave to rest until serving.

Heat a small frying pan over medium–low heat and add the butter. When the butter is bubbling, add the shallot and bacon, then cook, without colouring, for 2 minutes, or until soft and sweet. Add the peas and fish stock, then bring to the boil. Reduce the heat a little and simmer for 1–2 minutes, until the stock reduces slightly. Fold the lettuce through just before serving.

To serve, place the fish gently on a serving platter and spoon the pea, lettuce and bacon mixture over.

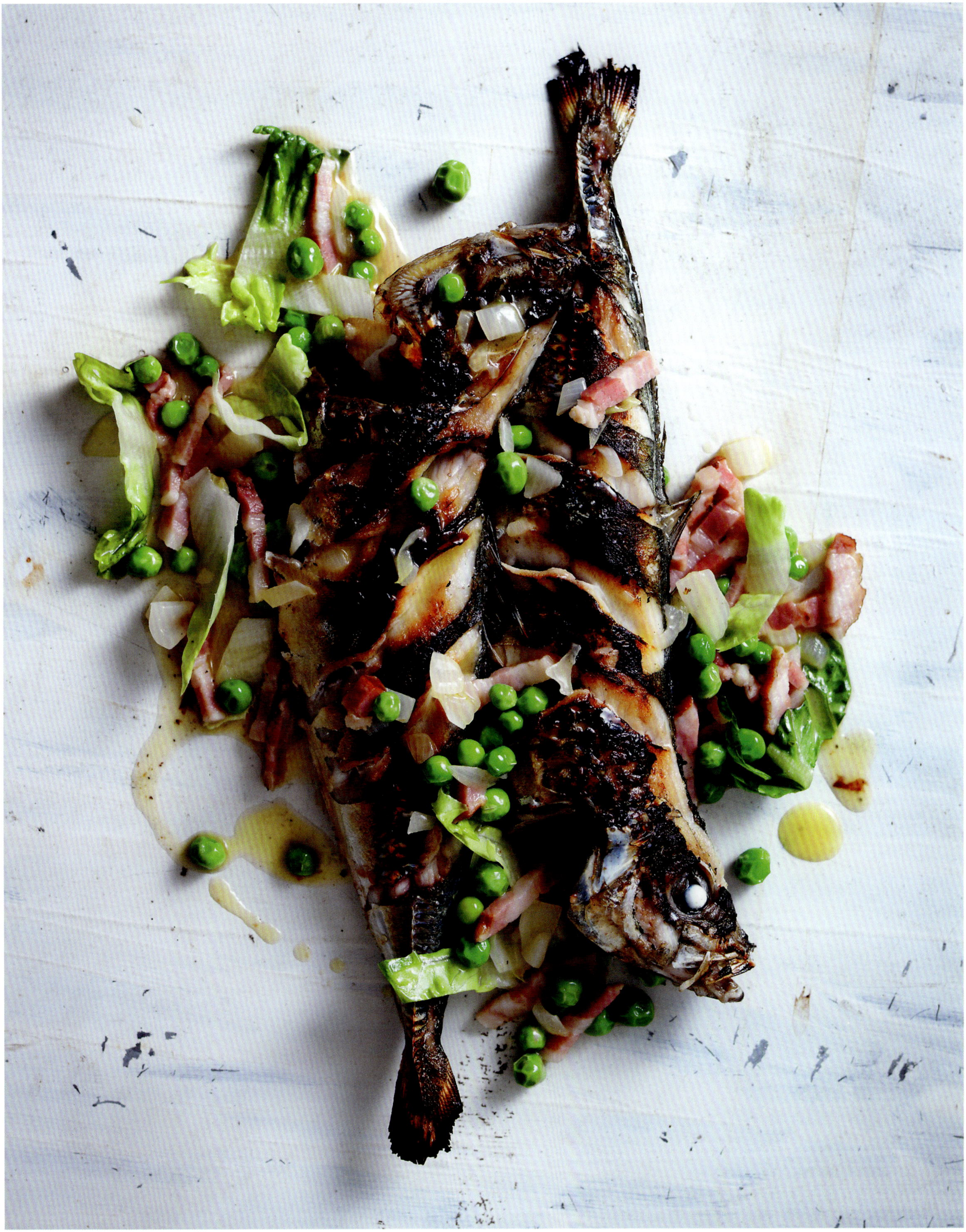

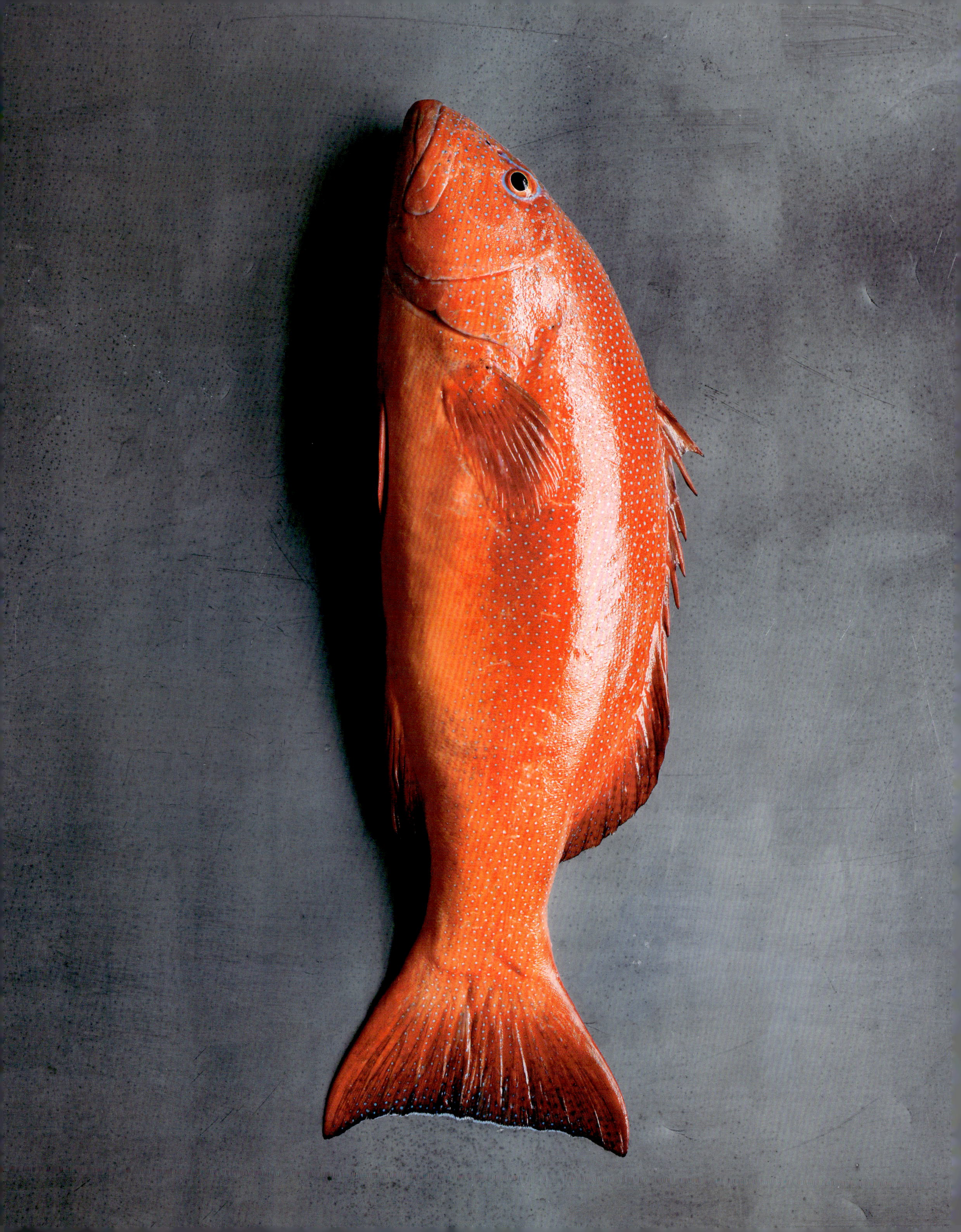

TROUT, CORAL

The coral trout (*Plectropomus leopardus*) is one of the truly iconic, premium northern Australian fish, with a reputation built on the sheer luxury of eating it.

It's not related to the orange-fleshed freshwater trout, but like the brown and rainbow trout, it has spots along its back. Its closest relatives are actually groupers and tropical cods.

Coral trout are bottom-dwellers around inshore and coastal reefs and islands in tropical waters. In Australia, they're found along the northern Queensland and Northern Territory coasts, and off Western Australia all the way south to Shark Bay. They're voracious eaters, and their preferred diet of crabs, prawns (shrimp) and live fish produces their sweet, delicate flesh.

They come in a variety of colours depending on the depth of water they live in. Fish from deeper waters are paler than those from shallow waters.

SEASONALITY Year round, with a peak in autumn–spring

CATCHING METHODS Handline, setline, trap, tropical mid-water trawl

COMMON LENGTH 30–50 cm (12–20 in)

COMMON WEIGHT 1–4 kg (2 lb 4 oz – 8 lb 13 oz)

IDENTIFIABLE FEATURES Elongated body with protruding lower jaw, sharp teeth, large eyes and bright red skin covered in small blue dots

SUSTAINABILITY Stock status good; managed at state and federal level

CORAL TROUT IN THE KITCHEN

This outstanding fish is often quite hard to obtain, as it's so popular in the high-paying Hong Kong and Singapore markets, where we sell them live. You can often buy it live in Chinatown markets.

Coral trout has a big flavour and gelatinous skin. This means you can eat it pan-fried with crisp skin, but when steamed the skin turns into a beautiful jelly. It's ideal in broths, and can be cooked on the bone, but it's not great raw.

Try it poached or steamed whole (a fish around 2 kg/4 lb 8 oz is ideal) – its natural sweetness provides a fantastic platform for other flavours. You can slow-steam it then add it to a tomato broth or a soup. It suits Asian ingredients, such as ginger, lime, spring onions (scallions) and coconut, and can even cope with stronger tastes such as fennel.

BEST COOKING METHODS Steamed, roasted, pan-fried with crisp skin (fillets, see page 437), grilled (broiled), in soup

TEXTURE Flesh soft to firm, with a broadly scalloping flake

AROMA Sweet, mild, with a light seaweed note

FLAVOUR Sweet, bright, with a hint of umami

APPEARANCE Flesh translucent grey–white when raw; arctic white once cooked

YIELD Flesh about 40% of whole weight

SUBSTITUTES Big-eye ocean perch, red emperor

Steamed coral trout tail with almonds, pomegranate and prunes

SERVES 4

1 tail of a large (2.25 kg/5 lb) coral trout (or a whole small fish)

160 ml (5¼ fl oz) lemon oil (see note page 25)

2 tablespoons blanched almonds, roughly chopped

seeds and juice of 1 small pomegranate

8 pitted prunes

2 tablespoons verjuice or sherry vinegar

sea salt and freshly ground black pepper, to taste

Preheat the oven to 200°C (400°F).

Score the trout tail well, with slashes a thumb-width apart down the length of the fish. This will ensure even cooking.

Place the fish on a wire rack in a roasting tin. Add about 80 ml (2½ fl oz/⅓ cup) of water and cover the tin securely with foil. Place on the stovetop over very low heat and bring to a gentle simmer, then immediately transfer the tin to the oven.

A 1.2 kg (2 lb 10 oz) tail will take about 15 minutes to cook, followed by a further 10 minutes of resting time out of the oven. If cooking a whole fish or a larger piece up to 2 kg (4 lb 8 oz), expect 25 minutes of cooking time, with 10 minutes of resting time. A 200 g (7 oz) piece of fillet will take 10 minutes to cook, with 4 minutes of resting time.

While the fish is cooking, make a simple vinaigrette by gently heating the lemon oil in a small saucepan over low heat for 1 minute. Remove the pan from the heat and transfer the oil to a medium mixing bowl. Toss in the almonds, pomegranate seeds and juice, prunes and verjuice. Season with a little salt and pepper, then toss well to combine. Set aside in a warm spot.

When the fish has rested, transfer it carefully to a platter and top generously with the vinaigrette.

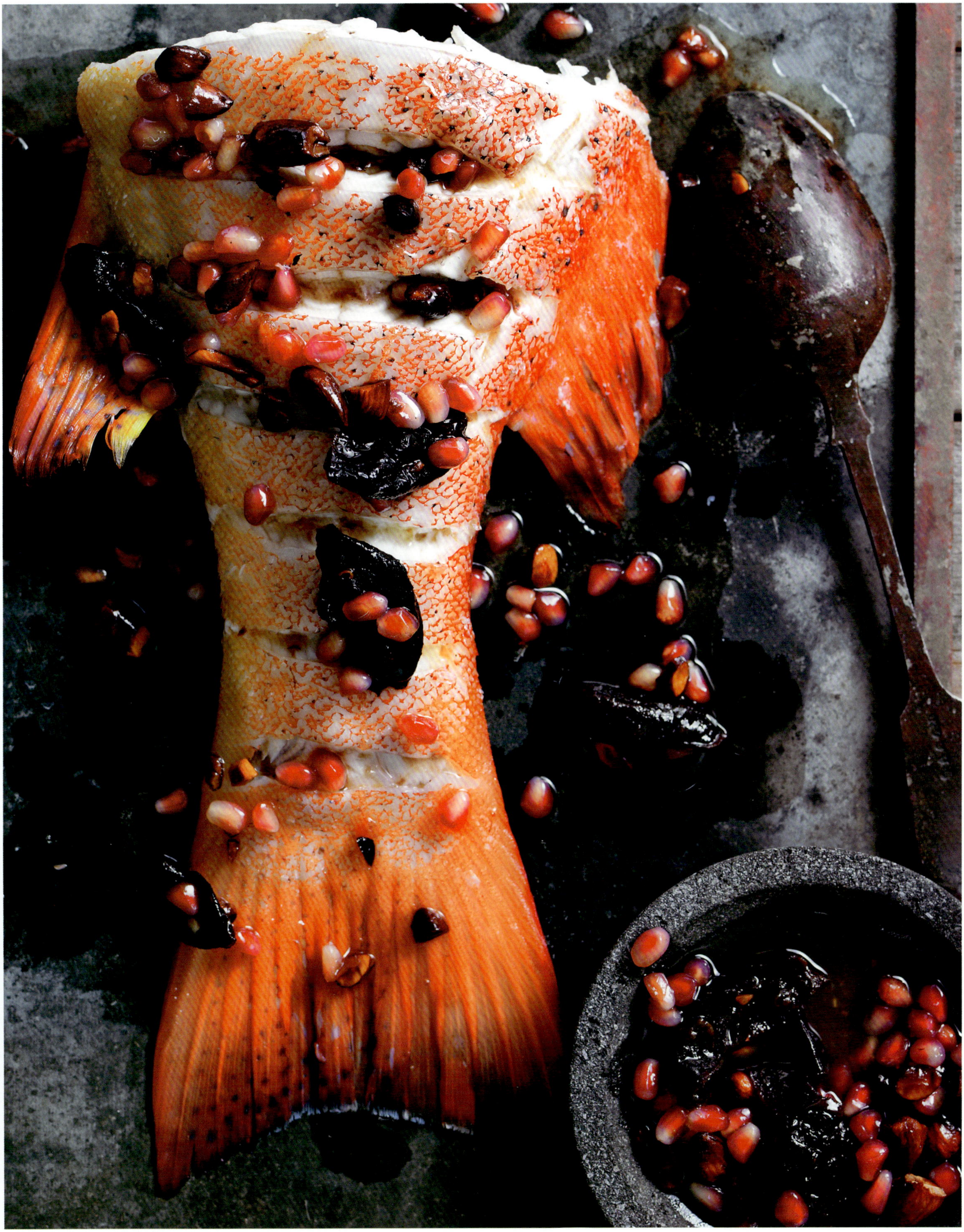

Ocean (left) and rainbow trout

TROUT, OCEAN & RAINBOW

Rainbow and ocean trout are the same species (*Oncorhynchus mykiss*), but rainbow trouts spend their lives entirely in fresh water whereas ocean trout are farmed in sea water. Native to the West Coast of the United States, they were successfully introduced to Australia and New Zealand in the late 1880s and became a staple in ocean farming in Tasmania a century later.

In nutrient-rich dams, rainbow trout can reach 2 kg (4 lb 8 oz) in two years and 3 kg (6 lb 12 oz) in three years, but in nutrient-poor or overstocked dams, growth may be much slower. They inhabit freshwater creeks, dams, rivers and lakes at 5–20°C (40–70°F); they need good-quality, clean water and are intolerant of low oxygen levels caused by heat and stagnation. Most farms are thus in New South Wales, Victoria and Tasmania, although some are in South Australia and Western Australia.

In the northern hemisphere, some trout migrate between fresh and salt water for breeding, but in Australia most are restricted to fresh water. Ocean trout are acclimatised to sea water at a young age and grown in marine conditions until maturity, mostly in Macquarie Harbour on the west coast of Tasmania.

Wild trout eat a range of insects, and small fish, including redfin perch. The diet of farmed fish ensures consistent growth, flavour and texture, and thus consistently high quality. Ocean trout are well regarded for their fat content, which is much higher than that of Atlantic salmon.

SEASONALITY Year round
CATCHING METHOD Farmed
COMMON LENGTH Rainbow: 15–25 cm (6–10 in); ocean: 35–50 cm (14–20 in)
COMMON WEIGHT Rainbow: 400–700 g (14 oz – 1 lb 9 oz); ocean: 2–3 kg (4 lb 8 oz – 6 lb 12 oz)
IDENTIFIABLE FEATURES Upper body dark olive green to bluish, sides lighter, belly silver–white, head and body heavily speckled; pink, red or orange markings along head and flanks
SUSTAINABILITY Highly sustainable (farmed)

OCEAN & RAINBOW TROUT IN THE KITCHEN

Rainbow trout used to be quite a prize in Australian restaurants. The chef would steam it whole then a waiter would bring it to the table, roll back the skin and serve portions of that amazing flesh to each guest. It's also brilliant smoked, and can be pan-fried, barbecued and even minced (ground) for fishcakes and fish balls. As a general rule the skin is not eaten, but is kept on during cooking to protect the soft, delicate flesh. Trout is best served with greens, nuts and vinaigrettes rather than big-flavoured vegetables. Green beans and hazelnuts is a classic accompaniment.

It's almost the fish of choice to smoke whole, but its buttery and fatty nature also makes it ideally suited to pâté. To hot-smoke 600–800 g (1 lb 5 oz – 1 lb 12 oz) of trout, make a brine of 12 litres (25 pt/48 cups) of water, 1.3 kg (3 lb) of table salt, 300 g (10½ oz) of raw (demerara) sugar and 1 tablespoon of molasses, stirred together warm to dissolve the sugar and salt, then cooled. Soak the whole trout in this brine for 24 hours. Drain, pat dry with paper towel and refrigerate for 3–4 hours.

Preheat the oven to 240°C (475°F) and spread 2 cups of hardwood smoking chips (available in hardware stores) over the base of a large roasting tin. Place a wire rack over the chips, sit the trout on the rack and cover the tin with foil. Bake for 30–35 minutes then remove the tin from the oven but leave the trout covered for a further 1 hour. Use the trout immediately to enjoy its soft, juicy texture, or refrigerate for later use.

There's enough fat under the skin to cook on the barbecue, but make sure you cook it whole, with the skin on to protect the flesh. Rainbow trout can easily be overcooked.

The best way to cook trout, however, is whole on the bone. Serve it a little under-done – still pink or taut on the bone. It will continue to cook even when you remove it from the heat. To plate it, flip it over, to ensure you're not eating overcooked fish.

Because of its higher fat content, ocean trout is more like Atlantic salmon than rainbow trout. It's ideal confit, cured, raw and even as fillets pan-fried with crisp skin. It's as versatile as salmon and can withstand almost all cooking methods, including Asian dishes from rice paper rolls to stir-fries; and many flavour combinations, particularly fennel, zucchini (courgette), potato and tomato.

BEST COOKING METHODS Poached, smoked, minced (ground), pan-fried with crisp skin (fillets, see page 437), barbecued

TEXTURE Medium soft, with a broadly scalloping flesh

AROMA Rainbow: earthy minerality, with bright fresh notes; ocean trout: rich iodine, with notes of egg yolk

FLAVOUR Rainbow: light, mild sweetness, with a hint of mushroom and boiled cabbage; ocean trout: deep, rich, mouth-filling, with a umami character and salty back palate

APPEARANCE Flesh light to bright orange when raw; pale orange once cooked

YIELD Fillets about 45% of whole weight

SUBSTITUTES Salmon

Ocean trout in filo pastry with mushroom duxelles, leek and sorrel sauce

For the mushroom duxelles, heat the vegetable oil in a large heavy-based saucepan over medium heat. Add the onion, garlic and thyme, then cook gently. When the onion starts to colour, add the mushrooms, butter, salt and pepper, then stir well to coat. Cover and cook for 10 minutes, or until the mushrooms have released all their juices, checking regularly to ensure the mixture is not catching on the base of the pan. Remove the lid and cook for a further 30 minutes, or until all the moisture has evaporated, then remove the pan from the heat and set aside in a warm place for 1 hour to dry out. While the mixture is still warm, pulse it in a food processor until finely chopped – do not purée. Set aside to cool completely. (The duxelles can be made a day ahead and kept in the fridge.)

Cut the leek lengthways down one side, then remove and separate the next four layers, including the green part – only these four layers are required. Reserve any remaining leek for another use. Bring a small saucepan of salted water to the boil over high heat. Blanch the four leek pieces for 30 seconds, or until soft. Remove immediately, refresh in iced water and drain well.

Lay the leek pieces out on a clean work surface with a long side facing you, and pat dry with paper towel. Place 3–4 tablespoons of mushroom duxelles on each leek piece and flatten gently with the back of a spoon, leaving about 4 cm (1½ in) clear at each end. Lay a trout fillet in the centre of each leek piece. Roll up the trout firmly in the leek, but leave the ends open. Trim the ends to neaten.

Separate the filo pastry into bundles of four sheets and lay each bundle flat on the work surface with a short side facing you. Place each piece of leek-wrapped trout on the centre of a filo bundle, about 3 cm (1¼ in) from the edge facing you. Carefully roll, folding in the sides neatly and brushing with a little melted butter to help the pastry stick. Brush each parcel well with melted butter and set aside.

RECIPE CONTINUED OVERLEAF >

SERVES 4

1 large leek (about 30 cm/12 in long), ends trimmed, tough outer layer removed, well washed
iced water, as required, to refresh
4 × 160 g (5¾ oz) thick ocean trout fillets, skin removed, pin-boned
16 sheets filo pastry (about 30 × 15 cm/12 × 6 in)
melted butter, for brushing
80 ml (2½ fl oz/⅓ cup) ghee (see note page 26)
1 heaped tablespoon ocean trout roe, to serve
sorrel leaves, to serve

MUSHROOM DUXELLES

1 tablespoon vegetable oil
1 large brown onion, peeled and sliced
6 garlic cloves, peeled
1 tablespoon picked thyme leaves
440 g (15½ oz) field mushrooms, roughly chopped
110 g (3¾ oz) butter
sea salt and freshly ground black pepper, to taste

SORREL SAUCE

250 ml (9 fl oz/1 cup) dry white wine
100 ml (3½ fl oz) Fish Stock (page 457)
250 ml (9 fl oz/1 cup) thin (pouring) cream
250 g (9 oz) chilled butter, cut into small cubes
12–16 sorrel leaves and stalks

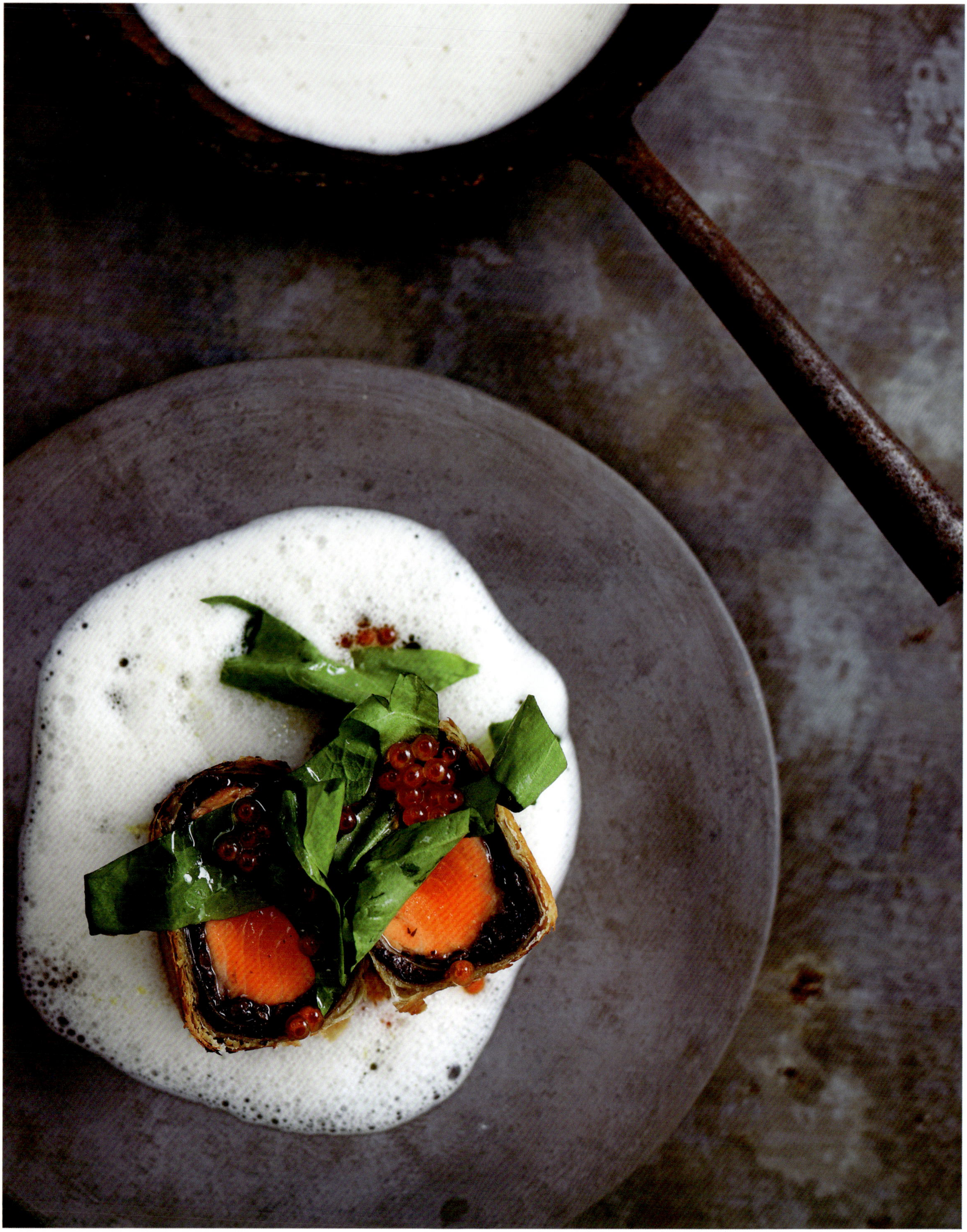

<< **RECIPE CONTINUED FROM PREVIOUS PAGE**

For the sorrel sauce, heat the wine in a medium saucepan over high heat. Boil until the wine has reduced by about half. Add the fish stock and cream, return to the boil, reduce the heat to medium and simmer until the sauce has reduced by half again. Reduce the heat to low and gradually add the butter, whisking constantly. Once all the butter has been added, continue whisking for 5 minutes. Remove the sauce from the heat, add the sorrel and set aside in a warm place.

Preheat the oven to 220°C (425°F).

Melt the ghee in a large heavy-based ovenproof frying pan over medium–high heat until a thin blue haze rises from the surface. Add the fish parcels, narrow side down, and pan-fry gently for about 1 minute, until golden. Turn and repeat with the opposite side. Lay the parcels flat in the pan and bake in the oven for about 4 minutes, until golden. Turn onto the remaining side and bake for a further 4 minutes, so that the parcels are now golden all over. Remove from the oven and rest the parcels in the pan for 5 minutes.

Meanwhile, blitz the sorrel sauce with a hand-held blender for 1 minute, or until frothy.

To serve, cut each ocean trout parcel in half using a sharp knife. Spoon the sorrel sauce onto each plate, then place a halved parcel on top. Scatter over the ocean trout roe and garnish with extra sorrel leaves.

Sugar-cured ocean trout

**1 LARGE SIDE OF TROUT
YIELDS 12–14 PORTIONS**

1 side filleted ocean trout, skin on, pin-boned
1 tablespoon chardonnay vinegar
60 ml (2 fl oz/¼ cup) lemon oil (see note page 25)
1 large handful flat-leaf (Italian) parsley leaves
1 large handful fennel fronds
2 teaspoons ocean trout roe
4–8 slices rye bread, toasted
165 g (5¾ oz/⅔ cup) ricotta

CURE
1 teaspoon salt per 100 g (3½ oz) fish
1 teaspoon caster (superfine) sugar per 100 g (3½ oz) fish
1 small handful finely chopped fennel fronds

Weigh the side of ocean trout to work out the quantities of salt and caster sugar required for curing, allowing 1 teaspoon of each per 100 g. If the fish weighs 800 g (1 lb 2 oz), for example, you'll need 2 tablespoons (8 teaspoons) of salt and 2 tablespoons of caster sugar.

For the cure, combine the salt, sugar and chopped fennel fronds in a bowl. Place the fish on a stainless-steel tray and rub the cure mixture generously into the flesh. Cover with plastic wrap and refrigerate for a minimum of 48 hours, turning it twice during that time. It's safe to leave the salmon refrigerated in the brine for up to 1 week without risk of over-curing.

Cut five slices from the cured ocean trout per portion. Arrange them carefully on a plate, slightly overlapping.

Make a simple vinaigrette by mixing the chardonnay vinegar and lemon oil in a medium bowl. (No seasoning is required here as the balance is perfect.) Add the parsley leaves and fennel fronds, then toss together gently.

Place the dressed salad on the fish slices. Scatter the roe over the top and serve the rye bread and ricotta on the side.

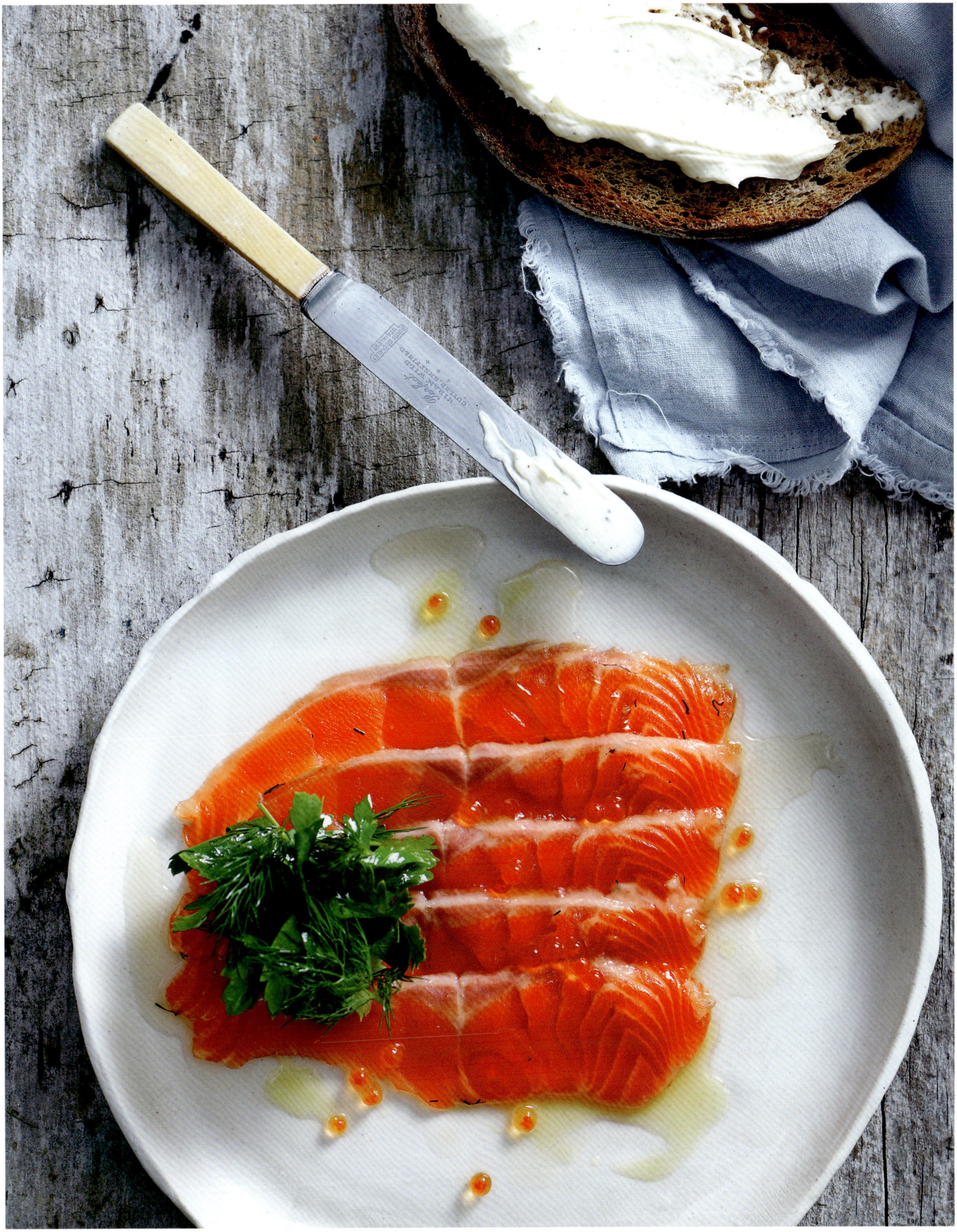

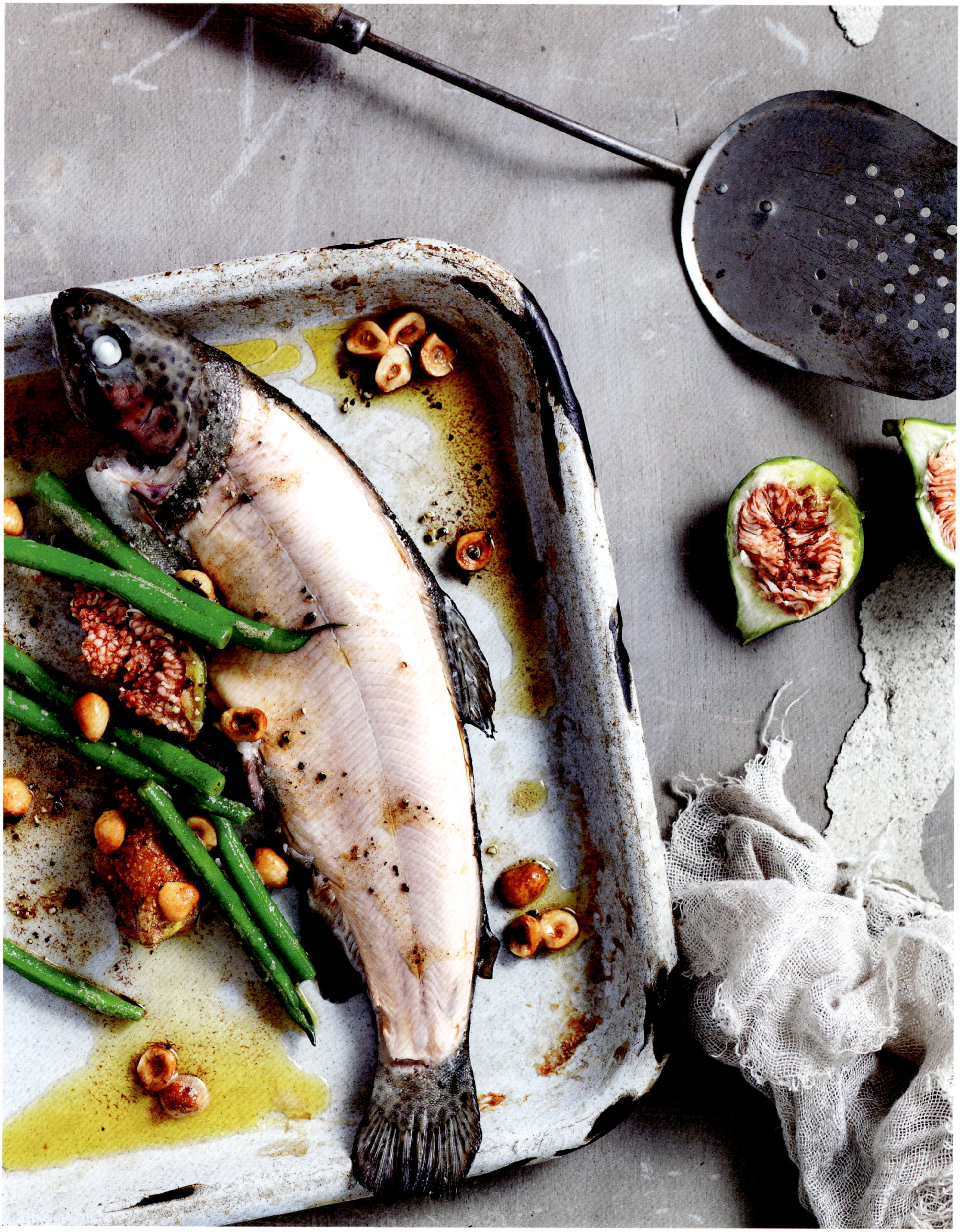

Steamed whole rainbow trout with green beans, figs and hazelnut butter

Place the whole trout in a prepared benchtop steamer (see note) and cook for 4 minutes.

Remove the trout from the steamer and carefully transfer to a tray or board. Using a very sharp paring knife, cut a tiny and subtle incision all the way around the edge of the top side of the fish. Peel off the skin carefully, using a tissue to assist with grip, and discard. Carefully transfer the skinned fish to a serving tray or platter.

Heat a medium frying pan over high heat. Add the butter and move the pan over the heat until the butter is nut brown. Quickly add the beans, figs and hazelnuts. Season with salt and pepper, then immediately pour half the bean mixture over the trout, retaining about half in the pan, off the heat.

When the first side of the trout has been served, turn it over carefully using a spatula. Remove the skin from the other side and top with the remaining bean mixture.

NOTES: When blanching beans that won't be cooked any further, take them beyond al dente to the point where they're soft to the bite and not squeaky, yet still vibrant green. At this point, the starches break down into sugars and the beans become sweet and extremely delicious.

We use a benchtop fish steamer for cooking the fish in this recipe. Cooking times may vary a little if you use a Chinese steamer, a double boiler or choose to steam in an oven, so take care not to overcook the fish.

SERVES 4 AS AN ENTRÉE

1 whole rainbow trout, gutted
80 g (2¾ oz) butter
125 g (4½ oz) green beans, trimmed, blanched and refreshed (see note)
2 large, ripe green figs, carefully torn in half lengthways
2 tablespoons roasted and peeled hazelnuts
sea salt and freshly ground black pepper, to taste

STRIPED TRUMPETER IN THE KITCHEN

Chefs will tell you that fresh striped trumpeter is the best fish in the world. It's great steamed and served with a lemon wedge and olive oil, because you want to taste the sheer beauty and elegance of this stunning fish. Although you want to keep it simple, you can also grill (broil), fry or bake it. If *super*-fresh it's a textural delight raw as sashimi.

Striped trumpeter caught off Tasmania and southern New Zealand are especially noted for their delicious fatty flesh, particularly during winter, when they inhabit extremely cold water. Although fatty, the flesh has a unique crunchy texture but a creamy mouthfeel. This versatile fish, is fantastic pan-fried with crisp skin or roasted, but when steamed the flavours explode, with a defined iodine zing.

BEST COOKING METHODS Steamed, pan-fried with crisp skin (fillets, see page 437), raw

TEXTURE White broadly scalloping flesh that can be meaty

AROMA Zippy iodine character with a clean note of fresh asparagus

FLAVOUR Rich, clean, with notes of fresh lobster and crab

APPEARANCE Opaque white flesh when raw; pearl white once cooked

YIELD Flesh 45–50% of whole weight

SUBSTITUTES Blue-eye trevalla, snapper

Charred striped trumpeter with pistachio and lime carrots

For the pistachio and lime butter, pulse the garlic with the pistachios in a food processor until roughly chopped. Add the butter, lime zest and juice, salt and pepper, then blend to mix. Set aside in the fridge (see note).

Preheat the oven to 200°C (400°F). Preheat a flat-top barbecue hotplate to high, or heat a flat stovetop grill pan over high heat.

Place the carrots on a baking tray, drizzle with a little olive oil and season with salt and pepper. Toss to coat. Place the tray in the oven.

Roast the carrots for 10 minutes, or until beginning to soften but still quite firm in the centre. Top with the pistachio and lime butter and roast for a further 10–15 minutes, until the carrots are perfectly cooked.

Meanwhile, season the trumpeter with salt. Splash a little olive oil on the grill plate and lay the fish on it, skin side down. Cook for 3–4 minutes – the aim is to achieve really dark skin on the fish without overcooking; a splash more oil halfway through will help achieve a better colour. Turn the fish gently using a spatula and sear for 30 seconds, then remove from the heat and set aside in a warm place to rest for 1–2 minutes.

Place the trumpeter fillets on a shared serving platter. Serve with the roasted carrots, pouring the melted butter over the carrots and fish. Offer the lime cheeks on the side.

NOTE: The pistachio and lime butter can be made in advance. Spoon the butter onto baking paper, use the paper to roll it into a log and wrap it tightly, then cover in plastic wrap. It will keep in the fridge for 1 month. Place the wrapped roll in a freezer bag and it will keep, frozen, for up to 6 months.

SERVES 4

500 g (1 lb 2 oz/2 bunches) baby carrots, stems trimmed, scrubbed
extra virgin olive oil, for cooking
sea salt and freshly ground black pepper, to taste
4 × 200 g (7 oz) striped trumpeter fillets, skin on, pin-boned
lime cheeks, to serve (see note page 144)

PISTACHIO AND LIME BUTTER
1 garlic clove, peeled and crushed
35 g (1¼ oz/¼ cup) pistachio nut kernels
100 g (3½ oz) butter, softened
grated zest and juice of 1 lime
sea salt and freshly ground black pepper, to taste

Yellowfin tuna loin

TUNA

Australian tuna offers a range of options – from the exotic and highly prized southern bluefin (*Thunnus maccoyii*) to the humble and inexpensive albacore (*Thunnus alalunga*) and skipjack (*Katsuwonus pelamis*) tunas. While they vary in their culinary uses, price and availability, their quality is second to none.

Tuna fisheries are among the largest and most important worldwide. The Australian tuna fishery accounts for nearly 60 per cent (by both volume and value) of finfish exports. Annually, nearly 15,000 tonnes are harvested, yielding some 37 million tuna steaks or 370 million pieces of sashimi. While much of this is exported, primarily to Japan, we in Australia and New Zealand also benefit from the local expertise.

Tuna are fast, graceful swimmers, with almost perfect streamlining, including eyes that retract to ensure they cut through the water. Southern bluefin tuna can swim at up to 70 km (44 mi) per hour when feeding. Tuna are fish of the open ocean rather than coastal waters, and are surface- rather than bottom-dwelling. They're constantly on the prowl for seafood, including other fish, crustaceans and molluscs.

As they're always on the move, they can eat up to a quarter of their body weight in a single day. This opportunistic feeding results in layers of fat throughout their muscles, which makes them incredibly delicious.

SEASONALITY Albacore: year round, with a peak in winter–spring; bigeye: year round from the east coast, with a peak in autumn–winter; southern bluefin: summer from SA; autumn to late spring from Tas., Vic. and NSW; yellowfin: year round from the east coast, with a peak in autumn–spring

CATCHING METHODS Albacore, bigeye and yellowfin: pelagic longline; southern bluefin: Danish seine for ranching

COMMON LENGTH Albacore: 50–90 cm (20–35½ in); bigeye and southern bluefin: up to 180 cm (71 in); yellowfin: 50–190 cm (20–75 in)

COMMON WEIGHT Albacore: 3–22 kg (6 lb 12 oz – 49 lb); bigeye: up to 120 kg (265 lb); southern bluefin and yellowfin: up to 100 kg (220 lb)

IDENTIFIABLE FEATURES See overleaf

SUSTAINABILITY Highly managed to be sustainable by law; several Australian fisheries have been certified sustainable by official agencies

COMMON TUNA SPECIES

Albacore tuna
Thunnus alalunga
Sometimes known as white tuna or chicken of the sea, the albacore has been much maligned in Australia over the years. But a reduction in the quotas for other species has forced tuna fishers to focus their attention on albacore, and they have discovered that when well handled, its flavour and texture are equal to the yellowfin. Much less expensive than yellowfin, bigeye or bluefin, good-quality albacore is readily available just about all year round but is in peak condition in winter. Much paler than other tunas, it's ideal both raw and braised or poached. Look for fish with a clean, pale crimson–pink, even flesh.

Albacore tuna can be recognised from their long pectoral (side) fins, which extend almost the entire length of their body. They have shorter dorsal (top) fins than other tuna and their tail fin is large by comparison. The back and belly can often both be steel grey.

Bigeye tuna
Thunnus obesus
Closely related to the yellowfin but with a tendency to swim further in search of food, the bigeye typically carries more fat than yellowfin during the winter months – it's known in Japan as 'the fat one'. Australian bigeye has built an enviable reputation and is highly sought after in certain Japanese markets (typically western Japan – Osaka and Kyoto). While the flesh doesn't have the vibrant colour of the yellowfin, it has a delicious flavour and firm texture, making it perfect for both sashimi and cooking. Seek out fish with a consistent colour and texture, and a clean, fresh smell.

The bigeye tuna is readily identifiable from its silvery steel skin and large head and eyes. It's easily differentiable from the yellowfin because its fins aren't yellow and its pectoral fins are shorter and stumpier.

Southern bluefin tuna
Thunnus maccoyii

The mighty southern bluefin is a short, stocky prize-fighter of a fish. Its stumpy pectoral and tail fins belie its strength, which comes from its rotund, dense body. The shimmering dark blue of its back and dorsal fins, combined with its large dark eyes, give it the regal look of the king of tunas.

Once the staple of the tuna-tinning industries in South Australia and New South Wales, the bluefin is now the most prized of all Australian tunas. While some wild bluefin makes its way to market from the east coast and from New Zealand, generally from late winter into spring, these days they're mostly caught by large boats in the Great Australian Bight. Whole schools are carefully netted live, then the fish and net are slowly towed back to Port Lincoln in South Australia.

The live bluefin tuna are kept in large floating pens and fattened on a diet of pilchards, squid and mackerel. When they've doubled in size, they're harvested and prepared for sashimi markets worldwide. Although the fish are caught in the early part of the year from January to March, they're generally fattened for three to six months, coming to market in June. The meat is a dark, rich burgundy colour, and the flesh is typically soft, due to its very high fat content, which makes it a highly prized sashimi fish.

Like other tuna fisheries, the bluefin fishery is highly controlled, and is managed on a strict licence and quota basis. The sustainable status of bluefin causes much anxiety among many sectors of the community, but the science from state, federal and international agencies confirms that stocks are now at a level environmentalists and fisheries managers agree indicates strong recovery. Fish caught off Australia and New Zealand is not only sustainable but consistently among the best handled in the world.

Yellowfin tuna
Thunnus albacares

The yellowfin tuna, the world's most valuable tuna, is found throughout the tropical and subtropical waters off both the east and west coasts of Australia. It accounts for more than 35 per cent of all tuna caught in Australia, and is typically caught by specialist longline fishing boats and handled with absolute care by fishers. The fish are graded according to their fat content, freshness and flesh colour. It's a highly prized sashimi fish, but over the past fifteen years or so has gained popularity as a grilling (broiling) fish.

The yellowfin is the easiest of all the tuna to identify. Not only is it found in our markets in the largest numbers, but it has large bright yellow dorsal, tail and anal fins, and a bright yellow streak running from head to tail. It has a small silver head, a silver belly, and dark shoulders and back.

Niçoise salad

SERVES 4 AS A SHARED SALAD OR ENTRÉE

2 kipfler (fingerling) potatoes, scrubbed, skin on
100 ml (3½ fl oz) extra virgin olive oil, plus 1 tablespoon extra
1 thyme sprig
2 small French shallots, peeled and finely diced
2 tablespoons cabernet vinegar
100 ml (3½ fl oz) lemon oil (see note page 25)
12 green beans, trimmed
iced water, as required, to refresh
400 g (14 oz) albacore tuna loin, skin off
sea salt and freshly ground black pepper, to taste
2 tablespoons ghee or clarified butter (see note page 26)
2 soft-boiled eggs, peeled and cut in half lengthways
2 cherry or small roma (plum) tomatoes, cut in half
4 white anchovies

Place the potatoes in a small saucepan with the 100 ml (3½ fl oz) of olive oil, the thyme and 100 ml of water. Bring to the boil over high heat, then reduce the heat to medium–low and cook until the potatoes are tender. Remove the potatoes from the saucepan and set aside to cool. Cut the cooled potatoes in half lengthways.

Heat the extra olive oil in a small frying pan over low heat. When just warm, add the shallot and cook gently, without colouring, for 2 minutes, or until soft and sweet. Add the vinegar and lemon oil, then mix well. Pour this shallot dressing into a small bowl and set aside.

Bring a medium saucepan of salted water to the boil over high heat. Add the beans and blanch for 2 minutes, or until just tender. Transfer the beans to a bowl of iced water to refresh. Set aside.

Season the tuna with salt and pepper. Heat a medium frying pan over high heat and add the ghee. When the ghee begins to smoke, place the tuna loin in the pan and sear it all over for 2 minutes. Remove the tuna from the pan and leave the tuna to rest for 5 minutes. Cut it into slices 2 cm (¾ in) thick.

Place the tuna slices in a bowl with the potato, beans, eggs, tomatoes and white anchovies. Pour the shallot dressing over and toss gently to coat the salad. Season with salt and pepper, then transfer to a serving platter.

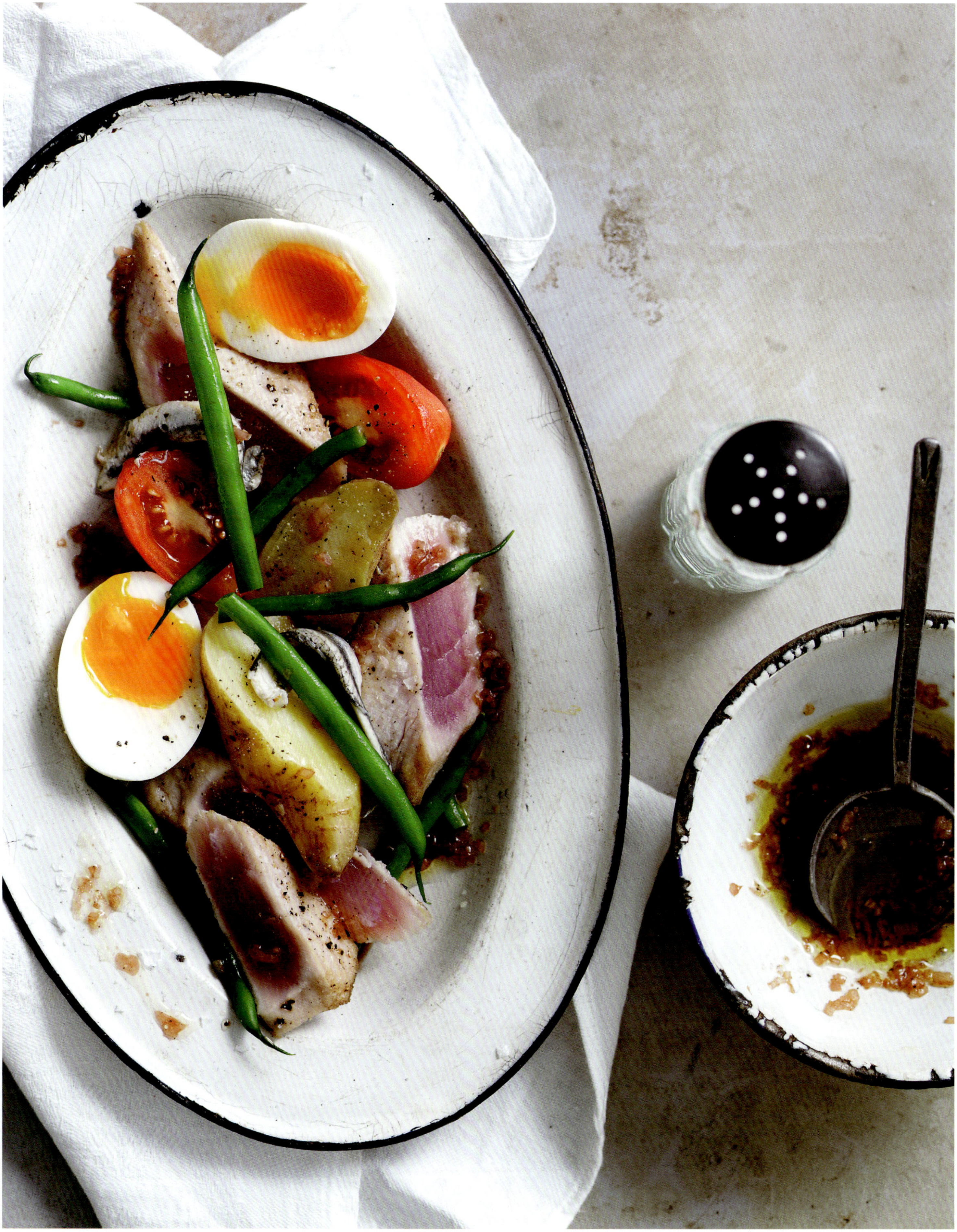

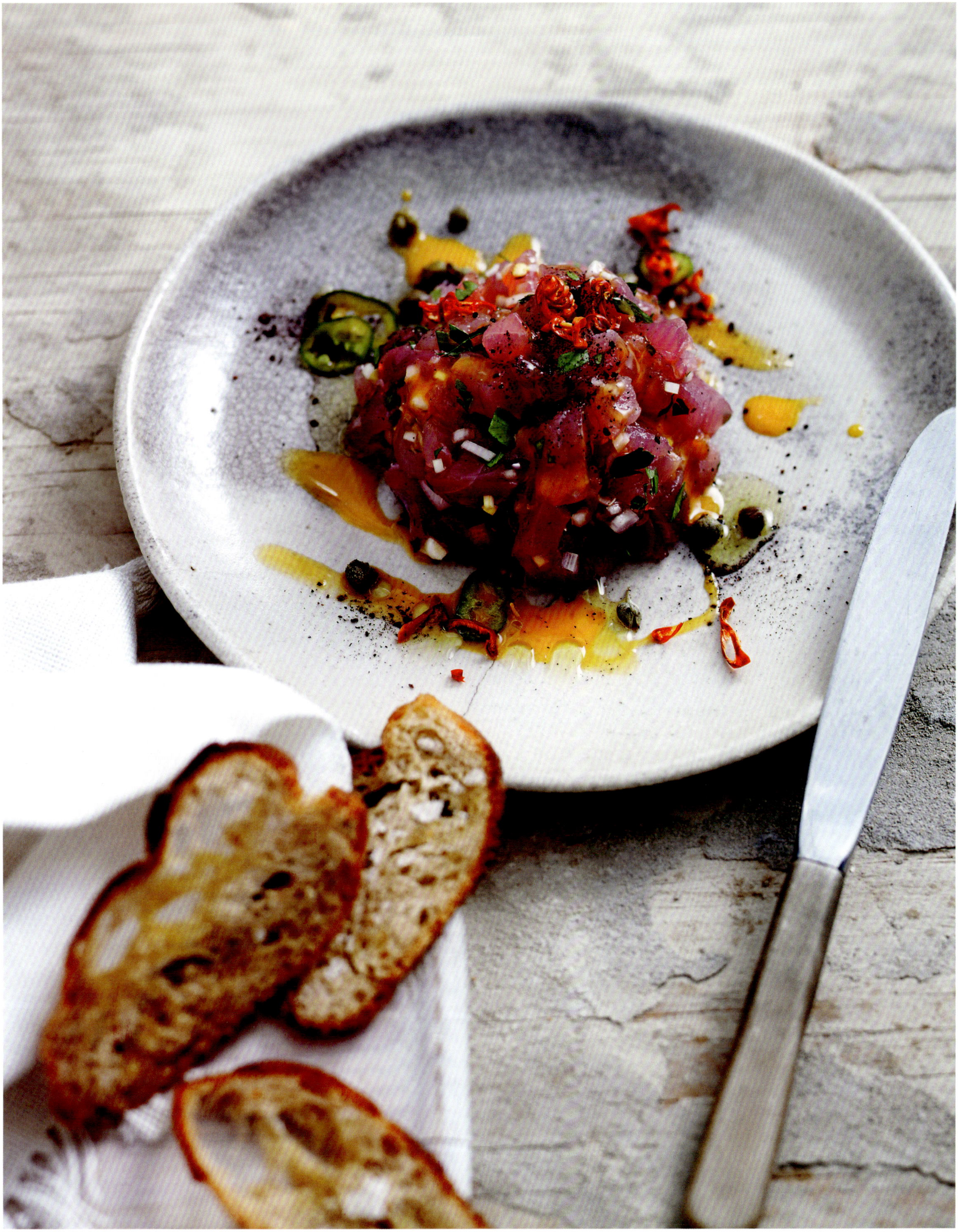

Tuna tartare

For the pickled green chilli, start by making the pickling liquid. Combine the vinegar, sugar and salt in a small saucepan over high heat and bring to the boil. Remove the pan from the heat and leave the liquid to cool.

Place the sliced chilli in a small bowl and cover completely with the pickling liquid. Leave to stand for 30 minutes – the chilli will be freshly pickled and ready for use.

Place the pepper berry in a spice grinder and grind to the consistency of salt. Add the sea salt and mix well to combine. The result should be a well-combined black salt, not two-toned. (Reserve a little for this recipe and keep the remainder in an airtight jar for future use.)

Cut the tuna steaks into 1 cm (½ in) thick slices then into 1 cm (½ in) dice. In a medium bowl, gently toss the tuna with the shallot, parsley and capers.

Arrange the tuna tartare carefully on serving plates. Sprinkle with the pepper berry salt and the pickled and dried chillies. Drizzle with egg yolk and add a good splash of lemon oil to finish.

Serve with crostini on the side for scooping.

NOTES: Native pepper berry, also known as mountain pepper and Tasmanian pepperberry, is dark blue to black with an intense peppery bite and a herbal aftertaste. It's available from specialty spice or gourmet grocery stores, or online from Indigenous food providores or growers.

For the pepper berry salt, use a 'wet' sea salt, such as fleur de sel. Any dried herb can be used in place of the pepper berry.

To make crostini, cut day-old Italian-style bread into 5 mm (¼ in) thick slices. Splash with olive oil and sprinkle with a little salt. Place on a baking tray and bake in a 130°C (250°F) oven for 20 minutes, or until crisp and just starting to colour. The cooking time will vary with the type of bread, so check every 5 minutes.

SERVES 4

200 g (7 oz) native pepper berry (see note)
100 g (3½ oz) wet sea salt (see note)
320 g (11¼ oz) skinless bluefin tuna steaks (cut from the top shoulder)
2 teaspoons chopped French shallot
2 teaspoons chopped flat-leaf (Italian) parsley
2 teaspoons drained and well-rinsed capers in vinegar
2 teaspoons pickled green chilli (see below)
pinch of dried red chilli (see note page 109)
4 egg yolks, beaten
1 tablespoon lemon oil, to finish (see note page 25)
crostini, to serve (see note)

PICKLED GREEN CHILLI
(Makes about 250 ml/9 fl oz/1 cup)
200 ml (7 fl oz) white wine vinegar
75 g (2½ oz/⅓ cup) caster (superfine) sugar
pinch of sea salt
2 long green chillies, seeds in, thinly sliced into rounds

Seared yellowfin tuna with agrodolce

SERVES 4

2 yellow witlof (chicory)
80 g (2¾ oz) butter, plus 40 g (1½ oz) extra
250 ml (9 fl oz/1 cup) Fish Stock (page 457)
pinch of sea salt, plus extra to serve
80 ml (2½ fl oz/⅓ cup) olive oil
4 × 200 g skinless yellowfin tuna steaks, about 3 cm (1¼ in) thick, cut from a thick piece of the loin

AGRODOLCE

2 tablespoons olive oil
2 French shallots, very finely diced
150 ml (5 fl oz) white wine vinegar
60 ml (2 fl oz/¼ cup) dry white wine
1 tablespoon currants
30 g (1 oz) caster (superfine) sugar

Preheat the oven to 200°C (400°F).

For the agrodolce, heat the olive oil in a medium saucepan over medium–low heat. Add the shallot and cook gently, without colouring, until very soft. Add the remaining ingredients and 60 ml (2 fl oz/¼ cup) of water, then stir well to combine. Increase the heat to medium and cook until the mixture has reduced by about three-quarters. Set aside to cool to room temperature.

Cut the witlof in half lengthways and remove the bitter core. Heat a shallow ovenproof frying pan over medium–low heat and add the butter. When melted, add the witlof halves and fry gently, cut side down, for 2 minutes, or until golden. Turn the witlof, add the stock and the salt, then transfer the pan to the oven to braise the witlof for 15–20 minutes, until tender. Remove from the oven and set aside in a warm place.

Heat a large ovenproof frying pan (or two smaller pans – it's essential that the fish is not overcrowded in the pan; see note) over medium–high heat and add the olive oil. When the oil is hot, add the tuna steaks and sear well for 2 minutes on each side, turning once, to create a good crust. Transfer to the oven and cook for a further 2 minutes. Remove from the oven and set aside to rest for 4 minutes. (Cooking times may vary depending on the size of the fish from which the steaks were cut; for more information, see page 437.)

Meanwhile, heat a small frying pan over medium–high heat and add the extra butter. When it starts to bubble and brown, add the witlof and coat well on both sides.

Cut the steaks in half crossways and place two pieces on each plate. Top one piece with a witlof half and the other with a good tablespoon of agrodolce. Sprinkle with sea salt and serve.

NOTE: If you don't have a pan large enough for all the steaks, or two smaller pans, cook the fish in two batches. Keep the first batch warm while you cook the second.

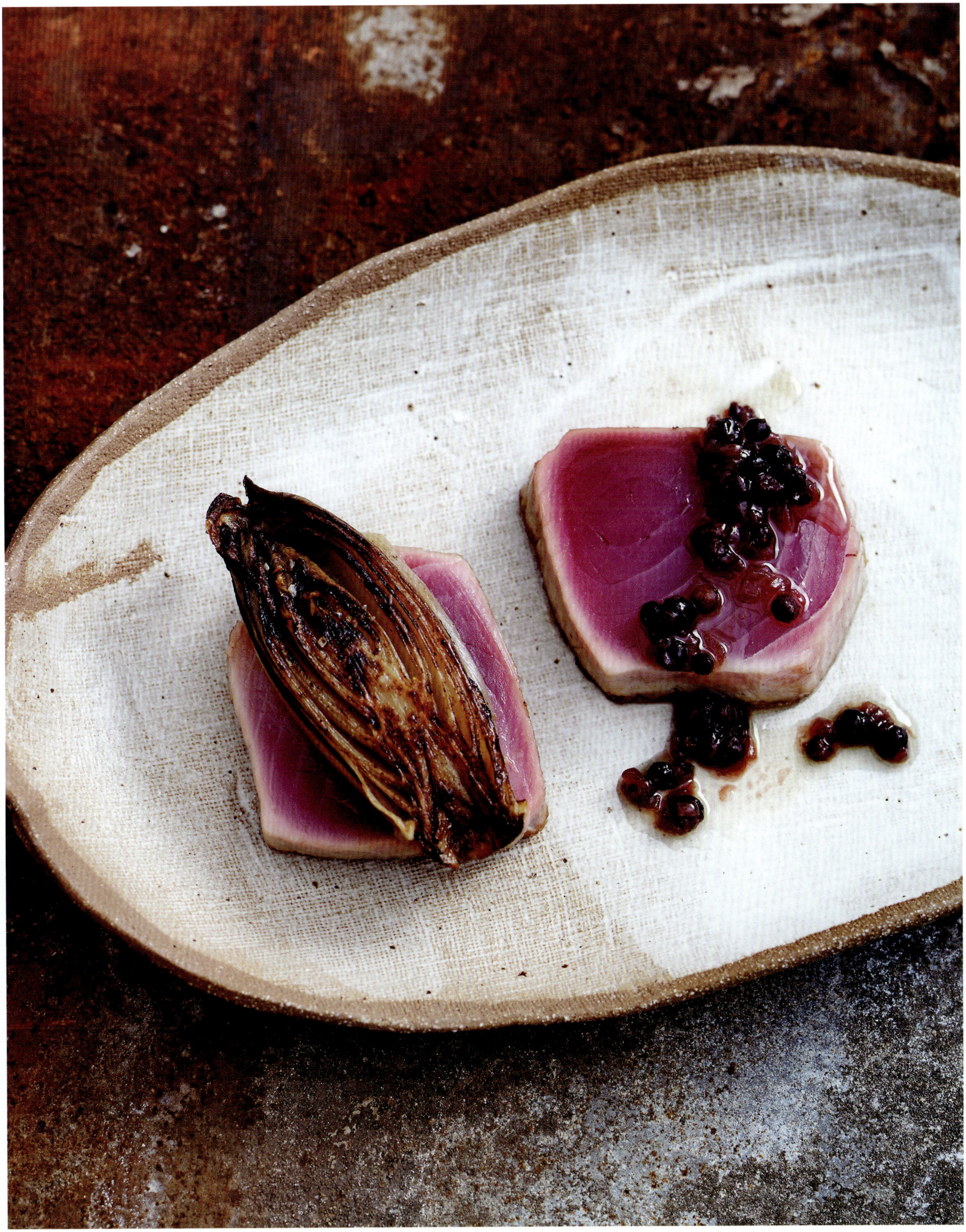

Blue warehou

WAREHOU

The silver warehou (*Seriolella punctata*), sometimes called spotted trevalla, is the lesser known cousin of the blue warehou (*Seriolella brama*), white warehou (*Seriolella caerulea*) and the much more famous blue-eye trevalla (see page 243).

It's caught in the deep cold-water trenches off the continental shelf, principally off the rugged west coast of Tasmania. Silver warehou has been a staple offering on fishmongers' slabs in Victoria and Tasmania for years, but is rarely seen in shops or restaurants north or west of the Murray River.

The similar blue warehou is found in slightly shallower waters along the south-eastern coast of Australia and around New Zealand at depths of 50–400 m (160–1300 ft). White warehou is more commonly caught off New Zealand.

SEASONALITY Year round, with a peak in June–September

CATCHING METHODS Bottom otter trawl, mid-water trawl

COMMON LENGTH 35–55 cm (14–22 in)

COMMON WEIGHT 500 g – 2.5 kg (1 lb 2 oz – 5 lb 8 oz)

IDENTIFIABLE FEATURES Short squat body, small head and eyes, short powerful tail; blue warehou: blue tinge to the back; silver warehou: much paler, with dark spots; white warehou: lighter again, without spots

SUSTAINABILITY Managed to a strict quota and regarded as sustainable

WAREHOU IN THE KITCHEN

In good condition, silver warehou offers a thick fillet with few bones and a culinary versatility belying its modest price, but it's fragile and can spoil quickly. Skinned deeply to remove the dark blood line, it yields a luscious white portion that when pan-fried is pale and flavoursome.

The high oil content can be overwhelming if the fish is the focus, but it makes warehous excellent for smoking and barbecuing. They do have a tendency to dry out, however, so they're ideal for marinating. They're great in a curry because they can hold the robust flavours. Warehou is also one of the rare fish that works with the potato scales recipe (page 244).

BEST COOKING METHODS Smoked, grilled (broiled), barbecued, baked, braised

TEXTURE Medium when raw, springy once cooked; fibrous if overcooked

AROMA Savoury umami with notes of champignon and cooked potato

FLAVOUR Rich and clean to full roast-meat tones

APPEARANCE White to light grey when raw; off-white or bright white once cooked

YIELD Skinless, boneless fillet about 45% of whole weight

SUBSTITUTES Blue-eye trevalla, hapuka

Yellow curry of warehou

SERVES 4

80 g (2¾ oz/½ cup) cashew nuts
dash of Chinese red vinegar
500 ml (17 fl oz/2 cups) Yellow Curry Sauce (page 456)
500 ml (17 fl oz/2 cups) Fish Stock (page 457)
4 × 200 g (7 oz) warehou fillets, skin on, pin-boned
8 ribbons pickled green papaya (see below), to serve
2 handfuls mixed Asian herbs, such as mint, Vietnamese mint, Thai basil and coriander (cilantro), to serve
steamed jasmine rice, to serve

PICKLED GREEN PAPAYA
(Makes about 500 ml/17 fl oz/2 cups)

1 small green papaya, peeled and cut in half, seeds removed
375 ml (13 fl oz/1½ cups) white wine vinegar
330 g (11½ oz/1½ cups) caster (superfine) sugar

For the pickled green papaya, shave the fruit into ribbons using a vegetable peeler. Combine the vinegar and sugar in a small saucepan over medium–high heat and bring to the boil. When the sugar has dissolved, remove from the heat, add the papaya and toss through. It will be ready to use in as little as 30 minutes (see note).

To roast the cashew nuts, preheat the oven to 180°C (350°F). Place the nuts in a heavy-based ovenproof frying pan and roast until just coloured. Remove the pan from the oven, add the Chinese red vinegar and place on the stovetop over medium heat. Reduce the vinegar until there is no liquid left. Spread the nuts on a tray and leave to dry (see note).

Heat the curry sauce with the fish stock in a medium saucepan over high heat and bring to the boil. Remove from the heat, add the fish, skin side up, and cover immediately. Leave the fish to poach for 2 minutes. Remove the lid, gently turn the fish using a spatula, then cover and leave for a further 2–3 minutes, depending on the size of the fish.

Remove the fish from the saucepan. Peel the skin off each fillet and discard. Place the fillets in serving bowls, then pour 125 ml (4 fl oz/½ cup) of the hot curry sauce into each bowl.

Garnish each bowl with ribbons of papaya, herb sprigs and cashew nuts. Serve with jasmine rice on the side.

NOTES: Pickled green papaya will keep in an airtight container in the fridge for up to 3 months. The pickling liquid can be strained and re-used.
  The roasted cashews will keep in an airtight container in the pantry for 3 days.

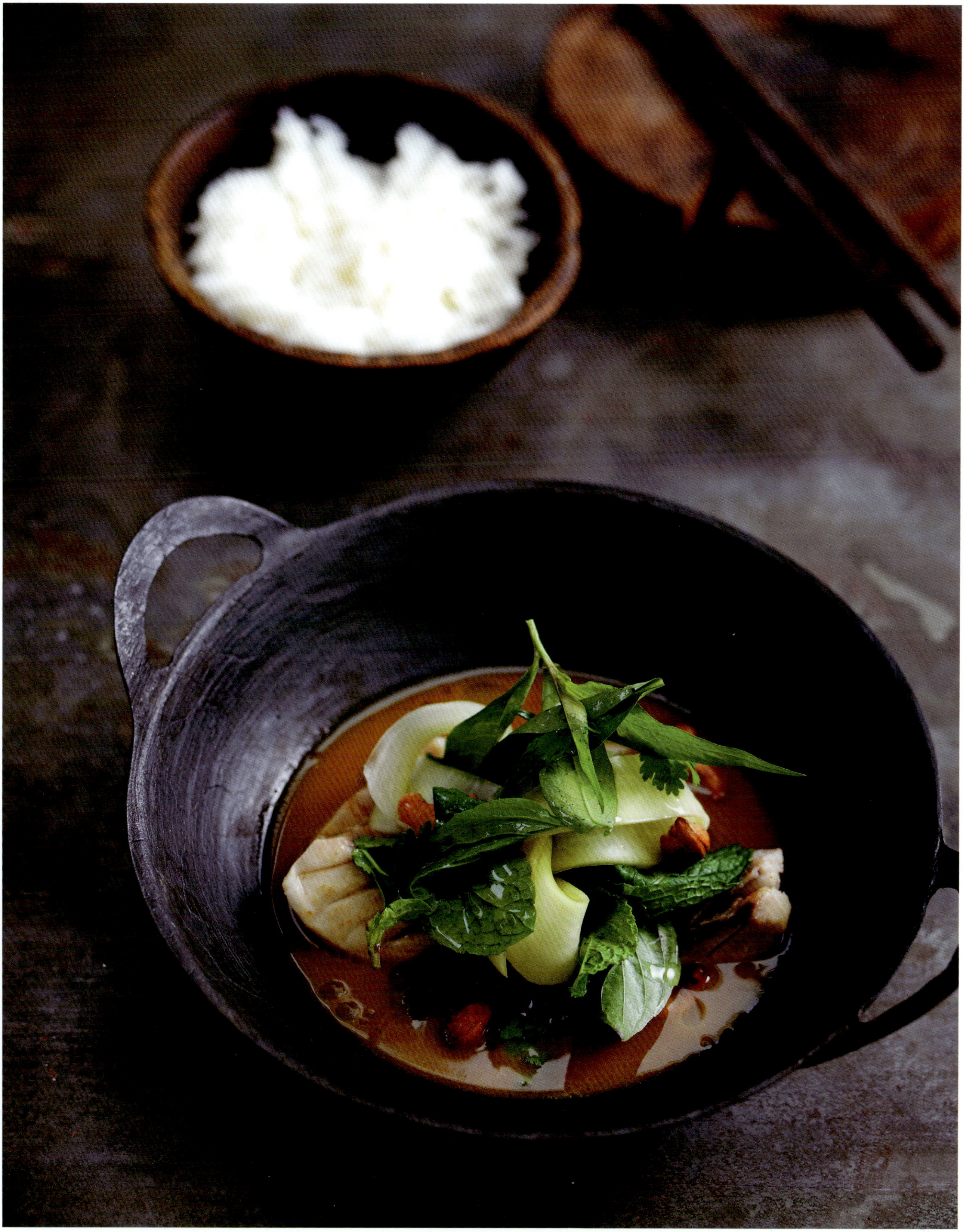

King George (left) and sand whiting

WHITING

Here in Australia, we catch about ten species of whiting, but two iconic southern species stand out: King George whiting (*Sillaginodes punctatus*), found off south-eastern Victoria, South Australia and south-west Western Australia; and the sand whiting (*Sillago ciliata*), common in southern coastal waters, from southern New South Wales to southern Western Australia, including north-east Tasmania.

The King George whiting has a delicate, sweet flavour and firm, tight texture similar to the renowned English Dover sole. Schooling in large numbers, it's native to shallow coastal and estuarine waters with muddy bottoms or grassy flats with sand. The upper body is dark brown or sometimes almost black, merging to light brown on the sides and silver on the belly. The sides are well studded with dark brown blotches.

Sand whiting, also known as summer whiting, inhabit the inshore tidal waters of eastern Australia, including beaches, sand bars, bays, coastal lakes, estuaries and rivers. They form large schools across sandbanks near river mouths and in the surf zone. They're silvery white on top with plain yellowish sides and dark blotches at the base of the fins. They're long and round, with a relatively long, conical snout.

The eastern school whiting (*Sillago flindersi*), sometimes referred to as redspot whiting, is much more modestly priced but its flesh is just as fine, sweet and tasty. It's actually several species, found off north Queensland and around the south coast up to Shark Bay in Western Australia. Once a bycatch of prawn trawling, it's now targeted specifically, largely due to its popularity in Japanese tempura. It has orange colouring and red diagonal stripes on the upper body.

SEASONALITY Year round, with a peak in summer; best in winter
CATCHING METHODS Handline, purse seine
COMMON LENGTH 20–30 cm (8–12 in)
COMMON WEIGHT 300–800 g (10½ oz – 1 lb 12 oz)
IDENTIFIABLE FEATURES King George: dark back, light brown sides with dark brown spots, silver belly; eastern school: orange body, red horizontal stripe with diagonal red stripes above; sand: long, round, silvery white back, yellowish sides, dark spots at fin base, long conical snout
SUSTAINABILITY Considered sustainable

WHITING IN THE KITCHEN

The King George whiting offers one of the world's finest fish-eating experiences. It's really sweet when cooked properly, and at its best when steamed whole. It's a thin fish, so another way to steam it is to take a medium-sized fillet, roll it from tail to top, secure it with a skewer, then steam it in a bamboo basket. Because the flesh is rolled up tight, the tail is protected from overcooking. It's often served as fish and chips, but it's much better crumbed than battered – no egg wash or flour, just panko breadcrumbs straight on the skin. Cook skin side down in hot ghee for 1 minute with a weight on top, then flip over and serve. Immaculate.

Although sand whiting is also sweet, it's the King George whiting's more savoury cousin. While it's good minced (ground) for fishcakes, little sand whiting can be rolled up and cooked on a barbecue under a cloche instead of a weight. This allows them to sear and steam gently at the same time. A minute each side is all you need.

The eastern school whiting is small (mostly 15–25 cm/6–10 in long), with fine scales and bones. This makes it slightly tricky to fillet, but it's worth the effort. The sweet, clean and tasty flesh is tight-grained, with a characteristic iodine grassiness. Beautiful pan-fried in butter, it can also be cooked whole, which is a good way to retain moisture in the flesh.

All whiting is versatile, and can be pot-roasted, barbecued, crumbed and fried or pan-fried, as long as you take a lot of care because it's so thin and delicate. All whiting is best with simple pairings, such as aioli (page 393) and lemon. Don't bother with vegetables, but a nice salsa – capers, cucumber, parsley, tomato and anchovies – works well, or simply try salt, lemon and a side of chips (page 459).

BEST COOKING METHODS Steamed, poached, crumbed and fried

TEXTURE Firm, with a small flake and tight grain

AROMA Clean, bright, the King George especially with notes of freshly cut grass and asparagus

FLAVOUR Sweet, clean, with a bright iodine zing and notes of grassy brightness

APPEARANCE Fillets translucent grey when raw; pearl white once cooked

YIELD Fillets about 40% of whole weight

SUBSTITUTES Garfish, yellowfin bream

Barbecued whole redspot whiting with sourdough crumbs and blackened citrus

Preheat a flat-top barbecue hotplate to medium, or heat a flat stovetop grill pan over medium heat.

Splash a little olive oil on the barbecue or grill and lay the four lemon halves on it, flesh side down. Cook for 2–3 minutes, or until they start to blacken. Turn and cook on the skin side for a further 2 minutes, or until the lemons are soft and nicely charred – don't be afraid to let the lemons really darken. Set aside and keep warm.

Heat a small heavy-based frying pan over medium heat and add the 60 ml (2 fl oz/ ¼ cup) olive oil. When the oil is hot, add the breadcrumbs, fennel seeds and chilli flakes, then cook, tossing frequently, until the crumbs are golden brown and well coated. Add the lemon zest and a pinch of salt, then remove the pan from the heat and set aside.

Drizzle the whiting with olive oil and season with salt and pepper. Cook the fish on the barbecue for 2 minutes on each side, or until golden and just cooked.

Transfer the fish to a serving platter, scatter the capers, pine nuts and fennel fronds over, and top with the breadcrumbs. Add the blackened lemon and finish with any remaining oil from the pan. The lemon can be squeezed over the fish when serving.

NOTE: Limes, blood oranges or ruby grapefruit, when in season, are delicious alternatives to lemons.

SERVES 4

60 ml (2 fl oz/¼ cup) extra virgin olive oil, plus extra for cooking and drizzling

2 lemons, ends trimmed, cut in half (see note)

15 g (½ oz/¼ cup) fresh coarse sourdough breadcrumbs

1 teaspoon fennel seeds

pinch of chilli flakes

grated zest of 1 lemon

sea salt and freshly ground black pepper, to taste

4 whole redspot whiting, gutted and cleaned

2 tablespoons drained salted baby capers, soaked for 30 minutes in cold water and well rinsed

50 g (1¾ oz/⅓ cup) pine nuts, lightly toasted in a dry frying pan

2 tablespoons roughly chopped fennel fronds

Rolled King George whiting with Asian mushrooms

SERVES 4 AS AN ENTRÉE

4 × 100–120 g (3½–4¼ oz) King George whiting fillets, skin on, pin-boned

vegetable oil, for cooking

4 fresh black fungus (wood ear) mushrooms, roughly torn

60 g (2¼ oz/1 cup) loosely packed mixed enoki and shimeji mushrooms

lemon oil, to serve (see note page 25)

sea salt and freshly ground black pepper, to taste

Fill a Chinese steamer, wok or saucepan with water and bring to the boil over high heat.

Lay the whiting fillets on a work surface. Gently roll up each fillet, skin side out, starting at the tail end. Secure the roll with a toothpick.

Place the rolled whiting in a metal or bamboo steamer basket lined with baking paper. Set the basket over the steamer, then cook, covered, for 4 minutes (see note).

While the fish is cooking, heat a heavy-based frying pan over high heat and add a splash of vegetable oil. When the oil is smoking, add all the mushrooms and fry, tossing constantly, for 30 seconds, or until they have softened and the enokis and shimejis have coloured slightly and crisped around the edges.

Remove the fish from the steamer. Place the rolled whiting on serving plates. Toss a little lemon oil, salt and pepper through the mushrooms in the pan, then spoon the mushrooms onto and around each roll. Serve immediately.

NOTE: Cooking times may vary according to the size of the fish and the thickness of the fillets, and whether you use a Chinese steamer or a double boiler, so take care not to overcook the fish.

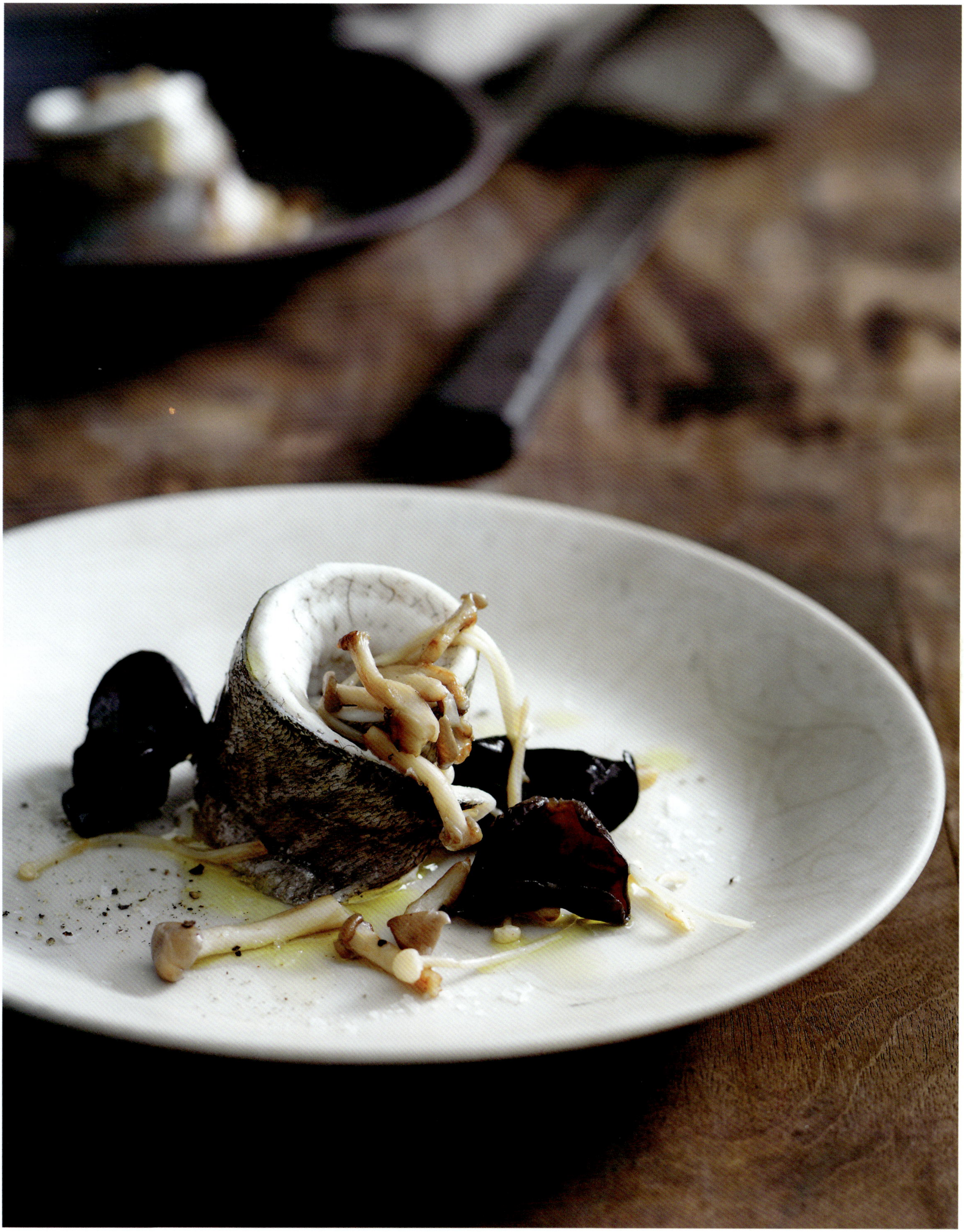

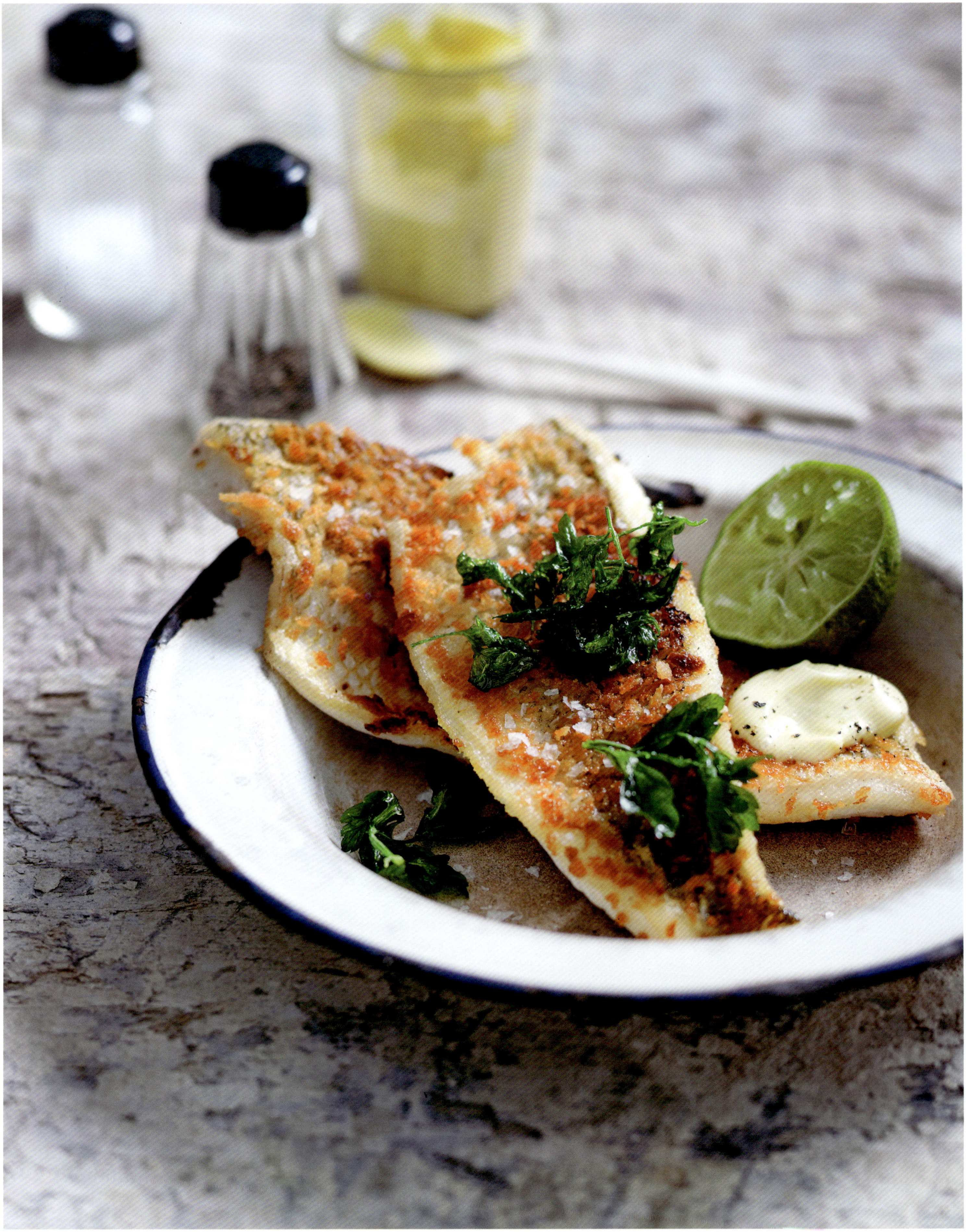

Crumbed sand whiting

Spread the breadcrumbs over a flat tray and lay each sand whiting fillet on the crumbs, skin side down. Coat the skin side only with crumbs, pressing quite firmly to ensure the crumbs stay on during cooking.

On a clean work surface, lay each fillet, flesh side down, on a sheet of baking paper large enough to cover it.

Heat a large cast-iron or heavy-based frying pan (or two smaller pans — it's essential that the fish is not overcrowded in the pan; see note) over medium–high heat. Add the 125 ml (4 fl oz) of ghee. When the pan is hot and the ghee translucent, place the fillets in the pan, crumbed side down, leaving the paper on the flesh side. Place a 1 kg (2 lb 4 oz) weight — such as a heavy pot or another pan — on top of the fillets and cook for 1 minute; they will be warm and the flesh slightly translucent.

While the fish is cooking, heat the extra ghee in a smaller frying pan over medium–high heat. When the ghee is translucent, add the parsley and fry for about 30 seconds, or until crisp. Immediately remove from the pan and drain on paper towel.

Remove the weight and the paper from the fish, then gently flip the fillets using a spatula and quickly seal the flesh side. Transfer to paper towel to drain.

Place two whiting fillets on each serving plate, and season with a squeeze of lime juice and a pinch of salt and pepper. Top with the fried parsley leaves and serve with a good dollop of mayonnaise.

NOTE: If you don't have a pan large enough for all the fillets, or two smaller pans, cook the fish in two batches. Keep the first batch warm while you cook the second.

SERVES 4

30 g (1 oz/½ cup) panko (Japanese-style) breadcrumbs

8 sand whiting fillets, skin on, pin-boned

125 ml (4 fl oz/½ cup) ghee (see note page 26), plus 80 ml (2½ fl oz/⅓ cup) extra

4 tablespoons flat-leaf (Italian) parsley leaves

2 limes, cut in half

sea salt and freshly ground black pepper, to taste

85 g (3 oz/⅓ cup) Mayonnaise (page 455), to serve

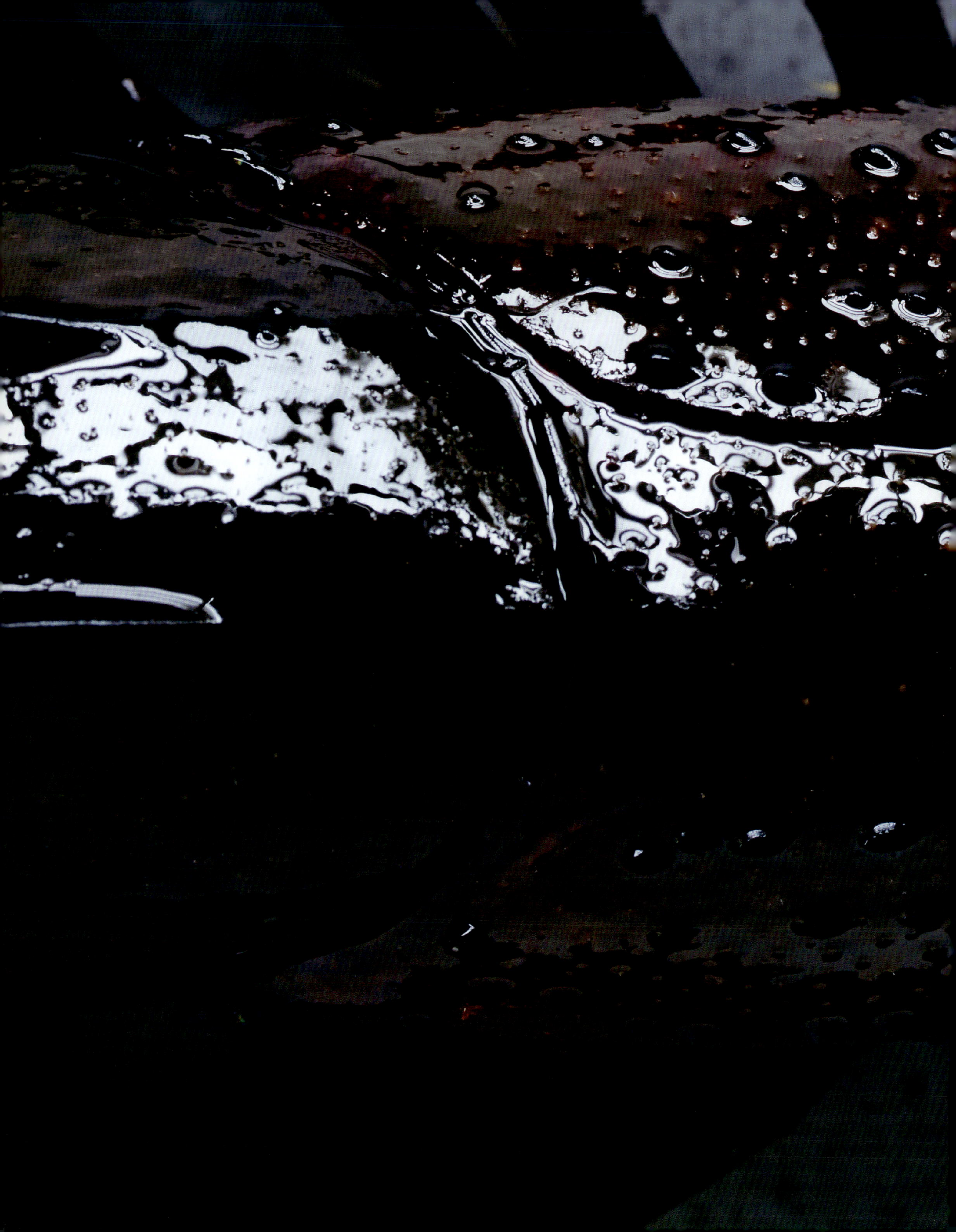

SHELLFISH
A–Z GUIDE
& RECIPES

Greenlip abalone

ABALONE

Abalone is rare, exotic, delicious and expensive. Blacklip (*Haliotis rubra*) or greenlip (*Haliotis laevigata*); wild or farmed; live, frozen or cooked and tinned – abalone is universally pricey. It's often misunderstood, though, especially in the West, where its cost and intolerance of poor handling make it a risky option for most home cooks.

Abalone is one of Australia's most important commercial fisheries, ranking second in export value only to rock lobster. Australia is currently the dominant player in the world abalone market, supplying around half of all wild-caught and 30 per cent of farmed abalone. Australian abalone is well regarded for its clean flavour and smooth texture, the key eating qualities sought by gourmets.

Abalone live on the rocky bottom of the sea and each species has a distinct habitat. The only harvesting technique is collection by divers, who mainly use the 'hookah' surface-to-water air-supply system and can spend up to seven hours in the water at a time. Winter temperatures below 12°C (54°F), combined with the physical demands on the diver's body, make diving extremely dangerous. Often the waters fished are also well known for sharks. Many divers, especially on the west coast of South Australia, dive in shark-proof cages, which can slow down the harvest and increase the decompression times required on resurfacing.

The predominant wild species in Australia are the greenlip and blacklip abalone, named for the colour of the large muscular foot under the shell. Other less common species in Australian waters include the brownlip (*Haliotis conicopora*) and Roe's (*Haliotis roei*) abalone. Farmed abalone can be blacklip or greenlip, and are generally much smaller than the minimum wild size.

SEASONALITY Year round, with peak demand at Chinese New Year

CATCHING METHOD Divers

COMMON SIZE Wild: 13–18 cm (5–7 in); farmed: 6–8 cm (2½–3¼ in)

COMMON WEIGHT Wild meat: 130–250 g (4½–9 oz); farmed meat: 25–35 g (1–1¼ oz)

IDENTIFIABLE FEATURES Ear-shaped shell with a row of holes along one side; muscular foot

SUSTAINABILITY Managed to a strict quota; stock status good

COMMON ABALONE SPECIES

Blacklip abalone
Haliotis rubra
Lives in a variety of habitats off the coasts of Western Australia, western and central South Australia and New South Wales. They can be found on reefs, usually hidden in caves, fissures and narrow crevices, but they prefer shallow waters and are rarely found deeper than about 10 m (35 ft). The frill around the muscular foot is black.

Brownlip abalone
Haliotis conicopora
Endemic to the south-west Western Australian coast, and found on rocks and reefs in deeper water up to 40 m (130 ft). In brownlip abalone, the muscular foot and frill are brown.

Greenlip abalone
Haliotis laevigata
Lives in several habitats, mainly on the eastern, southern and western coasts, in low reef areas at depths of 5–40 m (15–130 ft); rough waters at the base of granite cliffs and along the sides of clefts at depths of 10–25 m (35–80 ft); and shallower waters on rocky surfaces near seagrass beds. The large muscular foot has a bright green frill or lip.

Most in the know would agree that greenlip abalone has the silkiest texture and most pronounced iodine and seagrass flavours, which are as intense as cured Iberian jamón, as deep and soul-satisfying as a black truffle, and as rich and mouth-filling as foie gras.

Roe's abalone
Haliotis roei
Lives exclusively off south-west Western Australian, inshore to depths of 5 m (15 ft). They inhabit mainly shallow limestone reefs, especially around Perth, where they're a popular recreational catch. This smaller species is also known as redlip.

ABALONE IN THE KITCHEN

Abalone is an absolute luxury, thanks to its regal, velvety, firm, mushroomy texture and earthy flavour profile. The blacklip has an intense meaty taste, subtle sweetness and umami notes of miso soup. The greenlip has a round, full flavour, lingering sweetness and the mild umami character of a chicken consommé.

Abalone is exquisite either cooked or raw, but there's no point having a couple of shavings in a pasta dish because you won't taste it. The best way is to clean it up, slice it very thinly and dip it in boiling water for a few seconds – if you overcook it, it will be tough and inedible, and once the texture is gone, the flavour is gone too.

If you want to sauté abalone, just toss it with a bit of garlic. You can eat it raw, but it often takes the best sushi chefs to get it right. Abalone sashimi is indeed an experience – firm of texture and intense in taste, leaving an almost numbing sense of flavour in the mouth.

These days, tinned abalone is a great option. Although tinned greenlip abalone is often farmed and the flavour is slightly different from fresh, it will still give you a good idea of what abalone tastes like.

STORAGE AND HANDLING Handle fragile live abalone with care: wrap in a moist cloth and store in the vegetable crisper in the fridge for no longer than 12–14 hours or shuck and clean as quickly as possible, wrap tightly in plastic wrap and bury in ice until ready to use. Alternatively, buy frozen or blanched meat; thaw slowly from frozen overnight in a sealed container in the fridge, then use as soon as possible.

BEST COOKING METHODS Raw, slowly braised, quickly blanched or grilled (broiled)

TEXTURE Firm mushroom and cooked cheese

AROMA Vegetal, with notes of zesty iodine and funky braised cabbage

FLAVOUR Seagrass, savoury umami and a lingering sweetness

APPEARANCE The muscular foot, when cleaned of roe, gut and frill, looks like a white puck of meat

YIELD Meat about 35% of whole weight

SUBSTITUTES Tinned or poached abalone

Pan-fried abalone with zucchini and garlic

SERVES 4 AS AN ENTRÉE

2 live abalone
80 ml (2½ fl oz/⅓ cup) extra virgin olive oil
1 small garlic clove, peeled and finely crushed
2 baby green zucchini (courgettes), shaved into ribbons (using a mandoline or vegetable peeler)
pinch of sea salt
freshly ground black pepper, to taste
lemon oil, to serve (see note page 25)

Shuck the abalone (see page 439) and remove the meat from the shells. Slice the abalone meat as thinly as possible – the thinner the better.

Heat a large frying pan over medium–high heat and add 2 tablespoons of the olive oil. When the oil is hot but not smoking, add the garlic, zucchini and salt. Toss for about 1 minute, to coat and soften. While the zucchini skin is still a vibrant green, transfer the mixture and all the pan juices to a bowl and set aside.

Return the pan to high heat and add the remaining olive oil (see note). When the oil is smoking, add the abalone and fry quickly, about 30 seconds on each side. Immediately remove the abalone from the pan and transfer to the bowl with the zucchini.

Toss the abalone and zucchini mixture together and transfer to serving plates. Finish with pepper and a splash of lemon oil.

NOTE: You may need to use two frying pans for the abalone, or cook it in two batches, to avoid overcrowding the pan.

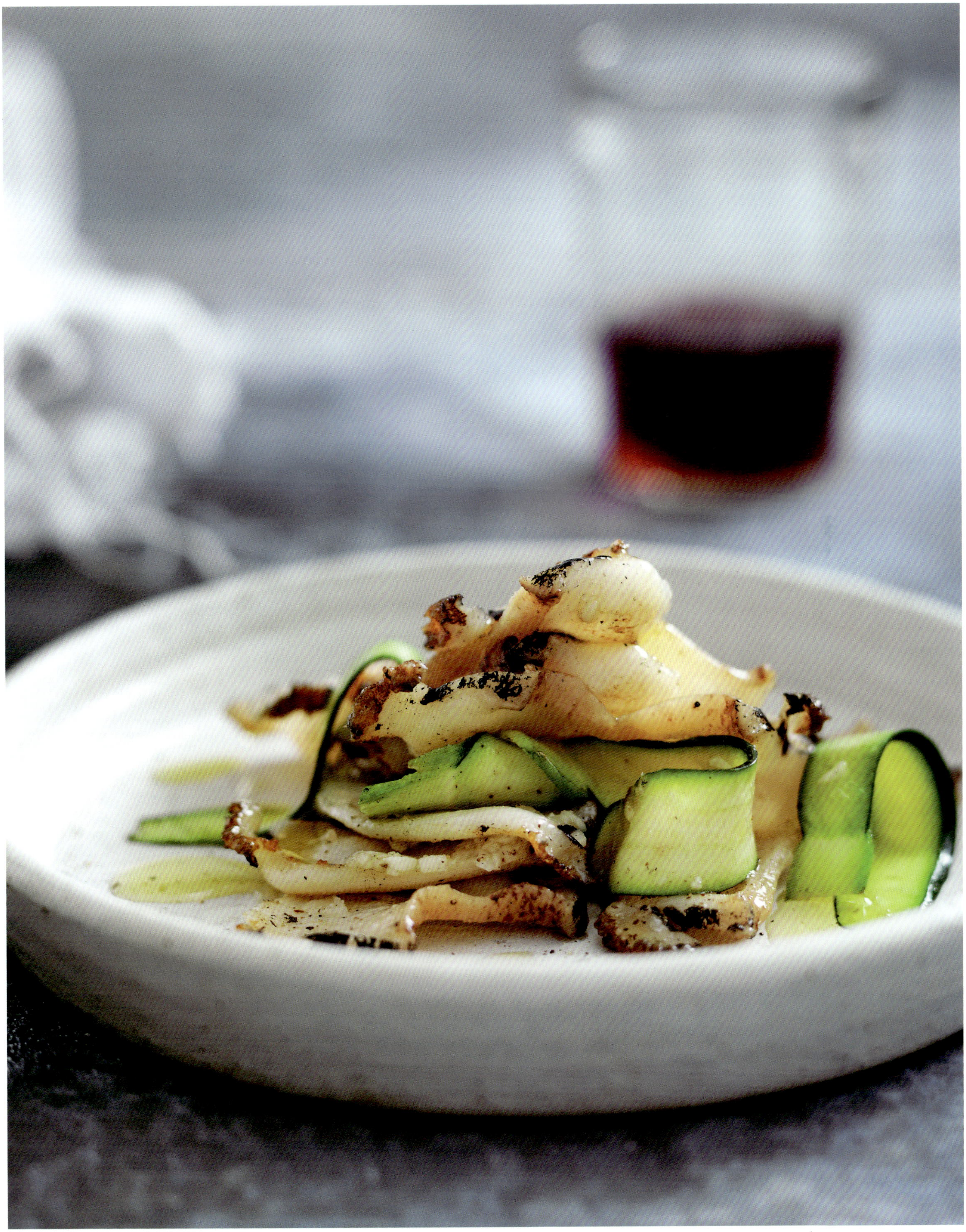

Balmain bug

BUGS

Some readers might think we're suggesting they make insects part of their everyday cuisine, but 'bug' is actually the colloquial Australian term for our slipper and shovel-nosed lobsters. These ubiquitous critters are some of our favourite crustaceans.

Closely related to rock lobsters, bugs are found throughout Australian inshore waters, mostly buried in sand and mud, sometimes in the seagrass beds off southern New South Wales. The two main commercial species both carry quirky regional identification. The Balmain bug (*Ibacus peronii*) is actually found throughout southern Australia rather than a single suburb of Sydney. Its broad round body and close-set eyes differentiate it from the generally longer Moreton Bay bug (*Thenus orientalis*), which is found not only in Moreton Bay near Brisbane but throughout northern Australia and in South Australia's Spencer Gulf.

Bugs don't survive well out of water and are mostly available cooked or frozen. Sometimes you'll find them live, however, in good fish markets and in tanks in the Chinatowns of Sydney, Melbourne and Brisbane. If you do come across live bugs, forget whatever you went to the fish market to buy and grab the bugs – you'll be in for a treat.

Like rock lobster, bugs are distinctly delicious, with a rich, sweet taste and firm texture. The Balmain bug can sometimes have an unmistakable 'garlic weed' or iodine aroma. This is a direct reflection of its feeding habitat and will by no means affect the flesh quality or deeper flavour.

SEASONALITY Generally year round, mostly frozen
CATCHING METHOD Mostly a bycatch of prawn (shrimp) trawl fisheries
COMMON HEAD WIDTH Balmain: 10–14 cm (4–5½ in); Moreton Bay: 8–12 cm (3¼–4½ in)
COMMON WEIGHT Balmain: 80–200 g (2¾–7 oz); Moreton Bay: 120–380 g (4¼–13½ oz)
IDENTIFIABLE FEATURES Flat, hard, brick-coloured shell with a prehistoric-looking profile, short legs, short broad antennae. Balmain: round, close-set eyes on top of head; Moreton Bay: longer and thinner.
SUSTAINABILITY As a bycatch of prawn fisheries, bug harvest numbers are limited; stocks of both species are deemed sustainable

Pipis

CLAMS

Australia might not have a rich clam culture like the countries surrounding the Adriatic Sea, or in Asia or the United States, but we've lately become more inclined to eat clams, especially in restaurants.

Clams are physiologically very different from mussels and oysters, which means they require a unique approach to sourcing, handling and use. While oysters and mussels extract nutrients from the free water around them, clams literally suck their food off the sand or mud in which they're buried. This means that while oysters and mussels are naturally sweet and soft, clams are naturally savoury and firm-textured. As clams have a much higher metabolic rate than oysters or mussels (given they're mostly muscle), they require high levels of food and oxygen – in other words, they need nutrient-rich water that's high in salinity and wave action.

Clams can be either subtidal, meaning they live underwater, or intertidal, meaning they're submerged for only part of each day. Subtidal clams will be inherently fattier than intertidal clams and therefore richer in taste, fuller in body and sweeter.

Clam fishing in Australia occurs mainly in New South Wales, Tasmania and South Australia, and is all done by hand, typically by raking the intertidal beach zone. Reduction of catching quotas in these fisheries has dramatically limited the volume of domestically produced clams coming to market.

Clams require purging (see page 317) before consumption, and any quality producer will have purged or de-sanded the clams in advance. As this can shorten the shelf life of a live clam, however, one school of thought suggests they should only be purged just before cooking.

COMMON CLAM SPECIES

Pipi
Plebidonax deltoides

Known in South Australia as the Goolwa cockle, the pipi has a cream to pale brown wedge-shaped shell, sometimes with green, yellow or purple bands. Found all around the southern Australian coastline from Moreton Bay in Queensland to Geraldton in Western Australia, they're hand-harvested using long rakes from the intertidal zone of sandy beaches with good surf.

One of the most important fisheries, certified by the Marine Stewardship Council, is in the Coorong, in South Australia.

SEASONALITY Year round from small Vic. fisheries; spring–autumn in SA and NSW
CATCHING METHOD Hand-raking
COMMON SIZE 3–6 cm (1¼–2½ in)
COMMON WEIGHT 20–40 g (¾–1½ oz)
IDENTIFIABLE FEATURES Shell cream to brown, wedge-shaped, with green, yellow or purple bands
SUSTAINABILITY Certified by the Marine Stewardship Council
STORAGE AND HANDLING Store live pipis in a moist cloth in the vegetable crisper in the fridge; use as soon as possible
BEST COOKING METHODS Raw, stir-fried, steamed, poached
TEXTURE Firm
AROMA Zesty oceanic character, with funky notes of braised cabbage
FLAVOUR Earthy mangrove, with a back-note of iodine
APPEARANCE Cream-coloured meat with a white adductor muscle
YIELD Meat 10–15% of whole weight
SUBSTITUTES Clams, vongole

Vongole
Katelysia spp. and *Venerupis* spp.

Vongole is the name mostly used for *Katelysia* or *Venerupis* clam species. These sand cockles are found mainly in South Australia, Tasmania and the South Island of New Zealand. They're harvested from tidal flats and estuary mouths on sheltered or sandy subtidal sediment to depths of about 5 m (15 ft). South Australia, home to Australia's largest vongole fishery, produces clams similar in appearance to the famed US little neck. *Katelysia* clams are hand-harvested by 'cocklers' who work the intertidal sandbanks of Coffin and Venus bays on the west coast of South Australia and in Tasmania. They have a light brown oval shell with concentric ridges containing white to yellow meat that sometimes has patches of purple.

SEASONALITY Year round, with a peak in autumn–winter
CATCHING METHOD Hand-harvested
COMMON SIZE 2–5 cm (¾–2 in)
COMMON WEIGHT 15–30 g (½–1 oz)
IDENTIFIABLE FEATURES Light brown oval shell with concentric ridges
SUSTAINABILITY Tightly controlled by quota
STORAGE AND HANDLING Wrap fragile live vongole in a moist cloth and store in the vegetable crisper; use as soon as possible. Thaw frozen raw clams slowly overnight in the fridge for best results.
BEST COOKING METHODS Raw, stir-fried, steamed, poached
TEXTURE Firm
AROMA Wet straw, with grassy notes
FLAVOUR Mildly sweet, with notes of champignon and braised cabbage
APPEARANCE Meat white to yellow, sometimes with patches of purple
YIELD Meat about 8% of whole weight
SUBSTITUTES Clams, pipi

Vongole

COMMON CLAM SPECIES (continued)

Surf clams

Although the term 'surf clam' can be applied to both intertidal and subtidal species, it's more commonly used for a range of subtidal clam species harvested wild off New Zealand beaches.

Each species – the storm clam, triangle or diamond shell and tua tua – has its own distinct flavour and texture, and each has captured the imagination of chefs for a range of dishes.

SEASONALITY Year round; in peak condition in autumn
CATCHING METHOD Bespoke hydraulic winnowing rake system
COMMON SIZE 3–6 cm (1¼–2½ in)
COMMON WEIGHT 30–50 g (1–1¾ oz)
IDENTIFIABLE FEATURES Rough cream, greyish white, pale yellow or light brown shell with sculpted concentric ridges
SUSTAINABILITY NZ clams certified by Friend of the Sea

Storm clam
Mactra murchisoni

Caught in the rugged surf zone surrounding New Zealand, the storm clam varies in size from golf ball to tennis ball. Its smooth round shell is cream with dark concentric rings. Inside the shell, the storm clam has two significant parts – a dark body that fills most of the shell and a clean white 'tongue' that has the texture of a prawn (shrimp) and the flavour of a scallop.

STORAGE AND HANDLING NZ clams are blanched before arrival in Australia and can be refrigerated for 21 days
BEST COOKING METHODS Raw, stir-fried, steamed, poached
TEXTURE Body: medium to firm; tongue: soft, yielding
AROMA Zesty oceanic and fresh-grass character, with notes of funky braised cabbage
FLAVOUR Body: rich notes of shiitake mushroom; tongue: scallop taste, bright zesty zing
APPEARANCE Smooth round cream shell with dark concentric rings, containing dark body and white 'tongue'
YIELD Meat 25–30% of whole weight
SUBSTITUTES Large diamond shell

Triangle or diamond shell
Spisula aequilateralis
Caught in the surf zone at 5–10 m (15–30 ft) it has a diamond-shaped khaki shell with light purple highlights. Ideal for use in 'spaghetti vongole', it has a delicious, rich, full-bodied yet clean liquor.

STORAGE AND HANDLING NZ clams are blanched before arrival in Australia and can be refrigerated for 21 days

BEST COOKING METHODS Raw, steamed, roasted, half-shell, stir-fried, in pasta

TEXTURE Medium to soft

AROMA Fresh crustacean and iodine character, with a note of steamed broccoli

FLAVOUR Sweet, rich, buttery and nutty, with notes of green melon

APPEARANCE Khaki, diamond-shaped shell with pale purple highlights

YIELD Meat 25–30% of whole weight

SUBSTITUTES Pipi, tua tua, vongole

Tua tua
Paphies donacina
A smooth, cream shell contains cream meat with a light pink hue around the edges. It's a lovely clam served au naturel, but can also take strong flavours. It works well in Asian and Mediterranean dishes.

STORAGE AND HANDLING NZ clams are blanched before arrival in Australia and can be refrigerated for 21 days

BEST COOKING METHODS Raw, steamed, roasted, half-shell, stir-fried, in pasta

TEXTURE Soft, creamy and mouth-filling

AROMA Light buttermilk and pine nut, with a grassy sweetness of fresh kelp

FLAVOUR Rich, mouth-filling and oceanic, with notes of clean citrus and light Japanese soy sauce

APPEARANCE Smooth, clean, cream shell containing cream meat with pale pink edges

YIELD Meat 30–35% of whole weight

SUBSTITUTES Diamond shell, pipi, vongole

Diamond shells

CLAMS IN THE KITCHEN

If you buy unpurged clams, submerge them in salt water made with 1 tablespoon of salt for each 1 litre (35 fl oz/4 cups) of water. Leave for 30 minutes, then rinse. Repeat this step twice and use the clams immediately.

As clams are mostly lean meat, they need either a fast and high heat or a slow, low and long heat. They're also excellent eaten raw or blanched, simply with a squeeze of lemon or an acid-based dressing, and they make a great addition to any raw plate.

When cooking fast, keep a close eye on the pan and remove each clam as it opens. When they've all opened, return the entire batch to the sauce, soup or pasta.

They're excellent in both Western and Eastern cuisine, but should be handled with some care. Try stir-frying, steaming, roasting, barbecuing or braising. They can carry strong flavours and are best cooked simply in a small amount of flavoured liquid, such as beer, sherry, cider or stock.

The rich, intense nature of clam meat also makes it excellent for sousing or pickling – the flesh doesn't denature under the acid of the pickle or brine as does that of a mussel or oyster.

Clams vinaigrette

SERVES 4–8

125 ml (4 fl oz/½ cup) dry white wine
3 garlic cloves, peeled and crushed
1 small brown onion, peeled and roughly chopped
1 small handful parsley stems
48 small clams (see note)
80 ml (2½ fl oz/⅓ cup) lemon juice
160 ml (5¼ fl oz) lemon oil (see note page 25)
2 red Asian shallots, very finely diced
sea salt and freshly ground black pepper, to taste
2 teaspoons finely chopped chives
crusty bread, to serve

To steam the clams open, combine the wine, garlic, onion and parsley stems with 125 ml (4 fl oz/½ cup) of water in a large saucepan with a tight-fitting lid and bring to the boil over medium–high heat. Toss in the clams, then cover and cook for 8–10 minutes, or until the clams open.

Remove from the heat and scoop the clams into a bowl using a slotted spoon. Discard the cooking liquid and any unopened clams, then allow the opened clams to cool before removing the top shell.

To make the vinaigrette, mix the lemon juice, lemon oil and shallot in a bowl. Season with salt and pepper.

Place the shucked clams on serving plates or on a platter and spoon the vinaigrette over the top. Finish with the chives and serve with crusty bread.

NOTE: Pipis, vongole and surf clams all work well in this recipe. Clams from New Zealand are sold par-cooked and pre-packed in Australia – they can be shucked and used immediately, although you can warm them through a little if you prefer.

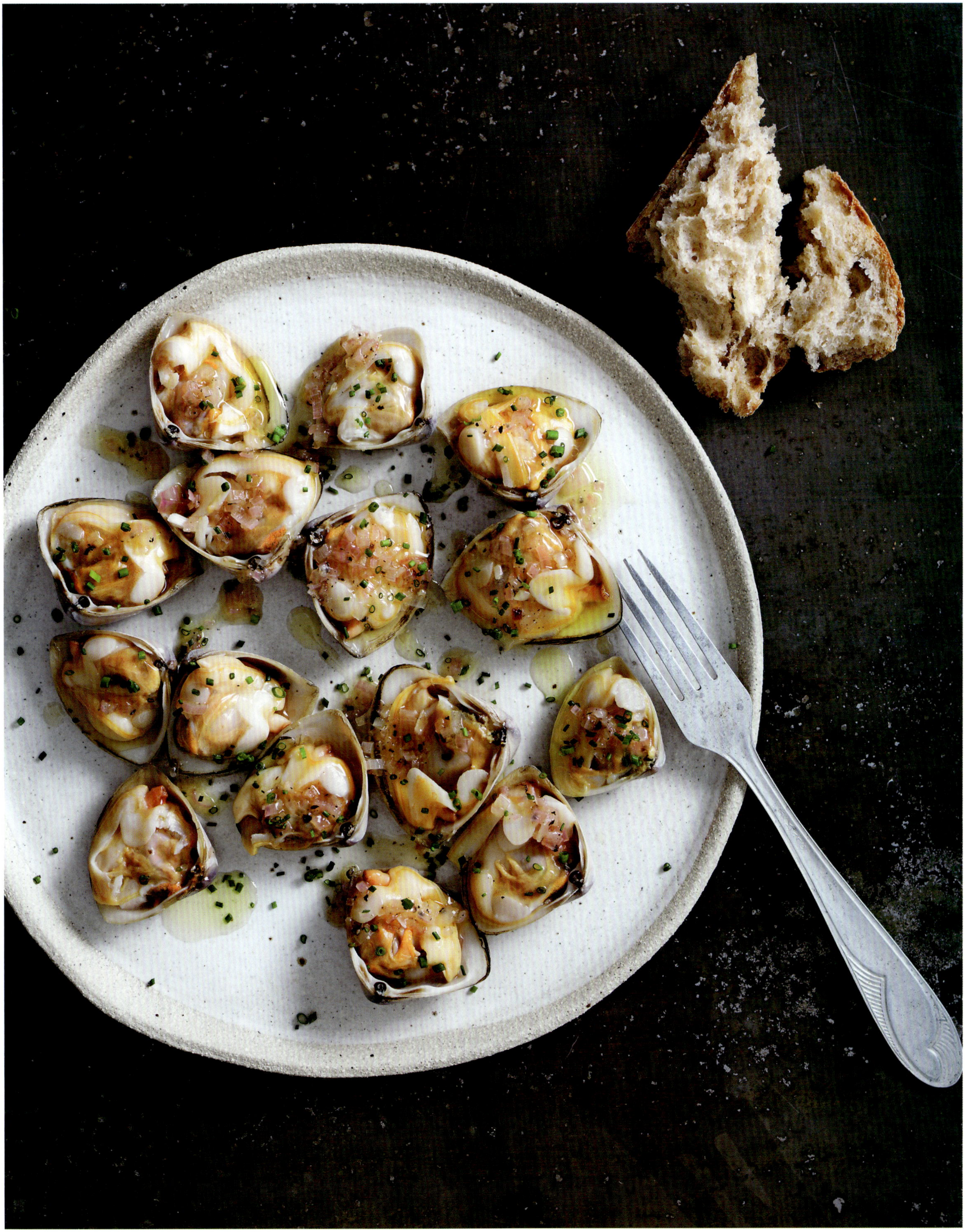

Spaghetti vongole

SERVES 4

sea salt, as required

400 g (14 oz) good-quality dried spaghetti

60 ml (2 fl oz/¼ cup) extra virgin olive oil

4 garlic cloves, peeled and finely chopped

1 long red chilli, split lengthways, seeds removed, finely chopped

1 kg (2 lb 4 oz) vongole (see note)

250 ml (9 fl oz/1 cup) dry white wine

1 large handful flat-leaf (Italian) parsley leaves

Bring a medium saucepan of water to the boil over high heat and add a good pinch of sea salt. Add the spaghetti, return the water to the boil, then reduce the heat to medium, maintaining a steady simmer. Cook the spaghetti, stirring regularly, according to the instructions on the packet until al dente.

Meanwhile, heat a large frying pan over medium heat. Add the olive oil, garlic and chilli to the pan, then fry gently, stirring constantly, for 3 minutes, or until the garlic begins to colour. Add the vongole and toss for about 3 minutes. Increase the heat to high, add the wine and cook for a further 1–2 minutes, until all the clams are open and the briny juices have mingled with the wine. (Discard any unopened vongole.)

Drain the spaghetti in a colander and transfer to the frying pan with the vongole. Add a good pinch of salt and the parsley, then toss well to combine. Remove from the heat and serve immediately on a shared platter or individual plates.

NOTES: Many other types of clam work beautifully in this dish.

Clams from New Zealand are sold par-cooked and pre-packed in Australia. Simply heat them through in the sauce before tossing with the spaghetti.

New England-style clam chowder

To steam the clams open, combine the wine, garlic, onion and parsley stems with 125 ml (4 fl oz/½ cup) of water in a large saucepan with a tight-fitting lid and bring to the boil over medium–high heat. Toss in the clams, then cover and cook for 8–10 minutes, or until the clams open (discard any that don't open).

Heat the olive oil and butter in a medium saucepan over medium heat. As the butter starts to bubble, add the bacon and cook, stirring, for about 4 minutes, until the bacon is fragrant and starting to colour and render slightly.

Reduce the heat to medium–low. Add the onion, leek, garlic and thyme, then cook, without colouring, for 4–5 minutes, until the vegetables are soft and sweet.

Add the potato, stock and bay leaves. Increase the heat to high to bring the stock to the boil. Once boiling, reduce the heat to medium and simmer the chowder gently for about 10 minutes, until the potatoes are soft.

Add the milk and cream, then stir in the clams with the reserved juices. Bring the chowder back to a gentle simmer for 30 minutes but do not boil. Season with pepper.

Spoon the chowder into bowls, top with the chopped parsley and serve with your favourite bread.

NOTES: Pipis, vongole and surf clams all work well in this recipe. Clams from New Zealand are sold par-cooked and pre-packed in Australia – they can be used straight from the packet.

SERVES 4

125 ml (4 fl oz/½ cup) dry white wine, plus 160 ml (5¼ fl oz) extra
1 garlic clove, peeled and crushed
½ small brown onion, peeled and roughly chopped
a few parsley stems
24 clams (see note)
80 ml (2½ fl oz/⅓ cup) extra virgin olive oil
40 g (1½ oz) butter
4 smoky bacon rashers
1 brown onion, peeled and finely diced
½ leek, white part only, trimmed, well washed and finely diced
4 garlic cloves, peeled and finely chopped
4 thyme sprigs
2 all-purpose potatoes (such as desiree), peeled and roughly chopped
250 ml (9 fl oz/1 cup) chicken stock
2 fresh bay leaves
500 ml (17 fl oz/2 cups) milk
250 ml (9 fl oz/1 cup) thin (pouring) cream
freshly ground black pepper, to taste
2 tablespoons chopped flat-leaf (Italian) parsley, to serve
bread, to serve

Blue swimmer crab

CRABS

Sweet, rich and delicious, this luxury is regarded by many as among the tastiest of seafoods. Here in Australia we have many species of crab, a dozen of which are popular in specific regions, from the famous mud crab (*Scylla serrata*) of tropical and subtropical mangroves and tidal flats, to the deepwater snow or crystal crab (*Chaceon bicolor*) that inhabits the subterranean abyss off the southern slopes of the continental shelf at depths of at least 600 m (1970 ft).

Crabs are aggressive feeders, scavenging on the seabed and gorging themselves on pretty much anything they can get their claws into. This scavenging renders their flesh beautifully sweet, but it also makes them home to many naturally occurring bacteria that, given the right environment, can flourish and cause spoilage. For culinary and safety considerations, careful handling from water to plate is more critical with crab than pretty much any other seafood.

SEASONALITY Blue swimmer: year round, with a peak in November–April; mud: year round, with a peak in Qld and NSW in January–April and in NT in May–August; spanner: year round, with a peak in Qld in August–October and a closure from 20 November to 20 December

CATCHING METHODS Blue swimmer: pot, prawn (shrimp) trawl; mud: trap, hand-harvest; spanner: trap

COMMON SHELL WIDTH Blue swimmer: 10–14 cm (4–5½ in); mud: 15–18 cm (6–7 in); spanner: 10–13 cm (4–5 in)

COMMON WEIGHT Blue swimmer: 200 g – 1 kg (7 oz – 2 lb 4 oz); mud: 500 g – 2 kg (1 lb 2 oz – 4 lb 8 oz); spanner: 350–650 g (12 oz – 1 lb 7 oz)

APPEARANCE See following pages

SUSTAINABILITY Stock status good

COMMON CRAB SPECIES

Blue swimmer crab
Portunus pelagicus
The blue swimmer crab, sometimes called the sand crab, is the most common crab in Australian waters. They're caught year round, with a peak supply coming from South Australia and Western Australia from November to April.

They're excellent and versatile eating crabs, with sweet, moist flesh. As they rarely live long after being removed from the water, they're one of the few crabs you can buy dead and uncooked. Bright blue when raw, they turn a brilliant orange when cooked, and the meat is quite easily extracted. Given you can get large chunks of meat from both the body and the claws, they're a great crab to serve whole.

When buying blue swimmer crab, make sure all the limbs are intact and firmly attached, and that it has a fresh sea aroma with no hint of ammonia.

STORAGE AND HANDLING Available pre-cooked or dead and raw; use fresh crabs immediately after purchase and don't freeze (for more, see 'Crabs in the kitchen', page 330)
BEST COOKING METHODS Barbecued; picked meat stir-fried, pot-roasted, in soups and broths
TEXTURE Moist, soft and yielding
AROMA Iodine sweetness, with a fresh grassy note
FLAVOUR Mild, delicate; body intensely savoury, claws nutty and sweet
APPEARANCE Shell bright blue when raw; brilliant orange once cooked
YIELD Picked flesh about 25% of whole weight
SUBSTITUTES Spanner crab, mud crab

Mud crab
Scylla serrata
Although the same species is found throughout South-East Asia, the mud crab of eastern and northern Australia has its own distinctive flavour and texture. They're caught year round, with a peak supply in New South Wales and Queensland from January to April, and in the Northern Territory from May to August. The meat is sweet and moist, with an unmatched flavour and texture.

Muddies can survive happily out of water and are best purchased live. They'll be tied tightly, but they should still be handled with care, as the powerful claws are dangerous. Select crabs that are heavy for their size, with all limbs intact and not blowing bubbles or emitting any liquid. Before cooking, place the still-tied crab in the freezer or fridge for an hour or two. This will send the crab to sleep, which is not only the most humane way to deal with them, but also ensures the cooked meat will be moist and tender.

STORAGE AND HANDLING Available cooked and live; live crabs should be snapping and feisty, with a strong mangrove aroma, and shouldn't be blowing bubbles or be limp. Store live crabs in a moist, warm environment – covered in a wet cloth in a bucket in the laundry. Bury under ice 30 minutes before cooking (for more, see 'Crabs in the kitchen', page 330).
BEST COOKING METHOD Pot-roasted
TEXTURE Soft, with a broad flake
AROMA Rich umami notes of shiitake mushroom and roasted carrot
FLAVOUR Rich umami notes of shiitake mushroom transforming to candied-vegetable sweetness
APPEARANCE Dark green to beige shell and white–tan belly when raw, bright orange shell and white–tan belly once cooked; look for a tan belly
YIELD Picked flesh 15–25% of whole weight
SUBSTITUTES Blue swimmer crab, spanner crab

Mud crab

Spanner crab

COMMON CRAB SPECIES *(continued)*

Spanner crab
Ranina ranina
Spanner crabs are found in only a few places throughout the world, including along the northern New South Wales and south-eastern Queensland coasts. These peculiar-looking crabs offer exceptional value for money, and their meat is among the sweetest of any crab in the world.

Spanner crabs can survive out of water for some time and so are best purchased live. Slow-moving and orange–red, they have ferocious-looking claws that are actually quite harmless and therefore don't need tying. They're especially popular in Asian restaurants, so an Asian fishmonger will probably carry them.

Select a crab that's a good weight for its size, with all limbs intact and a sweet, sea-like aroma. Spanner crab is also often available pre-cooked – make sure it's not dripping liquid or smelling of ammonia. Place live crabs in the freezer for 30–60 minutes to send them off to sleep and improve their eating qualities.

STORAGE AND HANDLING Wrap live crabs in a moist cloth and store in the vegetable crisper for no more than 24 hours; use as soon as possible. Freeze for 30–60 minutes before cooking. Store cooked whole crab in an airtight container in the vegetable crisper and use within 36 hours (for more, see 'Crabs in the kitchen', page 330).

BEST COOKING METHODS Salads, omelettes, pot-roasted

TEXTURE Firm, tight

AROMA Sweet, clean shellfish character with a lingering note of cooked egg white

FLAVOUR Oceanic sweetness with grassy notes of cooked scallop and prawn (shrimp)

APPEARANCE Wrench-shaped pincers, bright red shell with white underbelly both live and cooked

YIELD Picked flesh 15–25% of whole weight

SUBSTITUTES Blue swimmer crab, mud crab

CRABS IN THE KITCHEN

Most crabs are sold live, frozen or cooked. Blue swimmer crabs will, however, never be sold live. This is because they not only have a high fat content but also an extremely sensitive nervous system, which means their flesh becomes mushy if they die slowly. For other species, a live crab will without a doubt give you the best culinary outcome. If you live near a quality fish market or a Chinatown, you're in luck. Head there with a bucket and an open mind as to what crab you might buy.

Mud crabs are generally kept out of tanks, often in cardboard boxes among the vegetables in Chinese supermarkets. Their finger-snapping claws will be tied but you should still handle the crabs from the back, holding them firmly by their rear paddle flippers. You're looking for a crab that's heavy and healthy. You want it feisty, with no limp limbs, strange smells or bubbles coming out of its mouth. Pinch the leg between the last joint and the body; if the crab is healthy, this area of the leg will be full and resistant to the squeeze.

Spanner crabs will generally be stored in a tank, although some fishmongers prefer not to re-tank them once they've been dispatched. Spanner crabs are much weaker out of water than mud crabs but you still want them to be lively, fresh-smelling and not blowing bubbles.

Place live crabs in the bucket you brought and fold a damp cloth or newspaper over the top of the crab. You'll find the live crab will quickly relax, and a handful of ice on the cloth or newspaper will assist in keeping it comfortable. When home, place the bucket in a cool place, such as the laundry. An hour before use, remove the cloth or newspaper and bury the crab in ice to dispatch it humanely.

If buying cooked whole crabs, pick up several of the same size and choose the heaviest. Listen as you tap the shell lightly on the back – if it's a dull, dense thud, the crab will be full; if it's a light airy tap, it will be empty. Smell the cooked crab; if there are any notes of ammonia or forest floor, discard it and move on. You're seeking a clean, fresh aroma with an iodine zing. Place purchased cooked crab in your bucket and cover with ice. Use as quickly as possible.

If buying frozen whole crabs, check the production date and buy the 'freshest', most recently frozen possible. Aim to use them as soon as you can. Thaw in the fridge in an airtight container, resting the crabs on a drip tray above the base. When thawed, ensure that the crab has a fresh, clean aroma.

Cooking with blue swimmer crab
Blue swimmer crab produces delicious meat that's wonderful for soups and broths, salads and pasta. The legs are fantastic to barbecue because the shell is like porcelain. The texture is softer and looser than that of other crabs, and it therefore makes a great sauce or bisque and is brilliant with noodles or pasta.

See page 447 for how to prepare a blue swimmer crab for pot-roasting or stir-frying.

Cooking with mud crab
Mud crabs are *the* crabs to eat whole, especially pot-roasted. They have a very earthy flavour, but also a wonderful sweetness. A crab of 600–800 g (1 lb 5 oz – 1 lb 12 oz) is the best size and perfectly sweet. At 800 g – 1 kg (1 lb 12 oz – 2 lb 4 oz), you'd pick out the meat rather than serve whole. Crabs of 600 g and under are probably sweeter but offer considerably less meat.

The best meat comes from the claws, and you also get a good amount out of the belly and from behind the rear paddle flipper. It's a crab for Asian flavours, such as mango, chillies, lemongrass, caramelised garlic and black pepper.

See page 448 for how to prepare a mud crab for pot-roasting or stir-frying.

Cooking with spanner crab
This is *the* crab for meat. Its flesh is perfect in salads and omelettes, and also great pot-roasted. It's immensely sweet – what chefs would call salty–sweet. The best size for flavour and sweetness is 600–800 g (1 lb 5 oz – 1 lb 12 oz) but up to 1 kg (2 lb 4 oz) is good.

In a spanner crab most of the meat comes from the body itself rather than the claws, which offer intensely sweet meat but demand a lot of work to extract it. Spanner crab can stand alone, eaten only with bread and butter or fresh buttered tagliatelle. It can even take the heat out of chilli.

See page 449 for how to cook spanner crab, and page 450 for how to clean and pick a cooked spanner crab.

Crab salad

SERVES 4

280 g (10 oz) picked crabmeat from a 1 kg (2 lb 4 oz) cooked crab (see pages 449–50)
2 tablespoons Pickled Green Chilli (see page 281)
80 g (2¾ oz/½ cup) roasted cashew nuts, roughly chopped
40 g (1½ oz/⅓ cup) bean sprouts
1 small handful Thai basil leaves
1 small handful Vietnamese mint leaves
1 small green mango, peeled and shaved into ribbons using a vegetable peeler (see note)
80 ml (2½ fl oz/⅓ cup) lemon oil (see note page 25)
juice of 2 limes
1 teaspoon salted red chilli (see note page 247), julienned

Mix the crabmeat with the pickled green chilli, cashew nuts, bean sprouts, herbs and mango.

Dress with the lemon oil and lime juice. Toss gently and transfer to serving plates. Scatter over the salted red chilli and serve.

NOTE: Use any leftover green mango in a curry or pickle.

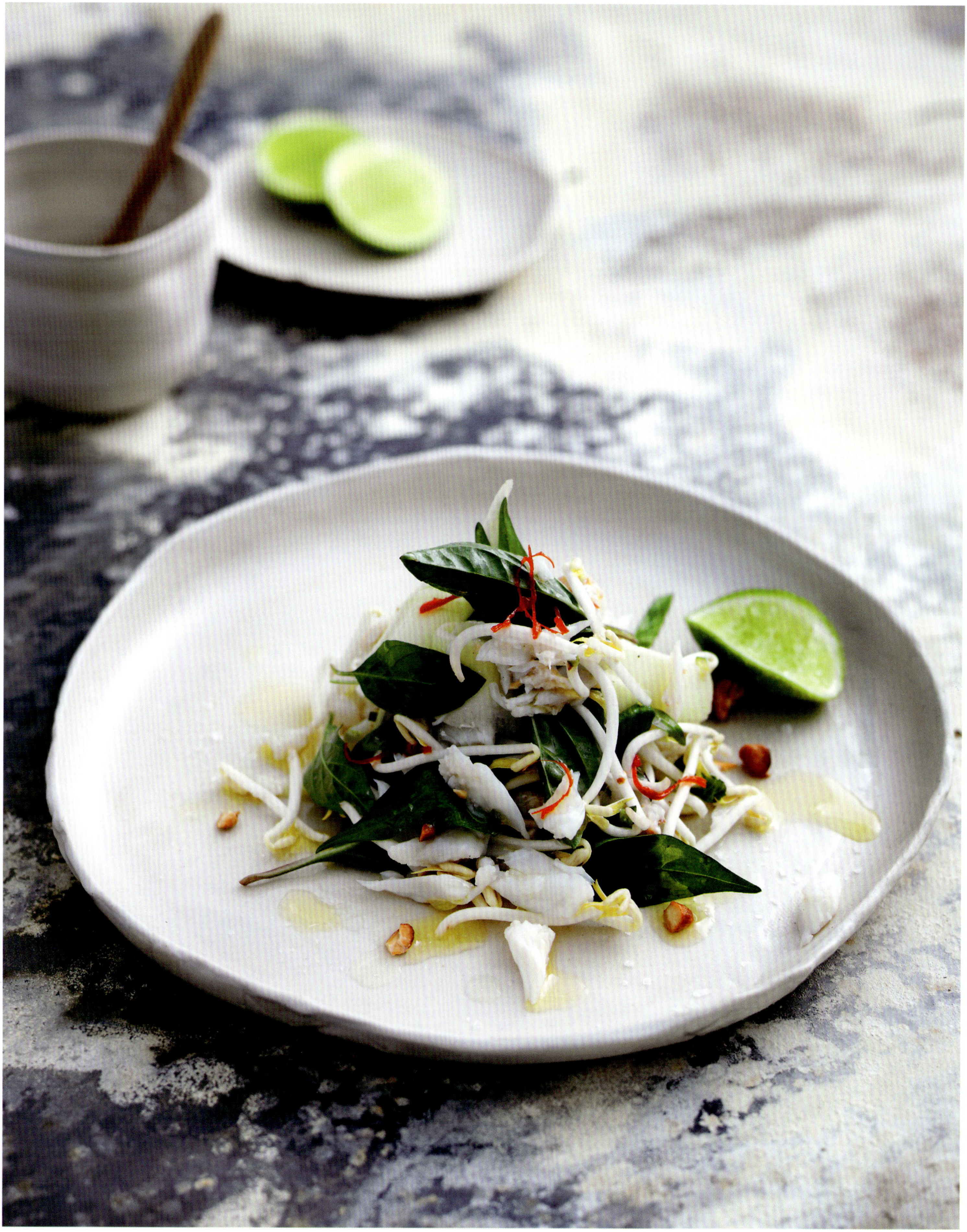

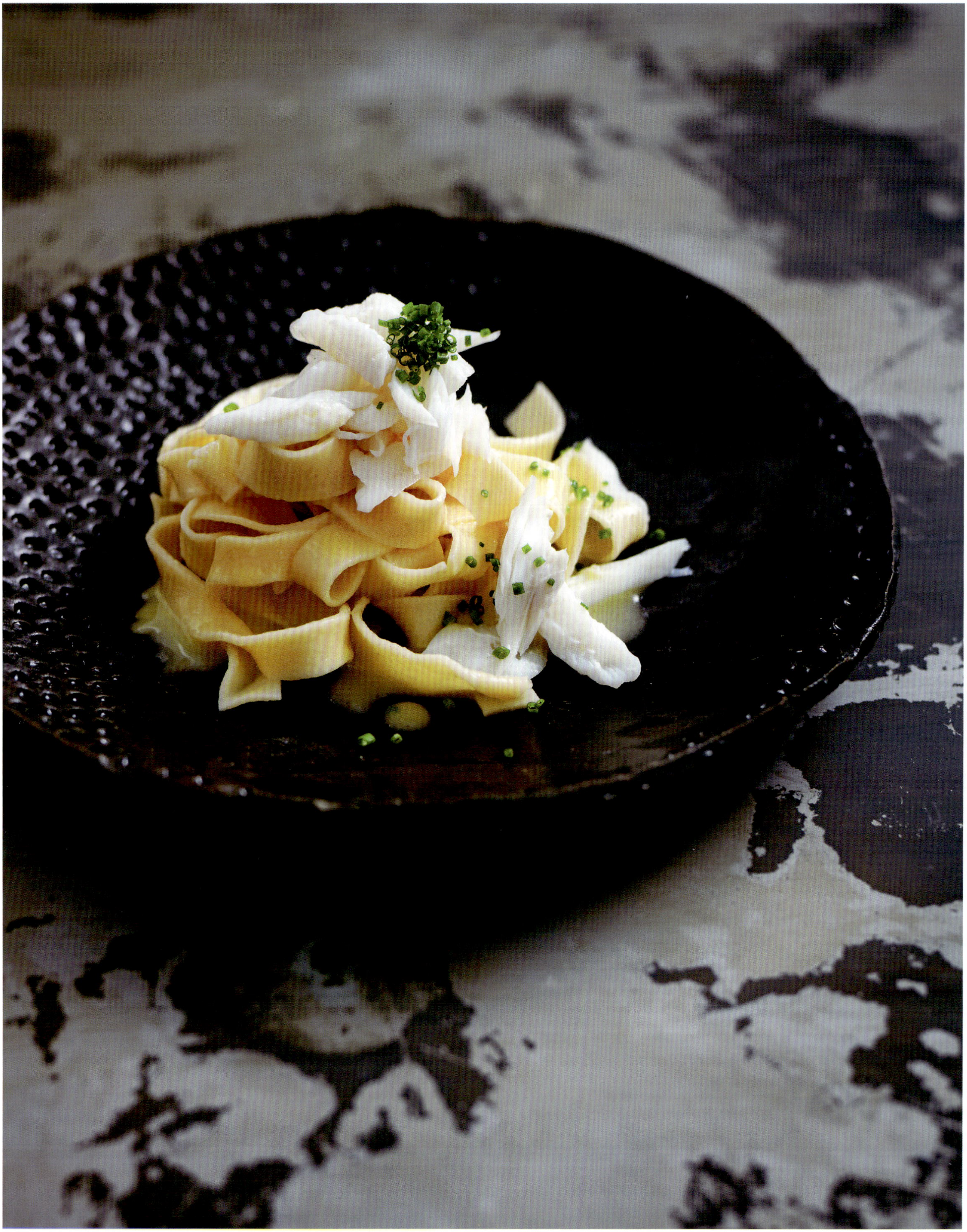

Spanner crab fettuccine

For the fettucine, mix the semolina and strong flour in a food processor until combined. Add the eggs, one at a time, blending to a sticky crumb consistency.

Turn the dough out onto a dusted work surface and knead it, using the palms and heels of your hands, for 1 minute, or until the dough just comes together. Wrap the dough in plastic wrap and set aside to rest for 30 minutes.

Roll the dough through a pasta machine while fresh. Flatten it to just thicker than the machine's thickest setting and dust it lightly with the semolina and flour mix. Feed the dough through the machine, supporting it with your hand as it comes out. Fold the dough into thirds and repeat the process three times.

Reduce the setting on the pasta machine a little and feed the dough through once more. Fold into thirds and repeat the process three more times. Reduce the setting once more and repeat the process of fold and feed until you eventually reach the thinnest setting on the pasta machine. Use the semolina and flour mix as necessary to prevent sticking. Cut the pasta in half if it gets too long.

Hang the pasta sheet over a clean broom handle balanced between two stable points, or over a towel rack, and leave it to air-dry for 5 minutes.

Place the pasta sheet on a lightly floured work surface and cut it into 15 cm (6 in) lengths. Dust each length lightly, then cut into 1 cm (½ in) strips using a sharp knife.

Air-dry the fettuccine over the broom handle or towel rail for 3 hours, as it will cook better if slightly dried rather than completely fresh. It will keep in an airtight container for 3 days. Bring a small saucepan of well-salted water to the boil over high heat. Add the fettuccine and cook in the boiling water for 5 minutes, or until al dente. Strain using a colander.

Melt the butter in a small frying pan over low heat. Add the fettuccine and chives, then toss gently. Transfer to serving plates, top with the crabmeat and serve immediately.

SERVES 4

200 g (7 oz) fresh fettuccine (see below)
80 g (2¾ oz) butter
1 tablespoon finely chopped chives
240 g (8½ oz) picked crabmeat from an 800 g (1 lb 12 oz) cooked spanner crab (see pages 449–50)

FETTUCCINE
(Makes about 600 g/1 lb 5 oz)
70 g (2½ oz) fine semolina
330 g (11½ oz) strong (00) flour
4 eggs
equal mix of semolina and plain (all-purpose) flour, for dusting

Pot-roasted spanner crab with caramelised garlic and cracked pepper

SERVES 2

1 teaspoon black peppercorns
120 g (4¼ oz) butter
10 garlic cloves, peeled
2 teaspoons caster (superfine) sugar
2 tablespoons Fish Stock (page 457), plus 125 ml (4 fl oz/½ cup) extra
1 × 800 g (1 lb 12 oz) whole spanner crab
sea salt, to taste
1 small handful flat-leaf (Italian) parsley leaves
bread, to serve (optional)

Preheat the oven to 180°C (350°C).

Heat the peppercorns in a small ovenproof frying pan in the oven for 3–4 minutes, or until the pepper is fragrant. Using a mortar and pestle, crush the peppercorns to 'cracked' stage – not completely finely ground. Place in a sieve over a bowl to separate the pepper husks from any powdered pepper. Reserve the cracked pepper for the crab and set the powder aside for another use.

Increase the oven temperature to 220°C (425°F).

To caramelise the garlic, heat a small frying pan over medium–low heat and add 40 g (1½ oz) of the butter. When the butter melts and begins to froth, add the garlic and toss to coat. Sprinkle with the sugar and keep tossing for 3 minutes, or until the garlic is golden. Add the 2 tablespoons of fish stock, then continue tossing and cooking the garlic for 5–7 minutes, until tender.

To prepare the crab, remove the top shell (see page 450), leaving the roe in and legs on. Cut the body into four pieces and crack each leg in three places.

Heat the remaining butter in a heavy-based ovenproof shallow saucepan over medium–low heat. Allow the butter to melt but not colour. Add the crab, fleshy side down, and heat through for 1 minute. Add the garlic, cracked pepper and extra fish stock, then cover the pan.

Transfer the pan to the oven and cook the crab for 4 minutes. Remove the crab using tongs and transfer to a plate or bowl. Set aside.

Return the saucepan to the stovetop and stir the butter sauce well using a wooden spoon for 2–3 minutes. Taste and add salt if required. Return the crab to the pan and coat with the sauce. Serve topped with the parsley. This dish is best with a chunk of fresh bread to mop up the sauce.

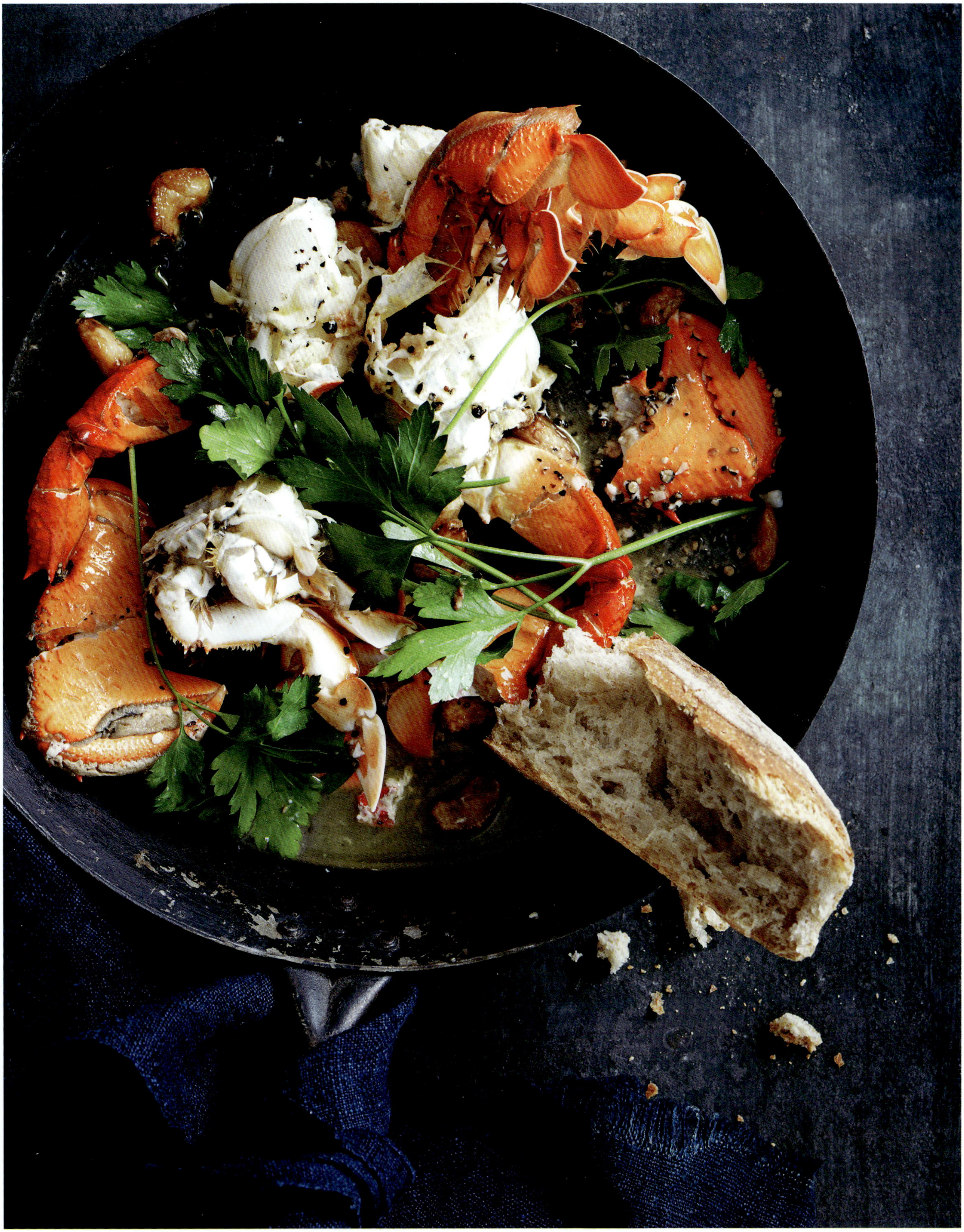

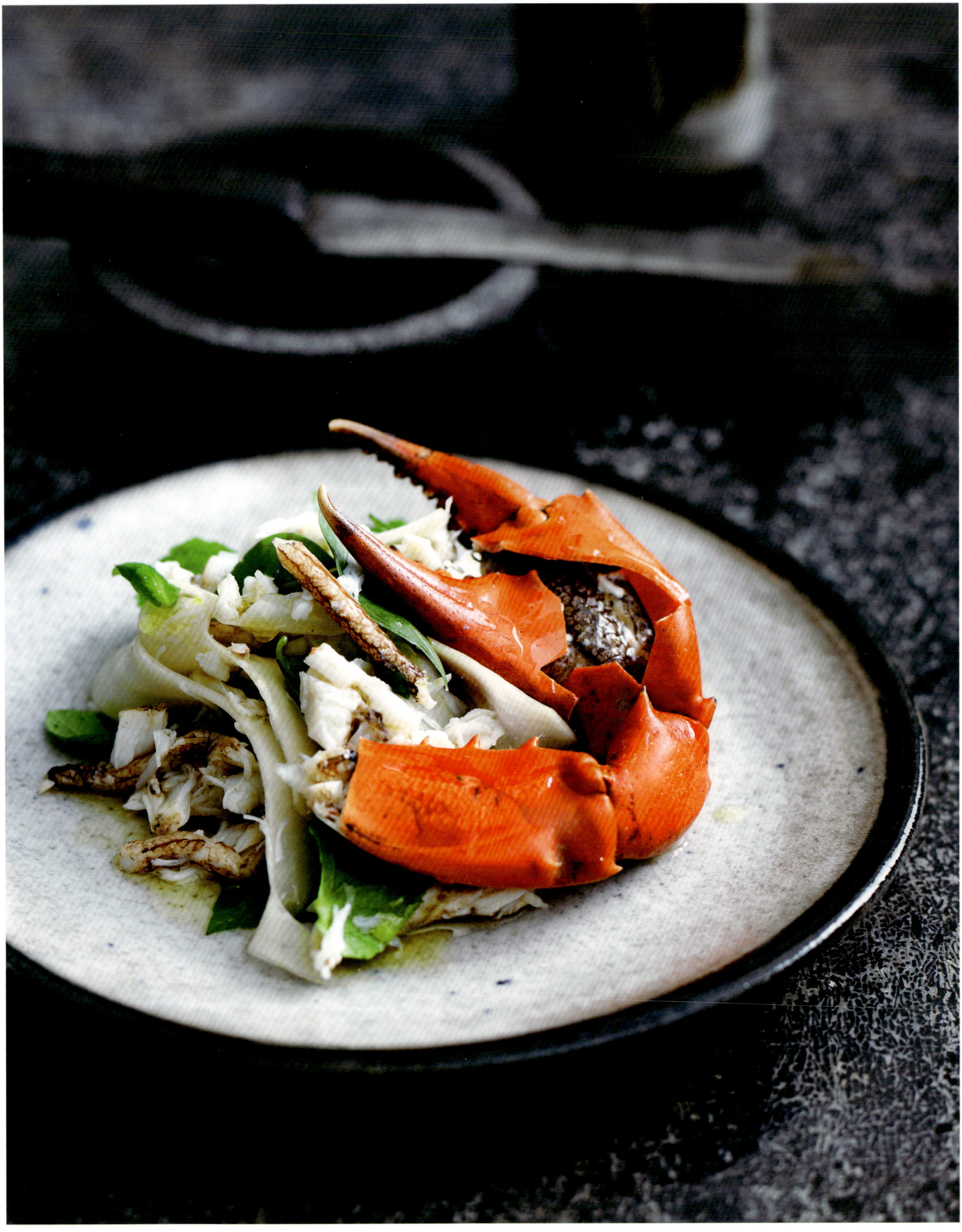

Mud crab with pickled green papaya

In a large bowl, mix together the mud crab claws and all the meat, with the pickled green papaya, herbs, a good splash of lemon oil and pepper to taste. Check to see if any salt is needed – this will depend on how heavily the cooking water was salted.

Serve the crab mixture on individual plates or a platter to share.

SERVES 2

1 × 700 g (1 lb 9 oz) live mud crab, cooked and picked (see page 449)

8 ribbons Pickled Green Papaya (see page 286)

1 small handful Thai basil leaves

1 small handful mint leaves

lemon oil, to serve (see note page 25)

sea salt and freshly ground black pepper, to taste

Wok-fried blue swimmer crab with pepper and egg

SERVES 4 AS AN ENTRÉE OR SHARED DISH

3 garlic cloves, peeled
3 coriander (cilantro) roots, well washed, roughly chopped
½ teaspoon white peppercorns
½ teaspoon caster (superfine) sugar
2 teaspoons fish sauce
250 ml (9 fl oz/1 cup) vegetable oil
3 blue swimmer crabs, cleaned, quartered and cracked, with shells (see page 447)
1 spring onion (scallion), trimmed, cut into long thin strips on the diagonal
2 eggs, lightly whisked
1 small handful coriander (cilantro) leaves, roughly chopped (optional)

Using a mortar and pestle, pound the garlic, coriander root and white peppercorns to a rough paste. Add the caster sugar and fish sauce, then stir until the sugar has dissolved. Refrigerate until ready to use.

Place a large wok on a wok burner over high heat and add the vegetable oil. Heat the oil to 180°C (350°F) – check with an oil thermometer. (For a guide to testing the oil temperature without a thermometer, see note.)

Working in batches if necessary, add the shells and quartered crab pieces to the wok (work carefully to avoid splashing the hot oil). Fry the crab, turning regularly (as this process is somewhere between shallow- and deep-frying, it's essential to keep turning the crab regularly, using a pair of long tongs, to ensure even cooking). After about 2 minutes, when the crab is still slightly undercooked, remove it from the wok and set aside to drain on paper towel.

Pour the oil from the wok and strain it into a suitable container for disposal. Take 60 ml (2 fl oz/¼ cup) of the oil and strain it back into the wok, then return the wok to the burner over high heat.

When the oil in the wok begins to smoke, add the reserved paste and stir-fry for 1 minute, or until fragrant and beginning to caramelise. Immediately return the crab to the wok and add 60 ml (2 fl oz/¼ cup) of water. Toss well for 4 minutes, or until the crab is heated through.

Remove the wok from the heat, add the spring onion and eggs, then toss through to coat the crab. Serve the crab on a large platter with the chopped coriander scattered over (if using).

NOTE: To test the temperature of the oil, drop a cube of bread into it. If it turns golden in 15 seconds, it's sitting perfectly on 180°C (350°F). If the bread takes only 10 seconds to turn golden, then the oil is around 190°C (375°F). If it takes 20–30 seconds to brown, the oil is too cold. Be patient and get the oil to the correct temperature before proceeding.

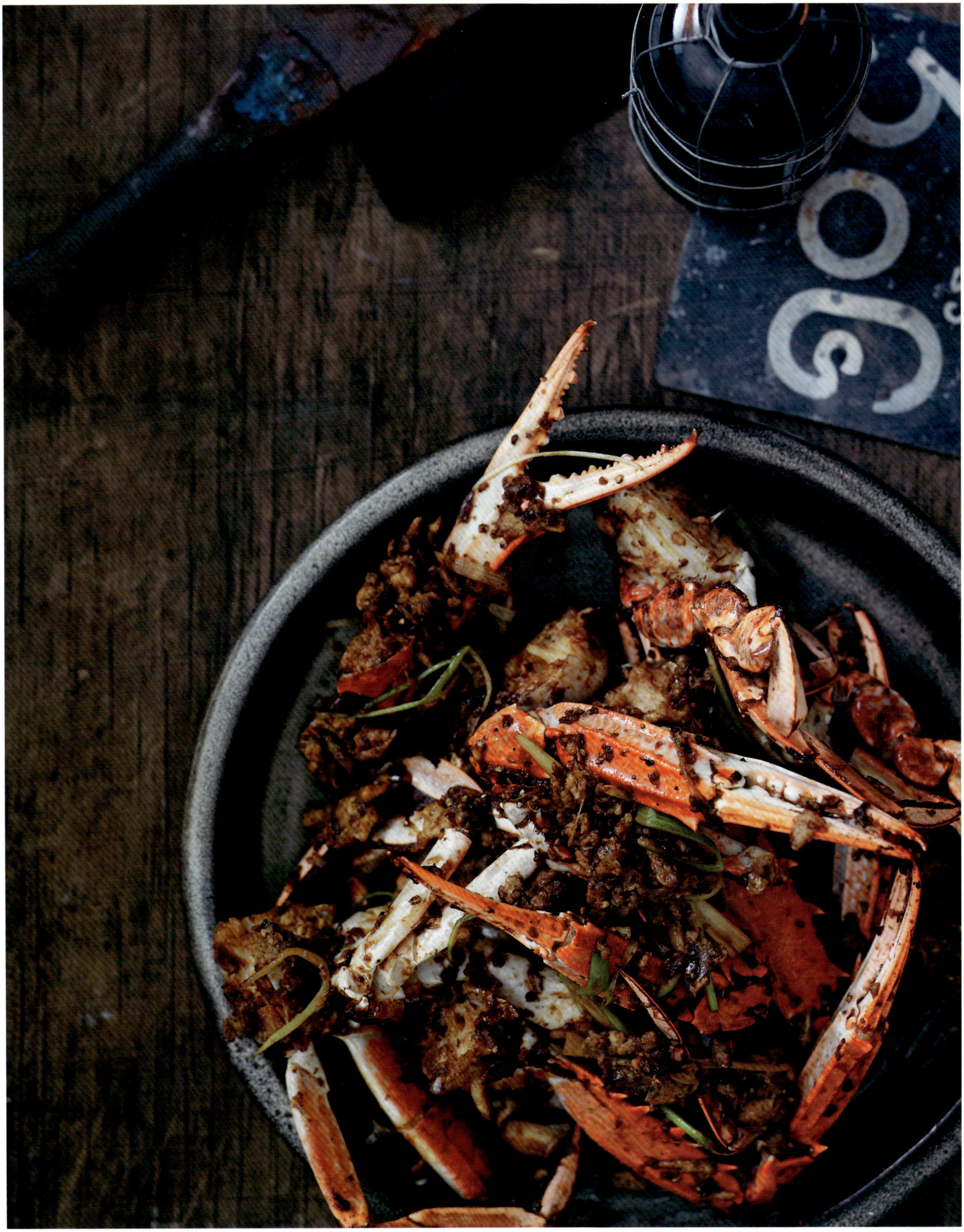

Marron

CRAYFISH, FRESHWATER

Australia has many freshwater crayfish, but the predominant types available are marron (*Cherax tenuimanus*), yabby (*Cherax destructor*) and redclaw (*Cherax quadricarinatus*). The reputation of Australian freshwater crayfish was particularly enhanced when acclaimed French chef Paul Bocuse declared the Western Australian marron one of the five great tastes in the world. Its flesh is deliciously sweet and mild.

Marrons are farmed in South Australia. Unlike yabbies and redclaws, which are quite comfortable in water of varying quality, marrons are sensitive and require cool, clean water at all times. The translucent raw flesh cooks to a pearly white, sometimes with a slight orange tinge.

Yabbies are native to New South Wales and Victoria. Those now available for sale are almost exclusively farmed in specially designed ponds and dams throughout southern Australia, including South Australia and Western Australia. Yabbies take on the conditions of the water in which they grow, so their quality and taste can vary. Check the source with your fishmonger, to ensure a clean, bright flavour.

The tropical cousins of yabbies, redclaws are found in north-flowing rivers and streams in Queensland and the Northern Territory, but are also farmed in New South Wales. Like yabbies, those available for sale are almost exclusively farmed and are readily available year round.

SEASONALITY Year round; best in winter when carrying extra fat
CATCHING METHOD Farmed
COMMON LENGTH Marron: 17–21 cm (6½–8¼ in); yabby: 12 cm (4½ in); redclaw: 10–16 cm (4–6¼ in)
COMMON WEIGHT Marron: 100–500 g (3½ oz – 1 lb 2 oz); yabby: 70 g (2½ oz); redclaw: 50–120 g (1¾–4¼ oz)
IDENTIFIABLE FEATURES Marron: shell mainly dark brown sometimes dark blue to black, spiny back, elongated claws; yabby: short and stocky, bright blue to green shell, large strong pincers; redclaw: dark brown to green shell, blue tinges on legs and forearms, red lower clipper
SUSTAINABILITY Highly sustainable (farmed)

FRESHWATER CRAYFISH IN THE KITCHEN

Marron

Beautiful flavour, beautiful texture. Marron has a cleaner taste than lobster, and some believe it's the true king of Australian shellfish. It's ideal cut in half and grilled (broiled; page 346), pot-roasted or in a salad – there's not much you can't do with it.

It shines with something as simple as a compound butter made with ginger and spring onions (scallions). Don't introduce flavours that are too big – caramelised garlic and black pepper is an ideal combo. In a salad, marron is best friends with peaches and nectarines, finger limes and watercress. It's also great with parsley and chives, or even in a curry.

Yabby and redclaw

Both are great and highly underrated, but they can be quite expensive. Their flavour is soft, delicate and earthy, and they're perfect with lemon and in a curry. They need to be purged before cooking or they'll taste dirty and grainy, although those available for sale have normally been purged before getting to market.

They're great poached in the shell in salted water. Once poached, you can peel them and use them in a salad, or serve them in a corn soup (opposite). To heat up poached and cooled yabby, heat some stock and Shellfish Oil (page 456) and warm it gently in that without boiling.

STORAGE AND HANDLING Can last for up to a week out of water, so are best purchased live – seek lively specimens with all their limbs intact and no damp-earth aroma; store in a lidded basket, cover them with a moist cloth, ideally covered with ice to slow them down and keep them cool. Make sure the lid is closed or you might find them on their way to the biscuits in your pantry.

BEST COOKING METHODS Grilled (broiled), pot-roasted, poached, baked

TEXTURE Marron: crispy, firm, not at all mushy; redclaw: moist, firm; yabby: firm, not mushy

AROMA Fresh, clean, with a light, vegetal grassiness or mushroom note

FLAVOUR Marron: sweet; yabby and redclaw: soft, delicate, earthy

YIELD Marron and yabby: flesh about 40% of whole weight; redclaw: flesh about 25% of whole weight

SUBSTITUTES Each for the others

Sweet corn soup with yabbies

Heat the olive oil and the 40 g (1½ oz) of butter in a medium saucepan over medium heat, then add the spring onion, garlic and celery with a good pinch of salt. Sauté gently, without colouring, for 5–6 minutes, until the vegetables are soft and sweet. Stir through the corn kernels and herbs, then cook for a further 2 minutes.

Add the cornflour paste and stir well. Add the milk and stock, then season well with salt and white pepper. Increase the heat to high and bring to the boil, then reduce the heat to low and simmer for 2 minutes, or until the soup is slightly thickened and the rawness of the cornflour has cooked out. Taste and adjust the seasoning with salt and pepper if necessary. Remove from the heat.

Using a hand-held blender, pulse the soup until it is about half-puréed, with some of the corn kernels still visible. Keep the soup hot while poaching the yabbies.

Bring a large saucepan or stockpot of salted water to the boil over high heat, then reduce to a simmer. Add the yabbies and poach for 8–10 minutes, until they turn red and the flesh springs back a little. Remove the pan from the heat and drain. While the yabbies are still warm but cool enough to handle, peel by twisting the heads and cutting down the side of the shells. Peel and discard the shells and remove the digestive tracts.

Place a small frying pan over high heat. Add the 80 g (2¾ oz) of butter and let it melt — it will quickly turn nut brown and begin to foam. Remove immediately from the heat.

Pour the hot corn soup into four bowls and top each with two yabbies. Spoon the brown butter over and finish with a pinch of salt and white pepper.

NOTE: If using live yabbies, put them to sleep before cooking by placing them in the freezer for 15 minutes.

SERVES 4

80 ml (2½ fl oz/⅓ cup) extra virgin olive oil

40 g (1½ oz) butter, plus 80 g (2¾ oz) extra to serve

2 spring onions (scallions), thinly sliced

4 garlic cloves, peeled and finely chopped

2 celery stalks, finely diced

sea salt and freshly ground white pepper

kernels of 4 cooked sweet corn cobs

2 thyme sprigs, leaves picked and finely chopped

2 tarragon sprigs, leaves picked and finely chopped

1 teaspoon cornflour (cornstarch), dissolved in 2 tablespoons water

500 ml (17 fl oz/2 cups) warm milk

500 ml (17 fl oz/2 cups) warm chicken stock

8 whole green purged yabbies (crayfish) (see note)

Grilled marron

SERVES 4

4 live marron

160 g (5¾ oz) butter, softened, plus extra to serve

2 tablespoons Preserved Lemon (page 461), julienned (from about ½ lemon, pulp removed, not rinsed)

2 tablespoons tarragon leaves

Preheat the oven grill (broiler) to high.

To kill the marron, place them in the freezer for 10–15 minutes to put them to sleep. Remove from the freezer and lay on a chopping board. Using a sharp knife, split each marron in half lengthways, from the tip of the nose to the tail. Remove the stomach and digestive tract, but do not wash the marron.

Place the marron on a baking tray, flesh side up, and brush each half with 20 g (¾ oz) butter.

Place the tray on the lowest shelf of the oven, as far from the heat source as possible, and cook for 2–3 minutes, or until the marron flesh is just cooked through and the protein has just set.

Serve the grilled marron with a little extra butter over the top, or on the side, with the preserved lemon and tarragon leaves scattered over.

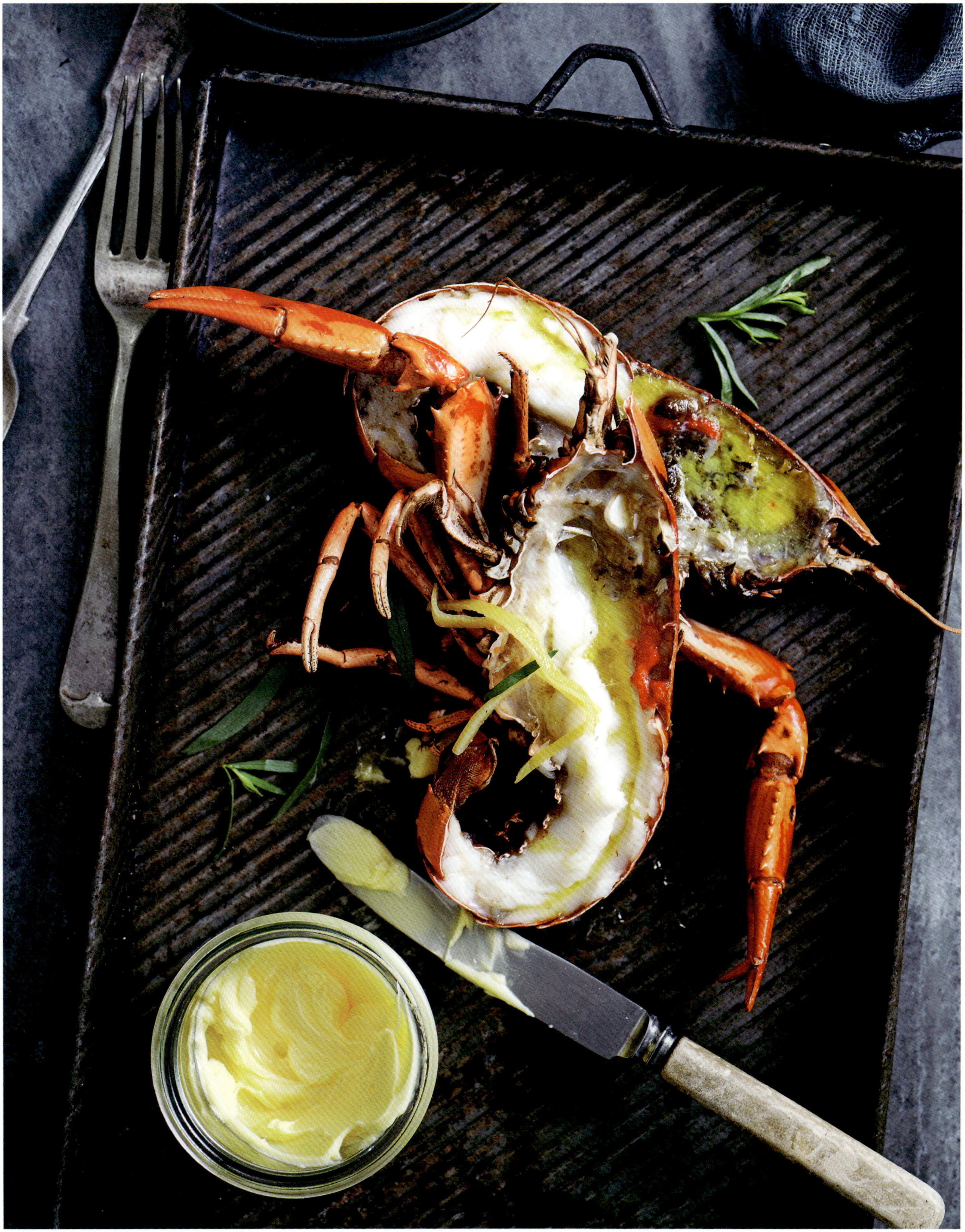

Eastern rock lobster

LOBSTER

The four main species of lobster found in Australia and New Zealand – the southern rock (*Jasus edwardsii*), western rock (*Panulirus cygnus*), eastern rock (*Sagmariasus verreauxi*) and tropical rock (*Panulirus ornatus*) – belong to the Palinuridae family and differ from true lobsters of the Nephropidae family in lacking cartoon-like pincers on their first pair of walking legs. Their reduced pincers are used to carry eggs.

Australia's lobster fisheries are some of our most valuable, primarily due to demand from Asia. As a result, they're among our most tightly regulated, and licence rights are closely guarded. Strict quotas ensure that undersized lobsters are returned to the ocean to mature to breeding age, while limited licences, boats and pot numbers help avoid overfishing.

The western rock lobster fishery is certified by the Marine Stewardship Council, while the other lobster fisheries have internal sustainability programs. Stringent regulations for catching and handling Australian lobsters ensure consistent quality.

SEASONALITY Eastern rock: year round, with peaks at Easter and Christmas; southern rock: SA closed end of May to start of October, Vic. closed June–November, Tas. closed May–October; tropical rock: closed October to end of January; western rock: closed July–November

CATCHING METHODS Eastern rock: traps and pots; southern rock: pots; tropical rock: divers, hand-held nets, spears; western rock: pots

COMMON LENGTH Eastern rock: 10–17 cm (4–6½ in); southern rock: 10–14 cm (4–5½ in); tropical rock: 7–11 cm (2¾–4¼ in); western rock: 8–11 cm (3¼–4¼ in)

COMMON WEIGHT Eastern rock: 800 g – 1.5 kg (1 lb 12 oz – 3 lb 5 oz); southern rock: 500 g – 4 kg (1 lb 2 oz – 8 lb 13 oz); tropical rock: 350 g – 1.5 kg (12 oz – 3 lb 5 oz); western rock: 400–900 g (14 oz – 2 lb)

IDENTIFIABLE FEATURES Eastern rock: smooth dark green shell with brownish orange legs; southern rock: orange–red, with pale yellow abdomen, or grey–greenish brown with a paler underside; tropical rock: light green with dark green bands and aqua spots; western rock: reddish purple shell with white spots along body, two prominent spines between the eyes, long antennae draping down back

SUSTAINABILITY All carefully managed by quota

COMMON LOBSTER SPECIES

Eastern rock lobster
Sagmariasus verreauxi
Eastern rock lobsters live from the inshore zone to the continental shelf at 2–200 m (6½–650 ft) along Australia's east coast from Tweed Heads in New South Wales, south around Tasmania, and to Port MacDonnell in South Australia. They usually move into deeper water in early winter, then return closer to the shoreline in late August.

They hide in holes and crevices around rocky areas and reefs, often taking cover in seaweed. They can grow to 8 kg (18 lb) but are mostly sold at 800 g – 1.5 kg (1 lb 12 oz – 3 lb 5 oz). They have a dark green body and brownish orange legs. The shell on their body is smooth and unsculpted.

The small commercial fishery uses baited traps and pots, and is managed under a quota system, producing only 150 tonnes per annum. This makes eastern rock lobster a genuine luxury. They're caught all year, with Easter and Christmas peaks.

Southern rock lobster
Jasus edwardsii
The southern rock lobster is found all around southern Australia, northern New South Wales and Western Australia. It lives in reef habitats, from shallow rock pools at 1–2 m (3¼–6½ ft) to deep underwater caves and trenches out to the continental shelf at about 250 m (800 ft). They tend to stay in the same place their whole life.

They're usually red or orange, with a paler yellowish abdomen, but can be greyish or greenish brown with a paler underside. Most are caught off South Australia, where they thrive in the cold nutrient-rich waters from Antarctica. They're selective feeders and slow-growing.

The fishery exclusively uses pots. Once graded for size, the live lobsters are held on board the boats in aerated sea water then returned to shore, re-tanked or cooked, and shipped to market.

Tropical rock lobster
Panulirus ornatus
The northern Australian tropical or painted lobster is a vivid light green with dark green bands and aqua spots. It's generally found at depths of less than 20 m (65 ft) and rarely more than 100 m (330 ft). They usually live in rocks and on coral reefs, but migrate in winter to the deeper waters of the eastern Torres Strait. At this time they're also found on seabeds surrounding the reefs.

They're primarily hand-collected by divers, using surface-supplied air (called a hookah system). Some, however, are collected at night on shallow reef flats, and others using hand-held nets or spears. The fishery is quite small, taking about 800 tonnes per annum, and is managed with both seasonal closures and quotas. Hand-harvesting means that the catchers are both selective and careful, and the environmental impact is minimal.

Western rock lobster
Panulirus cygnus
The western rock lobster is found only along the Western Australian coast, from Shark Bay south to Cape Leeuwin. It lives under rocks and in coral reefs to 200 m (650 ft), but most are caught at 35–60 m (110–200 ft), exclusively in baited pots.

It has a distinctive reddish purple shell with white spots along the body, two prominent spines between the eyes, and long flowing antennae that drape down its back. There are eight size grades from 350 g (12 oz) to 2 kg (4 lb 8 oz) or more, but most are 400–900 g (14 oz – 2 lb).

The fishery, Australia's most valuable and by far our largest, has been managed carefully since 1963. In 2000 it became the world's first fishery to be certified sustainable by the Marine Stewardship Council. The season is closed from July to November. The annual harvest is about 5000 tonnes.

LOBSTER IN THE KITCHEN

Lobster is a delicacy, only a step or two down from caviar. The meat is richer and more substantial than that of most seafood. Its taste is subtle compared to the marine-gaminess of mussels or clams, and although similar to crabs and prawns (shrimp), it stands alone in eating pleasure.

There's no need to clean lobster, and you don't want to cook it for long. The best cooking method is to cut it into medallions and pot-roast it (page 356), or chop it in half and throw it in the oven (page 355) or on the barbecue. Lobster sashimi, an amazing delicacy but illegal in New South Wales, tastes like saltwater puffed rice. To prepare sashimi, cut the tail off, cut into medallions and poach quickly.

You're better off cooking your own lobsters than buying them pre-cooked. Calculate the boiling time for a lobster by adding 2 minutes to the weight in grams divided by 100. This means that an 800 g (1 lb 12 oz) lobster should be cooked for 8 + 2 = 10 minutes. Make sure you salt the water.

Eastern rock lobsters at around 600 g (1 lb 5 oz) are the sweetest lobsters you can eat in Australia. Southern rock lobsters are large and have a more intense, punchier flavour and a firmer texture. Western rock lobsters are smaller, with a firmer texture and multiple layers of skin that must be dealt with carefully. The heads are ideal for a bisque, consommé or broth.

Tropical rock lobsters have a fairly low oil content and therefore should be handled with some care when cooking. Avoid methods involving high heat, as the meat will toughen.

Buy only from reputable seafood retailers. Your lobster should be highly active, flapping its tail when picked up, have all legs and feelers intact, the head firmly attached to the body, and should feel heavy for its size. Ensure the flesh hasn't come away from the shell. It should smell sweet, with no hint of an ammonia-like odour.

STORAGE AND HANDLING Wrap live creatures in a moist cloth and store in the vegetable crisper for no more than 24 hours, or freeze for 30 minutes then blanch before removing raw meat, wrapping tightly in freezer film then plastic wrap and sitting on a draining tray over ice in a sealed airtight container. If the lobster dies, blanch quickly then remove the raw meat, and wrap and store as above; use as soon as possible. Frozen lobster is best when processed and packed at the point of harvest; thaw slowly overnight in an airtight container in the fridge and use soon after.

BEST COOKING METHODS Pot-roasted medallions, barbecued, sashimi (except NSW)

TEXTURE Eastern rock: soft to medium; southern rock: delicate yet firm; tropical rock: firm; western rock: very firm

AROMA Rich umami character, with mild creamy notes and a bright iodine zing

FLAVOUR Eastern rock: sweet, rich, with a delicious umami character; southern rock: rich 'sea spray' character, zesty minerality and sweetness, with delicious notes of ripe melon and cashew and a lingering umami note; tropical rock: mild sweetness with a light egg-white aroma and iodine or seaweed zing on the palate; western rock: definite sweetness with a light note of saffron and iodine zestiness when raw, with a mild aroma of cooked cabbage with strong mineral notes once cooked

APPEARANCE Eastern rock: dark green shell, small legs; southern rock: deep maroon to mottled white shell; tropical rock: aqua shell, white tail; western rock: deep red shell, pale pink tail

YIELD Flesh 35% of whole weight

SUBSTITUTES Each for the others

Lobster and white nectarine salad

SERVES 8 AS AN ENTRÉE

1 × 1.4 kg (3 lb 2 oz) whole raw lobster (for humane treatment of live lobster, see page 446)
4 white nectarines
60 ml (2 fl oz/¼ cup) extra virgin olive oil
1 tablespoon chardonnay vinegar
sea salt and freshly ground black pepper, to taste
2 large handfuls watercress

Heat a large saucepan of water over high heat and bring to the boil. Gently lower the lobster into the water, reduce the heat to medium–high and cook at a rolling boil for 16 minutes (see note).

Remove the cooked lobster from the pot using a pair of long tongs and place it on a tray. Leave it to rest for at least 1 hour. (You can cook the lobster up to 2 hours ahead, preferably no longer. This way, it will not require refrigeration or icing and the flesh will be at its best.)

Cut the tail meat into eight medallions (see page 446) and place one of these medallions on each serving plate.

Run a small sharp knife cleanly around the centre of each nectarine and slide the two halves in opposite directions to separate them from the stone. Place half a nectarine beside each lobster medallion.

In a medium bowl, whisk together the olive oil, vinegar and a little salt and pepper. Add the watercress, toss gently and place a little on each plate.

NOTE: The rule of thumb with lobster is to cook it in boiling water for 1 minute per 100 g (3½ oz), plus 2 minutes. This means a 1.4 kg (3 lb 2 oz) lobster should cook for 14 + 2 = 16 minutes.

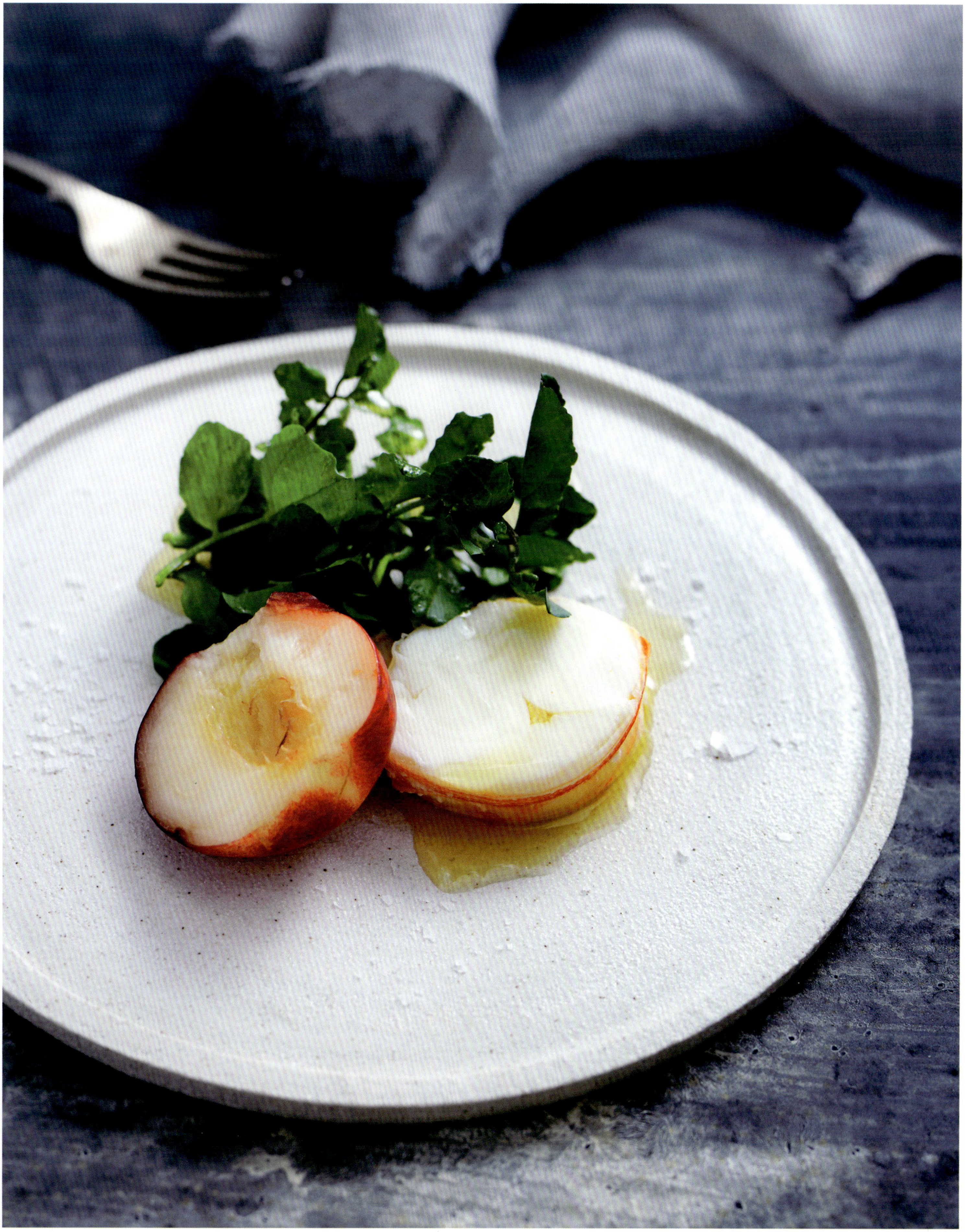

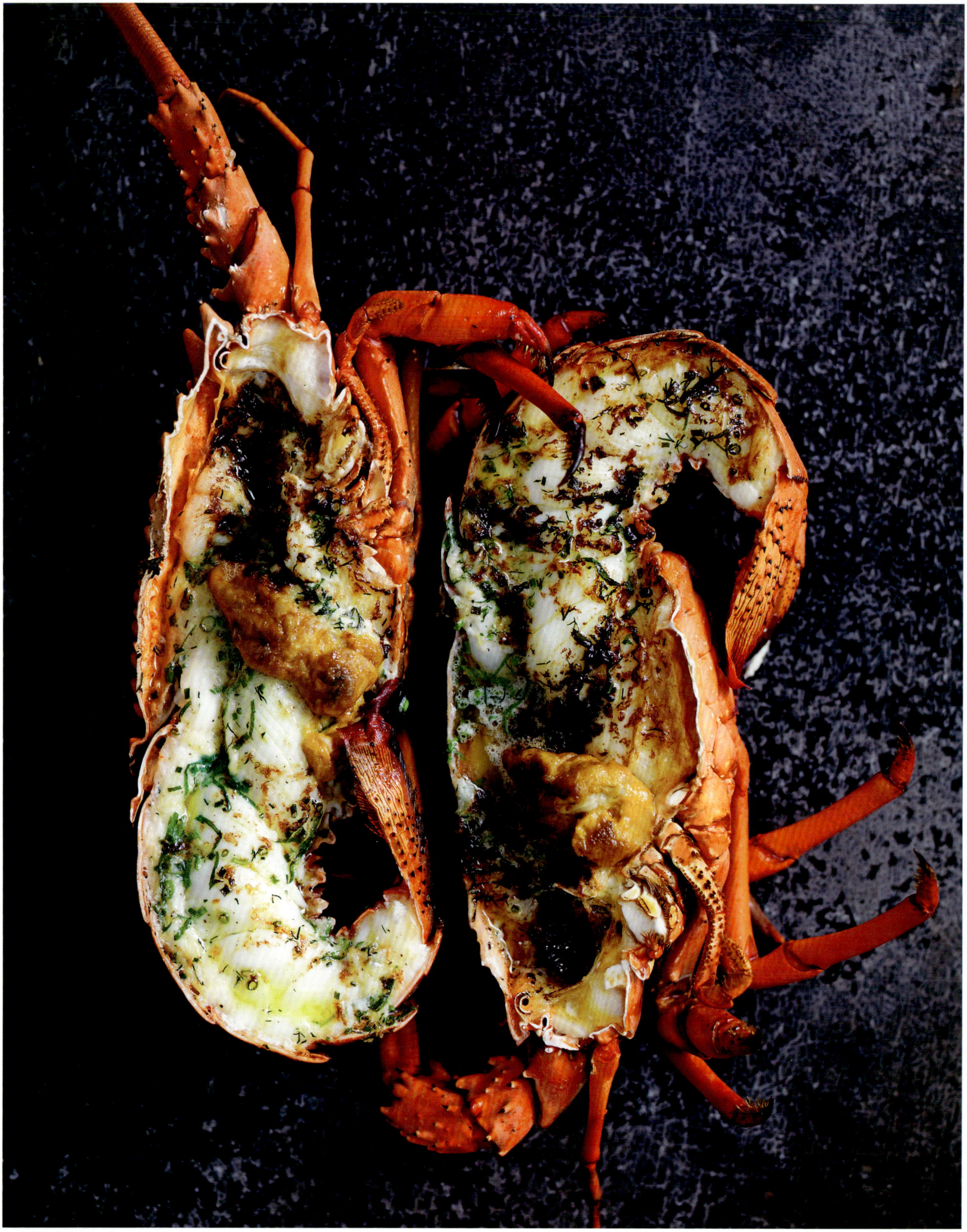

Roast lobster with herb butter

Preheat the oven to 200°C (400°F).

To make the herb butter, heat the vegetable oil in a small saucepan over low heat. Add the onion and garlic and cook, without colouring, for a few minutes until softened and sweet. Remove from the heat and set aside to cool.

Put the butter in a food processor with the onion and garlic, herbs, lemon juice, egg yolk, salt and pepper. Process until just combined. Wrap the butter in baking paper and refrigerate until ready to use (see note).

If you have a live lobster, kill it humanely (see page 446). Hold the lobster down firmly on a chopping board, shell up, using a tea towel (dish towel) for grip. Using a large sharp knife, cut the lobster in half lengthways, from head to tail, all the way through the shell. Remove the digestive tract, retain the tomalley (the soft green substance just behind the head) and set it aside.

Place the halved lobster on a baking tray, flesh side up, and top with the tomalley. Spread the herb butter over the lobster. Place the tray on the bottom shelf of the oven and cook the lobster for 6–7 minutes.

Remove the lobster from the oven and serve immediately.

NOTES: Use any soft herbs you like in this compound butter – it's a great way to use up left-over herbs. You can also add ingredients such as capers and anchovies as you choose.

The herb butter can be made in advance and stored until needed. Spoon the butter onto baking paper, use the paper to roll it into a log and wrap it tightly, then place it in a freezer bag. It will keep in the fridge for 1 month or in the freezer for up to 3 months. If you have any butter left over from this recipe, save it for a later use.

SERVES 2

1 × 1.2–1.4 kg (2 lb 10 oz – 3 lb 2 oz) whole live or cooked lobster

HERB BUTTER
1 tablespoon vegetable oil
¼ brown onion, peeled and finely diced
1 garlic clove, peeled and crushed
100 g (3½ oz) butter, softened
1 small handful flat-leaf (Italian) parsley leaves
1 small handful dill
1 small handful mixed tarragon, sage and oregano leaves (see note)
juice of ½ lemon
1 egg yolk
sea salt and freshly ground black pepper, to taste

Pot-roasted lobster with ginger, spring onion and pepper

SERVES 4

2 × 600 g (1 lb 5 oz) whole live or cooked lobsters
120 g (4¼ oz) butter
10 cm (4 in) piece young ginger, unpeeled, roughly sliced
2 tablespoons freshly ground black pepper
good pinch of sea salt
250 ml (9 fl oz/1 cup) Fish Stock (page 457)
4 spring onions (scallions), roughly torn

If you have live lobsters, kill them humanely. Separate the bodies of the lobsters from the heads, setting the heads aside (see page 446).

Preheat the oven to 200°C (400°F).

Firmly hold the body of one lobster down on a chopping board, using a tea towel (dish towel) for grip. Using a large sharp knife or a cleaver, cut through the shell to get five shell-on medallions, each 2–3 cm (¾–1¼ in) thick. Cut each lobster head into two or three pieces (see page 446 for preparing a lobster).

Heat 60 g (2¼ oz) of the butter in a large, deep ovenproof frying pan. (If you need to use two pans, simply divide the ingredients evenly between them.) When the pan is hot, add the lobster pieces and seal, tossing, for 1 minute. Add the ginger and toss through. Add the remaining butter, and the pepper, salt, fish stock and spring onion. Cover and transfer to the oven for 4 minutes.

Remove the lobster pan from the oven. Serve in the pan on a heatproof surface, or transfer the lobster, vegetables and sauce to a serving platter.

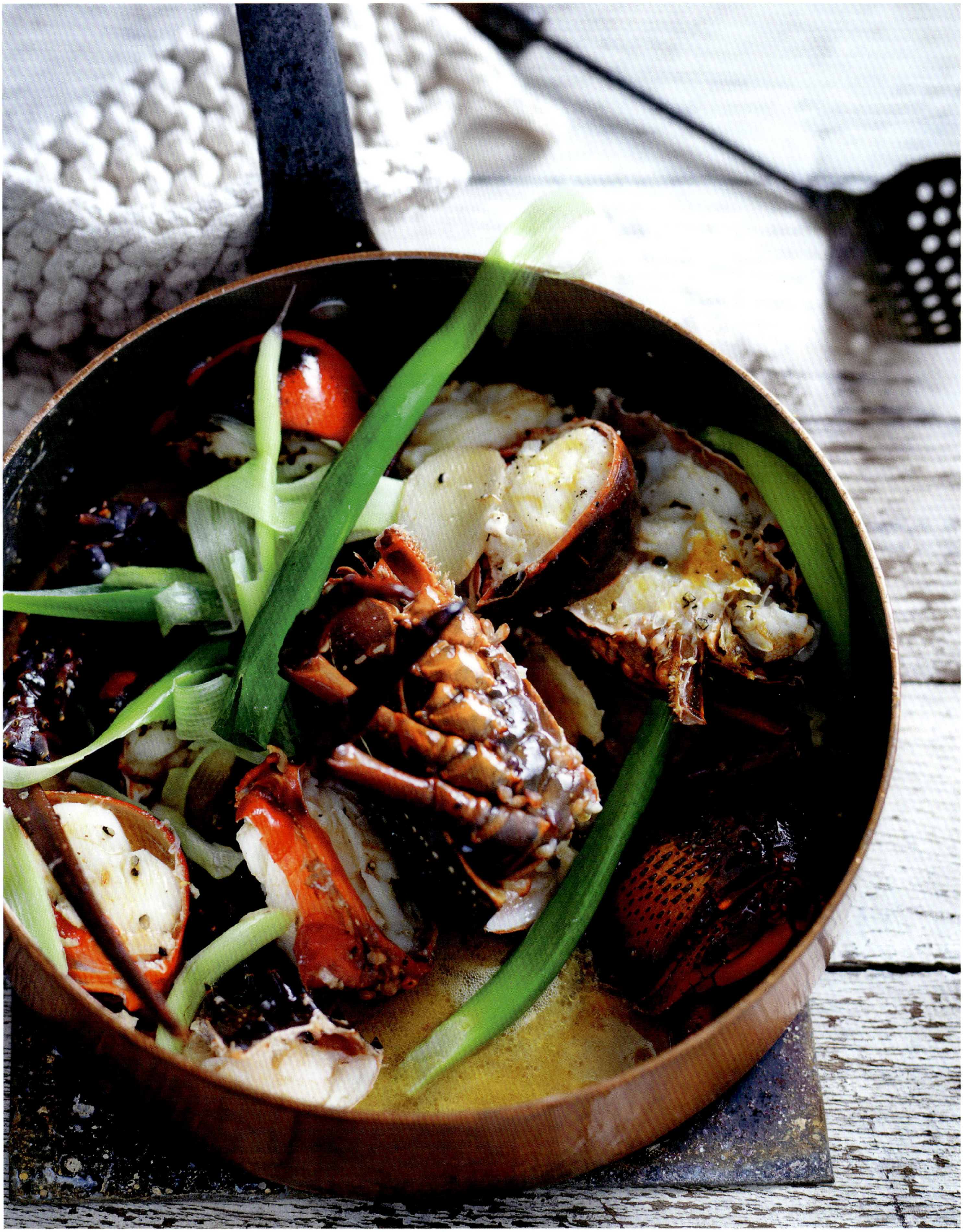

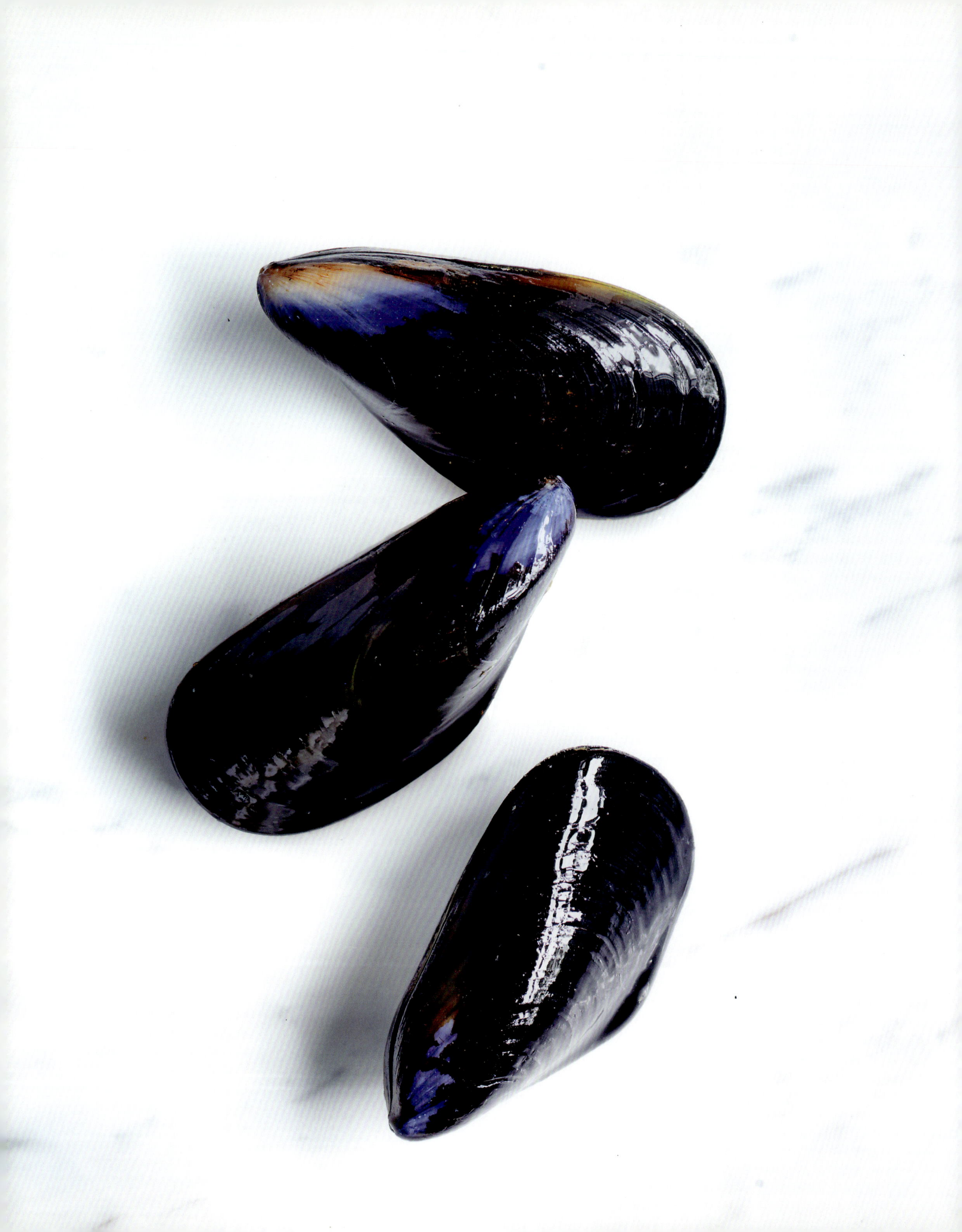

MUSSELS

Mussels are both sustainable and cheap. Those sold in Australia are all blue mussels (*Mytilus galloprovincialis*) farmed in clean waters in Boston Bay, South Australia, and Spring Bay, Tasmania. It's even thought they may improve the quality of the water they're grown in.

They're grown on longlines, where mussel spat is 'seeded' on ropes suspended from rafts at 2–15 m (5–50 ft) below the surface. Dead mussels simply fall off the line and harvested mussels need not be purged of sand or mud. You also don't have to throw away those that don't open. They're now sold pre-scrubbed, graded and de-bearded in packaging that keeps them in prime condition.

SEASONALITY Year round, with a peak in February–June in NSW, Tas. and Vic., June–September in SA and September–October in WA

CATCHING METHOD Farmed on longlines

COMMON LENGTH 5–9 cm (2–3½ in)

COMMON WEIGHT 20–30 g (¾–1 oz)

IDENTIFIABLE FEATURES Small, blue–black, smooth shell

SUSTAINABILITY Excellent (farmed)

MUSSELS IN THE KITCHEN

Machines don't do 100 per cent of the de-bearding job, so carefully grab the beard, slide it towards the hinged end of the shell, then pull it out. It's worth being patient, to avoid stripping the mussel apart.

Added tastes should complement rather than overpower the sweet, subtle mussel flavours. They're great in broths and curries. The small, sweet, tender mussels from South Australia are ideal cooked in a pot, in the natural juice that comes with them. Cooking them in wine can make them taste more like wine than mussel. If you need to add water, a little salted water is ideal. Turn them over with a spoon during cooking so they cook evenly. Serve in the pot and replace the lid between serves.

Larger mussels from Tasmania and Victoria have a more intense flavour and firmer texture. They're good cooked in a pot, but great in a salad, grilled (broiled), smoked and even au gratin.

STORAGE AND HANDLING Store pre-packed clean mussels in the middle part of the fridge. Wrap loose fresh mussels in a moist tea towel (dish towel), sit them in a bowl with ice on top, and store in the middle of the fridge. Use in a day or two. If some don't open during cooking, prise them open with a butter knife. Dead mussels smell awful – clearly, don't eat!

BEST COOKING METHODS Grilled (broiled), in a pot

TEXTURE Silky initial mouthfeel, then moussey

AROMA Clean, seaweed-like when raw; savoury notes of saffron once cooked

FLAVOUR Sweet, rich, mildly briny, with egg yolk

APPEARANCE Pot-ready should be de-bearded; cooked meat either orange (female) or white (male)

YIELD Meat 25–30% of whole weight

SUBSTITUTES None

Mussels with spring onions and butter

SERVES 4

80 ml (2½ fl oz/⅓ cup) mussel liquid (see note)
1 kg (2 lb 4 oz) mussels, cleaned and de-bearded
4 spring onions (scallions), cleaned and cut in half lengthways
150 g (5½ oz) unsalted butter
bread, to serve (optional)

Heat the mussel liquid in a large saucepan or double-handled mussel pot over high heat, covered. When the liquid is boiling and steam begins to appear, quickly add the mussels and spring onion. Cook, covered, stirring the mussels occasionally to keep them turning over.

When all the mussels have opened (the time will differ depending on the size of the mussel: South Australian mussels will take about 2 minutes and Tasmanian around 4 minutes), remove them from the heat and add the butter. Stir through to melt the butter and serve immediately, either in individual bowls or simply place the pan on the table. This dish is even better with some good bread to mop up the buttery sauce.

NOTE: No seasoning is required in this recipe due to the natural salt content of the mussels. If you're using mussels from a sealed packet, there'll be plenty of natural mussel liquid to use. Otherwise, wine, fish stock or a mixture of both are equally good, but you'll need no more than the amount noted above – there will usually be enough liquid naturally from the mussels for the purpose of this recipe. Make the most of this liquid where possible, as it has so much flavour.

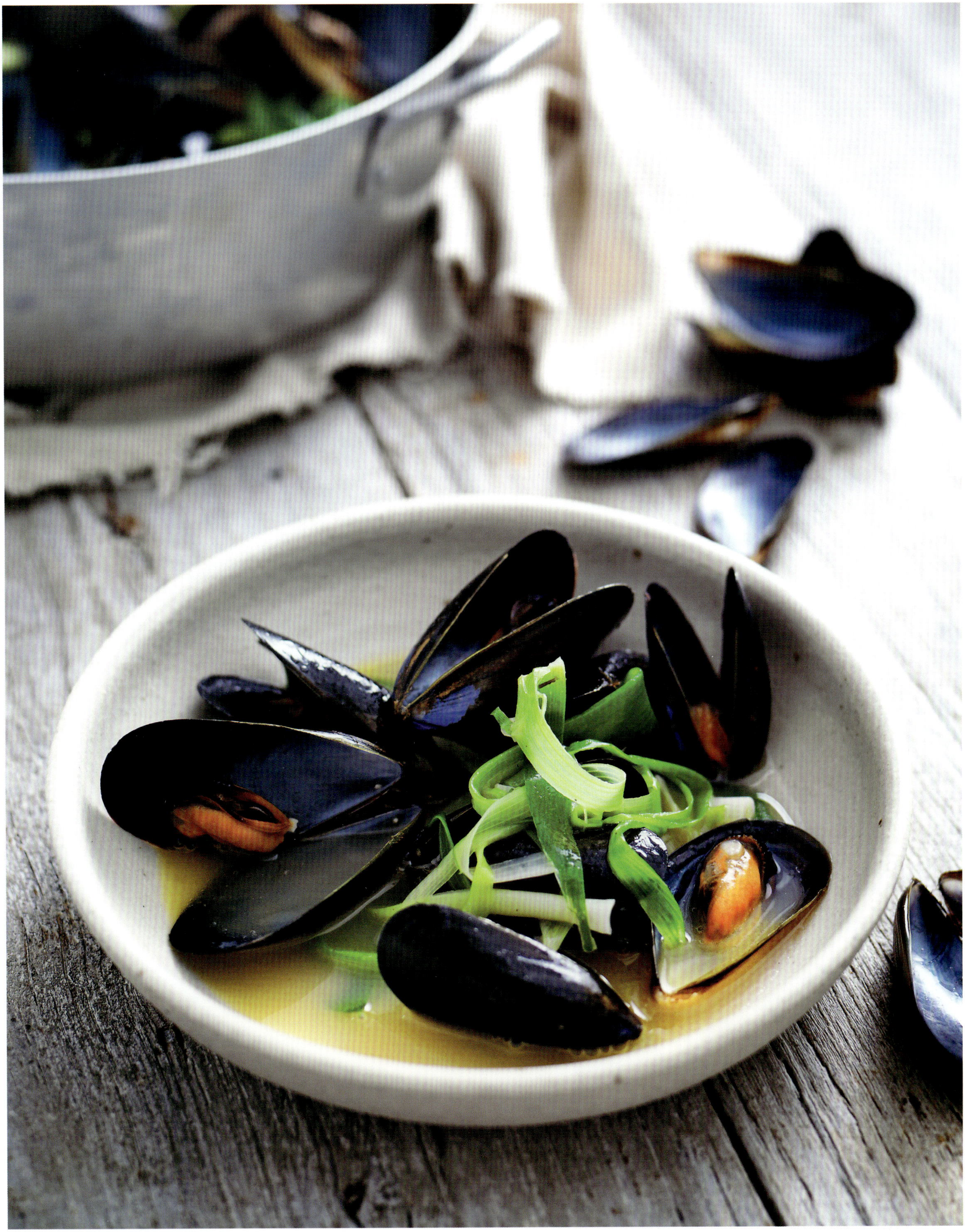

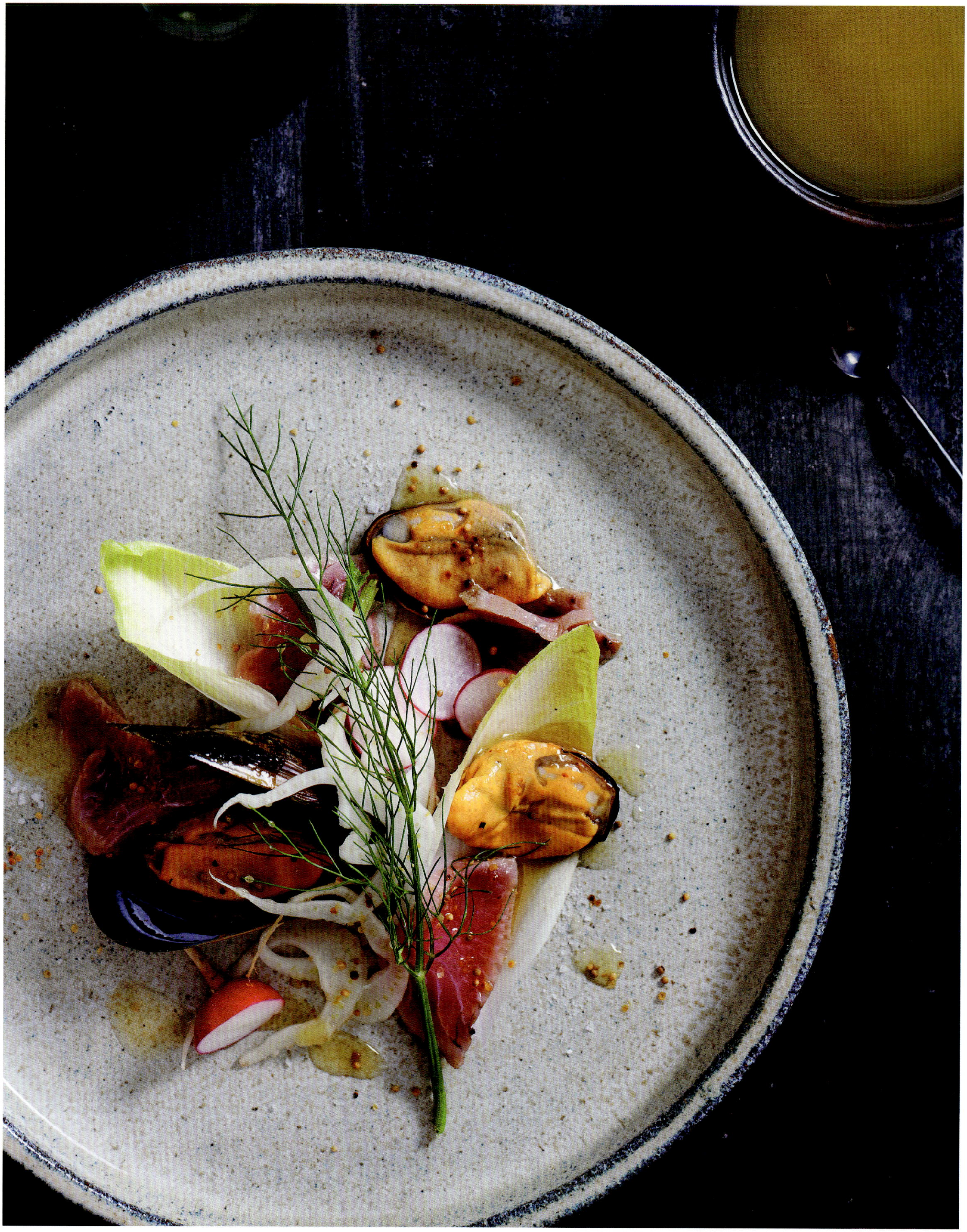

Mussel and seared tuna salad

To sear the tuna (see note), heat a large cast-iron or heavy-based frying pan over high heat and add the ghee. Season the tuna with salt and pepper, then place in the pan when the ghee begins to smoke. Sear the tuna on all sides for 2 minutes, then remove it from the pan and set aside to rest for 5 minutes. Cut into slices 1–2 cm (½–¾ in) thick.

To make a salad dressing, in a small bowl, whisk together the olive oil and vinegar with a good pinch of salt and pepper. Set the vinaigrette aside.

Heat the mussel liquid in a large saucepan or double-handled mussel pot over high heat, covered. When the liquid is boiling and steam begins to appear, quickly add the mussels. Cook, covered, stirring occasionally to keep the mussels turning over.

When all the mussels have opened (the time will differ depending on the size of the mussel: South Australian mussels will take about 2 minutes and Tasmanian around 4 minutes), remove them from the heat and transfer to a tray or large bowl to cool.

Remove eight of the mussels from their shells and discard the shells, leaving four mussels still in their shells.

In a large bowl, gently toss together all the cooked mussels with the braised tuna, witlof leaves, radish, fennel, mustard seeds and vinaigrette. Divide among serving plates and garnish each serve with a fennel frond.

NOTE: It's also great to braise the tuna for this dish. Heat a small saucepan of oil to 65°C (150°F) and infuse with chilli, lemon and bay leaf. Add the tuna, then remove from the heat and cool in the pan. Once cool, remove and sear over high heat.

SERVES 4

200 g (7 oz) tuna loin (the sinewy part), skin off

1½ teaspoons ghee (see note page 26)

sea salt and freshly ground black pepper, to taste

125 ml (4 fl oz/½ cup) extra virgin olive oil

2 tablespoons sherry vinegar

80 ml (2½ fl oz/⅓ cup) mussel liquid (see note page 360) or water

12 mussels, cleaned and de-bearded

8 yellow witlof (chicory) leaves

2 radishes, skin on, thinly shaved (preferably using a mandoline)

½ baby fennel bulb, thinly shaved (preferably using a mandoline)

1 teaspoon yellow mustard seeds, roasted and crushed

4 long fennel fronds, to serve

Baby octopus

OCTOPUS

Wild-caught Australian octopus is a standout in the sustainable seafood stakes. While general confusion reigns as to which seafood does or doesn't represent sustainable, local or organic production, the simple octopus ticks every box – fast-growing with a short lifecycle, a prolific breeder, zero bycatch.

Octopus (*Octopus* spp.) are found all around Australia, and several species are harvested commercially. These are not differentiated at market but are simply labelled either 'large' or 'baby'. This can be confusing, given much of the 'baby' octopus harvested on the east coast is mature and actually grows only to the size of a human fist.

It's common these days to buy both baby and large octopus cleaned and tenderised. Like squid and cuttlefish, octopus freezes well; unlike finfish and shellfish, it benefits from a slow freezing process, which assists with tenderisation by denaturing the proteins in the tough fibres.

SEASONALITY	Year round
CATCHING METHOD	Traps
COMMON LENGTH	Up to 80 cm (31½ in)
COMMON WEIGHT	Up to 2 kg (4 lb 8 oz)
IDENTIFIABLE FEATURES	White, grey and creamy skin
SUSTAINABILITY	Excellent

Octopus with sweet soy and sesame

SERVES 2–4 AS A SHARED ENTRÉE

2 kg (4 lb 8 oz) Western Australian octopus legs
sea salt, as required
65 g (2¼ oz) pomegranate tea, tied in muslin (cheesecloth)
½ teaspoon toasted sesame seeds, to serve

SWEET SOY SAUCE
100 ml (3½ fl oz) soy sauce
100 g (3½ oz) caster (superfine) sugar
1½ tablespoons mirin

To make the sweet soy sauce, combine the soy sauce, sugar and mirin with 1½ tablespoons of water in a small saucepan, then bring to a simmer over medium–low heat. Reduce the heat to low and simmer gently for 15–20 minutes, or until the sauce has reduced by half.

On a clean work surface, thoroughly massage the octopus with a handful of salt for 5 minutes. Rinse off the salt under cold running water.

Bring 4 litres (135 fl oz/16 cups) of water to the boil in a medium saucepan over medium–high heat, then add the wrapped tea. Gently lower the octopus into the tea broth, turn the heat down to low and cook at a gentle simmer for 35 minutes, turning regularly. Remove the octopus from the tea broth and set aside on a tray to cool.

Slice the cooled octopus into 12 thin slices. Lay the slices in a row on a platter or serving plates. Drizzle the sweet soy sauce over the centre. Serve topped with toasted sesame seeds and any extra sauce on the side.

NOTE: Pomegranate tea is available from tea retailers.

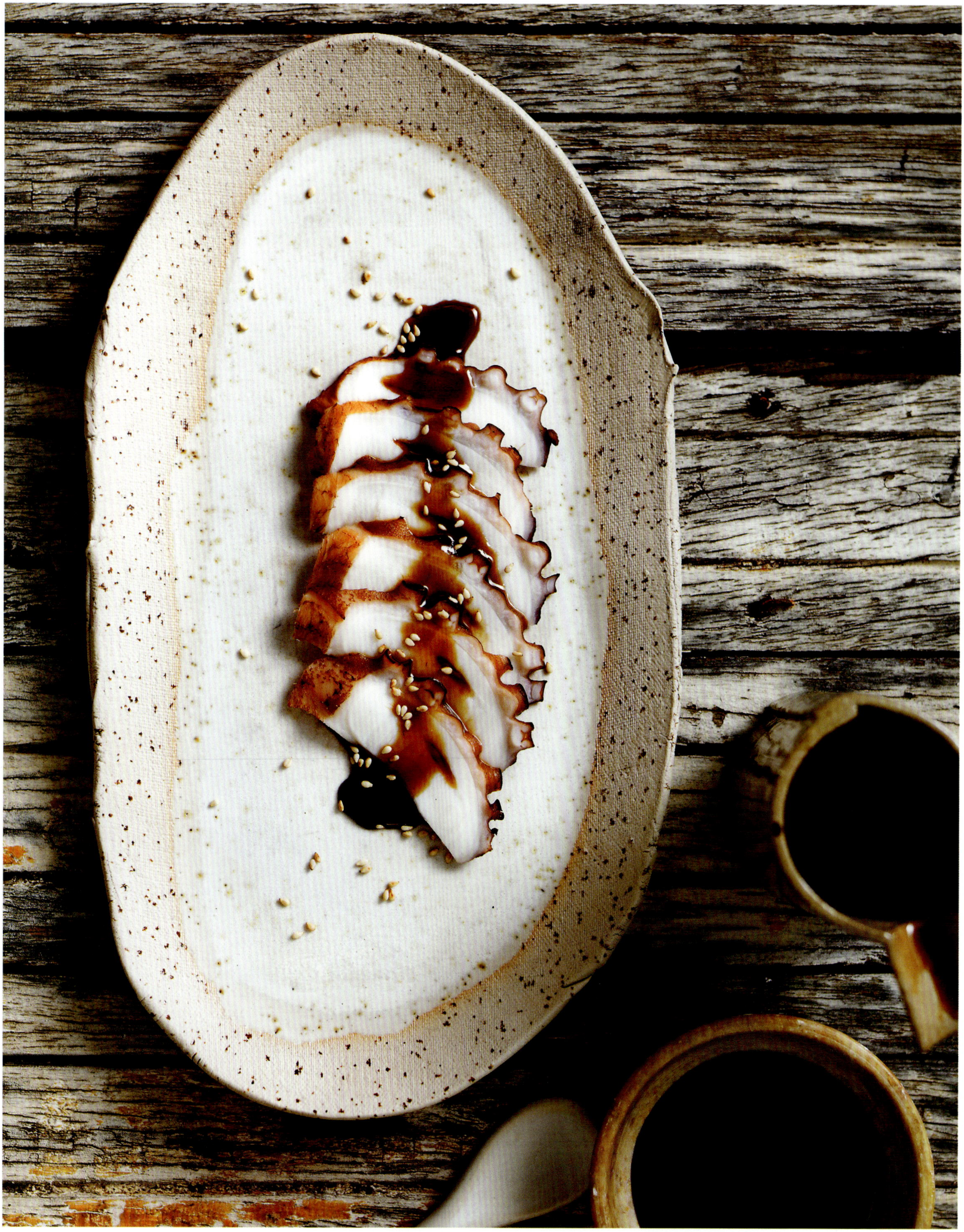

Angasi oysters

OYSTERS

Regarded as the world's best loved molluscs, oysters – of all varieties, from all regions and in all seasons – continue to capture the mouths, hearts and minds of the modern diner. No other seafood so inspires the imagination, polarises the palate and causes as much consternation among buyers, consumers and critics as the oyster.

Oyster farming has become the standout contemporary aquaculture industry. Farmers choose species and growing techniques specific to their region in order to produce oysters with the best possible flavour and texture. While regional variation can have a natural impact on availability and seasonal condition, the most important factor in final eating quality is the care taken by the farmer. Although oysters might look robust, they demand constant attention, and a good farmer has an intimate relationship with their crop throughout its life.

Oysters are farmed in Queensland, New South Wales, Victoria, Tasmania, South Australia and Western Australia, most commonly in the intertidal zone of coastal waters, where they're exposed at low tide. Depending on the local conditions, they're grown in suspended baskets or trays. Sometimes they're also grown in deeper subtidal waters, with the baskets or trays suspended from rafts or pontoons.

While oysters have limited culinary versatility, they are enjoying a renaissance among growers and consumers who care more about quality than quantity. Oysters are best enjoyed freshly shucked and are worth exploring by species, region, grower and season. All of these factors can have a vast impact on the taste of the oyster.

While the rock and angasi oysters (see following pages) are native to our waters, the introduced Pacific oyster is now the most prolifically farmed in both Australia and New Zealand.

COMMON OYSTER SPECIES

Angasi oyster
Ostrea angasi
The flat angasi, or native oyster as it's sometimes called, is a very special oyster indeed. Although it's one of the first known seafoods farmed in Australia – by Indigenous Australians, starting some 6000 years ago – the angasi has only recently become fashionable with modern farmers, due mainly to the comparative difficulty of growing it. Often sought by chefs, the angasi is hard to come by and expensive. Do try them if you ever have the chance. They require special care when shucking – see page 443.

SEASONALITY Best in winter
CATCHING METHOD Mainly basket-cultured
COMMON LENGTH Up to 10 cm (4 in)
COMMON WEIGHT 60–80 g (2¼–2¾ oz)
IDENTIFIABLE FEATURES Broad flat shell, flesh off-white with green tinges
SUSTAINABILITY Highly sustainable (farmed)

Pacific oyster
Crassostrea gigas
The Pacific oyster, originally introduced to Australia from Japan, is now the most prolifically grown oyster in Australia, primarily in Tasmania and on the west coast of South Australia, but more recently also in New South Wales. Typically it's large, with a spiky shell and clean white interior.

The Pacific oyster has a characteristic fresh, clean and salty flavour – just like being rolled in the surf. As it spends its entire life underwater, it's relatively easy to shuck and so is a good starting point for the novice opener (see page 442).

It's popular as a cooking oyster, particularly with Japanese and Chinese chefs, who consider its simple flavour and texture a great vehicle for flavours. It's most prolific in the cooler months, spawning in summer. Depending on the region it comes from, it's available from March to early December.

SEASONALITY Best March–December
CATCHING METHOD Mainly basket-cultured
COMMON LENGTH 6–8 cm (2½–3¼ in)
COMMON WEIGHT 60–80 g (2¼–2¾ oz)
IDENTIFIABLE FEATURES Deeply cupped, steely grey–black outer shell, brilliant white inner shell, meat bright white to light grey with black frill
SUSTAINABILITY Highly sustainable (farmed)

Pacific oysters

Sydney rock oysters

COMMON OYSTER SPECIES *(continued)*

Sydney rock oyster
Saccostrea glomerata
It's a strange name, really, for an oyster that grows naturally along some 1200 km (750 mi) of coastline from Moreton Bay in south-east Queensland to Mallacoota on the border of Victoria and New South Wales. It grows intertidally in the estuaries, lakes and inlets all along this stretch of the east coast of Australia.

The Sydney rock oyster is without doubt one of the world's great eating oysters. It has a lasting deep, rich and sweet flavour that's unknown in other oysters.

Generally speaking, the north coast of New South Wales has the best rock oysters in the summer months, and the south coast of New South Wales has the best in winter, although it's wise to check with your local supplier which is best on any given day.

SEASONALITY Best from NSW north coast spring–summer, from NSW south coast winter–spring
CATCHING METHOD Mainly basket-cultured
COMMON LENGTH 6–8 cm (2½–3¼ in)
COMMON WEIGHT 40–60 g (1½–2¼ oz)
IDENTIFIABLE FEATURES Craggy, irregular shell with a thin profile, outer shell light to purple and dark green, inner shell cream to dark ochre, meat cream to yellow with green hues
SUSTAINABILITY Highly sustainable (farmed)

OYSTERS IN THE KITCHEN

Angasi oyster
The angasi is big, very rich and very flavourful, with an almost meaty texture. It's hard to find consistent product in Australia. They must be really fresh and they don't mind a bit of topping – champagne and chives, for instance – because they have a bit more chew. The small ones are best.

Pacific oyster
If you think you don't like oysters, the Pacific is a great one to try because it's our mildest – almost like a mouthful of textured salty water. They're mild because they grow so fast, generally to full size in eighteen months. Because it's bigger, it's the best oyster to cook with. Don't give it too much heat, though, or it will become a rubber bullet – you just want to set the protein. The Pacific oysters from South Australia have a lot more flavour and are smaller, so they're the best ones to eat raw.

Sydney rock oyster
If there was ever an oyster you shouldn't cook, the Sydney rock oyster is it. It's almost a sin. They're magical as they are, completely on their own. Weather depicts the profile of an oyster – they'll taste different all year round. The flesh should have a good bite or even pop, and a bit of fat. It should be a little bit creamy but not excessively so – that means the oyster is spawning.

Sydney rock oysters take five or six years to grow to harvest and can last three weeks out of the water. A good oyster farmer will take them out, sit them in darkness, then put them back in the water and give them a tumble for 24 hours to remove any casualties. The second week is the premium time to eat an oyster.

Look for oysters that are even in shape, have clean shells, are free of overgrowth and have a pleasant oceanic aroma. Be sure to check that none of them is gaping or leaking liquor or, worse, emitting a foul odour. It's vital to take good care of oysters after buying and before opening. Oysters are surprisingly fragile and, like all molluscs, from the moment they're removed from their watery home, they're consuming their energy stores to survive. The more stressed they are, the more they consume, and the more they consume, the quicker they lose condition, which is most generally reflected in a loss of their delicious natural sweetness and mouthfeel.

STORAGE AND HANDLING Treat with care; angasi and Pacific: store at a humid 5–8°C (41–46°F); Sydney rock: store at a humid 12–14°C (54–57°F)
BEST COOKING METHODS Angasi and Sydney rock: raw; Pacific: raw, very lightly cooked
TEXTURE Angasi: firm; Pacific: medium soft; Sydney rock: medium soft
AROMA Angasi: funky vegetal notes of forest floor; Pacific: briny iodine zing; Sydney rock: rich note of clotted cream
FLAVOUR Angasi: rich and meaty; Pacific: mild, of salty water; Sydney rock: creamy
YIELD Flesh 20–40% of whole weight
SUBSTITUTES Each for the others

Oyster and sorrel soup

Shuck the oysters (see page 442) and refrigerate, covered, until required, being sure to retain the briny liquid.

Heat a medium saucepan over medium heat and add the butter. When the butter begins to bubble, add the onion and garlic, then cook, without colouring, for 5 minutes, or until soft.

Add the sorrel and stir it through well. Cook for 2 minutes, or until wilted.

Increase the heat to high, add the potato and stock, then bring to the boil. Reduce the heat to medium–low and simmer, covered, for 15 minutes, or until the potatoes are soft. Remove from the heat and set aside to cool at room temperature for about 20 minutes.

Using a food processor, blend the soup until completely smooth, then return the soup to low heat. Stir in the cream and heat gently, ensuring it does not boil. Season with salt and pepper.

Place three oysters and a little of their brine in each serving bowl. Pour the sorrel soup over the top and serve immediately.

NOTE: Sorrel can be difficult to find, but spinach makes a great alternative in this recipe.

SERVES 4

12 live Pacific oysters
60 g (2¼ oz) butter
1 brown onion, peeled and finely diced
2 garlic cloves, peeled and finely chopped
160 g (5¾ oz) young sorrel leaves, stems removed (see note)
1 large all-purpose potato (such as desiree), peeled and roughly chopped
750 ml (26 fl oz/3 cups) chicken stock
250 ml (9 fl oz/1 cup) thin (pouring) cream
sea salt and freshly ground black pepper, to taste

Oysters mignonette

SERVES 4

24 oysters, freshly shucked (see pages 442–43; see note)
2 teaspoons lemon oil (see note page 25)
brown bread, to serve
lemon cheeks, to serve (see note page 144)

MIGNONETTE DRESSING
1 small French shallot, peeled and very finely diced
100 ml (3½ fl oz) quality red wine vinegar
½ teaspoon freshly ground black pepper

For the mignonette dressing, combine the shallot, vinegar and pepper in a small bowl. Pour into a small serving bowl.

Arrange the oysters on a platter and splash over a little lemon oil. Serve the mignonette dressing on the side, with brown bread and lemon cheeks.

NOTE: All types of oyster are perfect in this recipe.

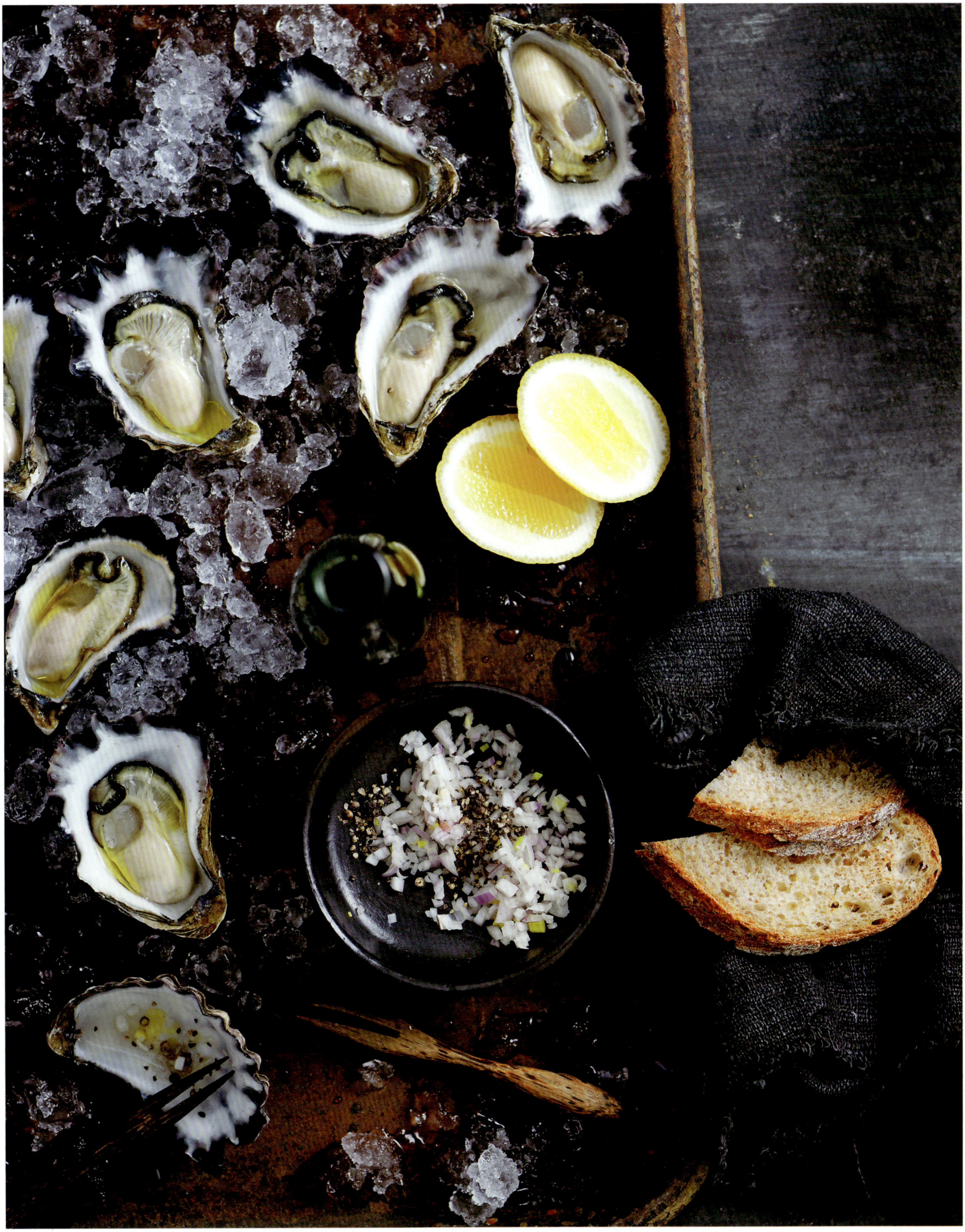

Banana prawn (top left), southern king prawn (top right), black tiger prawn (bottom right) and brown tiger prawn (bottom left)

PRAWNS

The highly managed Australian wild prawn (shrimp) fisheries have evolved into some of the most sustainable on the planet. Many stocks are now at their highest levels for years, and some species are also farmed. A vast range of species is caught, from shallow tropical waters to deep temperate seas. The main farms are in northern New South Wales, south-east Queensland and Far North Queensland. They ensure a consistent supply of high-quality prawns at very reasonable prices.

Generally, prawns hatch out in their millions in the open sea, then move into estuaries, lakes and inlets along the coast, where they find food on the muddy and sandy seabed, growing quickly before moving back out to sea. Small (school) prawns are netted inshore, in shallow bays, lagoons and rivers, but larger ones are usually caught in the deeper waters above the continental shelf, where they return to spawn.

Prawns are scavengers, eating pretty much anything they encounter. This gives them amazing flavour and texture, but is also one reason they require careful handling from harvest to plate. It's often best to buy frozen prawns, particularly if they're raw. The integrity and quality of a raw prawn packed and frozen from live will always be superior to one that has endured days of variable handling in a 'fresh' state.

When buying fresh prawns, look for vibrantly coloured tails and flesh glowing translucently through firm shells, with no discolouration at the base of the head or legs. They should neither look nor feel soggy; avoid buying any displayed floating in a pool of water in a plastic tray. If buying cooked prawns, ask to taste one. Inspect it first – check that it has all its legs, feelers and eyes, and that the tail has a firm springiness. Smell it – it should have a crisp, clean iodine aroma, with no signs of ammonia, old fish or brackish water. Finally, peel and taste it – it should be firm and sweet, with a long clean finish and no strong aftertaste.

Prawns are generally classified by size, the rather old-fashioned units for which are the number of pieces per imperial pound. U10 means you get about 10 pieces per lb (22 pieces per kg, which means each piece is about 45 g/1½ oz). U6–10 prawns could generally be described as jumbo prawns. U10–15 indicates 10–15 pieces per lb (22–33 pieces per kg or 30–45 g/1–1½ oz per piece). These and U15–20 would be described as large. U20–30 prawns are medium and U30 or more are small.

SHELLFISH A–Z GUIDE & RECIPES

COMMON PRAWN SPECIES

Banana prawn
Fenneropenaeus indicus
Caught during a few weeks, generally around April–May, and heavy summer rains usually mean a bumper season. They're trawled off northern Australia to highly managed plans by a fishery certified by the Marine Stewardship Council.

Translucent to yellow, with tiny dark spots and neat red legs, they have a sweet, firm-textured flesh preferred by Asian chefs seeking a sweet burst of flavour. They're also favoured by retailers, and although quite fragile are excellent value.

SEASONALITY	Short season in late autumn
CATCHING METHOD	Prawn trawl
COMMON LENGTH	12–20 cm (4½–8 in)
COMMON WEIGHT	20–30 g (¾–1 oz)
IDENTIFIABLE FEATURES	Translucent to yellow with tiny dark spots, red legs
SUSTAINABILITY	Northern prawn fisheries certified by the Marine Stewardship Council
STORAGE AND HANDLING	See page 385
BEST COOKING METHODS	Stir-fried, crumbed or battered and deep-fried, poached for salads
TEXTURE	Soft, moist
AROMA	Intense, complex, lightly earthy
FLAVOUR	Sweet, with notes of vanilla pod and green melon, and a zesty vegetal character
YIELD	Flesh 40–60% of whole weight
SUBSTITUTES	Each for the others

Blue endeavour prawn
Metapenaeus endeavouri
Live on the muddy seafloor to a depth of about 95 m (310 ft). They look similar to king prawns but have no spine under the head, making them much more fragile, and their legs are not blue.

These are great-value wild-caught prawns. They have a medium to strong, generally sweet flavour, a firm texture and low to medium oiliness.

SEASONALITY	Autumn to late spring
CATCHING METHOD	Prawn trawl
COMMON LENGTH	8–14 cm (3¼–5½ in)
COMMON WEIGHT	20–25 g (¾–1 oz)
IDENTIFIABLE FEATURES	Pink–apricot body and legs with dark tail; flesh translucent when raw, white with pinkish bands once cooked
SUSTAINABILITY	Northern and Shark Bay fisheries certified by Marine Stewardship Council
STORAGE AND HANDLING	See page 385
BEST COOKING METHODS	Poached in the shell in salt water for salads, grilled in the shell
TEXTURE	Firm, moist
AROMA	Funky deep aroma of champignon, with grassy back notes
FLAVOUR	Funky rich roast-meat character, with notes of shiitake mushroom
YIELD	Flesh 40–60% of whole weight
SUBSTITUTES	Each for the others

Eastern and western king prawns
Melicertus plebejus and *M. latisulcatus*
These delicious eating prawns, which are regarded by many as the true king of prawns, have an intensely sweet yet savoury character and rich, moist flesh. With their dramatic blue legs and tails, and green or coppery markings, they're also truly magnificent-looking prawns.

Eastern king prawns are caught mainly off northern New South Wales and south-eastern Queensland all year round, with peak catches from February to June. Western king prawns are caught mainly in the Exmouth Gulf and Shark Bay regions of north-west Western Australia, and the Spencer Gulf and west coast of South Australia. They're caught mainly during spring and summer. The fisheries are highly managed, and certified sustainable by the Marine Stewardship Council.

SEASONALITY Eastern king: peak in late summer to early winter; western king: 10–12-day periods in November, December, March, April and June
CATCHING METHOD Prawn trawl
COMMON LENGTH 10–16 cm (4–6¼ in)
COMMON WEIGHT 45 g (1½ oz)
IDENTIFIABLE FEATURES Pink–apricot body with green or coppery colourations, blue legs and tail
SUSTAINABILITY Spencer Gulf, Exmouth Gulf and Shark Bay fisheries certified by Marine Stewardship Council
STORAGE AND HANDLING See page 385
BEST COOKING METHODS Boiled, steamed, grilled (broiled), stir-fried, deep-fried, roasted
TEXTURE Firm, moist
AROMA Oceanic, with light notes of green melon
FLAVOUR Sweet, salty, churned-butter rich, with a lingering aftertaste
YIELD Flesh 40–60% of whole weight
SUBSTITUTES Each for the others

Redspot king prawn
Melicertus longistylus

Redspot prawns are reef prawns closely related to king prawns, although often smaller. They have a distinctive red spot on each side of their body and are typically lighter in flavour and softer in texture than king prawns.

Caught mainly off the central Queensland coast in the Gladstone to Bowen region, they like to stay within 30 km (19 mi) of coral reefs. Redspots are a popular choice in restaurants because they're great value and attractive-looking.

SEASONALITY Year round, with peaks in autumn
CATCHING METHOD Prawn trawl
COMMON LENGTH 10–14 cm (4–5½ in)
COMMON WEIGHT 20–25 g (¾–1 oz)
IDENTIFIABLE FEATURES Pale brown, bluish tail, red spot on either side of body
SUSTAINABILITY Managed sustainably
STORAGE AND HANDLING See page 385
BEST COOKING METHODS Boiled, grilled (broiled) or roasted in the shell
TEXTURE Firm, moist
AROMA Oceanic, with grassy notes
FLAVOUR Sweet, grassy, with notes of green melon
YIELD Flesh 40–60% of whole weight
SUBSTITUTES Each for the others

Royal red prawn
Haliporoides sibogae

Trawled in deep water in daylight at 250–850 m (820–2800 ft), mostly off the New South Wales south coast, but found off the east and west coasts.

They're pink to red, raw and cooked, with a thick, hard shell, but soft, sweet, creamy meat. They can spoil quickly and so are usually sold as frozen meat. They're a cheap alternative for chopped or minced (ground) prawn meat and also great raw or in a stir-fry.

SEASONALITY Year round, with a peak in spring
CATCHING METHOD Prawn trawl
COMMON LENGTH 7–10 cm (2¾–4 in)
COMMON WEIGHT 25 g (1 oz)
IDENTIFIABLE FEATURES Pink to red body, thick hard shell
SUSTAINABILITY Managed sustainably
STORAGE AND HANDLING See page 385
BEST COOKING METHODS Roasted, deep-fried, shallow-fried, stir-fried, dumplings or ravioli
TEXTURE Firm, moist
AROMA Notes of egg white, light oceanic zing
FLAVOUR Soft, rich, notes of mushroom and potato
YIELD Flesh 40–60% of whole weight
SUBSTITUTES Each for the others

Prawn cocktail

SERVES 4

320 g (11¼ oz/1 cup) salt
20 raw banana prawns (shrimp) (see note)
iced water, as required, to refresh
100 g (3½ oz/4 cups) shredded iceberg lettuce
lemon oil, to dress (see note page 25)
sea salt, to taste
cocktail sauce (see note), to serve

To cook the prawns, use the standard rule for cooking shellfish: for every 2 litres (68 fl oz/8 cups) of water, add 160 g (5¾ oz/½ cup) of salt. Be sure not to overcrowd the pot – 20 prawns to one pot is the absolute maximum; for this number of prawns, use 4–5 litres (135–169 fl oz/16–20 cups) of water.

In a medium–large saucepan with a tight-fitting lid, heat the water and salt over high heat. When it reaches a rapid boil, add the prawns and cover. Return to the boil, then stir, cover and boil, for a further 2–3 minutes. It's important that the water stays at a continuous rapid boil – this will yield prawns with a crisp bite.

Drain the prawns in a colander and immediately plunge them into a bowl of iced water to refresh. When completely cool, remove from the water and peel.

Divide the shredded lettuce into four and make heaped portions on four plates. Place the prawns on top, curled over the iceberg, top to tail and side by side. Drizzle the prawns and lettuce with lemon oil and season well with salt. Serve with the cocktail sauce on the side.

NOTES: You could use cooked prawns in this recipe and omit the first step.

There are many great commercial cocktail sauces available, but it's also quite easy to make your own: combine two parts Mayonnaise (see page 455) with one part tomato sauce (ketchup), then season as you wish with one or more of worcestershire sauce, Tabasco sauce, horseradish and cayenne pepper. It will keep for 3 days in the fridge.

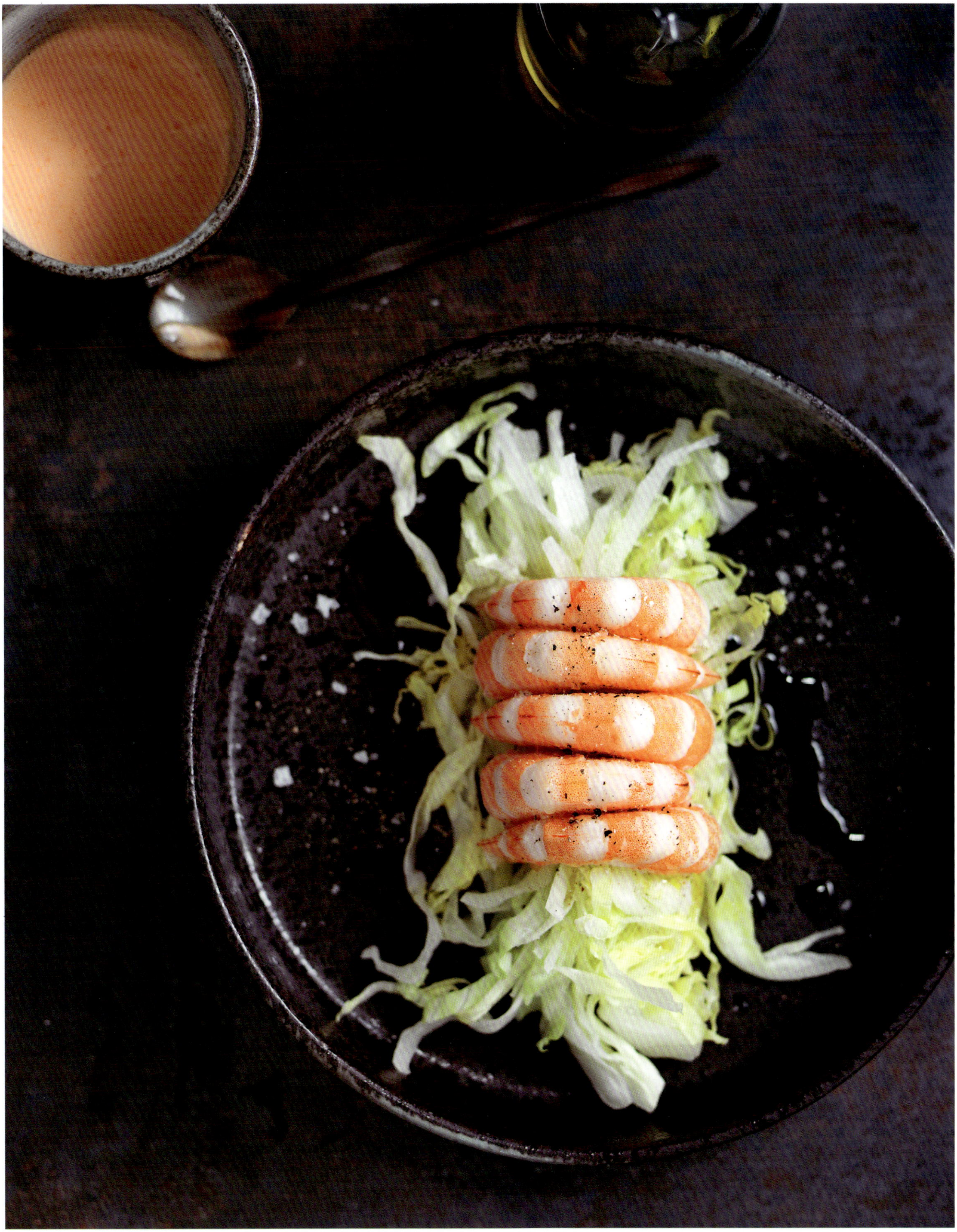

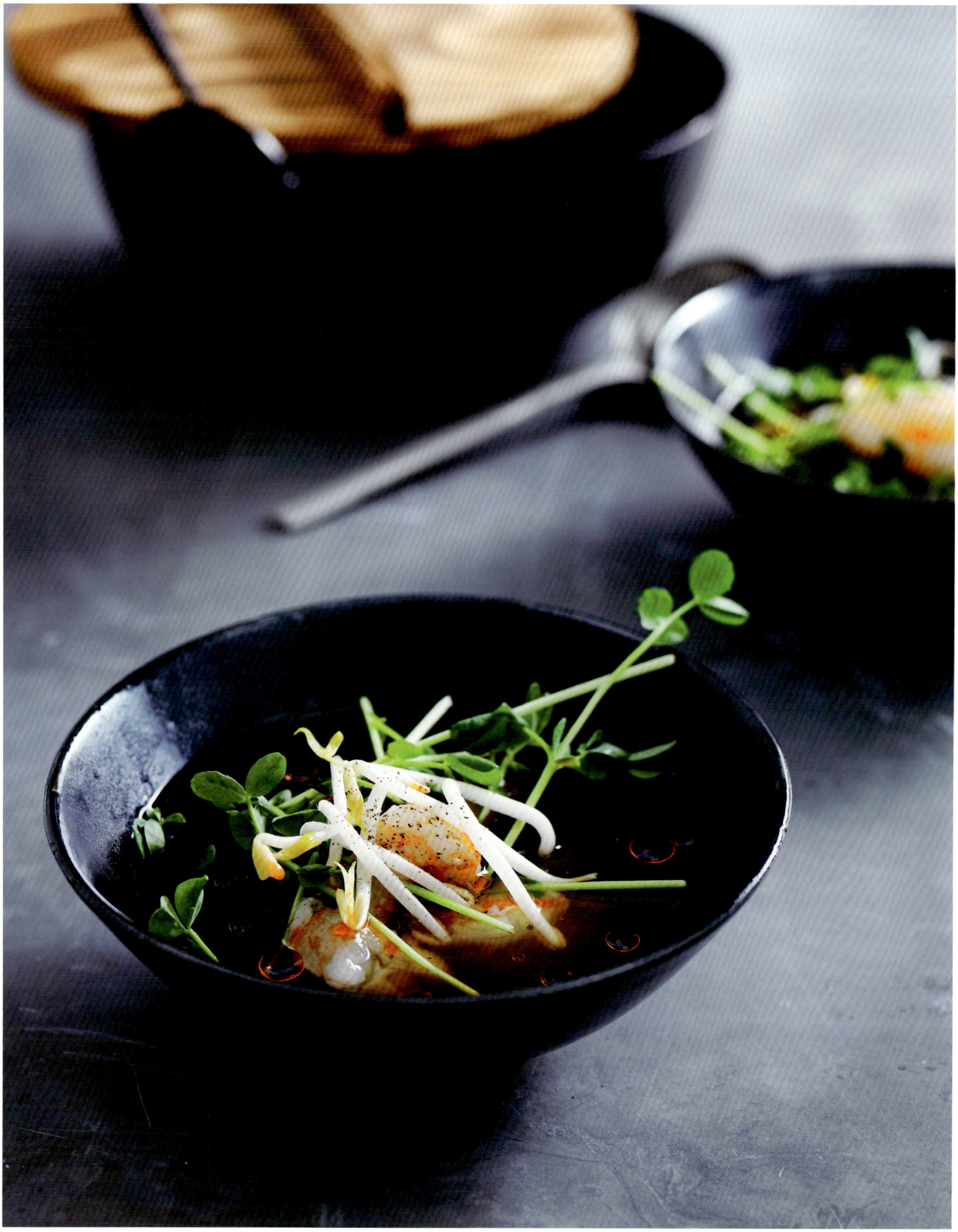

King prawn broth with sprouts

For the prawn broth, place the prawn heads in a colander to drain, ensuring they are as dry as possible.

Heat the vegetable oil in a large saucepan over medium–high heat. Add the onion, carrot, garlic, ginger, peppercorns and chilli, then fry, stirring frequently, for 10 minutes, or until a deep golden brown and well caramelised.

Increase the heat to high and slowly add the prawn heads, a handful at a time so you don't create a stew. Stir well and fry, scraping the caramelised bits from the base of the pan as you go – this is colour and flavour, and a vital part of the sauce, but take care not to burn it. Add the tomato, salt, wine and stock, then bring to the boil. Reduce the heat to medium–low and keep on a rolling simmer for 3 hours.

Rest a sieve just inside the top of the pan to push the solids down, then very carefully ladle out 1–1.5 litres (35–52 fl oz/4–6 cups) of prawn broth into a medium saucepan (the remaining liquids and solids can be used to make shellfish sauce; see page 458).

Bring the broth to the boil over high heat, then remove the pan from the heat. Add the prawns to the broth, turning after 1 minute to blanch them lightly.

Place three prawns in each serving bowl. Ladle over the broth and top with the snow pea sprouts and bean sprouts. Splash a few drops of shellfish oil over each bowl, sprinkle with pepper and serve immediately.

NOTES: Crab shells or legs left over from steaming make a great addition to this recipe. They add a whole new level of flavour to the sauce.

Be sure to use fresh tomatoes, as tinned tomatoes will turn the sauce cloudy.

SERVES 2

6 raw king prawns (shrimp), peeled, deveined, split down the back
1 small handful snow pea (mangetout) sprouts
1 tablespoon young bean sprouts
½ teaspoon Shellfish Oil (see page 456), to serve
pinch of freshly ground black pepper, to serve

PRAWN BROTH

2 kg (4 lb 8 oz) prawn (shrimp) heads, cleaned (see note)
125 ml (4 fl oz/½ cup) vegetable oil
1 large onion, peeled and roughly chopped
1 large carrot, peeled and roughly chopped
80 g (2¾ oz) garlic cloves, peeled and bruised with the back of a knife
6 cm (2½ in) piece ginger, peeled and roughly chopped
70 g (2½ oz/½ cup) black peppercorns
2 long red chillies, seeds in, roughly chopped
2 ripe tomatoes, roughly crushed (see note)
2 heaped tablespoons sea salt
3 litres (101 fl oz/12 cups) dry white wine
2 litres (68 fl oz/8 cups) Fish Stock (page 457) or water

Prawn omelette with spinach, enoki, bean sprouts and oyster sauce

SERVES 1–2

boiling water, for rinsing
2 eggs, at room temperature
1 teaspoon light soy sauce
1 teaspoon hot water
sesame oil, for frying
6 raw king prawns (shrimp), peeled, deveined, split down the back (see note)
½ small handful baby English spinach leaves
20 g (¾ oz/¼ cup) enoki mushrooms
30 g (1 oz/¼ cup) young bean sprouts
20 g (¾ oz) butter, softened
1 handful mixed Asian herbs, such as shiso, Vietnamese mint, Thai basil, coriander (cilantro)
1 tablespoon oyster sauce, or to taste

Preheat the oven to 180°C (350°F).

Rinse a mixing bowl and whisk with boiling water to sterilise both the bowl and the whisk. This also helps the eggs make a good, frothy sabayon. Pour out the water and break the eggs into the hot bowl, then whisk in the soy sauce. Whisking continuously, add the hot water until the eggs are thick and frothy, almost at sabayon stage.

Heat a 20 cm (8 in) non-stick ovenproof omelette pan over medium heat, adding a splash of sesame oil. Place the prawns in the pan and seal gently, without colouring. Add the spinach, enoki and bean sprouts. Toss for about 30 seconds, or until the vegetables are warmed through, then turn all the ingredients into a medium bowl and set aside in a warm place.

Wipe the pan with paper towel and return it to the stovetop over medium heat. Add the butter and quickly add the beaten egg mixture. Shake well in the pan for about 20 seconds, then top with the cooked ingredients. Transfer to the oven for 2–3 minutes, or until just set.

Remove the omelette from the oven and add the Asian herbs. Place a serving plate on top of the pan and carefully turn the pan upside down, inverting the omelette onto the plate and folding in half at the same time. Spoon over the oyster sauce and serve.

NOTE: Most types of prawn will work well in this recipe, particularly banana and redspot.

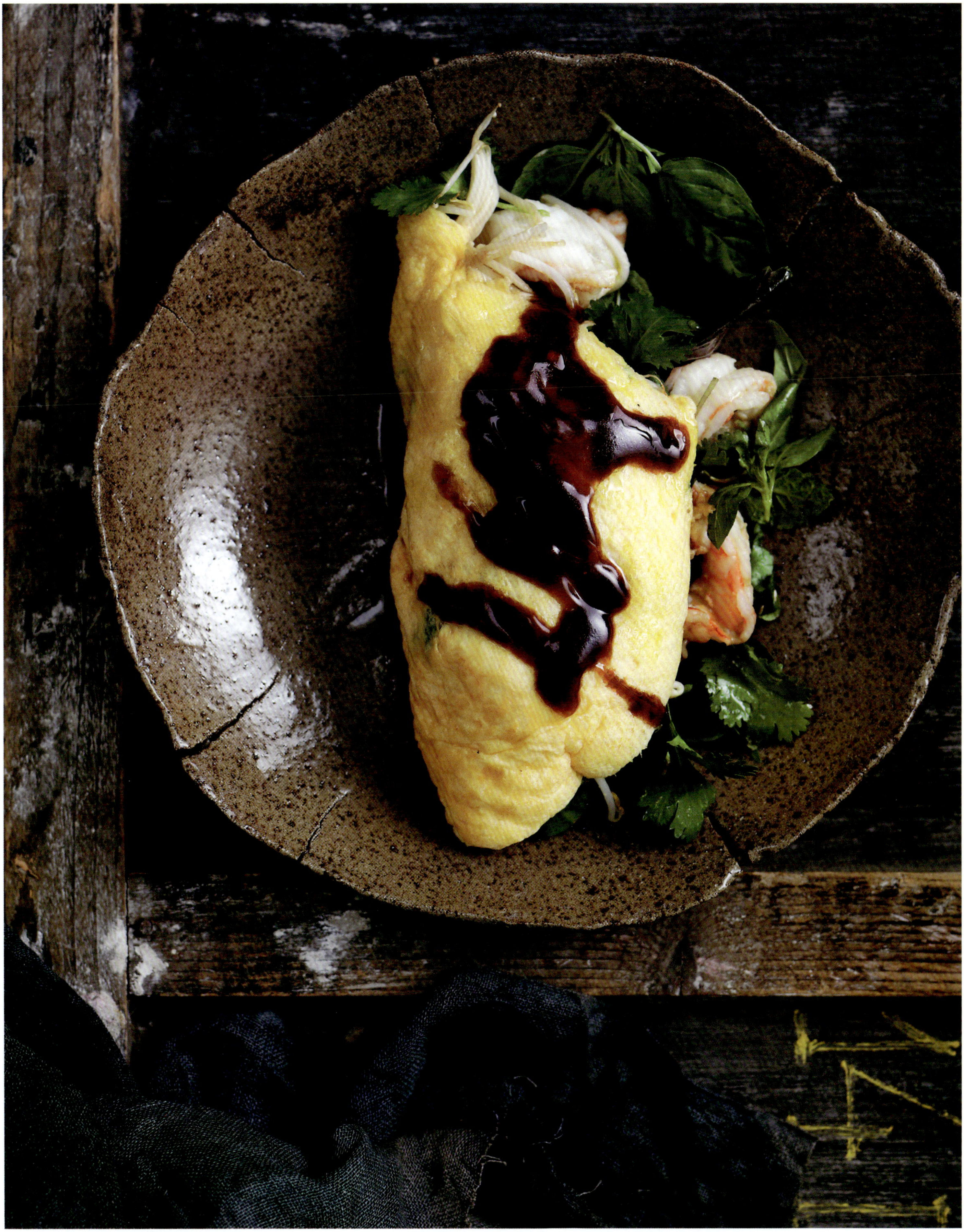

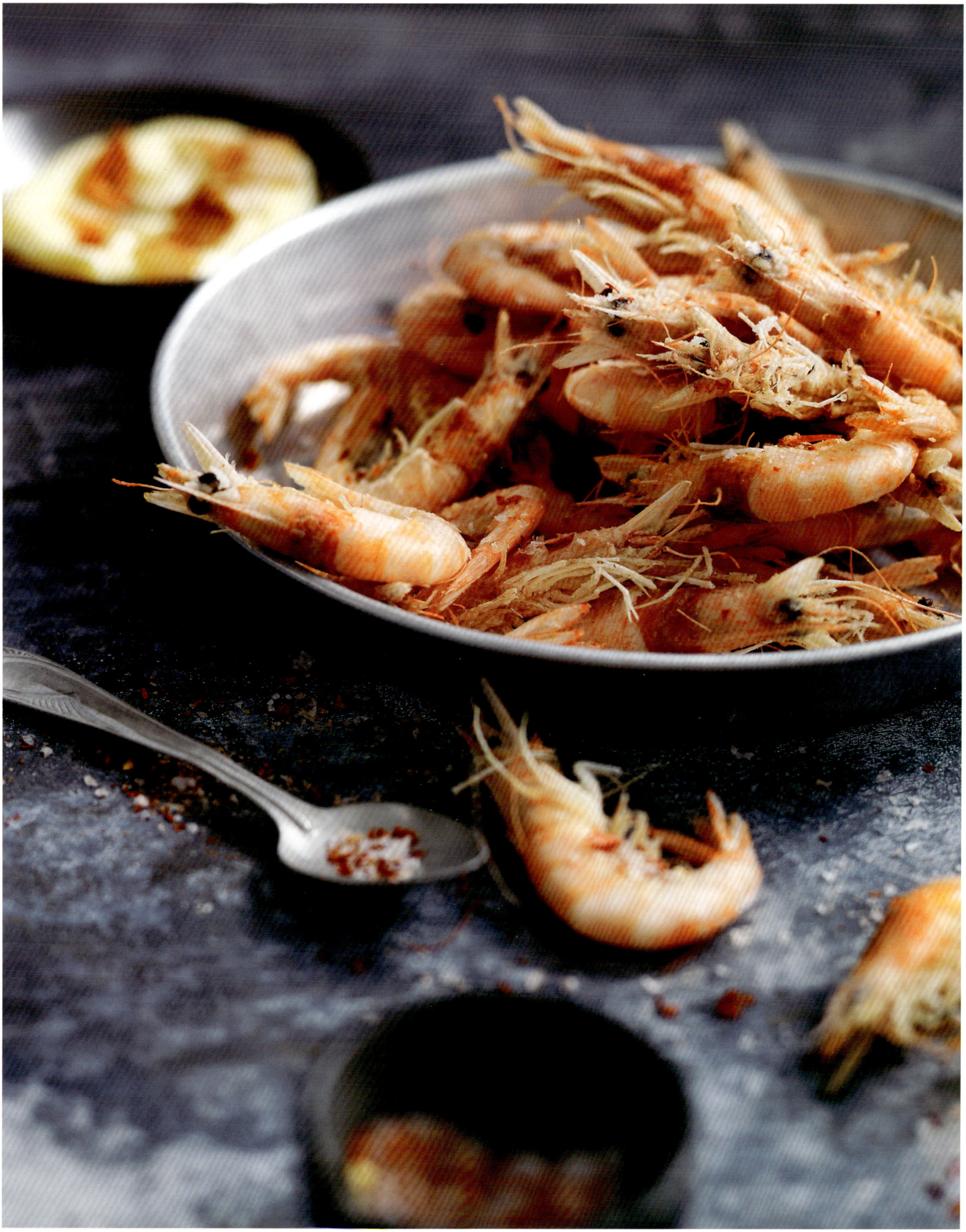

Deep-fried school prawns with aioli and chilli salt

To make the chilli salt, mix together the dried red chilli and sea salt. Using a mortar and pestle, crush the mixture roughly and set aside.

To make the aioli, caramelise the garlic by heating a small frying pan over medium–low heat and adding the butter. When the butter melts and begins to froth, add the garlic and toss to coat. Sprinkle with the sugar and keep tossing for 3 minutes, or until the garlic is golden. Add the fish stock, then continue tossing and cooking the garlic for 5–7 minutes, until tender. In a small bowl, crush the caramelised garlic using the back of a spoon, then stir through the mayonnaise. Cover and refrigerate.

Half-fill a 6 litre (203 fl oz/24 cup) saucepan (see note) with vegetable oil and place over high heat. Heat the oil to 180°C (350°C) – check with an oil thermometer. (For a guide to testing the oil temperature without a thermometer, see note.)

Place the rice flour in a large bowl. Dust the prawns with the flour then carefully drop them into the hot oil. Deep-fry for about 1 minute, until perfectly crisp. Remove and drain on paper towel.

Transfer the prawns to a serving bowl, sprinkle with some of the chilli salt and scatter the spring onions over (if using), then toss well. Serve with the aioli and the remaining chilli salt on the side.

NOTES: When deep-frying in a saucepan, it's advisable to keep the oil level a good 10 cm (4 in) below the rim of the pan. The other option for deep-frying is, of course, an electric deep-fryer. The used oil can be strained, cooled and refrigerated for later use.

To test the temperature of the oil without a thermometer, drop a cube of bread into the saucepan. If the bread turns golden in 15 seconds, the temperature is sitting perfectly on 180°C (350°F). If the bread only takes 10 seconds to turn golden, then the oil is around 190°C (375°F). If it takes 20–30 seconds to brown, the oil is too cold. Be patient and bring the oil to the correct temperature before proceeding.

SERVES 2–4

vegetable oil, for deep-frying
rice flour, for dusting
500 g (1 lb 2 oz) raw school prawns (shrimp)
2 tablespoons chopped spring onions (scallions) (optional)

CHILLI SALT

1 teaspoon dried red chilli (see note page 109)
1 teaspoon sea salt

AIOLI

20 g (¾ oz) butter
4 garlic cloves, peeled
1 teaspoon caster (superfine) sugar
1 tablespoon Fish Stock (page 457)
120 g (4¼ oz/½ cup) Mayonnaise (page 455)

Buttered prawns with nectarine and radicchio

SERVES 4

150 g (5½ oz) butter
12 medium raw prawns (shrimp), peeled and deveined
4 radicchio leaves
2 yellow nectarines, cut in half and stone removed
1 teaspoon chopped chives

Gently heat the butter in a large frying pan over low heat. Before the butter has completely melted, add the prawns to the pan – the butter can bubble, but ensure it remains over low heat and doesn't colour, as the prawns should be just warmed through and cooked without colouring at all. Keep gently tossing and basting the prawns in the butter for 2–3 minutes.

Place a radicchio-leaf cup on each plate and add a nectarine half to each. Top each with three prawns and drizzle over ample melted butter from the pan. Scatter the chives over and serve.

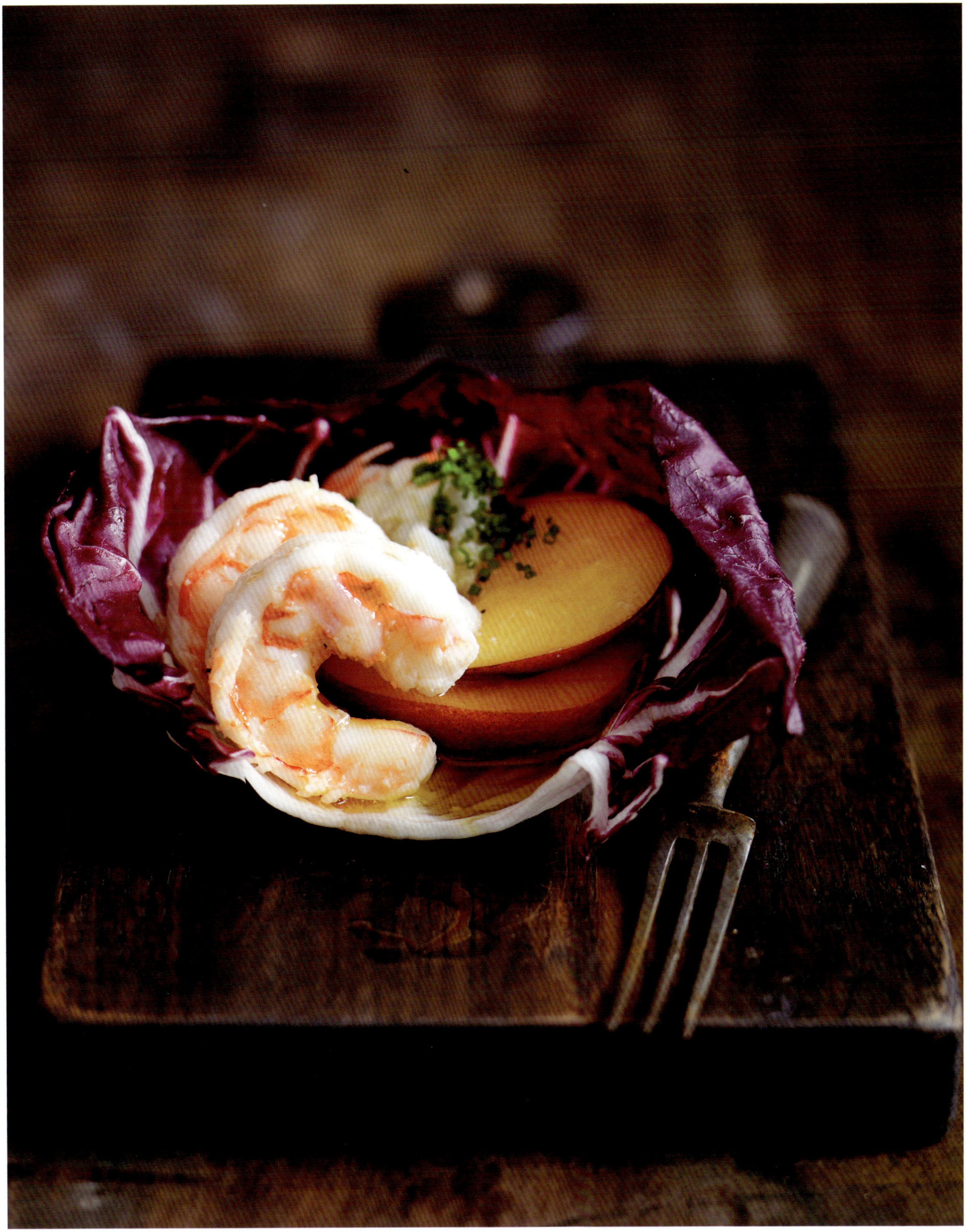

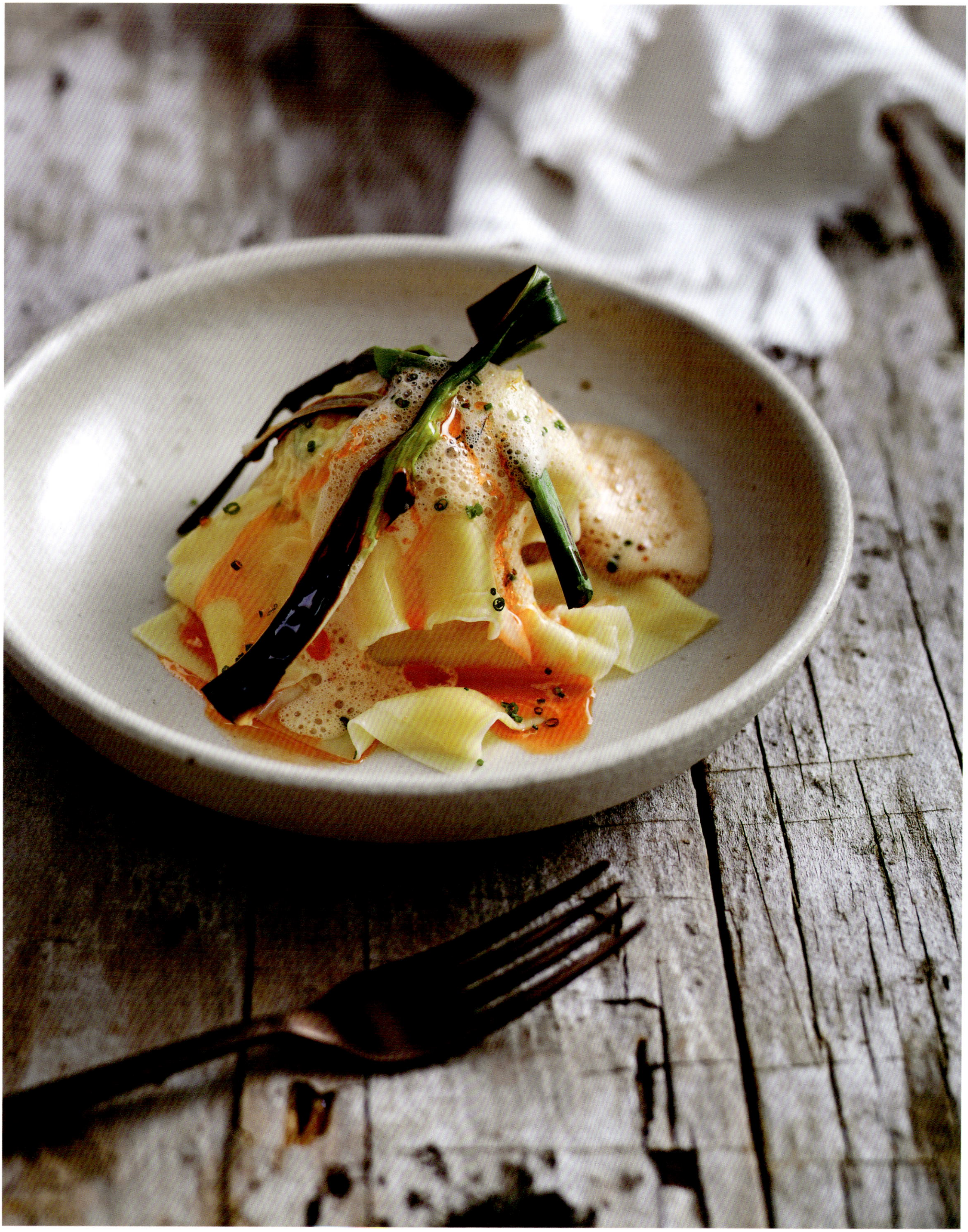

Tiger prawn ravioli, grilled spring onions and shellfish sauce

Process the fish in a food processor on medium speed for 1 minute, or until it forms a smooth paste. Add the egg, then reduce the speed to slow and gradually pour in the cream. Don't overwork the mixture at this point or it will split. Season well with salt and pepper. Transfer to a large mixing bowl then use your hands to mix through the prawn meat and julienned spring onion.

To make the ravioli, lay a won ton wrapper on a clean work surface. Place a heaped teaspoon of filling in the centre and dab the edges of the wrapper with a little water. Place another won ton wrapper directly on top and press the edges down gently, cupping your hands around the filling to create a secure mound in the centre. Cover and refrigerate while you prepare the remaining ravioli. (Refrigerate the ravioli in a single layer.)

To cook the ravioli, bring a saucepan of water to the boil over high heat (see note). Reduce the heat to medium, then, when the water is simmering, add the ravioli and blanch gently for 2 minutes on each side. Remove the pan from the heat immediately.

Using a slotted spoon, transfer the ravioli from the pan to a cold work surface or tray. After 1 minute, carefully turn each one over – this will create perfectly set and cooked ravioli.

While the ravioli is cooking, bring the shellfish sauce just to the boil in a small saucepan over high heat. Remove from the heat then, using a hand-held blender, whizz the hot sauce rapidly to create a little volume and aeration.

To serve, place two ravioli on each plate. Carefully spoon over the shellfish sauce, add the grilled spring onions and top with a scattering of chopped chives and a teaspoon of shellfish oil.

NOTE: This recipe makes about 16 portions, or 32 individual ravioli – it's much easier to make the filling in this quantity. Use a saucepan big enough to blanch all the ravioli at once. Freeze any ravioli you don't use in meal-sized batches in freezer bags for up to 3 months. Cook the ravioli from frozen without thawing in a pan of simmering (not boiling) water, for 4 minutes on each side, then rest on a cold work surface as described above.

MAKES 32 RAVIOLI (see note)

250 g (9 oz) boneless, skinless snapper fillet or offcuts or other low-fat white fish fillet

1 egg

250 ml (9 fl oz/1 cup) thick (double) cream

sea salt and freshly ground black pepper, to taste

1 kg (2 lb 4 oz) finely diced raw tiger prawn (shrimp) meat

4 spring onions (scallions), green ends only, finely julienned, plus 4 extra whole spring onions, grilled until soft and golden in a dry frying pan

64 square egg won ton wrappers

160 ml (5¼ fl oz) Shellfish Sauce (page 458)

½ teaspoon chopped chives

1 teaspoon Shellfish Oil (page 456) per serve (2 ravioli)

Indian prawn and eggplant curry

SERVES 4

1 large eggplant (aubergine), cut into large dice
80 g (2¾ oz) sea salt, plus extra to taste
125 ml (4 fl oz/½ cup) vegetable oil, plus extra for frying
1 cinnamon stick
6 cardamom pods, lightly crushed using a mortar and pestle
1 brown onion, peeled and roughly chopped
4 garlic cloves, peeled and finely chopped
2 cm (¾ in) piece ginger, peeled and finely chopped
2 long green chillies, split lengthways, seeds removed, finely chopped
2 teaspoons ground turmeric
1 tablespoon chilli powder
1 teaspoon garam masala
2 ripe tomatoes, roughly chopped
12 large raw king prawns (shrimp), peeled, deveined and cut into 2 cm (¾ in) lengths
2 tablespoons malt vinegar
6 curry leaves
freshly ground black pepper, to taste
chopped coriander (cilantro) leaves, to serve
cooked basmati rice, to serve
Indian bread, to serve

Place the chopped eggplant in a medium mixing bowl, sprinkle with 35 g (1¼ oz/¼ cup) of the sea salt and cover with cold water. Leave to soak for 1 hour.

Briefly rinse the eggplant under cold running water, then drain in a colander and turn out onto a tray lined with paper towel. Leave to dry for 5 minutes.

Half-fill a deep heavy-based frying pan with vegetable oil and heat over medium–high heat. When the oil begins to smoke, wipe any excess moisture from the eggplant and fry until dark, in batches if necessary. Remove the eggplant using a slotted spoon and drain on a tray lined with fresh paper towel. Set aside.

Return the frying pan to medium heat, re-using any oil remaining from frying the eggplant and adding more if required. When the oil begins to shimmer, add the cinnamon stick and cardamom pods, then toss for 30 seconds to flavour the oil.

Add the onion, garlic, ginger and green chilli, then fry, stirring constantly, for 2–3 minutes, until the vegetables are soft and beginning to caramelise. Stir through the remaining salt, and the turmeric, chilli powder and garam masala, then add the tomato and stir to combine. Cook for 2–3 minutes.

Add the prawns and vinegar, then cook for a further 1 minute, or until the prawns change colour. Add the fried eggplant and the curry leaves, stirring to combine. Reduce the heat to low and cook for a further 3 minutes. Taste for seasoning and adjust with salt and pepper if necessary.

Serve with coriander leaves, basmati rice and your favourite Indian bread.

Hot and sour prawn soup

Place the stock in a medium–large saucepan over high heat. Add the tomato, lemongrass, lime leaves, galangal and chilli, then bring to the boil. Reduce the heat to medium and simmer for 3–4 minutes.

Add the mushrooms and simmer for a further 3 minutes.

Increase the heat to high, add the chilli paste and stir through with the sugar and fish sauce. Add the prawns and cook for 2–3 minutes, until they turn pink. Remove from the heat.

Season the soup with lime juice and taste for a balance of hot, salty, sour and a touch of sweet. Adjust if necessary with more chilli paste, sugar, fish sauce and/or lime juice.

Ladle the soup and prawns into four bowls and top with the coriander. Serve with chilli oil on the side.

NOTE: Thai chilli paste (nam prik pao) is available from Asian supermarkets.

SERVES 4

1 litre (35 fl oz/4 cups) chicken stock
2 large ripe tomatoes, roughly chopped
3 lemongrass stems, white part only, outer layers removed, bruised
8 kaffir lime leaves, crushed in your hands
2 galangal slices
4 long red chillies, split lengthways, seeds removed
240 g (8½ oz) small whole button mushrooms (or straw or oyster mushrooms)
2 teaspoons Thai chilli paste, or to taste (see note)
1 tablespoon caster (superfine) sugar, or to taste
2 tablespoons fish sauce, or to taste
12 raw king prawns (shrimp), heads and tails on, body peeled
juice of 1–2 limes, or to taste
15 g (½ oz/½ cup) loosely packed coriander (cilantro) leaves
chilli oil, to serve

Tasmanian scallops

SCALLOPS

Milky translucent when raw, opaque white when cooked, intensely sweet and rich, scallops are true luxury. Of the three main commercial species harvested in Australia, the two most significant are the Tasmanian or commercial scallop (*Pecten fumatus*), caught off Victoria and Tasmania, and the saucer or Queensland scallop (*Amusium balloti*), caught in temperate tropical waters off Western Australia and Queensland. A smaller fishery exists in South Australia for the exotic purple-shelled and purple-roed queen scallop (*Chlamys bifrons*), which is hand-harvested by divers off Kangaroo Island and the west coast. The traditional harvesting of scallops using scallop dredges results in most of them being drowned during harvest; hand-harvested scallops are typically better able to survive and are inevitably less gritty.

Scallops feed on plankton, and local variations in plankton species lead to regional variation in scallop flavour. Live scallops should be treated with care from the moment they leave the water, as they quickly start consuming their own sugar stores and losing their great sweetness. They can also imbibe their own waste, fast rendering them musty and earthy. Unless they're kept in tanks to extend their shelf life, they won't remain in top condition for any longer than 48 hours after harvest.

Inside the shell, scallops have a large adductor muscle and the roe, sometimes referred to as the 'coral'. They're hermaphrodites, so the roe can be either orange (female) or white (male) or a combination. Saucer scallop roe is removed with the gut during processing.

SEASONALITY Tasmanian: mainly winter to early summer; queen: year round; saucer: year round, with various regional closures
CATCHING METHODS Tasmanian and saucer: dredge; queen: divers
COMMON SIZE 7–9 cm (2¾–3½ in)
COMMON WEIGHT 13–17 g (½–¾ oz)
IDENTIFIABLE FEATURES Tasmanian: 'classic' ribbed shell with white interior; queen: rough shell with bright purple interior, female roe bright purple; saucer: smooth, even shell with concentric growth rings
SUSTAINABILITY Stock status good

SCALLOPS IN THE KITCHEN

Fresh scallops are amazing raw. Alternatively, simply put them on a tray under the grill (broiler) for a minute or two to set the protein, then drizzle over olive oil and add a pinch of chopped chives. Avoid overcooking scallops. If you prefer your seafood cooked through, transfer the scallops from the heat to a warm place to finish cooking.

If you can't rely on the scallops being absolutely fresh, you're better off buying them still frozen rather than freshly thawed. You can tell if a scallop has been frozen and thawed from its texture. A fresh scallop will be very firm. If it moves to the touch and is soft, it's been frozen.

Say you go to the shop and buy a couple of dozen fresh scallops. On the first night eat them raw or slightly cooked. Thereafter they'll last in your fridge for about six days, but each day the flavour and texture will change. From day three you should cook them with other flavours.

Saucer scallops should only be seared rather than cooked through, or the protein will toughen. They're also superb eaten raw – if you get them live or really fresh they're great for carpaccio. They have a completely different texture from Tasmanian scallops.

With Tasmanian scallops, make sure you eat the roe and the scallop meat together – it's glorious. The roe is like an accompaniment that makes the meat sweet and saucy. Tasmanian scallops are beautiful raw, sushi-nigiri style. Simply open them up (see page 440), carefully cut away the frill and gut, then put them back in the shell and bang. They should be creamy and the roe a sweet joy.

Sometimes you'll find a lot of sand in a scallop once you open it up. If you do wash them, don't do it in fresh water – the scallop will soak it up like a sponge and it will wash all the flavour out. Use a brine made as described on page 385.

STORAGE AND HANDLING Scallops readily absorb other aromas and flavours. Wrap fresh meat in paper towel, then sit on a drip tray over ice in an airtight container in the vegetable crisper. Gently thaw frozen scallops overnight in the fridge, in an airtight container lined with paper towel.

BEST COOKING METHODS Raw, pan-seared, steamed, sautéed, grilled (broiled)

TEXTURE Silky soft with a gelatinous foamy character when raw; firm (tough if overcooked) once cooked

AROMA Caramel sweetness with hints of ozone-like seaweedy freshness

FLAVOUR Intensely sweet, vanilla-like, with notes of iodine and green seaweed

APPEARANCE Translucent, glistening white flesh with (or without) orange or white roe when raw; arctic white or creamy yellow flesh with orange or dark cream roe once cooked

YIELD Flesh and roe 15% of whole weight

SUBSTITUTES None

Pan-seared saucer scallops with speck, brussels sprouts and brown butter

Remove the scallops from their shells and set the scallop meat aside on paper towel. Wipe the scallop shells clean.

Heat half the olive oil in a large heavy-based frying pan over medium heat. Add the speck and sauté for 2 minutes, or until it begins to crisp. Add the brussels sprouts and toss to coat. Season with the lemon juice and pepper. Remove the pan from the heat. Spoon the mixture into a small bowl and set aside in a warm place.

Wipe the pan clean with paper towel and place it over high heat. Add the remaining olive oil and when a thin blue haze rises from the surface of the oil, add the scallops. Sear for 1 minute without moving them, then gently turn them over and cook for a further 1 minute. Remove the scallops from the pan and set aside on paper towel to drain.

Return the pan to high heat.

Place the scallop shells on four serving plates. Add a scallop to each shell and top with a tablespoon of the speck and brussels sprout mixture.

When the pan is hot, add the butter and let it melt – it will quickly turn nut brown and begin to foam. Remove immediately from the heat and spoon a little over each scallop. Serve straight away.

SERVES 4

16 saucer scallops on the half shell
120 ml (4 fl oz) extra virgin olive oil
60 g (2¼ oz) speck, finely diced
4 brussels sprouts, thinly shaved using a mandoline
juice of ½ lemon
sea salt and freshly ground black pepper, to taste
100 g (3½ oz) butter

Grilled scallops with ginger spring onion oil

SERVES 4

24 Tasmanian or queen scallops on the half shell, with roe

GINGER SPRING ONION OIL
30 g (1 oz) ginger, peeled and roughly chopped
30 g (1 oz) garlic cloves, peeled and roughly chopped
2 spring onions (scallions), green ends only, roughly chopped
200 ml (7 fl oz) vegetable oil
1 tablespoon white soy sauce (see note page 305)

Preheat an oven grill (broiler) to high.

For the ginger spring onion oil, roughly crush the ginger and garlic using a large mortar and pestle. Add the spring onion and pound lightly.

Heat the vegetable oil in a small saucepan over high heat. When the oil begins to smoke, carefully pour the hot oil into the mortar to scorch the vegetables and create a loose sauce. Stir through the white soy sauce.

Place the scallops on a baking tray on the bottom shelf of the oven and grill for 2 minutes. Remove from the oven, add about ⅓ teaspoon of ginger spring onion oil to each scallop and serve.

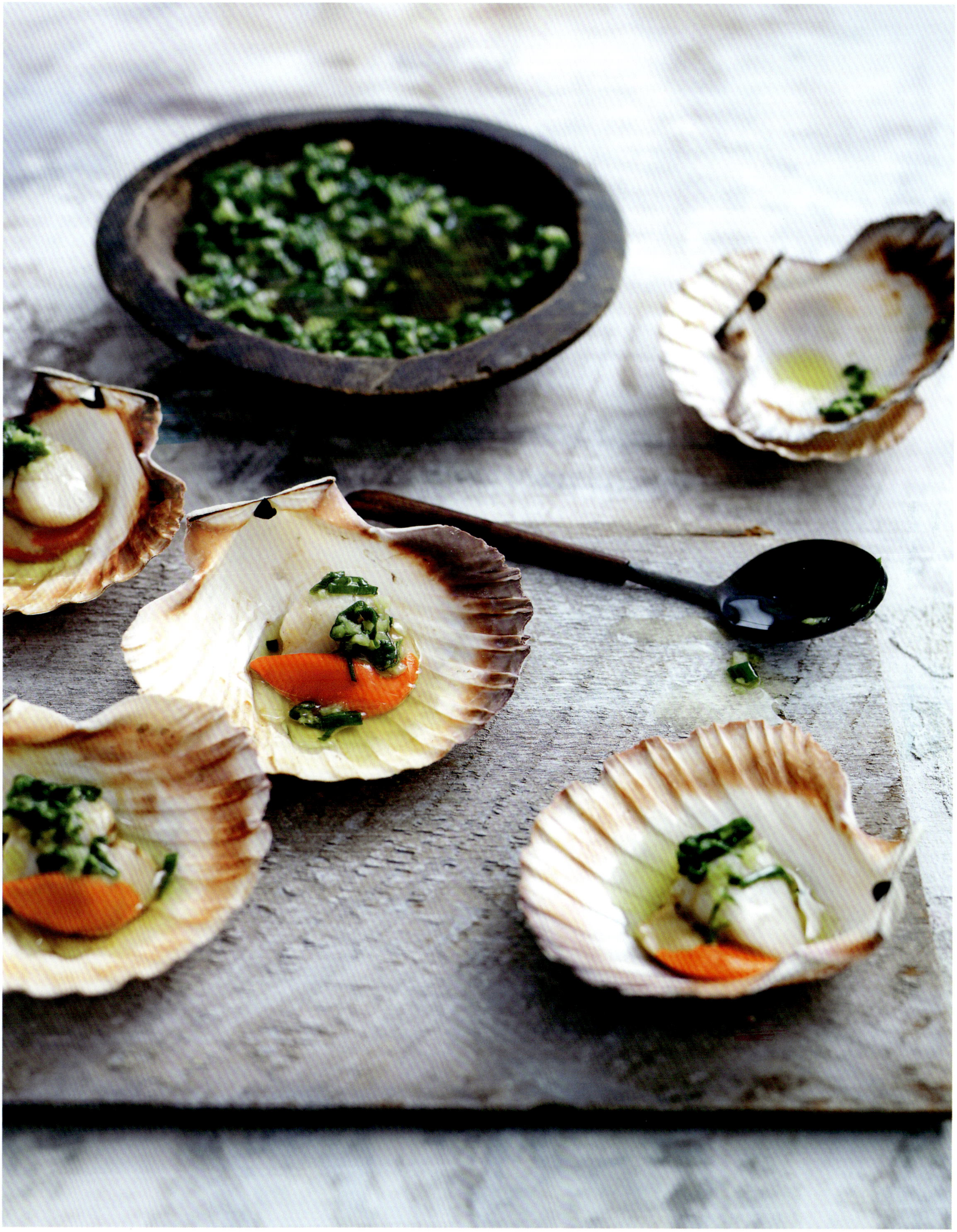

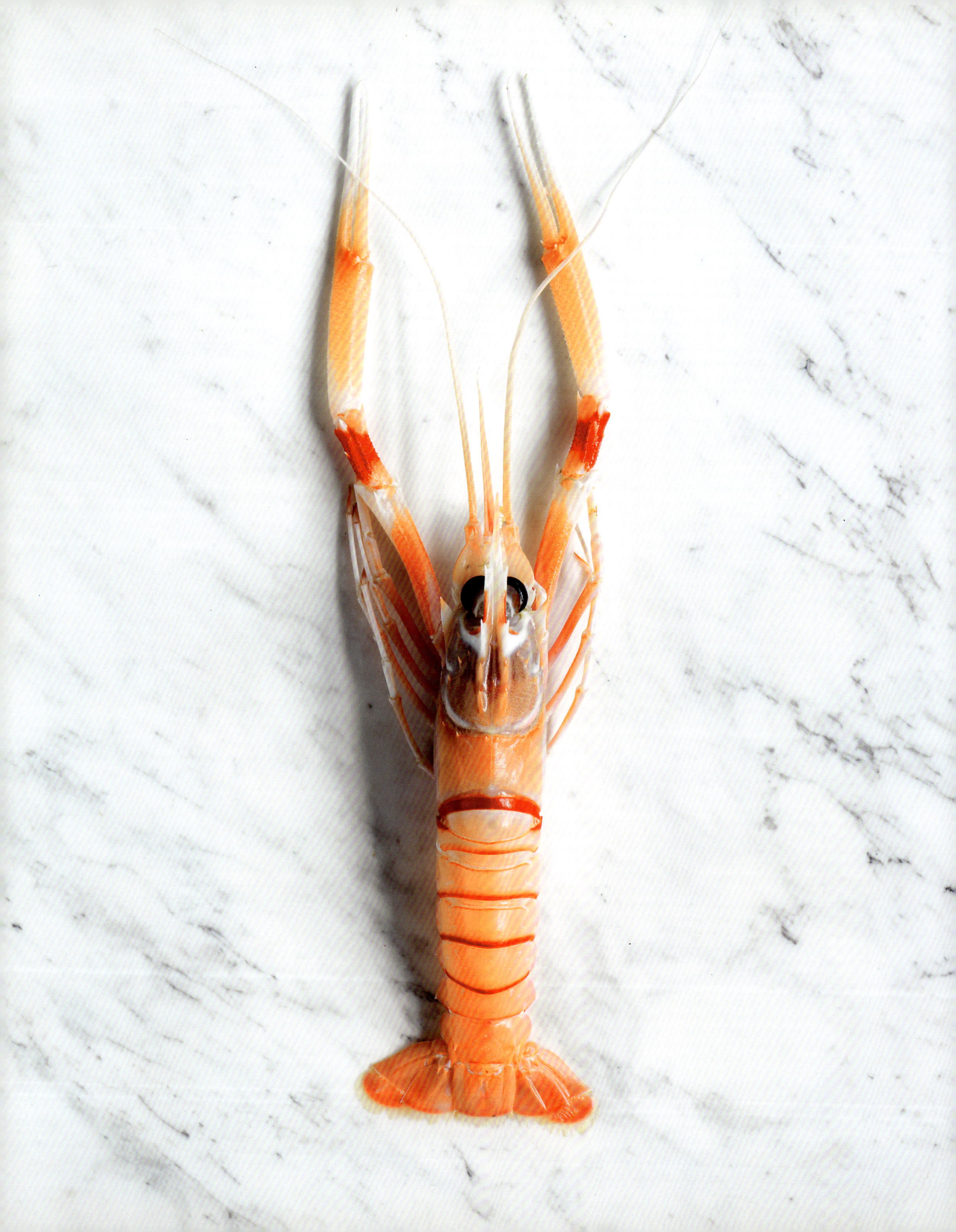

SCAMPI

Scampi (*Metanephrops australiensis*) are spectacular crayfish found in the deep cold waters off north-west Western Australia and all around New Zealand as far as the Chatham Islands. They're very similar to the lobster known in many parts of Europe as langoustine (*Nephrops norvegicus*) but also as scampi. Like their northern-hemisphere cousins, Australian scampi have two long feelers and are usually the size of a large prawn or yabby but have a taste and texture more like that of a crayfish or lobster.

Caught at depths of 150–650 m (490–2100 ft), the scampi is an adept predator, feeding on other crustaceans and small fish. Because of their fragile, thin shells and the fact that they're caught in deep water a long way from market, scampi are frozen raw on the catching boats and packed with their tails folded under and their feelers laid back against their body. By the time they reach the surface they're already black in the head area due to oxidisation, so you must always use them the same day you thaw them, because they'll continue to oxidise quickly.

Often they're displayed on ice in fish shops, slowly defrosting. Consume or cook them as soon as possible after purchase and never refreeze them. Their roe is a brilliant azure blue, with a crisp texture and a bright iodine zing. If it's there, make sure you enjoy it.

Scampi fishing in Australia and New Zealand is sustainable and tightly managed.

SEASONALITY Early summer and early autumn
CATCHING METHOD Bottom trawl
COMMON LENGTH 9–14 cm (3½–5½ in)
COMMON WEIGHT 50–100 g (1¾–3½ oz)
IDENTIFIABLE FEATURES Long, thin body, light orange shell, thin bright orange pincers and legs, large protruding black eyes
SUSTAINABILITY Managed to a strict quota

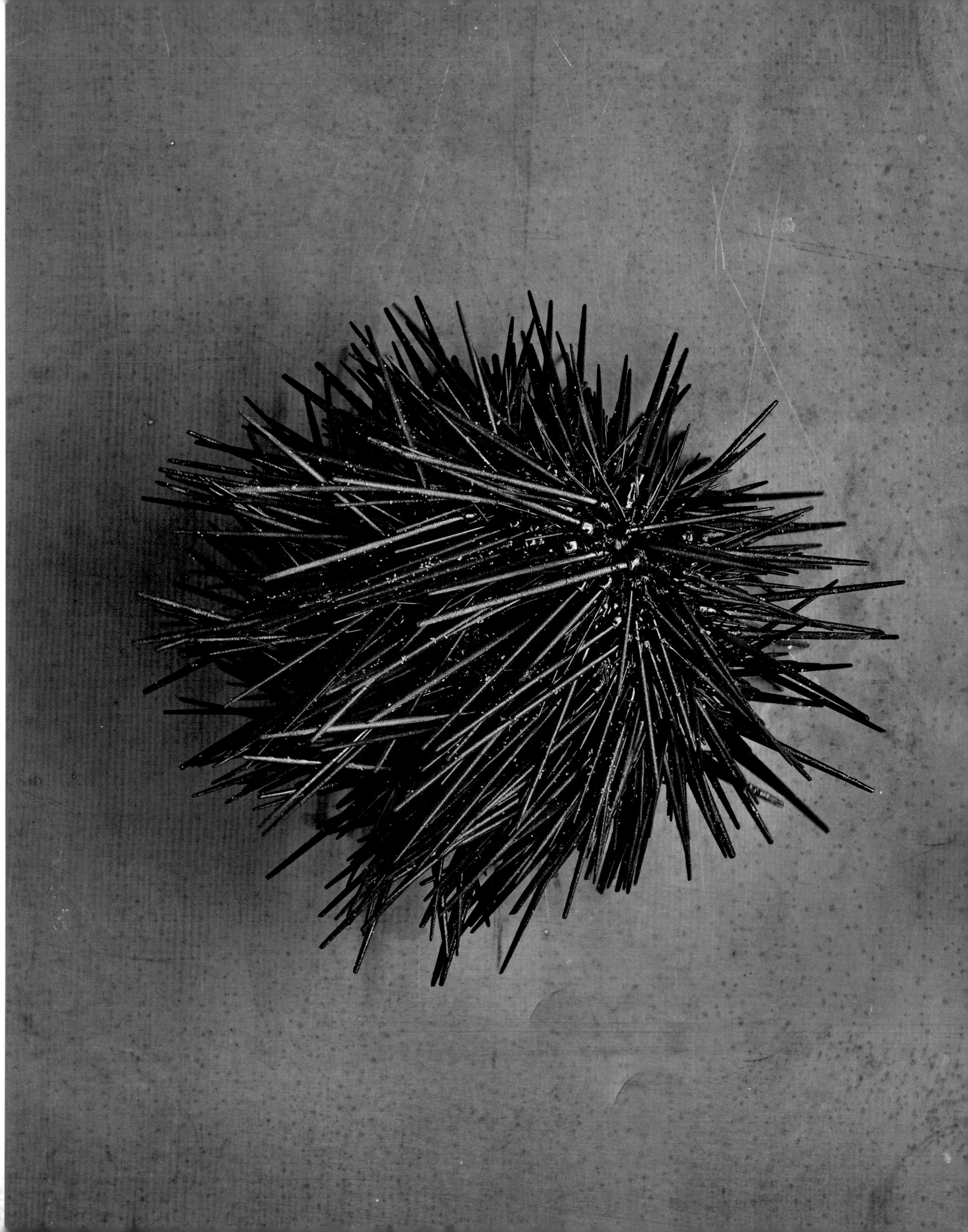

SEA URCHIN

What's sold as 'sea urchin' is the five-lobed roe of a range of spiny creatures of that name, and is their only edible part. Sea urchins are found on ocean floors all over the world, and are especially well suited to the subtropical, temperate waters of southern Australia. They have a rounded body with long spines they use for protection, trapping food particles floating in the water. Most feed on the algae of their region, which means they truly reflect their 'merroir' (marine environment).

Purple sea urchins (*Heliocidaris erythrogramma*) are endemic to coastal waters off southern Queensland, New South Wales, Victoria, Tasmania, South Australia and Western Australia. They live at depths of up to 35 m (115 ft), but are most common shallower than 10 m (35 ft). As animals of the sea floor, they're often found attached to rocky reefs, stones, seagrass beds, in crevices and burrows, and on sandy mud bottoms. They seem to avoid full exposure to wave motion.

A freshly shucked urchin is one of the great food experiences. The briny, sweet flavour and creamy yet firm texture are at their peak in the mid- and post-winter period. The roe is highly sought after in both France and Japan, where it's typically served raw, but in Australia it has only recently become valued as a culinary experience.

Sea urchin roe is most commonly known by its Japanese name, uni. The best is produced for the Japanese market and shipped as 'dry uni', which means it's not shipped in brine, it's of a consistent grade and it's more expensive. Uni has historically been graded based on colour, texture and freshness. The highest grade is bright yellow–gold, with a firm texture and natural residual sweetness. The next grade is a more muted yellow, has a softer texture and is less sweet. The lowest grade, referred to as vana, is often the parts left over after processing.

SEASONALITY Year round; best quality depends on microclimate; generally best in September–December in southern NSW, Vic. and Tas.
CATCHING METHOD Divers; mostly split on the boat to remove the roe
COMMON SIZE 7–8 cm (2¾–3¼ in)
COMMON WEIGHT 80–90 g (2¾–3¼ oz)
IDENTIFIABLE FEATURES Roe five-lobed, yellow to grey
SUSTAINABILITY Very sustainable

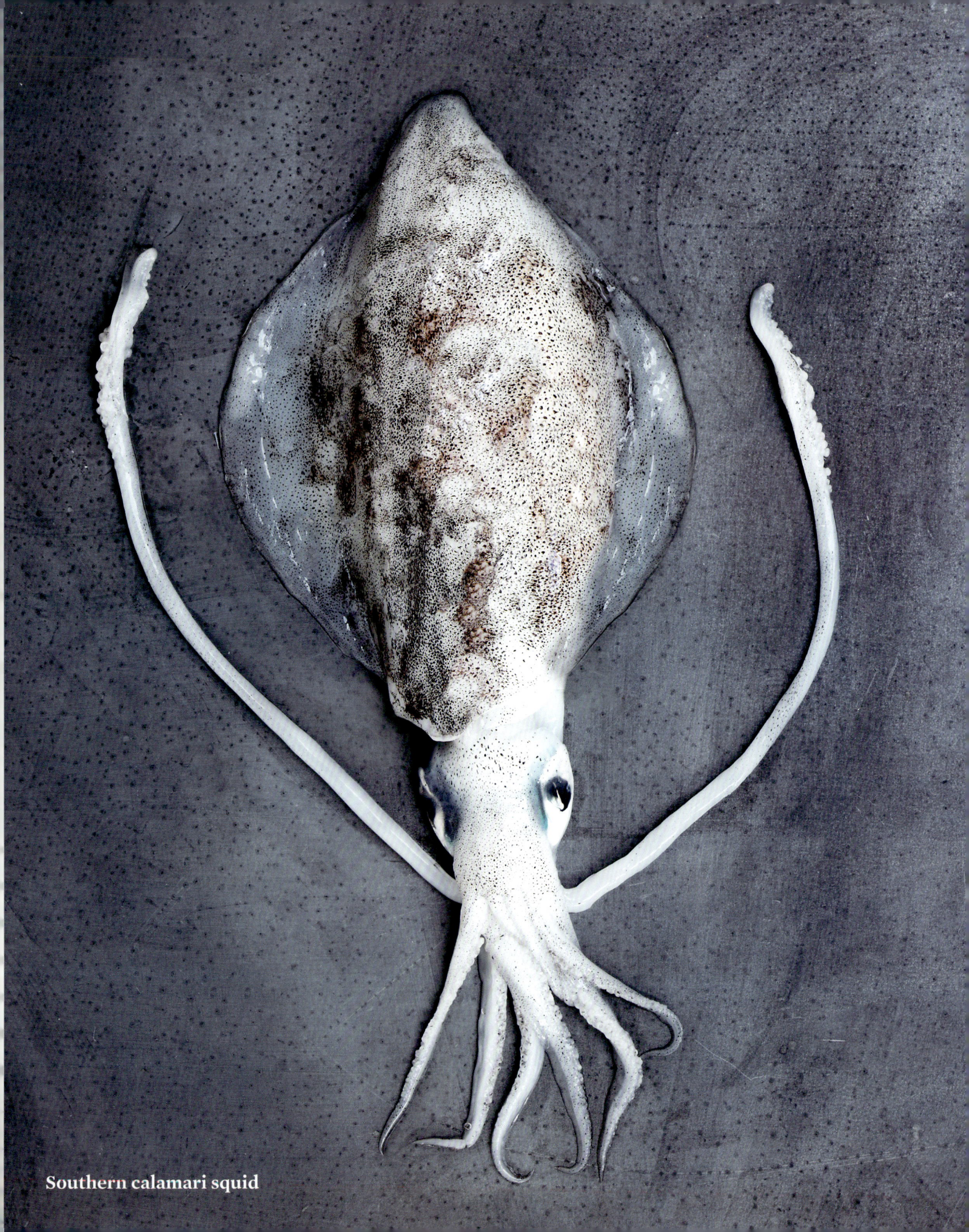

Southern calamari squid

SQUID & CUTTLEFISH

Squid and cuttlefish are cephalopods (Latin for 'head foot') and closely related to octopus. In Australia, the Italian word for squid, calamari, has been appropriated in some markets to represent the squid species with long extended fins, especially the southern calamari squid (*Sepioteuthis australis*) from southern New South Wales, Victoria, Tasmania and South Australia.

Cuttlefish are closely related to squid but their body is broader and contains the hard plate called a cuttlebone that's well known from budgie cages. In life, the cuttlebone aids in buoyancy. The main cuttlefish species harvested commercially in Australia is the Australian giant cuttlefish (*Sepia apama*).

Both squid and cuttlefish have ten tentacles and, like their cousin the octopus, they also release dark ink into the water when they sense danger. They range from 2.5 cm (1 in) to 13 m (43 ft), but squid are most commonly eaten at less than 30 cm (12 in). Most cuttlefish are 15–25 cm (6–10 in), but the largest grows to 50 cm (20 in).

When it comes to sustainability, squid and cuttlefish tick every box – they're fast-breeding, fast-growing and have a very efficient metabolism. Their meat is firm and white, with a mild, slightly sweet and almost nutty flavour.

COMMON SQUID & CUTTLEFISH SPECIES

Southern calamari squid
Sepioteuthis australis
Available wild-caught, these popular squid have white flesh and grey to luminescent green skin. Their rounded side fins run almost the full length of their body, and they have eight shorter and two longer tentacles.

Most of the commercial catch comes from South Australia, where they're handline jigged, although some are a bycatch of the Spencer and St Vincent gulf prawn (shrimp) fisheries. Other fisheries are in southern New South Wales, Victoria and Tasmania, but these are less predictable.

The white flesh is thick, moist and sweet, but the price has increased significantly in the past five years. They are available year round, although the quality is best in late winter and spring.

SEASONALITY Year round; best in late winter to spring
CATCHING METHOD Squid jig
COMMON HOOD LENGTH 16–20 cm (6¼–8 in)
COMMON WEIGHT 300–500 g (10½ oz – 1 lb 2 oz)
IDENTIFIABLE FEATURES Grey to luminescent green skin, long rounded side fins, eight shorter and two longer tentacles
SUSTAINABILITY Stock status very good

Gould's squid or arrow squid
Nototodarus gouldi
Available wild-caught and found on the continental shelf around southern Australia (including Tasmania), these are the most prolifically caught squid in Australia. They have brownish pink skin with a purple–blue stripe running along the hood.

They're mainly caught in Bass Strait and western Victoria by squid jigging, and also between Botany Bay and western Victoria as a bycatch of trawling.

The flesh can be tough and requires careful preparation and cooking, but it's full-flavoured, inexpensive and plentiful. It often comes as ready-cleaned hoods, which makes it easy to use.

SEASONALITY Year round
CATCHING METHOD Squid jig
COMMON HOOD LENGTH 20–25 cm (8–10 in)
COMMON WEIGHT 300–500 g (10½ oz – 1 lb 2 oz)
IDENTIFIABLE FEATURES Brownish pink skin, purple–blue stripe running along the hood
SUSTAINABILITY Stock status very good

Gould's squid or arrow squid

Queensland northern squid

COMMON SQUID & CUTTLEFISH SPECIES (continued)

Queensland northern or bigfin reef squid
Sepioteuthis lessoniana
Found not just in Queensland but throughout northern Australia, these squid have long side fins running almost the full length of their thick dark brown–green bodies.

They're mainly caught by squid jigging at night, but are also a bycatch of prawn (shrimp) trawling and inshore net fisheries off northern Australia. Most prolific in winter, this squid is typically sold frozen whole and is moderately priced.

Its clean, sweet flavour and thin flesh make it one of the most popular squids for cooking salt and pepper squid.

SEASONALITY	Year round; most plentiful in winter
CATCHING METHOD	Squid jig
COMMON HOOD LENGTH	20–30 cm (8–12 in)
COMMON WEIGHT	500 g – 1 kg (1 lb 2 oz – 2 lb 4 oz)
IDENTIFIABLE FEATURES	Thick, dark brown–green body, long side fins
SUSTAINABILITY	Stock status very good

Australian giant cuttlefish
Sepia apama
Found throughout southern Australia, cuttlefish have a far more aggressive feeding pattern than squid, delivering a creamier and richer flavour.

They're still mainly a bycatch of the prawn trawl fisheries in New South Wales and Victoria, but targeted fishing has resulted in a more consistent year-round availability.

Cuttlefish are prolific producers of ink, and the ink sac can be removed intact relatively easily. The flavour is nuttier than squid ink.

SEASONALITY	Year round
CATCHING METHOD	Prawn trawl
COMMON HOOD LENGTH	8–12 cm (3¼–4½ in)
COMMON WEIGHT	80–150 g (2¾–5½ oz)
IDENTIFIABLE FEATURES	Reddish brown skin with white markings, pale fins, eight shorter and two longer tentacles
SUSTAINABILITY	Stock status very good

SQUID & CUTTLEFISH IN THE KITCHEN

For the best, most tender outcome when preparing squid or cuttlefish, double-skin them. It's common to use a scourer (see page 451) to get the second skin off, which can take a long time, but you can actually peel it off. Dry it after taking the first skin off, then simply make a little nick with a knife and peel off the second skin. Once you've done this, you can eat them raw.

Raw, as sashimi and sushi, is the best option with squid and calamari. It has bite and a creamy, chewy mouthfeel. They're also fantastic quickly sautéed, but take care not to cook them for too long or they'll be rubbery and unpleasant. Cook up some chilli and thyme in hot butter, then throw the chopped squid straight in and flip it twice. Don't do any more than this or wait for it to colour up, or it will be overcooked.

If cooking squid salt and pepper style, you need to work very quickly. Dip it in flour at the last minute or it will soak up all the flour and go gluggy. Dust it only lightly, then drop it straight into extremely hot oil – close to 200°C (400°F). Remember, you're frying the flour, not the squid.

All squid is fantastic raw. Southern calamari is generally a larger squid, and that gives you a better yield and a bigger taste. Gould's squid is better for calamari rings and fried calamari, but you can also stuff it and bake it. Choose cuttlefish if you're looking for great flavour and texture.

STORAGE AND HANDLING Keep dry and deal with fresh animals quickly. Store whole for no more than 24 hours, on a drip tray over ice in an airtight container. Once cleaned (see pages 451–52), use immediately or wrap tightly in freezer film then plastic wrap and store in the vegetable crisper. Use within 24 hours or freeze.

BEST COOKING METHODS Raw, sautéed, steamed, poached, grilled (broiled), fried, braised

TEXTURE Meltingly tender, rich, mouth-filling, creamy

AROMA Light egg white with grassy notes of green melon

FLAVOUR Mild milky notes with an oceanic zing and a finish of fresh cream

APPEARANCE Cleaned flesh translucent white when raw; arctic white once cooked

YIELD Cleaned hoods and tentacles about 40% of whole weight

SUBSTITUTES None

Australian cuttlefish

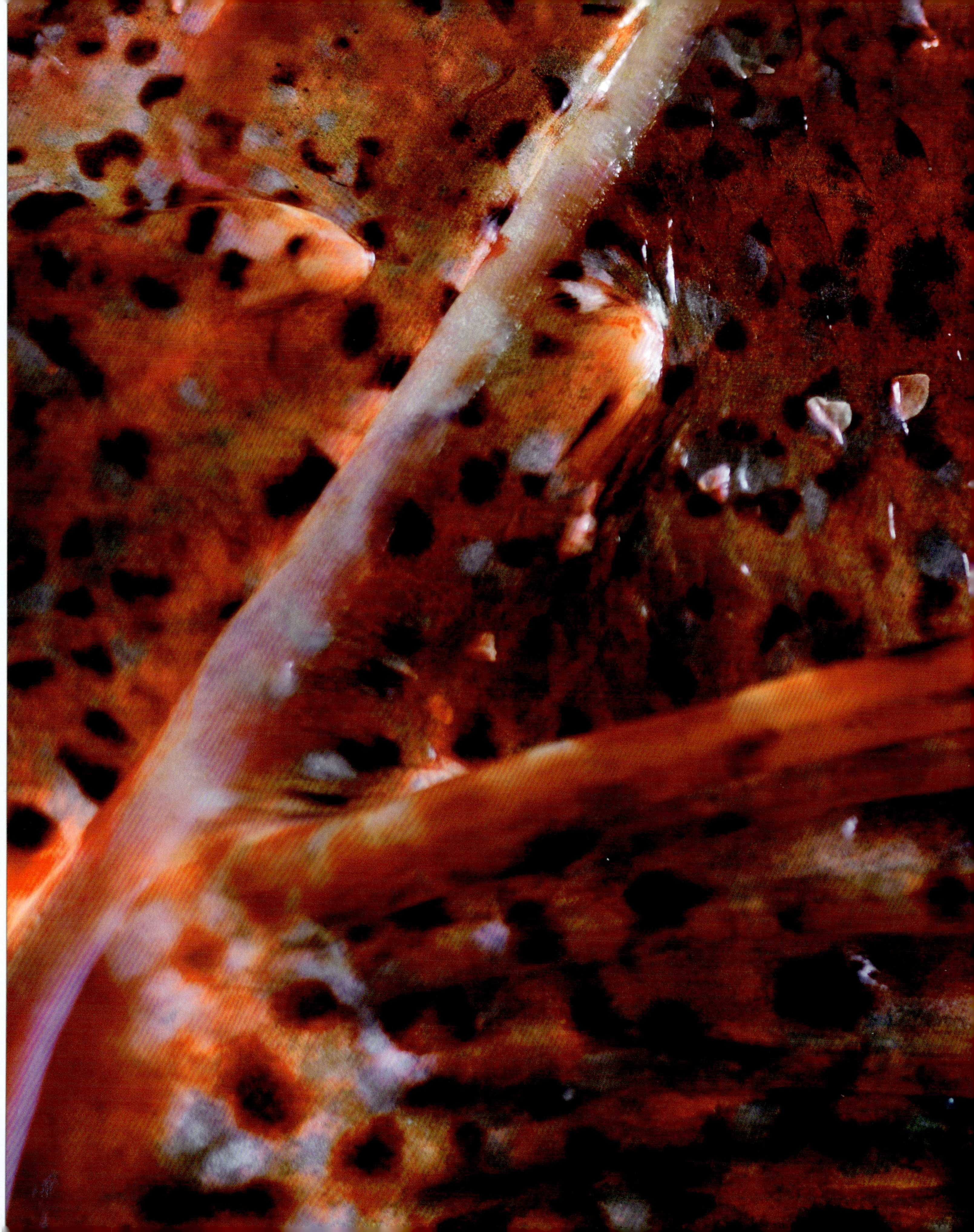

PREPARATION & COOKING TECHNIQUES

HOW TO SCALE, CLEAN AND FILLET A ROUND FISH

Filleting small round fish such as snapper and bream is an exercise in precision. Try scaling in a sink, laundry tub or outside under running water or – magician like – inside a plastic garbage bag. Make sure your knife is very sharp and take your time.

Holding the head firmly, draw a fish scaler from the tail towards the head in firm, light strokes. Repeat from shoulder to belly.

With a clean, moist kitchen wipe, remove all loose scales.

Insert a sharp knife into the anal vent and make an incision from the belly to the bottom of the head and through the jaw.

Lifting the gill plate, cut the gills away from the head by pushing the knife firmly through the attaching cartilage below the lip.

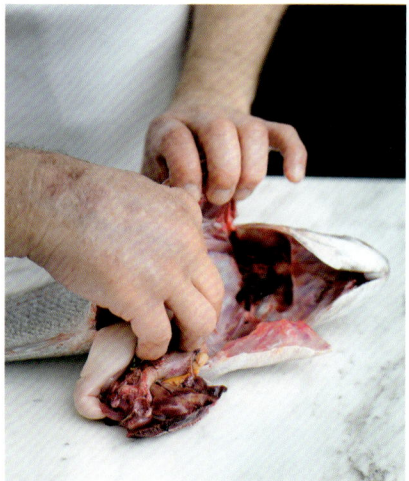

Holding the gills and head firmly, remove the gills and guts by drawing them down from head to anal vent. Pull firmly to tear out in one piece. Wipe the internal cavity dry.

Place a filleting knife behind the pectoral fin and draw the knife from the belly to the back of the head.

To make the shoulder fillet, hold the body down firmly, then insert the knife into the flesh behind the head. Using the backbone as a guide, draw the knife gently towards the tail.

Gently lift the shoulder fillet, then insert the knife behind the ribcage towards the belly and draw the knife along the backbone towards the tail.

Holding the tail firmly, place the knife behind the ribcage and slide it towards the head, keeping it as close to the spine as possible. Remove the fillet.

Using the rib bones as a guide, gently draw the knife from top to bottom of the belly and remove.

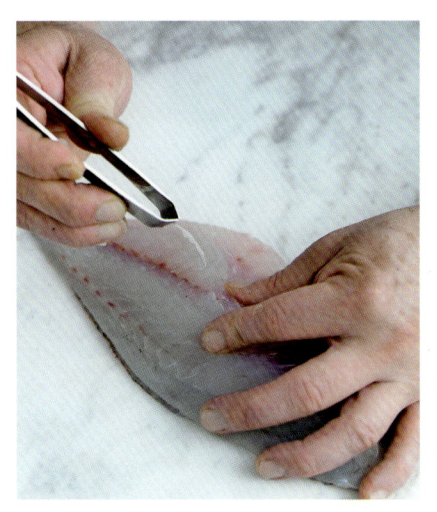

Working from tail to shoulder, gently squeeze the flesh around each of the pin bones down the centre and extract them using a pair of fish tweezers.

Retain the head, frame, wings and trim for use in stock, and check the guts for liver and roe.

PREPARATION & COOKING TECHNIQUES **429**

HOW TO DRESS A WHOLE ROUND FISH

'Dressing' or preparing a whole round fish is a simple task. Follow these steps after scaling and gutting (see page 428) to have a fish ready for the pan or barbecue.

Using sharp, thick-bladed scissors, cut the pectoral, dorsal, anal and tail fins back to the line of the body.

Score the skin diagonally to an even distance from the bones – deep at the shoulder and shallower at the tail. Gradually widen the cuts – one finger apart, then two, then three.

HOW TO DRESS A WHOLE FLAT FISH

Flat fish are always best cooked on the bone. With a simple bone structure and no fine pin bones like round fish, cooked flesh is easy to remove from the bones either in the kitchen or on the plate at the table.

Using sharp, thick-bladed scissors, trim the tail fin back to the line of the body.

Following the curve of the fish, cut off the remaining fins as close to the body as possible.

HOW TO FILLET A DORY

The dories are great cooked on the bone – their tight, fine-grained flesh cooks beautifully when protected from the heat by the bones. But filleting a dory is a relatively simple task once you know how and can yield a clean, boneless piece of fish that's simple to cook and easy to eat.

When filleting dories, it's best to depart from the usual practice and leave the fish whole, with the gut in. This helps the body retain its shape and allows for easier cutting.

Using a long sharp knife, cut through the flesh on the shoulder of the fish to the backbone, running the knife evenly around the back of the head.

Cut through the fish behind the pectoral fins and collar.

Using the backbone as a guide, cut evenly along the back of the fish from head to tail across the top fillet.

Following the backbone, draw the knife through the flesh. Take care to avoid the sharp, hard spikes at the bottom of the dory.

Pull the fillet carefully away from the bone and remove. Trim the belly skin and ribcage from the fillet.

PREPARATION & COOKING TECHNIQUES **431**

HOW TO SKIN AND FILLET, JAPANESE STYLE

This method is suitable for large round fish, including yellowtail kingfish, and for mackerel. Japanese chefs prefer to scale fish they're using for sashimi to ensure no scales get near the flesh at final preparation. This can be achieved either using the usual scaling method (see page 428) or by cutting the thin layer of scales attached to the skin using a very sharp Japanese knife, traditionally a one-sided fuguhiki blade. Perhaps visit your local Japanese restaurant and watch carefully to see a Japanese master in action.

Draw the blade of a sharp knife along the pectoral line (the horizontal centreline of the side of the fish), pressing the blade gently against the skin to remove a strip of scales.

Lift removed string of scales while continuing to slide the knife towards the head until you have scaled all the way to the gills.

Continue this technique to scale the whole of both sides.

Remove the head by cutting firmly and cleanly behind the pectoral fin to the top of the shoulder. Turn the fish over and repeat the cut, then remove the head by pulling sharply.

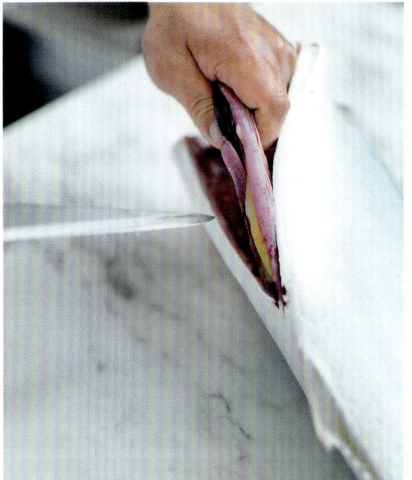

Insert the knife in the anal vent and draw the blade towards the head. Remove the guts and wipe the cavity with a clean, moist kitchen wipe.

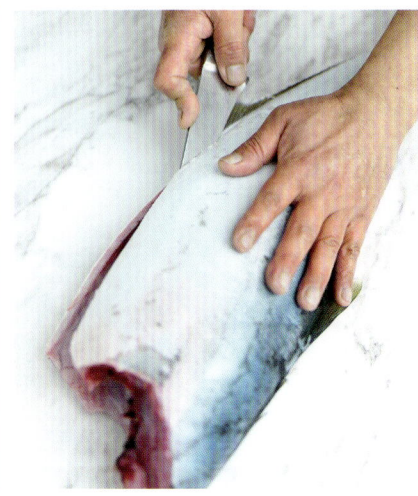

Insert the knife into the belly cavity and draw the blade along the belly fillet, using the backbone as a guide, from belly to tail in one firm cut.

Turn the fish around so the tail is facing away from you then draw the knife from tail to shoulder along the top side of the fillet, using the backbone as a guide.

Holding the tail firmly, draw the knife along the backbone and remove the fillet from the spine.

Place the knife under the ribcage at the shoulder and draw the knife towards the belly, using the bones as a guide and gently pulling the ribcage away from the flesh.

Holding the shoulder of the fillet, draw the knife down the belly flap and remove. (Keep the belly flap – it's excellent for sashimi, ceviche and other raw preparations.)

Using three fingers as a guide, slice across the fillet to produce a classic restaurant-style darne (transverse or slanted slice).

A finished sliced fillet.

PREPARATION & COOKING TECHNIQUES

HOW TO CUT SASHIMI FROM A FILLET

Use this method to cut sashimi from a scaled, skin-on fillet.

Draw the knife from shoulder to tail above the central blood and pin-bone line. Remove the top loin.

Invert the belly loin and draw the knife from tail to shoulder on the other side of the blood and pin-bone lines.

Pulling firmly on the skin at the tail end and holding the knife flat, slide the knife from tail to shoulder to skin the loin. Repeat with the other loin.

For classic sashimi cuts, place the heel of the knife against the top of the loin and draw gently downwards in one stroke with the tip of the knife finishing against the chopping board.

HOW TO CUT A SAKU BLOCK FROM TUNA

The Japanese have a saying for fish butchery: *kasshu hoju* – 'cutting is the most important, cooking comes second'. Cutting changes the taste and texture of the fish, and this is nowhere more apparent than when preparing tuna for sashimi. How it's done makes a huge difference in terms of taste, texture *and* appearance.

Saku are rectangular pieces of fish from which individual sashimi slices are cut. A good relationship with a fishmonger is vital for securing a premium block of tuna. Ideally, it should include the belly portion.

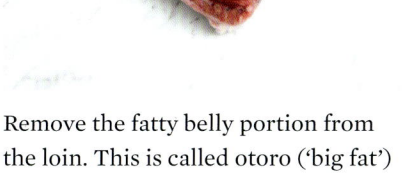

Remove the fatty belly portion from the loin. This is called otoro ('big fat') and is the most highly prized part of the fish.

Remove the ribcage from the block of tuna and trim, taking care not to waste any of the delicious meat.

Remove the dark blood line from the inside central bone side then, cutting along the outer sinew line, remove the top part of the loin from the skin side. This is called the akami ('red meat').

Trim the sinew from the skin side of the chutoro ('medium fat') belly piece. Remove the skin, but retain it to scrape off any remaining flesh.

Cut along the akami block at about two fingers' width to produce a saku block. Cut firmly through the loin and, using the skin as a guide, cut across the loin to remove the saku block.

Holding the belly portion firmly, run the knife along the thick skin to remove from the flesh. Turn and remove the sinew from the other side.

For classic sashimi cuts, place the heel of the knife against the top of the loin and draw gently downwards in a single stroke, so the tip of the knife finishes against the chopping board.

PREPARATION & COOKING TECHNIQUES

HOW TO CURE SALMON

This is the method used to make the King Salmon Pastrami on page 195.

Using a mortar and pestle, crush your chosen spices to a fine powder.

Pass the spices through a fine-mesh sieve and collect the fine dust. Reserve the rough spice shells that won't pass through the sieve.

Measure the crushed spices, then measure out equal amounts of salt and sugar. Mix all three together in a bowl.

Rub the spice mixture generously into the flesh on both sides. Cover with plastic wrap and refrigerate for 48 hours to 1 week, turning twice during that time.

Wipe the cured fish clean with paper towel. Crush the reserved spice husks using a mortar and pestle then coat both sides of the salmon with this spice mixture.

Wrap the cured fillet in freezer film, then tightly in plastic wrap. It will be excellent for 2 weeks.

438 AUSTRALIAN FISH & SEAFOOD COOKBOOK

HOW TO SHUCK AN ABALONE

You may as well use the best abalone you can, and that, of course, is a live one. Abalone has a tight-grained, firm muscle and needs to be treated with care. This method is for when you're planning to cook the abalone quickly over high heat.

Hold the abalone, shell side down, in the palm of your hand with the foot facing up. Slide a serving spoon under the body, using the shell as a guide to push right across and release the body.

Pull the gut and roe from the main body of the abalone. You may need to cut it gently using a sharp paring knife.

Using a clean scourer, gently scrub the cover of dark algae from the base of the foot, then trim the leathery frill from the edges, taking care not to waste too much precious meat.

Cut the bulbous 'top' of the abalone from the base of the foot.

Cut thin slices from the abalone body using either a very sharp mandoline or a thin sharp knife.

PREPARATION & COOKING TECHNIQUES

HOW TO CLEAN A SCALLOP

A fresh, live scallop has an incomparably sweet flavour combined with a buttery, custardy texture that's never matched by a pre-shucked scallop. Live scallops are hard to find and quite fragile, but if you can get them, shuck them before they die and you'll be guaranteed a delicious treat.

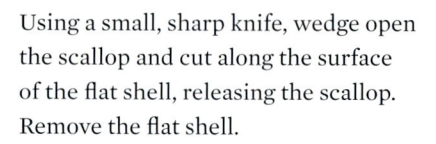

Using a small, sharp knife, wedge open the scallop and cut along the surface of the flat shell, releasing the scallop. Remove the flat shell.

Using the curved shell as a guide, carefully cut the scallop body, gut and 'frill' or mantle away from the shell and push off the shell. Gently wash the shell in salty water to remove any grit.

Gently pull the mantle and gut sac from the main scallop body, being careful *not* to pull the orange- or cream-coloured roe away from the scallop body.

Gently snip the tough side muscle from the opposite side of the scallop body to the roe and replace the meat and roe on the cleaned curved shell.

A cleaned scallop.

440 AUSTRALIAN FISH & SEAFOOD COOKBOOK

HOW TO CLEAN A COOKED BUG

The ancient-looking bug can be difficult to eat if not removed from the shell before serving. Preparing it in advance makes it so much more enjoyable to eat. Start with a bug that has been cooked then refreshed in iced water. Work with a sharp knife.

Lay the bug on its back. Insert the knife between head and body, then gently cut through the skin. Turn over and repeat on the other side, cutting the skin between the shell and the flesh.

Gripping the head firmly, pull the tail to remove it from the head.

Using a clean, moist kitchen wipe, turn the bug tail upside down in one hand and squeeze to break apart the shells covering the abdomen.

Gently pull the shell from either side of the bug, extracting the meat.

Gripping the base of the digestive tract and shell firmly, draw the tail flesh away, removing the entire length of the tract.

Using clean paper towel, gently wipe the flesh, particularly around the top of the tail, removing any remaining gut or liver marks.

PREPARATION & COOKING TECHNIQUES

HOW TO SHUCK AN OYSTER

This requires a special tool: the oyster knife – a short, stout, rigid blade embedded in a fat, round handle that provides a strong, non-slip grip.

Leave the natural coating of mud on the outside of unopened oysters to keep them moist and comfortable. Store Pacific oysters at 5–8°C (41–46°F) (i.e. the crisper) and rock oysters at 12–14°C (54–57°F) (the laundry). Before opening, scrub well and bury in ice for 30 minutes. This chills the oyster and relaxes it for opening.

ROCK AND PACIFIC OYSTERS

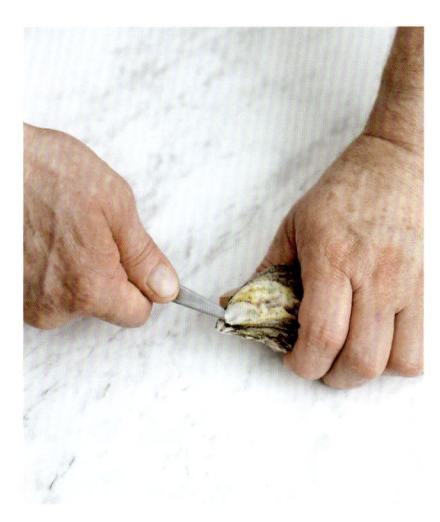

Holding the oyster with the hinge out and the flat surface up, insert the tip of the oyster knife into the hinge and gently wiggle the knife until it has purchase between the two shells.

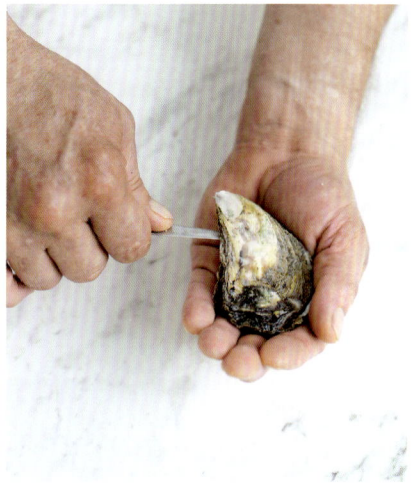

Holding the oyster firmly, quickly twist the knife clockwise until you hear a crack or feel the hinge break as the two shells separate.

Gently slide the knife across the inside of the top shell until it snips the adductor muscle on the upper right-hand side of the shell (at about 2 o'clock). Gently lever off the top shell.

Slide the oyster knife under the oyster in the bottom shell and gently snip the adductor muscle there.

Using the flat of the blade, gently roll the oyster over in the shell, so its belly is facing up.

A shucked oyster.

ANGASI OYSTERS

Angasi oysters are quite fragile and require specialist handling. Keep them tightly packed with a weight on top and store in the coldest part of the fridge. Opening the oyster on the top shell reduces the chance of piercing the sulfur bubble that can be on the bottom shell.

Holding the oyster with its hinge to the rear and the slightly concave side down, slide the knife through the front of the oyster and, using the bottom shell as a guide, move the knife across the shell until you hit the adductor muscle in the top right-hand corner.

Gently snip the muscle and remove the top shell with the oyster attached.

HOW TO SHUCK A CLAM

It's easier to use a bread and butter knife than an oyster shucker. Open your clams over a sink, or preferably a bowl if you want to use the brine inside.

Push the knife between the top and bottom shell from the front, not the hinge. Twist the knife from side to side until it moves, then pop the top shell off. Remove the top shell and cut the adductor muscle to release the clam meat.

HOW TO PEEL A PRAWN

Raw prawns (shrimp) are fragile, oxidising quickly and going black in the head and shell either when fresh or when thawed from frozen. This oxidisation creates that funky 'off prawn' character, which, if the shell is left on, can cause an unpleasant aroma and flavour of ammonia. It's best to get the head and shell off as soon as possible, then store the flesh in a cool, dry place. Use the shells for stock or sauce before they oxidise.

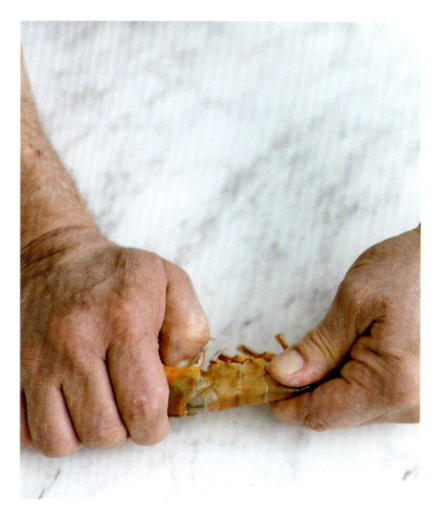

Holding the tail firmly in one hand, place your other thumb under the base of the head and gently but firmly pull the head away, taking care not to rupture the liver or gut.

Place your thumb under the front three legs and rotate the prawn to release the top half of the shell.

Pinch the base of the tail and pull the flesh to remove the remaining shell.

Using a sharp knife, make an incision through the top of the tail and, using a tissue, grasp the digestive tract and gently pull it away from the flesh.

Slice through the top of the prawn flesh to three-quarters depth and butterfly the prawn open.

HOW TO SKEWER A RAW PRAWN

Cooking a raw prawn with the shell on is ideal for high-heat cooking – such as a grill (broiler) or barbecue – or for when a prawn is to be used in a salad or sushi after steaming or boiling. When prawns are cooked over high heat, the flesh will naturally tighten, causing the prawn to take on the classic crescent shape. To avoid this, use a skewer to ensure a straight prawn.

Pre-soak a bamboo skewer in salt water, then insert it into the anal vent of the prawn and slide along the body.

Use the underside of the shell as a guide, so as not to tear the internal prawn flesh.

A skewered prawn.

HOW TO PREPARE A LIVE LOBSTER

Use this method to prepare lobster for pot-roasting or stir-frying. A whole live lobster is always best. Make sure they're lively when you purchase them, ideally from a tank. Place under ice or in the freezer for 30 minutes to send them to sleep – not only is this humane, but the resulting flesh will taste sweeter and be less tough. Don't discard the head and legs. The keen diner can always pick the meat from them both, but they also release an incredible flavour when used in cooking.

Using a sharp cleaver or large knife, dispatch the chilled lobster by chopping off the front of the head and the feelers with a firm blow directly behind the feelers.

Flatten out the tail and, holding the head firmly, use a sharp knife to cut the skin that connects the shells between the head and abdomen. Turn over and repeat on the underside.

Holding the head and tail firmly, gently rotate the tail and draw the head and tail apart.

Stand the head on end and, using a cleaver, strike a firm blow through the middle. Clean the gut from the split head and cut each side of the head into three pieces.

Using the shell segments as a guide, use a cleaver to cut through the shell top and bottom to produce even medallions of lobster in shell.

HOW TO PREPARE A RAW BLUE SWIMMER CRAB

Use this method to prepare blue swimmer crab for pot-roasting or stir-frying. The blue swimmer is one of the few crabs sold raw and dead. While this doesn't result in a rapid deterioration of quality (as it would for, say, a mud crab), a raw blue swimmer is best used for pot-roasting and stir-frying. The blue swimmer crab has a basic anatomy, making it simple to turn into easy-to-use, easy-to-eat pieces.

Lay the whole crab on its back and pull the abdomen away from the body by pushing a thumb under the top shell and pulling.

Remove the gut from the body and tear the grey lungs – the 'dead man's fingers' – from the top of the body. Rinse in salty water.

Cut the cleaned body in half using a sharp knife.

Using the back of the knife, crack the front and rear sections of the claws.

Cut each crab half into three pieces, using the shell segments as a guide. Remove the claws in one piece.

A prepared blue swimmer crab.

PREPARATION & COOKING TECHNIQUES

HOW TO PREPARE A LIVE MUD CRAB

Use this method to prepare mud crab for pot-roasting or stir-frying. The mud crab is ideal for these cooking methods, as its thick shell protects the delicate flesh inside. Mud crabs are best purchased live then left under ice or in the freezer for 30 minutes to 1 hour before handling. This both ensures humane treatment and sweet, soft meat.

Lay the iced mud crab on its back and, using a solid cleaver, cut straight through the midline.

Pull the top shell from the body of each crab half and remove the gut, leaving the liver and roe.

Remove the grey lungs – the 'dead man's fingers'.

Remove and set aside the liver and roe.

Cut each crab half into three sections, using the shell segments as a guide.

Using the back of a heavy cleaver or knife, crack the claws at three points.

A prepared mud crab.

448 AUSTRALIAN FISH & SEAFOOD COOKBOOK

HOW TO COOK AND PICK WHOLE CRAB

There's a formula for cooking whole crabs (or any shellfish) if you intend to store them for later use: 1 minute of cooking time per 100 g (3½ oz), plus a further 4 minutes, then cool it in ice.

If you intend to use the crab within 6 hours of cooking, the formula is: 1 minute of cooking time per 100 g (3½ oz), plus a further 2 minutes, then rest the crab for a further 2 minutes. This allows you to cut and 'shake' the crab. This is the simplest way to get the meat out, as the proteins have not yet had a chance to set on the shell and there's no need for a crab pick.

BLUE SWIMMER CRAB

Buy pre-cooked crabs for a salad or to stir through pasta at the last minute and remove meat as for a spanner crab (see page 450). Cooked blue swimmer crab can sometimes be slightly tough, so don't overheat if reheating.

To cook a whole raw blue swimmer crab, bring a large saucepan of well-salted water to the boil over high heat. Carefully lower the crab into the water, then cover and cook for the time indicated by the formula given. Prepare the crabmeat as indicated on page 447 (this will give a flesh yield of about 25 per cent of the whole weight).

MUD CRAB

Place the crab in the freezer for 30 minutes to 1 hour to put it to sleep.

Bring a medium saucepan of well-salted water to the boil over high heat. Place the crab in the rapidly boiling water and cook for the time indicated by the formula given. Remove the crab from the boiling water and plunge into iced water, then leave to stand until completely cold.

To remove the claws and legs, twist them until they dislodge. Crack the large claws with a cleaver or the back of a heavy knife. Cut along the length of the legs with scissors and pick the meat out using a skewer. Pull the top shell off the body and discard. Briefly rinse the body to remove any shell fragments, then cut it in half or quarters and extract the meat with a skewer.

SPANNER CRAB

Bring a large saucepan of water to a rapid boil over high heat.

Carefully lower the crab into the water, then cover and cook for the time indicated by the formula given. If necessary you can cook a few crabs at a time, but not too many or the water will lose heat.

Prepare the crabmeat as indicated overleaf. Picking this way will give a flesh yield of about 25 per cent of the whole weight. That means an 800 g (1 lb 12 oz) crab will yield 200 g (7 oz) of meat, or a 1.1 kg (2 lb 7 oz) crab about 280 g (10 oz), enough for a salad for four.

HOW TO CLEAN AND PICK A COOKED SPANNER CRAB

Crabmeat picked from a just-cooked crab has an unmatched sweetness and texture. With all crab, it's best to pick the meat while the crab is still warm, so the fat inside the shell will be retained in the meat. The cleaning process takes time but the result is well worth the effort.

Holding the bottom and top of the crab firmly, wedge a thumb under the base of the top shell and pull the top shell away. Discard the top shell and gut.

Remove the claws and legs by twisting them where they join the body. Set the claws and legs aside.

Rinse the body briefly in fresh water.

Lay the cleaned crab body on its belly and cut in half down the midline.

Gently squeeze each crab half and push the meat away from the shell. Try to make one piece of meat per body segment.

Use a sharp knife to cut each claw into three sections at the joints.

Using scissors, cut through the claw pieces, pushing the meat from each section. Pick the legs using scissors and a crab pick.

HOW TO CLEAN A SQUID

This is a messy job, and not for the squeamish or impatient. But given really fresh squid mostly comes only whole, it's a necessary task. This method is more complex than many others, but the result is unmatched.

Work near a clean sink with a bowl of iced salty water handy to rinse, dip and clean as you go. Dip your fingers in table salt to gain purchase on the flesh and skin. Be sure not to waste the tentacles and wings.

Gripping the head and body firmly in opposite hands, gently pull the head away from the body, releasing the head, tentacles, gut and ink sac – leave these to one side.

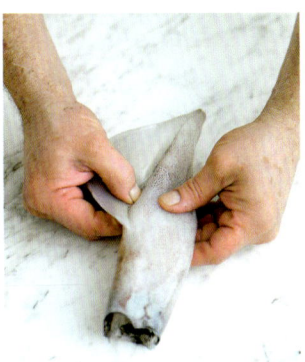

Slide your thumb between the base of the wing and the main body, tearing the cartilage connecting the wing to the body. Carefully pull away the skin and wing. Repeat with the other wing.

Remove any other skin remaining on the hood. Reach inside the hood and pull out the clear 'quill'.

Insert a sharp knife into the hood and cut through it gently, leaving a single V-shaped piece of flesh.

Using the back of a knife, scrape away any remaining ink or gut.

Using a clean scourer, remove the inner skin on both the inside and the outside of the split hood. Or peel off the skin (see page 420).

Using a sharp knife, cut the cleaned hood into strips or finely cross-score the inside of the cleaned hood.

To prepare the tentacles, cut away the upper head and eyes then push the central hard beak out from the base.

To prepare the wings, remove the skin from them and scrub the inner skin as for the hood. Using a sharp knife, cut the cartilage away from the wing flesh.

PREPARATION & COOKING TECHNIQUES

HOW TO CLEAN A CUTTLEFISH

Although this is a slightly messier job than cleaning a squid, in some ways it's also easier, as the firm fleshy piece of meat is less likely to tear. Before you start, prepare a bowl of iced salted water (brine slurry) to have handy, along with a dish of salt to dip your fingers into for gaining traction when handling the cuttlefish. Like squid, cuttlefish have an outer and an inner skin, both of which should be removed to ensure a soft flesh. After removing the ink sac, retain it for later use.

Holding the cuttlefish body firmly, tear the thin layer of skin covering the cuttlebone and, pulling firmly, remove the cuttlebone.

Insert your thumbs under the gut and ink sac, then gently loosen them from the flesh. Pulling gently yet firmly, remove the gut, head and tentacles without bursting the ink sac.

Holding the flesh and skin firmly in opposite hands (with salted fingers for grip), pull the skin from the flesh, releasing the single 'hood' of flesh.

Using a sharp knife, gently scrape the outside of the flesh to release the inner skin. Once the skin has been released, grip firmly and peel away. Turn the hood over and repeat on the inside.

Cut the cleaned hood into strips or finely cross-score on the inside.

HOW TO TENDERISE AND BLANCH OCTOPUS

Most octopus is cleaned and frozen before shipping. Octopus spoils quickly, so it's otherwise difficult to maintain high quality and, unlike squid, octopus does not noticeably lose quality when frozen.

Octopus can be tough, and so must be tenderised. This is the method best suited to a large octopus.

Put the octopus in a colander positioned over a sink or large bowl, then cover the tentacles with about 65 g (2¼ oz/½ cup) of salt per 1 kg (2 lb 4 oz) of tentacles.

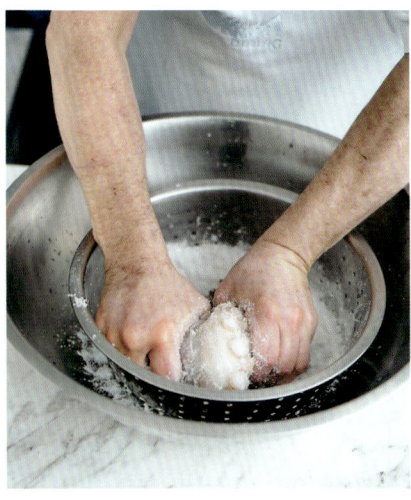

Massage the salt into the tentacles, as though kneading bread dough, for 5 minutes.

Bring 3 litres (101 fl oz/12 cups) of water to the boil. Wrap 3 tablespoons of earl grey tea in muslin (cheesecloth), add to the boiling water, then plunge in the massaged octopus.

Fully immerse the octopus and remove three times, then push it under and add a weight to stop the tentacles floating. Boil for 45 minutes. Remove from the water, cool, then refrigerate.

PREPARATION & COOKING TECHNIQUES

SAUCES, STOCKS & ACCOMPANIMENTS

The ideal pairing to beautifully cooked fish and seafood is the right sauce or accompaniment.

Whether rich and creamy, sharply acidic or with a hit of spice, the recipes on the following pages will give you plenty of ideas for the perfect partner to your dish. Also included here are classic stocks and delicious pickles, salsas and sides.

The sauces and accompaniments listed below can be found with their partner recipes:

Agrodolce (page 282)
Aioli (page 393)
Beer batter (page 83)
Beetroot and chilli relish (page 140)
Chilli jam (page 107)
Chilli salt (page 393)
Cucumber and anchovy salsa (page 97)
Fried red Asian shallots (page 109)
Garlic butter (page 409)
Ginger spring onion oil (page 404)
Herb butter (page 355)

Mousseline sauce (page 196)
Nuoc cham (page 181)
Pickled green chilli (page 281)
Pickled green papaya (page 286)
Pistachio and lime butter (page 271)
Rocket pesto (page 423)
Rouille (page 184)
Sambal matah (page 309)
Sauce gribiche (page 84)
Sea urchin butter (page 413)
Tartare sauce (page 83)

Mayonnaise

MAKES 1 LITRE (35 FL OZ/4 CUPS)

6 egg yolks, at room temperature
generous pinch of sea salt, plus extra as needed
100 ml (3½ fl oz) white wine vinegar
1 heaped tablespoon Dijon mustard
1 litre (35 fl oz/4 cups) vegetable oil

Place the egg yolks in the bowl of an electric mixer then whisk to combine. Whisk in the salt, vinegar and mustard.

Whisking continuously, slowly drizzle in the oil to form an emulsion. As the emulsion becomes stable, add the oil in a steadier stream. Taste for seasoning and add a little more salt if required. Transfer to an airtight container to store. (It will keep in the fridge for 3 days.)

NOTES: You can halve the quantities if you wish; if so, mix the mayonnaise by hand in a bowl, using a whisk.

To make lime mayonnaise, simply mix through freshly squeezed and strained lime juice, to taste.

Green goddess is a herb-packed version – where mayonnaise fits, green goddess pretty much fits as well. To 235 g (8½ oz/1 cup) mayonnaise, add 125 g (4½ oz/½ cup) sour cream, along with 1 bunch finely chopped chives, ½ bunch finely chopped chervil and ½ bunch finely chopped tarragon. Add lemon juice to taste, and season with sea salt and freshly ground white pepper. White anchovies are a great optional extra – start with 50 g (1¾ oz), and add more to your taste, up to 150 g (5½ oz).

Ponzu sauce

MAKES ABOUT 700 ML (24 FL OZ)

300 ml (10½ fl oz) light Japanese soy sauce
100 ml (3½ fl oz) mirin
80 g (2¾ oz) caster (superfine) sugar
140 ml (4¾ fl oz) yuzu juice
100 ml (3½ fl oz) lemon juice
10 g (¼ oz/1 cup loosely packed) dried bonito flakes (katsuobushi)

Combine the soy sauce, mirin, sugar, yuzu juice and lemon juice in a small saucepan over high heat. When the mixture begins to boil, remove the pan from the heat.

Add the bonito flakes to the soy mixture, then cover and leave to cool at room temperature.

Strain the cooled sauce, discarding the bonito flakes. Ponzu sauce will keep for up to 10 days in an airtight container in the fridge.

NOTE: Mirin and yuzu juice are available in Japanese grocery stores or Asian supermarkets.

Shellfish broth and sauce

MAKES ABOUT 5 LITRES (170 FL OZ/20 CUPS)

This recipe has two distinct elements that are used in a number of recipes in this book: the clear or consommé-style broth (as used in the Mixed Seafood and Vegetable Pot with Rouille on page 184 and the King Prawn Broth with Sprouts on page 389); and the thicker shellfish sauce (as used in Tiger Prawn Ravioli, Grilled Spring Onions and Shellfish Sauce on page 397), which makes a perfect base for a bisque.

2 kg (4 lb 8 oz) prawn (shrimp) heads, cleaned
125 ml (4 fl oz/½ cup) vegetable oil
1 large onion, peeled and roughly chopped
1 large carrot, peeled and roughly chopped
80 g (2¾ oz) garlic cloves, peeled and bruised with the back of a knife
6 cm (2½ in) piece ginger, peeled and roughly chopped
70 g (2½ oz/½ cup) black peppercorns
2 long red chillies, seeds in, roughly chopped
2 ripe tomatoes, roughly crushed (see note)
2 heaped tablespoons sea salt
3 litres (101 fl oz/12 cups) dry white wine
2 litres (68 fl oz/8 cups) Fish Stock (page 457) or water

Place the prawn heads in a colander to drain, ensuring they are as dry as possible.

Heat the vegetable oil in a large saucepan over medium–high heat. Add the onion, carrot, garlic, ginger, peppercorns and chilli, then fry, stirring frequently, for 10 minutes, or until the vegetables are a deep golden-brown and well caramelised.

Increase the heat to high and slowly add the prawn heads, a handful at a time so you don't create a stew. Stir well and fry, scraping the caramelised bits from the bottom as you go – this is a vital part of the sauce, so take care not to burn it. Add the tomato, salt, wine and stock, then bring to the boil. Reduce the heat to medium–low and keep on a rolling simmer for 3 hours.

Rest a sieve just inside the top of the pot to push the solids down. Very carefully ladle out 1–1.5 litres (35–52 fl oz/4–6 cups) of liquid – this is the consommé-style clear shellfish broth – into a clean saucepan for immediate use, or an airtight container (see note).

Strain the remaining liquid into a bowl and reserve.

Crush the vegetables, prawns and spices in the pot using a pestle or pass them through a food mill to form a paste. Add this mixture to the reserved liquid and combine – this is the shellfish sauce. Use immediately or transfer to an airtight container (see note).

NOTES: Crab shells or legs left over from steaming are a great addition to this recipe. They add a new level of flavour to the sauce.
  Be sure to use fresh tomatoes, as tinned tomatoes will turn the sauce cloudy.
  The clear shellfish broth will keep in the fridge in an airtight container for 3 days, or in the freezer in portion-sized containers for up to 3 months.
  The shellfish sauce will keep in the fridge in an airtight container for 3 days, or in the freezer in portion-sized containers for up to 3 months.

Chips

SERVES 4

500 g (1 lb 2 oz) all-purpose potatoes (such as sebago), scrubbed, skin on
vegetable oil, for deep-frying
fine sea salt, to serve

Slice the potatoes into 8 mm (3/8 in) thick rounds, then cut into batons 12 × 12 mm (1/2 × 1/2 in) thick (place them in a bowl of cold water as you go to prevent browning). Remove the chips from the water and transfer to an uncovered plastic container. Store in the fridge until ready to blanch. (The chips can be cut the night before, but if so, keep them in water.)

Half-fill a deep-fryer basket with the chips. Place in a deep-fryer filled with cold vegetable oil, then set it to 140°C (275°F). After about 5 minutes, the oil will start to bubble and steam will rise from the chips – as soon as the chips develop a thin, blistered crust, turn off the fryer but leave the chips to continue cooking. The crust will become thicker and may colour slightly. (During the final fry, this crust will help the chips develop a golden, crunchy exterior and a soft, fluffy interior.) Repeat, in batches, if necessary. Cool the blanched chips to room temperature in a plastic container, then refrigerate, uncovered.

When ready to serve, preheat the deep-fryer to 180°C (350°F). Half-fill the basket with the blanched chips and fry for about 3 minutes, or until golden and crisp. Drain the chips on paper towel, season with salt and serve immediately.

NOTES: To deep-fry in a saucepan, place a medium pan half-filled with vegetable oil over high heat. Heat the oil to 180°C (350°C) – check with an oil thermometer. (For a guide to testing the oil without a thermometer, see note page 461.)

When deep-frying in a saucepan, it's advisable to keep the oil level 10 cm (4 in) below the rim.

Cooked potatoes are a high-risk food for food poisoning, so refrigeration to maintain freshness is of the utmost importance.

Crushed peas

SERVES 4

40 g (1 1/2 oz) butter
2 French shallots, peeled and finely diced
1 teaspoon chopped garlic
400 ml (14 fl oz) Fish Stock (page 457)
1 kg (2 lb 4 oz) fresh green peas
ice, for cooling

Melt the butter in a medium saucepan over medium–low heat. Add the shallot and garlic, then cook, without colouring, for 5–10 minutes, until sweet and translucent. Add the fish stock, then increase the heat to high and bring to the boil. Add the peas, return to the boil, then reduce the heat to medium–low and simmer for 2 minutes. Remove the pan from the heat.

Using a conical sieve, strain the peas over a container to catch the stock. Reserve the stock. Place the peas in a bowl over ice and crush them with a fork (the ice will arrest the cooking process, helping the peas retain their vibrant colour). Add a little stock to make a coarse purée, but take care not to over-crush. Set the purée aside in a warm place. (It can be made up to a day ahead and reheated with a little more fish stock, if needed.)

Salsa verde

MAKES ABOUT 375 ML (13 FL OZ/1½ CUPS)

1 slice fresh ciabatta (or similar bread), crust removed, roughly chopped
2 tablespoons milk
1 large handful flat-leaf (Italian) parsley leaves
½ small handful tarragon leaves
½ small handful coriander (cilantro) leaves
1 anchovy fillet
1 tablespoon drained and well-rinsed capers in vinegar
juice of 1 lemon
100 ml (3½ fl oz) extra virgin olive oil
1 hard-boiled egg, peeled and finely chopped
sea salt and freshly ground black pepper, to taste

Place the bread in a small mixing bowl and add the milk. Set aside for 10 minutes for the bread to soak and soften.

Place the herbs, anchovy, capers, lemon juice and soaked bread in a food processor and blend to a slightly rough paste. With the motor running, quickly but gradually add the olive oil to combine and emulsify.

Transfer the salsa to a medium mixing bowl and stir through the egg. Season with salt and pepper.

The salsa will keep in an airtight container in the fridge for 3 days.

Salted fish

fish end scraps (see note), fillet or belly and offcuts, skin off, pin-boned
1 level tablespoon table salt per 100 g (3½ oz) fish scraps
thyme sprigs (or any other herbs, such as chopped bay leaves), to taste
garlic cloves, chopped, to taste
ginger scraps, to taste

Weigh the fish before you begin, then measure out 1 level tablespoon of salt for every 100 g (3½ oz) of fish.

In a deep stainless-steel tray, mix the salt with the thyme sprigs, chopped garlic cloves and ginger scraps. Add the fish pieces and barely cover with water.

Cover with plastic wrap and refrigerate for a minimum of 1 week. After the first week, transfer the salt fish to a clean airtight container, discarding the herbs. It will keep in the fridge for 3 months.

To prepare the salt fish for cooking, place it in a large bowl or tray and shake it vigorously to remove as much excess salt as possible. Remove any blood lines at this point, using a sharp knife. Transfer the fish to another bowl and submerge it in cold water. Cover with plastic wrap and refrigerate for 24 hours. The fish will swell up during this time.

Drain the fish. Fill a deep frying pan with fresh, unsalted water and bring to the boil over high heat. Once the water is boiling, remove the pan from the heat and add the fish. Poach for 2 minutes then remove the fish using a slotted spoon. The salt fish is now ready to use.

NOTE: Any white-fleshed fish and some other species, such as groper, trevalla, snapper and dory, can be used to make salt fish. This is a great way to use fish end scraps and meat from the head of a whole fish – the pieces don't need to be the same size. It's not necessary to trim blood lines before salting – trimming post-salting will achieve a better finish.

Salt-roasted vegetables

ENOUGH FOR ABOUT 1 KG (2 LB 4 OZ) OF VEGETABLES

600 g (1 lb 5 oz) plain (all-purpose) flour, plus extra for dusting
150 g (5½ oz) egg whites (from about 4 eggs)
420 g (15 oz) fine salt
whole vegetables of your choice (see note)

Place the flour, egg whites, salt and 260 ml (9 fl oz) of water in the bowl of an electric mixer. Using the dough hook attachment, mix on medium speed until a firm, smooth dough forms. Remove the dough, wrap it in plastic wrap and leave to rest at room temperature for 30 minutes.

Unwrap the dough and place it on a lightly floured work surface. Roll out to a thin, even thickness, about 5 mm (¼ in) thick for smaller vegetables and 1–2 cm (½–¾ in) for larger varieties.

Scrub the vegetables well, or remove any outer leaves as necessary – skins can stay on. Place a square of baking paper on a cast-iron baking tray or in a heavy-based, ovenproof shallow frying pan and lay the vegetables on top. Carefully drape the dough over each vegetable and wrap, ensuring each vegetable is completely encased in dough.

The cooking temperature and time required will vary depending on the vegetables chosen and may take a little practice. Most large root vegetables and cabbages will take 8 hours to cook at 180–190°C (350–375°F). When cooked, remove from the oven and leave to rest for 30 minutes. To serve, crack open the crust and scoop the vegetable out with a spoon.

NOTE: Many vegetables are suited to this salt-crust baking technique – celeriac, cabbage, pumpkin (winter squash), yam and beetroot (beet) work particularly well.

Sushi rice

SERVES 10–20

200 ml (7 fl oz) Japanese red vinegar (see note)
1 teaspoon Japanese table salt (see note)
3 teaspoons caster (superfine) sugar
1 kg (2 lb 4 oz) sushi rice

Mix the vinegar, salt and sugar together in a small bowl and set aside.

Put the rice in a large bowl, then gently wash it twice, rinsing well and pouring out the starchy water each time. Cover with fresh water and set aside to soak for 30 minutes at room temperature. Rinse the rice well once more, then transfer to a rice cooker. Add 1.25 litres (44 fl oz/5 cups) of cold water and cook for 30 minutes, then switch off and leave the rice in the cooker, covered, to rest for a further 30 minutes.

Spoon the rice into a large metal bowl. Drizzle the vinegar mixture over and, using a wooden spoon, cut the liquid through the rice in a gentle waving motion for 8 minutes. The idea is to incorporate the liquid evenly without overworking the rice.

Set the rice aside to cool to body temperature (37°C/99°F) – it should feel slightly warm when you touch it with your knuckles. Return it to the rice cooker to maintain a constant temperature – sushi rice should be served at this temperature, as it assists in releasing the fish oils. The rice can be kept safely in the rice cooker for up to 4 hours – if not used in this time it should be discarded.

Working with wet hands to prevent sticking, take about 12 g (½ oz) of cooked rice and mould it by gently squeezing it in the cup of your hand, then clasping the rice inside your hand to firm up the ball. Don't squeeze too tightly or too loosely; the rice needs to be firm enough to hold together but loose enough that it falls apart easily when eaten.

NOTE: You'll find Japanese red vinegar and table salt in Asian supermarkets.

INDEX

A

abalone
    Abalone shabu shabu 305
    Australian fisheries 299
    blacklip 299, 301
    brownlip 299, 301
    farmed 199
    greenlip 299, 301
    harvesting 299
    Pan-fried abalone with zucchini and garlic 302
    Roe's abalone 299, 301
    shucking 439
    tinned 301
Acanthopagrus australis (yellowfin bream) 45, 46
Acanthopagrus berda (pikey bream) 45
Acanthopagrus butcheri (black bream) 45, 46
accompaniments
    Chips 459
    Court bouillon 457
    Crushed peas 459
    Garlic butter 409
    Jasmine rice 460
    Pickled cucumbers 460
    Potato crisp 461
    Preserved lemon 461
    Salt-roasted vegetables 463
    Salted fish 462
    Sauce gribiche 84
    Shellfish broth and sauce 458
    Shellfish oil 456
    Sushi rice 463
    see also mayonnaise; sauces
Agrodolce 282
albacore tuna (*Thunnus alalunga*) 273, 274, 276
    Niçoise salad 278
alfonsino (*Beryx splendens*) 115
Amusium balloti (saucer or Queensland scallop) 401, 402
anchovies
    Cucumber and anchovy salsa 97
angasi oyster (*Ostrea angasi*) 371, 372, 376
angel shark (*Squatina australis*) 211
Anguilla australis (shortfin eel) 71
Anguilla reinhardtii (longfin eel) 71
Antarctic toothfish (*Dissostichus mawsoni*) 239
Aprion virescens (green jobfish) 227
Aptychotrema rostrata (eastern shovelnose ray) 215
aquaculture 10–11, 371
Argyrosomus japonicus (mulloway) 153–4
Arrhamphus sclerolepis (snubnose garfish) 93
arrow (Gould's) squid (*Nototodarus gouldi*) 416
Atlantic salmon (*Salmo salar*) 193, 194
    Atlantic salmon sushi and sashimi 199
Australian giant cuttlefish (*Sepia apama*) 415, 419
avocado
    Guacamole 213

B

Balmain bug (*Ibacus peronii*) 307, 308, 309
banana prawn (*Fenneropenaeus indicus*) 382, 385
bar cod (*Epinephelus ergastularius*) 29–30
    Salted bar cod salad with poached egg, wild rocket and salmon roe 32
Barbecued whole redspot whiting with sourdough crumbs and blackened citrus 291
Barbecued yellowtail scad with peas, lettuce and bacon 252
barramundi (*Lates calcarifer*) 23–4
    Barramundi with crushed peas and sour cream 26
    Steamed barramundi with tomato consommé 25
bass groper (*Polyprion moeone*) 29–31
    Bass groper with salt-roasted celeriac and yoghurt 31
batter
    Beer batter 83
Beetroot and chilli relish 140
belachan 167, 309
Beryx decadactylus (imperador) 115–16
Beryx splendens (alfonsino) 115
Bidyanus bidyanus (silver perch) 171–2
big-eye ocean perch (*Helicolenus barathri*) 161
    Steamed whole big-eye ocean perch with coconut, chilli and lime broth 162
bigeye trevally (*Caranx sexfasciatus*) 249
bigeye tuna (*Thunnus obesus*) 273, 274, 276
black bream (*Acanthopagrus butcheri*) 45, 46
black kingfish *see* cobia
blacklip abalone (*Haliotis rubra*) 299, 301
blacktip shark (*Carcharhinus limbatus*) 211
blue cod (*Parapercis colias*) 35–6
    Blue cod fillets with steamed celery and lettuce 36
blue endeavour prawn (*Metapenaeus endeavouri*) 382
blue mackerel (*Scomber australasicus*) 135–6
blue morwong or queen snapper (*Nemadactylus valenciennesi*) 51
blue swimmer (sand) crab (*Portunus pelagicus*) 326, 330, 331, 447

Wok-fried blue swimmer crab with pepper and egg 340
blue warehou (*Seriolella brama*) 285
blue-eye trevalla (*Hyperoglyphe antarctica*) 243
    Blue-eye trevalla roasted on potato scales, with baby beetroot and ricotta 244
    Brandade 102
    Grilled blue-eye trevalla medallions with curried chickpeas 247
bluefin trevally (*Caranx melampygus*) 249
blue-spotted flathead (*Platycephalus caeruleopunctatus*) 80
blue-spotted goatfish (*Upeneichthys vlamingii*) 147
blue-striped goatfish (*Upeneichthys lineatus*) 147
bonito (*Sarda australis*)
    Bonito sashimi with seaweed tempura 41
    Bonito tataki 42
    leaping 39
    oriental or striped 39
Bottarga (salted fish roe) 191
    bottarga di muggine 189
    bottarga di tonno 189
bottom longlines 14
Brandade 102
breadcrumbs, fried 208
bream 45–8
    Bream with bok choy, parsley root and salted red chilli 48
    Carpaccio of deep-sea bream with ponzu sauce 52
bream
    black 45, 46
    pikey 45
    yellowfin 45, 46
brill, New Zealand (*Colistium guntheri*) 87
broadbill *see* swordfish
broth
    Hot and sour prawn soup 399
    King prawn broth with sprouts 389
brownlip abalone (*Haliotis conicopora*) 299, 301
bugs
    Balmain 307, 308, 309
    Bugs with sambal matah and ground roast rice 309
    cleaning cooked 441
    extracting meat 308
    Moreton Bay 307, 308, 309
Buttered prawns with nectarine and radicchio 393, 394
butters
    Garlic 409
    Herb 355
    Pistachio and lime 271
    Sea urchin 413

C

Cabbage salad 213
Callorhinchus milii (elephant shark) 211
Caranx melampygus (bluefin trevally) 249
Caranx sexfasciatus (bigeye trevally) 249
Carcharhinus limbatus (blacktip shark) 211
Carcharhinus obscurus (dusky shark) 211
Carpaccio of deep-sea bream with ponzu sauce 52
caviar 189
Centroberyx affinis (redfish) 179–81
Chaceon bicolor (deepwater snow or crystal crab) 325
Charred pearl perch with radicchio and pine nuts 168
Charred striped trumpeter with pistachio and lime carrots 271
Cheilodactylus fuscus (red or banded morwong) 51
Chelidonichthys kumu (gurnard) 105–9
Cherax destructor see yabbies
Cherax quadricarinatus (redclaw) 343, 344
Cherax tenuimanus (marron) 343, 344
chickpeas
    Curried chickpeas 247
chilli
    Beetroot and chilli relish 140
    Chilli jam 107
    Chilli salt 393
    dried red chillies 109
    Salted red chilli 247
chinook salmon *see* king salmon
Chips 459
Chlamys bifrons (purple-shelled and purple-roed queen scallop) 401
clams 313
    Clams vinaigrette 318
    Mixed seafood and vegetable pot with rouille 184
    New England-style clam chowder 323
    New Zealand 318, 321, 322
    par-cooked 184
    pipi (Goolwa cockle) 312
    purging 311, 317
    raw 317
    Roasted clams with parsley, garlic and spring onions 321
    shucking 443
    Spaghetti vongole 315, 322
    steaming open 318
    storm 314
    'surf' 314–15
    triangle or diamond shell 314, 315
    tua tua 314, 315
    vongole 312
Classic fish pie 232
cleaning fish and seafood
    cooked bug 441
    cooked spanner crab 450
    cuttlefish 452
    scallop 440
    squid 451
cobia (*Rachycentron canadum*) 55–7
    Fijian kokoda (fish salad) 57
Colistium guntheri (New Zealand brill) 87
Colistium nudipinnis (New Zealand turbot) 87
condiments
    Agrodolce 282
    Beetroot and chilli relish 140
    Chilli jam 107
    Chilli salt 393
    native pepper berry salt 281
    Nuoc cham 181
    Pickled green chilli 281
    Pickled green papaya 286
    Rouille 184
    Sambal matah 309
    togarashi 90
Conger conger (European conger eel) 71
cooking fish
    crisp skin 437
    filleting 19
    steaming 267
    tough fish syndrome 175
coral trout (*Plectropomus leopardus*) 255–6
    Steamed coral trout tail with almonds, pomegranate and prunes 256
Coryphaena hippurus (mahi mahi) 143–4
Court bouillon 457
crab
    blue swimmer 326, 330, 331, 447
    catching 15
    cooking and picking 331, 449
    Crab salad 332
    deepwater snow or crystal 325
    dispatching 326
    frozen 330
    mud 325, 326, 330, 331, 448
    Mud crab with pickled green papaya 339
    Pot-roasted spanner crab with caramelised garlic and cracked pepper 336
    pre-cooked 330
    spanner 329, 330, 331, 450
    Spanner crab fettuccine 335

spoilage 325
storing live 316, 330
Wok-fried blue swimmer crab with pepper and egg 340
Crassostrea gigas (Pacific oyster) 372, 376
crayfish, freshwater
    buying live 344
    farmed 343
    see also marron; redclaw; yabbies
crimson snapper (*Lutjanus erythropterus*) 227
crostini 281
Crumbed ling with salad greens and lemon dressing 133
Crumbed sand whiting 295
Crushed peas 459
cucumber
    Cucumber and anchovy salsa 97
    Pickled cucumbers 460
curing salmon 438
curries
    Curried chickpeas 247
    Indian prawn and eggplant curry 398
    South Indian curry of mullet 151
    Yellow curry of warehou 286
Curry paste 151
cuttlefish *see* squid and cuttlefish
Cybiosarda elegans (leaping bonito) 39

D

Daikon salmon roll 199
dashi 305
Dasyatidae (rays) 215–16
Deania calcea (roughskin dogfish) 211
deep-frying
    Deep-fried flathead and chips with home-made tartare sauce 83
    Deep-fried school prawns with aioli and chilli salt 393
    deep-fryers 130, 133, 393
    oil level 393
    re-using oil 213
    safety 173
    in saucepan 130, 133
    testing temperature 130–1, 133, 173, 393
deepwater flathead (*Neoplatycephalus conatus*) 80
dhufish (*Glaucosoma hebraicum*) 165–6
    Penang-style laksa with whole dhufish 167
Dissostichus eleginoides (Patagonian toothfish) 239
Dissostichus mawsoni (Antarctic toothfish) 239
dory *see* john dory; mirror dory
dressing a whole flat fish 430

dressing a whole round fish 430
dressings
    Mignonette 378
    Salad 241
droplines 14
dry-filleting 19
dusky flathead (*Platycephalus fuscus*) 80
dusky shark (*Carcharhinus obscurus*) 211

E

eastern fiddler ray (*Trygonorrhina fasciata*) 215
eastern king prawn (*Melicertus plebejus*) 382
eastern red rock cod 183
eastern rock lobster (*Sagmariasus verreauxi*) 349, 350, 351
eastern school (redspot) whiting (*Sillago flindersi*) 289, 290
    Barbecued whole redspot whiting with sourdough crumbs and blackened citrus 291
eastern sea garfish (*Hyporhamphus australis*) 93
eastern shovelnose ray (*Aptychotrema rostrata*) 215
eel
    European conger 71
    longfin 71
    Pan-fried with tomatoes and garlic 76
    saltwater 72
    shortfin 71, 72
    Smoked eel and green peppercorn pâté 75
    smoking 72
eggplant
    Indian prawn and eggplant curry 398
elephant shark (*Callorhinchus milii*) 211
endangered species 157
Epinephelus ergastularius (bar cod) 29–30, 32
Escabeche of yellowtail kingfish 121
Etelis carbunculus (ruby snapper) 227, 228, 230
European conger eel (*Conger conger*) 71

F

farmed fish 15, 153
    see also aquaculture
Fenneropenaeus indicus (banana prawn) 382, 385
Fijian kokoda (fish salad) 57
filleting 19
    a dory 431
    a round fish 428–9, 431

fish
    catching and handling 12–15
    cleaning and scaling 428
    'dressed' 19, 430
    endangered species 157
    farmed 15, 153
    filleting 19, 428–9, 431
    freezing 18, 19
    killing 15, 228, 249
    oceanic species 13
    Salted fish 462
    sea slime 19
    seasonality guide 464–5
    selecting and storing 18–19
    skinning and filleting, Japanese style 432–3
    sustainable 16
    see also cooking fish; soup
Fish stock 457
Fish tacos 213
fishing
    Australian industry 9–10
    lines 13–14
    methods 12–15
    nets 12–13
    as a sport 10
    sustainability 16, 18
    trawls 14
flake 212
flathead 79–81
    blue-spotted 80
    Deep-fried flathead and chips with home-made tartare sauce 83
    deepwater 80
    dry-filleted 81
    dusky 80
    Flathead with sauce gribiche 84
    grassy 80
    sand 80
    tiger 80
flounder 87–8
    Pot-roasted whole flounder with togarashi 90
    sand flounder 87
    yellowbelly 87
food poisoning 139
freezing fish 18, 19
fried breadcrumbs 208
Fried whole gurnard with chilli jam 107
Furgaleus macki (whiskery shark) 211

G

Galeorhinus galeus (school shark) 211
garfish
    eastern sea 93
    Grilled garfish fillets with cucumber and anchovy salsa 97

for sashimi 93
Sicilian-style 94
snubnose 93
southern sea 93
for sushi 93
three-by-two 93
garlic
  caramelising 336
  Garlic butter 409
  wild 68
gemfish (*Rexea solandri*) 99–100
  Brandade 102
  Gemfish with preserved lemon and oregano 101
Genypterus blacodes (pink ling) 129
Genypterus tigerinus (rock ling) 129
Ginger spring onion oil 404
Glaucosoma hebraicum (dhufish) 165–6, 167
Glaucosoma scapulare (pearl perch) 165–6, 168
goldband snapper (*Pristipomoides multidens*) 227
golden or yellowfin perch (*Macquaria ambigua*) 171
Goolwa cockle (pipi) 312
Gould's (arrow) squid (*Nototodarus gouldi*) 416
grassy flathead (*Platycephalus laevigatus*) 80
Green goddess mayonnaise 455
green jobfish (*Aprion virescens*) 227
greenlip abalone (*Haliotis laevigata*) 299, 301
grey mackerel (*Scomberomorus semifasciatus*) 139
grey morwong (*Nemadactylus douglasii*) 51
Grilled blue-eye trevalla medallions with curried chickpeas 247
Grilled garfish fillets with cucumber and anchovy salsa 97
Grilled marron 346
Grilled scallops with ginger spring onion oil 404
Grilled scampi with garlic butter 409
Guacamole 213
gummy shark (*Mustelus antarcticus*) 211
  Fish tacos 213
gurnard (*Chelidonichthys kumu*) 105–6
  Fried whole gurnard with chilli jam 107

H

Haliotis conicopora (brownlip abalone) 299, 301
Haliotis laevigata (greenlip abalone) 299, 301
Haliotis roei (redlip abalone, Roe's abalone) 299, 301
Haliotis rubra (blacklip abalone) 299, 301
Haliporoides sibogae (royal red prawn) 383
handlines 13
hapuka (New Zealand groper, *Polyprion oxygeneios*) 111–12
  Steamed hapuka with mushrooms, soy and bok choy 113
Harissa-painted Murray cod 159
Helicolenus barathri (big-eye ocean perch) 161
Helicolenus percoides (reef ocean perch) 161
Heliocidaris erythrogramma (sea urchin) 411–13
Hemiramphus robustus (three-by-two garfish) 93
Herb butter 355
hook and line trolling 13
Hot and sour prawn soup 399
Hyperoglyphe antarctica (blue-eye trevalla) 243–7
Hyporhamphus australis (eastern sea garfish) 93
Hyporhamphus melanochir (southern sea garfish) 93

I

Ibacus peronii (Balmain bug) 307, 308, 309
ike jime (killing method) 15, 179, 228, 249
imperador (*Beryx decadactylus*) 115–16
  One-pot imperador with fig and verjuice 116
Indian prawn and eggplant curry 398
Isurus oxyrinchus (mako shark) 211

J

jackass morwong or tarahiki (*Nemadactylus macropterus*) 51
Jasmine rice 460
Jasus edwardsii (southern rock lobster) 349, 350, 351
jobfish
  green jobfish 227
  rosy jobfish or king snapper 227
  Spanish-flag jobfish 227
  see also snapper, tropical
john dory (*Zeus faber*) 59, 60
  filleting 19
  John dory with caramelised spring onions 67
  Pan-fried john dory liver on toast 63
  Pot-roasted whole john dory with wild garlic 68

K

Katelysia spp. (vongole) 312
Katsuwonus pelamis (skipjack tuna) 273
killing fish 15, 228, 249
King George whiting (*Sillaginodes punctatus*) 289, 290, 295
King prawn broth with sprouts 389
king salmon (*Oncorhynchus tshawytscha*) 193
  King salmon pastrami 195
  King salmon poached in court bouillon with mousseline sauce 196
king snapper or rosy jobfish (*Pristipomoides filamentosus*) 227
kingfish *see* yellowtail kingfish

L

Laksa paste 167
laksa
  Penang-style laksa with whole dhufish 167
latchet (*Pterygotrigla polyommata*) 105
Lates calcarifer (barramundi) 23–6
Latris lineata (striped trumpeter) 269–71
leaping bonito (*Cybiosarda elegans*) 39
leatherjacket
  Leatherjacket with potato, fennel, olives and pancetta 127
  ocean jacket 125
  sixspine leatherjacket 125
  yellowstriped leatherjacket 125
lime
  Lime mayonnaise 455
  Pistachio and lime butter 271
lines 13–14
ling
  Brandade 102
  Crumbed ling with salad greens and lemon dressing 133
  Ling burger 130
  pink ling 129
  rock ling 129
Linguine with sea urchin butter 413

INDEX **469**

lobster
    Australian fisheries 349
    catching 15
    cooking 351, 352
    eastern rock 349, 350, 351
    frozen 351
    killing 351
    Lobster and white nectarine salad 352
    Pot-roasted lobster with ginger, spring onion and pepper 356
    preparing 446
    Roast lobster with herb butter 355
    sashimi 351
    southern rock 349, 350, 351
    tropical rock 349, 350, 351
    western rock 349, 350, 351
longfin eel (*Anguilla reinhardtii*) 71
Lutjanus carponotatus (Spanish-flag jobfish) 227
Lutjanus erythropterus (crimson snapper) 227
Lutjanus malabaricus (saddletail snapper) 227
Lutjanus monostigma (one-spot snapper) 227
Lutjanus sebae (red emperor) 175–6

M

Maccullochella peelii peelii (Murray cod) 157–9
mackerel
    pickled mackerel 136
    see also blue mackerel; grey mackerel; school mackerel; Spanish mackerel
Macquaria ambigua (golden or yellowfin perch) 171
Macquaria australasica (Macquarie perch) 171
Mactra murchisoni (storm clam) 314
mahi mahi (*Coryphaena hippurus*)
    Mahi mahi with caramelised onion and tahini 144
    tempura 143
mako shark (*Isurus oxyrinchus*) 211
mangrove jack 175
marron (*Cherax tenuimanus*) 343, 344
    Grilled marron 346
mayonnaise 455
    Green goddess mayonnaise 455
    Lime mayonnaise 455
Melicertus latisulcatus (western king prawn) 382
Melicertus longistylus (redspot king prawn) 383
Melicertus plebejus (eastern king prawn) 382
Mendolia family 205
Metanephrops australiensis (scampi) 407–9
Metapenaeus endeavouri (blue endeavour prawn) 382
Metapenaeus macleayi (school prawn) 384
Meuschenia flavolineata (yellowstriped leatherjacket) 125
Meuschenia freycineti (sixspine leatherjacket) 125
Meuschenia trachylepis (yellowfin leatherjacket) 125
Mignonette dressing 378
mirror dory (*Zenopsis nebulosa*) 59, 60
    Mirror dory fillet with chips and salad 64
miso
    Toothfish in white miso 240, 241
Mixed seafood and vegetable pot with rouille 184
Moreton Bay bug (*Thenus orientalis*) 307, 308, 309
morwong
    blue morwong or queen snapper 51
    grey morwong 51
    red or banded morwong 51
Mousseline sauce 196
mud crab (*Scylla serrata*) 325, 326, 330, 331
    Mud crab with pickled green papaya 339
    preparing 448
mullet, red 147
    Red mullet with tomato, onion and basil 148
    South Indian curry of mullet 151
mullet, thin-lipped sea
    bottarga di muggine 189
mulloway (*Argyrosomus japonicus*)
    farmed 153
    Mulloway with pan-fried brussels sprouts, bacon and sage 154
    sashimi 153
    'soapies' 153
Murray cod (*Maccullochella peelii peelii*) 157–8
    Harissa-painted Murray cod 159
    skin-on cooking 158
mushrooms
    Mushroom duxelles 261
    Rolled King George whiting with Asian mushrooms 292
mussels (*Mytilus galloprovincialis*)
    debearding 359
    Mussel and seared tuna salad 363
    Mussels with spring onions and butter 360
    unopened 359, 363
Mustelus antarcticus (gummy shark) 211, 213
Mytilus galloprovincialis (mussels) 359, 360, 363

N

native pepper berry salt 281
Nelusetta ayraud (ocean jacket) 125
Nemadactylus douglasii (grey morwong) 51
Nemadactylus macropterus (jackass morwong, tarahiki) 51
Nemadactylus valenciennesi (blue morwong, queen snapper) 51
Neoplatycephalus conatus (deepwater flathead) 80
Neoplatycephalus richardsoni (tiger flathead) 80
nets 12–13
New England-style clam chowder 323
New Zealand clams 318, 321, 322
New Zealand flathead *see* gurnard
Niçoise salad 278
northern (black) jewfish (*Protonibea diacanthus*) 153
Nototodarus gouldi (Gould's/arrow squid) 416
Nuoc cham 181

O

ocean jacket (*Nelusetta ayraud*) 125
ocean trout (*Oncorhynchus mykiss*) 259–60
    Ocean trout in filo pastry with mushroom duxelles, leek and sorrel sauce 261
    Scrambled eggs on brioche with ocean trout roe 190
    Sugar-cured ocean trout 264
oceanic species 13
octopus (*Octopus* spp.)
    'baby' 365
    blanching and tenderising 365, 366, 453
    Octopus with sweet soy and sesame 368
    Pickled baby octopus 367
    'sashimi' 366
oil 130, 133
    Ginger spring onion oil 404
    testing temperature 181, 461, 393
omelette
    Prawn omelette with spinach, enoki, bean sprouts and oyster sauce 390

Oncorhynchus mykiss (trout, ocean and rainbow) 259–67
Oncorhynchus tshawytscha (king salmon) 193, 196
One-pot imperador with fig and verjuice 116
one-spot snapper (*Lutjanus monostigma*) 227
oriental or striped bonito (*Sarda orientalis*) 39
Ostrea angasi (angasi oyster) 371, 372, 376
oysters
    angasi (native) oyster 371, 372, 376
    buying 376
    cooking 372
    farmed 371
    Oyster and sorrel soup 377
    Oysters mignonette 378
    Pacific oyster 372, 376
    shucking 372, 442, 443
    Sydney rock oyster 371, 375, 376

P

Pacific oyster (*Crassostrea gigas*) 372, 376
Pagrus auratus (pink snapper) 219–20
Pan-fried abalone with zucchini and garlic 302
Pan-fried cuttlefish with salted chilli and basil 424
Pan-fried eel with tomatoes and garlic 76
Pan-fried john dory liver on toast 63
Pan-fried sardines with broccolini, fried bread and capers 208
Pan-fried squid tubes with rocket pesto 423
Pan-roasted snapper with cherry tomatoes, zucchini and basil 223
Pan-seared saucer scallops with speck, brussels sprouts and brown butter 403
Panulirus cygnus (western rock lobster) 349, 350, 351
Panulirus ornatus (tropical rock lobster) 349, 350, 351
papaya
    Pickled green papaya 286
Paphies donacina (tua tua) 314, 315
Parapercis colias (blue cod) 35–6
pasta
    freezing 397
    Linguine with sea urchin butter 413
    Spaghetti vongole 315, 322
    Spanner crab fettuccine 335
    Tiger prawn ravioli, grilled spring onions and shellfish sauce 397

pastes
    Curry paste 151
    Laksa paste 167
pastrami
    King salmon pastrami 195
Patagonian toothfish (*Dissostichus eleginoides*) 239
pâté
    Salmon pâté 203
pearl perch (*Glaucosoma scapulare*) 165–6
    Charred pearl perch with radicchio and pine nuts 168
peas
    Crushed peas 459
Pecten fumatus (Tasmanian or commercial scallop) 401
pelagic longlines 13
Penaeus monodon (tiger prawn) 384, 385
Penang-style laksa with whole dhufish 167
Perca fluviatilis (redfin perch) 171
perch *see* big-eye ocean perch; golden perch; Macquarie perch; pearl perch; redfin perch; reef ocean perch; silver perch
pesto
    Rocket pesto 423
Pickled baby octopus 367
Pickled cucumbers 460
Pickled green chilli 281
Pickled green papaya 286
Pickled mackerel 136
pie
    Classic fish pie 232
pikey bream (*Acanthopagrus berda*) 45
pink ling (*Genypterus blacodes*) 129
pipi (Goolwa cockle, *Plebidonax deltoides*) 312
Pistachio and lime butter 271
Platycephalus bassensis (sand flathead) 80
Platycephalus caeruleopunctatus (blue-spotted flathead) 80
Platycephalus fuscus (dusky flathead) 80
Platycephalus laevigatus (grassy flathead) 80
Plebidonax deltoides (Goolwa cockle; pipi) 312
Plectropomus leopardus (coral trout) 255–6
pole and line 13
Polyprion moeone (bass groper) 29–31
Polyprion oxygeneios (hapuka/hapuku or New Zealand groper) 111–12
Ponzu sauce 455
Portunus pelagicus (blue swimmer sand crab) 326, 330, 331, 447
Potato and speck salad 200
Potato chips 459

Potato crisp 461
potato scales 437
Pot-roasted lobster with ginger, spring onion and pepper 356
Pot-roasted spanner crab with caramelised garlic and cracked pepper 336
Pot-roasted whole flounder with togarashi 90
Pot-roasted whole john dory with wild garlic 68
prawns
    banana prawn 382, 385
    blue endeavour prawn 382
    Buttered prawns with nectarine and radicchio 393, 394
    buying cooked 381, 385
    buying fresh 381, 385
    cooking 385, 386
    Deep-fried school prawns with aioli and chilli salt 393
    eastern king prawn 382
    frozen 381, 385
    Hot and sour prawn soup 399
    Indian prawn and eggplant curry 398
    King prawn broth with sprouts 389
    Mixed seafood and vegetable pot with rouille 184
    peeling 444
    Prawn cocktail 386
    Prawn omelette with spinach, enoki, bean sprouts and oyster sauce 390
    redspot king prawn 383
    royal red prawn 383
    school prawn 384
    size and sweetness 381, 385
    skewering a raw prawn 445
    storing 385
    tiger prawn 384, 385
    Tiger prawn ravioli, grilled spring onions and shellfish sauce 397
    western king prawn 382
    wild prawn fisheries 381
preparation
    blue swimmer crab 447
    live lobster 446
    live mud crab 448
    potato scales 437
    skate wing 436
Preserved lemon 461
Pristiophorus cirratus (saw shark) 211
Pristipomoides filamentosus (king snapper or rosy jobfish) 227
Pristipomoides multidens (goldband snapper) 227
Protonibea diacanthus (northern/black jewfish) 153

Pseudocaranx dentex (silver trevally) 249, 251
Pterygotrigla polyommata (latchet) 105
purple-shelled and purple-roed queen scallop (*Chlamys bifrons*) 401

Q

queen snapper
    blue morwong or queen snapper (*Nemadactylus valenciennesi*) 51
    Queensland northern or bigfin reef squid (*Sepioteuthis lessoniana*) 419
    Queensland or saucer scallop (*Amusium balloti*) 401, 402

R

Rachycentron canadum (cobia) 55–7
rainbow trout (*Oncorhynchus mykiss*)
    Steamed whole rainbow trout with green beans, figs and hazelnut butter 267
Rajidae (skate) 215–16
Ranina ranina (spanner crab) 329, 330, 331, 336
rays *see* skate and rays
red emperor (*Lutjanus sebae*) 175–6
    Red emperor with mushrooms and yoghurt 176
red or banded morwong (*Cheilodactylus fuscus*) 51
Red mullet with tomato, onion and basil 148
red rock cod (*Scorpaena cardinalis*) 183–7
    Mixed seafood and vegetable pot with rouille 184
redclaw (*Cherax quadricarinatus*) 343, 344
redfin perch (*Perca fluviatilis*) 171
redfish (*Centroberyx affinis*) 179–81
    Vietnamese-style fishcakes with nuoc cham 181
redspot *see* eastern school whiting 289, 290
redspot king prawn (*Melicertus longistylus*) 383
reef jacket
    sixspine leatherjacket (*Meuschenia freycineti*) 125
    yellowfin leatherjacket (*Meuschenia trachylepis*) 125
    yellowstriped leatherjacket (*Meuschenia flavolineata*) 125
reef ocean perch (*Helicolenus percoides*) 161

relish
    Beetroot and chilli relish 140
Rexea solandri (gemfish) 99–102
Rhombosolea leporina (yellowbelly flounder) 87
Rhombosolea plebeia (sand flounder) 87
Rhynchobatus australiae (white-spotted guitarfish) 215
rice
    ground roast rice 309
    Jasmine rice 460
    Sushi rice 463
Roast lobster with herb butter 355
Roasted clams with parsley, garlic and spring onions 321
Rock cod cutlets in crazy water 187
rock ling (*Genypterus tigerinus*) 129
Rocket pesto 423
roe
    Bottarga (salted fish roe) 189, 191
    caviar 189
    Scrambled eggs on brioche with ocean trout roe 190
Roe's abalone (*Haliotis roei*, redlip) 299
Rolled King George whiting with Asian mushrooms 292
roughskin dogfish (*Deania calcea*) 211
Rouille 184
royal red prawn (*Haliporoides sibogae*) 383
ruby snapper (*Etelis carbunculus*) 227, 228
    Ruby snapper en papillote with zucchini, tomato and garlic 230

S

Saccostrea glomerata (Sydney rock oyster) 371, 375, 376
saddletail snapper (*Lutjanus malabaricus*) 227
Sagmariasus verreauxi (eastern rock lobster) 349, 350, 351
Salad dressing 241
salads
    Cabbage salad 213
    Crab salad 332
    Fijian kokoda (fish salad) 57
    Lobster and white nectarine salad 352
    Niçoise salad 278
    Potato and speck salad 200
    Toothfish in white miso 240, 241
Salmo salar (Atlantic salmon) 193, 194
salmon
    Atlantic salmon 193, 194
    Atlantic salmon sushi and sashimi 199
    curing 438
    Daikon salmon roll 199
    farmed 193

    Salmon pâté 203
    Salmon with potato and speck salad 200
    Salmon rillettes 203
    Salmon sashimi 199
    Tasmanian 193
    wild 193
    see also king salmon
salsa
    Cucumber and anchovy salsa 97
Salsa verde 462
salt
    chilli salt 393
    native pepper berry salt 281
Salt-crusted whole snapper 229
Salt-roasted vegetables 463
Salted fish 462
    Brandade 102
    Salted bar cod salad with poached egg, wild rocket and salmon roe 32
salted fish roe (Bottarga) 191
Salted red chilli 247
saltwater eel 72
Sambal matah 309
sand crab *see* blue swimmer crab
sand flathead (*Platycephalus bassensis*) 80
sand flounder (*Rhombosolea plebeia*) 87
sand whiting (*Sillago ciliata*, summer whiting) 289, 290
    Crumbed sand whiting 295
Sarda australis (bonito) 39–42
Sarda orientalis (oriental or striped bonito) 39
sardines (*Sardinops sagax*) 205–6
    Pan-fried sardines with broccolini, fried bread and capers 208
    Sardines on toast 207
sashimi
    Atlantic salmon sushi and sashimi 199
    Bonito sashimi with seaweed tempura 41
    cutting from a fillet 434
    garfish 93
    lobster 351
    mahi mahi 143
    mulloway 153
    octopus 366
    Salmon 199
    Silver trevally sashimi 251
    Snapper sushi and sashimi 224
    squid and cuttlefish 420
    trevally 249, 250
    yellowfin tuna 271, 275, 277
saucer or Queensland scallop (*Amusium balloti*) 401, 402
sauces
    cocktail 386
    Mousseline sauce 196
    Ponzu sauce 455

Salsa verde 462
Sauce gribiche 84
Sorrel sauce 261
Sweet soy sauce (home made) 368
Tartare sauce 83
Yellow curry sauce 456
saw shark (*Pristiophorus cirratus*) 211
scallops
   cleaning 440
   frozen 402
   Grilled scallops with ginger spring onion oil 404
   harvesting 402
   Pan-seared saucer scallops with speck, brussels sprouts and brown butter 403
   purple-shelled and purple-roed queen scallop 401
   raw 402
   roe (coral) 401, 402
   saucer or Queensland scallop 401, 402
   shelf life 401
   Tasmanian or commercial scallop 401
scampi (*Metanephrops australiensis*)
   extracting meat 408
   Grilled scampi with garlic butter 409
   roe 407
scarlet sea perch 175
school mackerel (*Scomberomorus queenslandicus*) 139
school prawn (*Metapenaeus macleayi*) 384
school shark (*Galeorhinus galeus*) 211
Scomber australasicus (blue mackerel) 135–6
Scomberomorus commerson (Spanish mackerel) 139–40
Scomberomorus munroi (spotted mackerel) 139
Scomberomorus queenslandicus (school mackerel) 139
Scomberomorus semifasciatus (grey mackerel) 139
Scorpaena cardinalis (red rock cod) 183–7
Scrambled eggs on brioche with ocean trout roe 190
Scylla serrata (mud crab) 325, 326, 330, 331, 339, 448
sea slime 19
sea urchin (*Heliocidaris erythrogramma*)
   buying live 412
   roe (uni) 411, 412
   Sea urchin butter 413
seafood
   buying and storing 18–19
   consumption 9
   frozen 18
   exported 9
   hand collection 14–15
   imported 9

sustainability 16, 365
Seared swordfish with caramelised pickled onions and charred eggplant 236
Seared yellowfin tuna with agrodolce 282
seasonality guide 464–5
Sepia apama (Australian giant cuttlefish) 415, 419
Sepioteuthis australis (southern calamari squid) 415, 416
Sepioteuthis lessoniana (Queensland northern or bigfin reef squid) 419
Seriola lalandi lalandi (yellowtail kingfish) 119–20
Seriolella brama (blue warehou) 285
Seriolella caerulea (white warehou) 285
Seriolella punctata (silver warehou) 285
setlines (trotlines) 13
shark
   angel shark 211
   aroma 211, 212
   blacktip shark 211
   dusky shark 211
   elephant shark 211
   flake 212
   gummy shark 211
   mako shark 211
   marinating 212
   roughskin dogfish 211
   saw shark 211
   school shark 211
   spikey dogfish 211
   whiskery shark 211
Shellfish broth and sauce 458
Shellfish oil 456
shortfin eel (*Anguilla australis*) 71, 72
shucking abalone 439
shucking clams 443
shucking oysters 372, 442, 443
Sicilian-style garfish 94
Sillaginodes punctatus (King George whiting) 289, 290, 295
Sillago ciliata (sand/summer whiting) 289, 290
Sillago flindersi (eastern school/redspot whiting) 289, 290, 291
silver perch (*Bidyanus bidyanus*) 171–2
   Vietnamese-style whole fried silver perch 173
silver trevally (*Pseudocaranx dentex*) 249
   Silver trevally sashimi 251
silver warehou (*Seriolella punctata*) 285
sixspine leatherjacket (*Meuschenia freycineti*) 125
skate (Rajidae) and rays (Dasyatidae)
   eastern fiddler ray 215
   eastern shovelnose ray 215
   preparing 436
   Skate grenobloise 216

white-spotted guitarfish 215
skewering a raw prawn 445
skinning and filleting, Japanese style 432–3
skipjack tuna (*Katsuwonus pelamis*) 273
Smoked eel and green peppercorn pâté 75
snapper
   ruby snapper 227, 228
   Ruby snapper en papillote with zucchini, tomato and garlic 230
snapper, pink (*Pagrus auratus*) 219–20
   barbecuing 220
   Pan-roasted snapper with cherry tomatoes, zucchini and basil 223
   Snapper with buttered greens 221
   Snapper sushi and sashimi 224
snapper, queen
   blue morwong or queen snapper 51
snapper, tropical
   Classic fish pie 232
   crimson snapper 227
   goldband snapper 227
   green jobfish 227
   king snapper or rosy jobfish 227
   one-spot snapper 227
   ruby snapper 227, 228, 230
   saddletail snapper 227
   Salt-crusted whole snapper 229
   Spanish-flag jobfish 227
snubnose garfish (*Arrhamphus sclerolepis*) 93
'soapies' (mulloway) 153
sorrel
   Oyster and sorrel soup 377
   Sorrel sauce 261
soup
   fish for 147
   New England-style clam chowder 323
   Oyster and sorrel soup 377
   Sweet corn soup with yabbies 345
   see also broth
South Indian curry of mullet 151
southern bluefin tuna (*Thunnus maccoyii*) 273, 275, 276–7
   Tuna tartare 281
southern calamari squid (*Sepioteuthis australis*) 415, 416
southern rock lobster (*Jasus edwardsii*) 349, 350, 351
southern sea garfish (*Hyporhamphus melanochir*) 93
soy sauce, 'white' 404
Spaghetti vongole 315, 322
spangled emperor 175
Spanish mackerel (*Scomberomorus commerson*) 139–40
   Mackerel with beetroot and chilli relish 140
   Pickled mackerel 136

Spanish-flag jobfish (*Lutjanus carponotatus*) 227
spanner crab (*Ranina ranina*) 329, 330, 331, 336
    cleaning cooked 450
    Spanner crab fettuccine 335
spikey dogfish (*Squalus megalops*) 211
Spisula aequilateralis (triangle or diamond shell clam) 314, 315
spotted mackerel (*Scomberomorus munroi*) 139
Squalus megalops (spikey dogfish) 211
Squatina australis (angel shark) 211
squid and cuttlefish
    arrow squid 416
    Australian giant cuttlefish 415, 419
    bigfin reef squid 419
    cleaning 452
    double-skinning 420
    Gould's squid 416
    Pan-fried cuttlefish with salted chilli and basil 424
    Pan-fried squid tubes with rocket pesto 423
    Queensland northern 419
    sashimi and sushi 420
    southern calamari squid 415, 416
squid jigging 13, 41, 419
Steamed barramundi with tomato consommé 25
Steamed coral trout tail with almonds, pomegranate and prunes 256
Steamed hapuka with mushrooms, soy and bok choy 113
Steamed whole big-eye ocean perch with coconut, chilli and lime broth 162
Steamed whole rainbow trout with green beans, figs and hazelnut butter 267
stock
    Fish stock 457
storm clams (*Mactra murchisoni*) 314
striped trumpeter (*Latris lineata*) 269–71
    Charred striped trumpeter with pistachio and lime carrots 271
Sugar-cured ocean trout 264
summer whiting *see* sand whiting
'surf clams' 314–15
sushi
    Atlantic salmon 199
    garfish 93
    Snapper sushi and sashimi 224
    squid and cuttlefish 420
Sushi rice 463
sustainability 16, 325
Sweet corn soup with yabbies 345
Sweet soy sauce (home made) 368
swordfish (*Xiphias gladius*, broadbill) 235–6
    Seared swordfish with caramelised pickled onions and charred eggplant 236
Sydney rock oyster (*Saccostrea glomerata*) 371, 375, 376

T

Tacos 213
    Fish tacos 213
tamarind water 181
tarahiki
    jackass morwong or tarahiki (*Nemadactylus macropterus*) 51
Tartare sauce 83
Tasmanian or commercial scallop (*Pecten fumatus*) 401
Tasmanian salmon 193
tataki
    Bonito tataki 42
techniques
    cleaning a cooked bug 441
    cleaning a cooked spanner crab 450
    cleaning a cuttlefish 452
    cleaning a round fish 428
    cleaning a scallop 440
    cleaning a squid 451
    cooking and picking whole crab 449
    curing salmon 438
    cutting a saku block from tuna 435
    cutting sashimi from a fillet 434
    dressing a whole flat fish 430
    dressing a whole round fish 430
    filleting a dory 431
    filleting a round fish 428–9
    pan-frying fillets with crisp skin 437
    peeling a prawn 444
    preparing a blue swimmer crab 447
    preparing a live lobster 446
    preparing a live mud crab 448
    preparing a skate wing 436
    preparing potato scales 437
    scaling a round fish 428
    shucking an abalone 439
    shucking a clam 443
    shucking an oyster (angasi) 443
    shucking an oyster (rock and Pacific) 442
    skewering a raw prawn 445
    skinning and filleting, Japanese style 432–3
    tenderising and blanching octopus 365, 366, 453
tempura
    mahi mahi (*Coryphaena hippurus*) 143
tenderising and blanching octopus 365, 366, 453

Thenus orientalis (Moreton Bay bug) 307, 308, 309
three-by-two garfish (*Hemiramphus robustus*) 93
Thunnus alalunga (albacore tuna) 273, 274, 276
Thunnus albacares (yellowfin tuna) 271, 273, 275, 277, 282
Thunnus maccoyii (southern bluefin tuna) 273, 275, 276–7, 281
Thunnus obesus (bigeye tuna) 273, 274, 276
tiger flathead (*Neoplatycephalus richardsoni*) 80
tiger prawn (*Penaeus monodon*) 384, 385
    Tiger prawn ravioli, grilled spring onions and shellfish sauce 397
togarashi 90
toothfish
    Antarctic 239
    Patagonian 239
    Toothfish in white miso 240, 241
tough fish syndrome 175
Trachurus novaezelandiae (yellowtail scad) 249, 250, 252
trawling 14
trevalla, blue-eye *see* blue-eye trevalla
trevally
    bigeye trevally 249
    bluefin trevally 249
    cooking on the bone 250
    raw 250
    sashimi 249, 250
    silver trevally 249, 251
    yellowtail scad 249, 250, 252
triangle or diamond shell clam (*Spisula aequilateralis*) 314, 315
tropical fish (provenance) 227
tropical rock lobster (*Panulirus ornatus*) 349, 350, 351
trout
    on the bone 260
    hot-smoking 260
    see also coral trout; ocean trout; rainbow trout
Trygonorrhina fasciata (eastern fiddler ray) 215
tua tua (*Paphies donacina*) 314, 315
tuna
    albacore (*Thunnus alalunga*) 273, 274, 276, 278
    bigeye (*Thunnus obesus*) 273, 274, 276
    bottarga di tonno 189
    braising 363
    cutting a saku block 435
    Mussel and seared tuna salad 363
    skipjack (*Katsuwonus pelamis*) 273
    southern bluefin (*Thunnus maccoyii*) 273, 275, 276–7

Tuna tartare 281
yellowfin (*Thunnus albacares*)
271, 273, 275, 277, 282
turbot, New Zealand (*Colistium nudipinnis*) 87

U

uni (sea urchin roe) 411, 412
Upeneichthys lineatus (blue-striped goatfish) 147
Upeneichthys vlamingii (blue-spotted goatfish) 147

V

vegetables
Salt-roasted vegetables 463
Venerupis spp. (vongole) 312
Vietnamese-style fishcakes with nuoc cham 181
Vietnamese-style whole fried silver perch 173
vongole (*Katelysia* spp. and *Venerupis* spp.) 312

W

warehou
blue (*Seriolella brama*) 285
silver (*Seriolella punctata*) 285
white (*Seriolella caerulea*) 285
Yellow curry of warehou 286
western king prawn (*Melicertus latisulcatus*) 382
western rock lobster (*Panulirus cygnus*) 349, 350, 357
whiskery shark (*Furgaleus macki*) 211
white warehou (*Seriolella caerulea*) 285
white-spotted guitarfish (*Rhynchobatus australiae*) 215
whiting
Barbecued whole redspot whiting with sourdough crumbs and blackened citrus 291
Crumbed sand whiting 295
eastern school whiting (redspot) 289, 290
King George whiting 289, 290
Rolled King George whiting with Asian mushrooms 292
sand whiting (summer whiting) 289, 290, 295
Wild kingfish with barbecued leek and pickled beetroot 122
wild salmon 193

wok
testing oil temperature 340
Wok-fried blue swimmer crab with pepper and egg 340

X

Xiphias gladius (swordfish) 235–6

Y

yabbies (*Cherax destructor*) 343, 344
Sweet corn soup with yabbies 345
yakitori 242
Yellow curry of warehou 286
Yellow curry sauce 456
yellowbelly flounder (*Rhombosolea leporina*) 87
yellowfin bream (*Acanthopagrus australis*) 45, 46
yellowfin leatherjacket (*Meuschenia trachylepis*) 125
yellowfin or golden perch (*Macquaria ambigua*) 171
yellowfin tuna (*Thunnus albacares*) 273
sashimi 271, 275, 277
Seared yellowfin tuna with agrodolce 282
yellowstriped leatherjacket (*Meuschenia flavolineata*) 125
yellowtail kingfish (*Seriola lalandi lalandi*) 119–20
Escabeche of yellowtail kingfish 121
Wild kingfish with barbecued leek and pickled beetroot 122
yellowtail scad (*Trachurus novaezelandiae*) 249, 250
Barbecued yellowtail scad with peas, lettuce and bacon 252

Z

Zenopsis nebulosa (mirror dory) 59, 60, 64
Zeus faber (john dory) 59, 60, 63, 67, 68

ACKNOWLEDGEMENTS

We'd like to thank the following awesome fisheries, catchers, managers, cooks, thieves and pirates who have provided assistance, advice, stewardship and general thoughts on our book. You legends!

The team at the Fisheries Research and Development Corporation, in particular Patrick Hone, Pete Horvat, John Wilson and Crispian Ashby. Professor Colin Buxton, University of Tasmania; Dr Daryl 'Mr Shark' McPhee, Bond University; and Dr Janet Howieson, Curtin University. Ian Lyall, aquaculture manager, NSW and Steve McCorrie, oyster manager, Port Stephens Fisheries Institute, NSW Department of Primary Industries; and Robbie Moxham and Mark Bulley, rock oyster farmers. The team at Sydney Fish Market, in particular Erik Poole; Rob Cleminson; and Frank, Stan, Rod, Kev and the lads on the auction floor.

Peter Jecks, Abacus Fisheries; Gary Kessel and Simon Little, Westmore Seafoods; David Carter, Martin Xcell, Clayton Nelson and Dylan Skinns, Austral Fisheries; Andy Puglisi and Andy Dyer, Kinkawooka Shellfish; Rick Kolega, Segol Seafoods; Pavo Walker, Walker Seafoods; Dave 'Scratchy' Caracciolo, Mackay Reef Fisheries; Les Apps, Fraser Isle Spanner Crab; Isaac Piper, Cloudy Bay Clams; Con Liaros, Poulos Brothers; Greg Bishop and Tom Searle, Lee Fish; Patrick Caleo, Marine Stewardship Council; Paolo Bray, Friend of the Sea; Lucas Barrowman, Monterey Bay Aquarium; Kim 'Barrel' Skeer, Southern Rock Lobster; Jimmy Mendolia, Fremantle Sardines; Dave 'Bucky' Buckland, scallop and abalone diver; Dave Gallot, south-east trawl fisherman; Richie Bagnato, Sydney trawl fisherman; Hagen Stehr, Aquaculture, and Trent Gregory, Farm Manager, Cleanseas; Brendan Guidera, the 'Oyster Whisperer', Pristine Oysters; John Moloney, Pacific Reef Fisheries; Ryan Morris, ATTSU Divers NSW; Narito Ishii, seafood distributor; Ken Sadamatsu, Masuya Restaurant; Martin Benn, Sepia; Jared Ingersoll, chef; Colin Barker, The Boathouse; Neil Perry, Rockpool; Cheong Liew, chef; Q.C. Wong, chef, Golden Century; Michael Bacash, Bacash Restaurant; Jules Crocker, seafood distributor; Greg Isimedes, seafood distributor; Andrew Boyd, seafood distributor; Frank Theodore, seafood distributor; Con Andronis, seafood distributor; Paul Catalano, seafood distributor; Tom Angelakis, seafood distributor; Alan Lee, seafood retailer; Craig 'Freckle' Gream, Bay Seafoods; Mitch Tonks, fish chef and author; Rick Stein, fish chef and author; Pete Manifes, fish cook.

Ben Dearnley for the incredible photography and Michelle Noerianto for the fantastic food styling. Sue Hines, Jane Morrow, Hugh Ford, Barbara McClenahan, Virginia Birch, Nicola Young, Karen Lateo and the entire team at Murdoch. Probably the hardest project we've all been part of – but we made it!

John would like to thank
Prue, Harry and George Susman – apologies for not being at sporting events, social occasions and backyard cleaning sessions. Couldn't do any of this without you guys.

Anthony would like to thank
Hodgie – your understanding of seafood is almost as frightening as the way you throw frying pans. Swannie – you deserve an Order of Australia for translating Hodgie-speak into these incredible recipes; you made us look good. Susman – you're the king of seafood, an awful but enthusiastic dancer, an inspiration and a great mate; this wouldn't have happened without you. Mum, for your misguided belief in me – you legend. Ziggy and Scout for making every day hilarious – you ning-nongs. And finally, Hester Gascoigne – you are everything.

Sarah would like to thank
Jeremy, business partner extraordinaire and the most enthusiastic human being I know – thanks for your patience and understanding through the writing and testing process. Your generosity was sincere and appreciated, your humour nutty! You make a workday a joyous thing. To my husband, Dan, the deepest heart I know. Between the early coffee runs and the chilled 5 pm beer, you somehow keep things normal. Your belief in (nearly) everything I do is astounding, your whacky sense of humour is a thing of wonder and you make life fun every day. I'm loving living our dream with you. Hunter and Daisy – my fur kids – unconditional love at its best; nothing compares. Sus, Huck and Hodgie – thanks, guys. You're the best. Working with you three has been the most weirdly wonderful challenge. Stoked to be a part of the team.

Stephen would like to thank
My amazing son Jared. Greg Doyle (Pier). Mark Eather and John Susman for introducing me to export fish all those years ago, which ignited my passion for sourcing the best-quality fish, and the best methods to cook them. And finally, all the staff at Fish Face, who put up with me during the writing of this book.

ABOUT THE AUTHORS

John 'Suso' Susman

Now with almost 30 years' experience in the seafood industry, John grew up in South Australia, in an extended family of manic fishermen, dairy farmers and horticulturalists. With a father who was part Indiana Jones, part Keith Floyd, every holiday was full of catching and cooking seafood. Whether handlining for King George whiting on the Fleurieu Peninsula, raking for blue swimmer crabs in the Gulf St Vincent or trapping yabbies on the River Murray, from the start his love of good seafood was innate.

During his years of floundering around at university completing various useless studies, John ventured into restaurants at a crucial stage in the evolution of the industry. Cutting his teeth alongside the likes of Cheong Liew, Tim Pak Poy, Christine Manfield, Phillip Searle and Margie Harris gave him a thorough knowledge and passion for what it takes to prepare, cook and present great food. John's knack for developing bonds with some of the most influential people in food has seen him work around the world, from J. Lelande in Paris, to Japan and the Americas. Back in Australia, he set up the legendary Flying Squid Brothers, an integrated scallop-fishing business that became Australia's first water-to-plate operation. These days he's the 'fishhead' of seafood-industry agency Fishtales.

Consistently regarded as a foremost authority on seafood, not only in Australia, but globally, John regularly appears on television and radio, and in print media. In 2004, he was admitted into the Fairfax Australian Food Industry Hall of Fame for his services to the Australian food industry, while in 2012 he was named Outstanding Providore of the Year by *delicious.* magazine.

Favourite seafood: *King George whiting, along with all the other species in this book!*

Anthony 'Huck' Huckstep

An award-winning journalist and writer, Huck was spawned in a brooding broth of mullets, distortion and Sunday roasts in Sydney's western suburbs. His passion for produce and its culinary applications is matched only by his unhealthy appetite for music that most find unpalatable – which makes Huck one of the most left-of-centre food writers in Australia.

National restaurant critic and columnist for *delicious.* magazine, food and drink writer for *The Australian*, *Qantas Magazine* and *GQ Australia*, he also co-founded MetalMouth, an annual dinner that deconstructs the heavy metal and fine dining contradiction by celebrating the beauty of both in the heaviest culinary experience on earth. He spent 13 years editing the award-winning title *Foodservice Magazine* – named 2011 Australian B2B Magazine of the Year during his tenure. Over many years the last notch on his belt was reviewing for the *SMH Good Food Guide*. He penned Luke Mangan's *The Making of a Chef* and the narrative for *Sepia: The Cuisine of Martin Benn*.

Favourite seafood: *Sea urchin roe*

Sarah 'Swannie' Swan

Born in Auckland, 'Swannie' moved to Australia in her late teens and took up an apprenticeship in Sydney before heading to London to travel and work in restaurants and bars. Upon returning to Australia during the 1990s, she worked in the kitchens of the Bayswater Brasserie with Tony Papas and Michael Klausen, The Bathers' Pavilion with Genevieve Harris, Wokpool with Kylie Kwong and onto Rockpool and XO with Neil Perry. An eventual shift out of the kitchen saw Sarah work on the Rockpool Group websites and social media, and closely with Neil on his books, television shows and media commitments.

In late 2011, she moved to Byron Bay with her husband Dan and spaniel Hunter (soon to be joined by fur sister Daisy) and settled into a sea/tree change. During 2014, Sarah opened 100 Mile Table cafe and catering business in Byron's Arts and Industry Estate with business partner Jeremy Burn. She's been loving it from day dot. Byron, its lifestyle and accessibility to incredible produce and people makes her a happy camper.

Favourite seafood: *Sydney rock oysters*

Stephen 'Hodgie' Hodges

Hodgie was born into hospitality. His grandfather was a fisherman and his parents ran pubs for Miller's Hotels. In fact, he practically lived in pubs – washing pots and flipping steaks – until he was 14. He started his apprenticeship at Sydney's infamous Bourbon and Beefsteak in the late 1970s, before working with mentor Ron Hughes at Our Pleasure restaurant. Hughes's suggestion that Hodgie go and work with his best friend Greg Doyle at Puligny's led to a series of influential establishments from the duo. After four years they opened Riley Street Bistro in the Forresters Hotel, Surry Hills, before opening East Side Bar and Grill in Kings Cross. In 1990, Doyle and Hodges opened Pier in Rose Bay, which won Best Seafood Restaurant year on year. It was here that seafood became Hodgie's focus, and he hasn't looked back.

In 2002 Hodgie left Pier and the following year opened Fish Face in Darlinghurst, a casual dining space where all the attention was on the fish on the plate. He soon became known as one of the best fish cooks, not only in Australia, but on the planet. In 2011, Fish Face was named the *SMH Good Food Guide*'s Best Seafood Restaurant. In 2014, Hodgie opened Fish Face Double Bay, but closed both Fish Faces during 2015. Hodgie currently works with seafood specialists Sydney Fresh Seafood.

Favourite seafood: *Bass groper*

Published in 2016 by Murdoch Books, an imprint of Allen & Unwin

Murdoch Books Australia
83 Alexander Street
Crows Nest NSW 2065
Phone: +61 (0) 2 8425 0100
Fax: +61 (0) 2 9906 2218
murdochbooks.com.au
info@murdochbooks.com.au

Murdoch Books UK
Ormond House
26–27 Boswell Street
London WC1N 3JZ
Phone: +44 (0) 20 8785 5995
murdochbooks.co.uk
info@murdochbooks.co.uk

For Corporate Orders & Custom Publishing, contact our Business Development Team at salesenquiries@murdochbooks.com.au.

Publishing Consultants: Terry Durack and Jill Dupleix
Publisher: Jane Morrow
Editorial Managers: Barbara McClenahan, Virginia Birch
Design Manager: Hugh Ford
Project Editor: Nicola Young
Photographer: Ben Dearnley
Stylist: Michelle Noerianto
Food Editor: Karen Lateo
Production Manager: Alexandra Gonzalez and Rachel Walsh

Text © John Susman, Anthony Huckstep, Sarah Swan and Stephen Hodges 2016
The moral rights of the authors have been asserted.
Design © Murdoch Books 2016
All photography © Ben Dearnley 2016, except for photograph on page 211 © Caroline McCredie

All rights reserved. No part of this publication may be reproduced, stored in a retrieval system or transmitted in any form or by any means, electronic, mechanical, photocopying, recording or otherwise, without the prior written permission of the publisher.

A cataloguing-in-publication entry is available from the catalogue of the National Library of Australia at nla.gov.au.

ISBN 978 1 74336 295 2 Australia
ISBN 978 1 74336 328 7 UK

A catalogue record for this book is available from the British Library.

Colour reproduction by Splitting Image Colour Studio Pty Ltd, Clayton, Victoria
Printed by C & C Offset Printing Co. Ltd., China
Reprinted in 2017

IMPORTANT: Those who might be at risk from the effects of salmonella poisoning (the elderly, pregnant women, young children and those suffering from immune deficiency diseases) should consult their doctor with any concerns about eating raw eggs.

OVEN GUIDE: You may find cooking times vary depending on the oven you are using. For fan-forced ovens, as a general rule, set the oven temperature to 20°C (35°F) lower than indicated in the recipe.

MEASURES GUIDE: We have used 20 ml (4 teaspoon) tablespoon measures. If you are using a 15 ml (3 teaspoon) tablespoon add an extra teaspoon of the ingredient for each tablespoon specified.